Water Management in Ancient Greek Cities

Frontispiece. Schubring's map of the waterlines of Akragas, based on his investigations in the 1860s. Surface drainage is shown by slightly thicker lines than underground waterpassages, and the rivers at left and bottom are labled "fluss." The Fluss Hypsas widens out into the artificial (?) lake labled "Fischteich" which the ancient writers said was used for growing fish and water fowl. The ridge of temples makes a dark almost-horizontal line below center. Compare with Fig. 15.2. (See p. 209 for detailed description of this map.)

Water Management in Ancient Greek Cities

Dora P. Crouch

New York   Oxford
OXFORD UNIVERSITY PRESS
1993

Oxford University Press

Oxford   New York   Toronto
Delhi   Bombay   Calcutta   Madras   Karachi
Kuala Lumpur   Singapore   Hong Kong   Tokyo
Nairobi   Dar es Salaam   Cape Town
Melbourne   Auckland   Madrid

and associated companies in
Berlin   Ibadan

Library of Congress Cataloging-in-Publication Data
Crouch, Dora P.
Water management in ancient Greek cities / Dora P. Crouch.
p.   cm.   Includes bibliographical references and index.
ISBN 0–19–507280–4
1. Municipal water supply—Greece—Management—History.
2. Cities and towns, Ancient—Greece.   I. Title.
TD275.AIC76   1993
628.1′0938—dc20   91–29246

All photos not otherwise credited are by the author. Drawings are by
Michael Frachioni (Figure 18.1); Barbara Harris (Figure 16.12), Paula Fish
(Figures 11.4, 15.2, 17.4, 17.6, 17.8, 17.9, 17.11, 21.2, 22.3, and re-drawing of
12.5, 12.6), and Brian Kreuger (Figures 5.1, 8.1, 8.7, 11.5, 11.6, 12.1, 12.2,
13.4, 17.7, and re-drawing of 7.2, 10.1, 13.1, 15.2, 22.7, 22.8, as well as cor-
rections and relettering of many others).

9 8 7 6 5 4 3 2 1

Printed in the United States of America
on acid-free paper

For Homer Thompson
who urged me to write it
and for my mother Peggie
and daughter Jane

Preface

There has to be a first historian of any subject.
—C. Vann Woodward
The Perils of Writing History

A "decent Respect to the Opinions of Mankind"[1] indicates that this book should begin with a few paragraphs setting it in context. What the book is as well as what the book is not may be sketched and some justification offered.

In architectural and urban history as they have been practiced during the last fifteen or twenty years, there has been a great deal of interest in the impact of technological developments on urban form and functioning. Both American cities and English post-industrial-revolution cities have been studied in relation to the railroad, the location and impact of factory districts, the location and impact of maritime districts, and more recently, the impact of electrification and of the automobile. Studies have considered the particulars of how the provision of water influenced the growth of cities like Philadelphia or Cincinnati.

Little of this approach to urban history has spilled over into the study of premodern cities. Yet such agglomerations were surely as dependent on water supply, as constrained by transportation, and so on, as their modern counterparts.

This book is a first attempt to examine ancient Greek cities from this protechnical point of view. It has the virtue of freshness, but it suffers from the difficulties of bending to its purpose data that were accumulated for very different purposes. The ancient authors were almost no help, as they simply do not discourse on these matters in any depth or length. Archaeological data from ancient Greek cities seem to a modern urban historian to be episodic and object-oriented, where one would long for a systemic approach. Yet it is only from archaeological data and from personal inspection of the sites that the modern investigator can learn detail after detail about ancient Greek water management. The details

1. Preamble to the Declaration of Independence.

eventually add up to general understanding, especially when illuminated by the light shed on location and function by the geological subspeciality called karst geology.

This, then, is not a book about what the ancient authors wrote. Nor is it a book about the arguments between modern classicists and historians who deal with ancient times as to arrangements within Greek cities. Rather, it is a book about the cities themselves, considered in a new light. Looking at ancient Greek cities as places where life was a little less precarious, where one could live longer and more safely, we ask, How this was accomplished? An important answer is that municipal control of water, with multiple sources, gave communal life a decided advantage over rural life. It was an evolutionary development that permitted larger numbers of individuals and more of their culture to survive.

As an urban historian, then, but one trained in the architecture and urbanism of Greece and Rome, I have dared to sketch the outlines of a comparative study of the interaction between the management of water and the process of urbanization in the ancient Greek world. Such a preliminary survey cannot take the place of the fuller studies that I know need to be done, but may inspire them. Ancient cities were not simply a few buried walls or a few allusive documents. Rather, they were four-dimensional, increasingly complex, centers of multifarious activity. If we truly take this into our imagination as well as our cognition, we will realize that ancient urban history has barely begun to be written. Many disciplines will need to work together on this project, producing both a number of case studies and a series of generalized topical studies.

In the increasingly self-conscious conditions of historiography today, many have realized that not all historical studies are or need to be chronological. This is a history of ancient Greek times, that considers issues topically rather than in order of their happening. Largely unavoidable because of the gaps in coverage, this arrangement is also patterned on some models in modern urban history such as Norma Evenson's *Two Brazilian Capitals: Architecture and Urbanism in Rio de Janeiro and Brasilia* (New Haven: Yale University Press,1973). In ancient urban history, one may cite William MacDonald's masterly *An Architecture of the Roman Empire:* Vol. II *An Urban Appraisal* (New Haven: Yale University Press, l986), where examples from many areas and centuries are carefully selected and grouped around a theme such as "Urban Armatures" (chapter II).

An important underlying assumption of this book is that there are no immutable rights to intellectual property. Cities of Greece and Rome do not belong to the classicists, the geology of Mediterranean lands does not belong to the geologists, nor does hydraulic engineering belong to the engineers. Nothing human is alien to me, and as a historian I press into service what ever I can understand that will illuminate and help others to understand the Greek past and our present. The stories of how our forebears faced the challenge of living in large groups in a fragile and unforgiving landscape are germane to our own time of severe resource constraints. From the enthusiastic reception given to the portions of this work I have presented as papers at international meetings of water policymakers, engineers, and geologists, it seems that those who can make operational use of these findings readily appreciate them. It is my hope that those who can make intellectual use of them will be equally receptive.

Glendale, Cal.   D.P.C.
August 1992

Acknowledgments

My first encounter with the public realm was in Port Huron, Michigan, where my mother, Margaret Lowber Polk, led a group from the League of Women Voters in lobbying for a new water system for the city, and getting it built. Her cleanliness compulsion has descended to me in intellectual form, and to my daughter Jane Crouch Thapa, an environmental engineer who has helped me with readings, introductions, and discussions based on her experience in building modest water and sanitation systems in Nepal for the Peace Corps. My thesis advisor, Professor Susan Downey of UCLA, encouraged me to consider how water was a major determinant in the growth pattern of Palmyra, introduced me to Homer Thompson, and generally induced me to do better than I thought I could. Homer Thompson, who challenged me to tackle Greek water systems, has been unfailingly supportive, illuminating, and kind.

I am grateful to Berkeley for the Faculty Research Grant that enabled me to begin this project in 1970; to Rensselaer for sabbaticals that helped me pursue it; and to the American Association of University Women without whose Educational Foundation Fellowship I could not have made the essential field trip in 1985. In 1980–81, I held a fellowship at the Center for Advanced Study in the Visual Arts at the National Gallery of Art in Washington, D.C., which enabled me to read a great deal of accumulated material, and to write on Morgantina's water system for the *American Journal of Archaeology.* This stimulating year was one of the most productive I have ever had, and I thank Dean Henry Millon and Associate Dean Shreve Simpson for their support of a project with an apparently tenuous relationship to the visual arts, and for the pleasure of their company.

At Rensselaer, colleagues Paul Hohenberg (an economic historian turned urban historian), Donald Aulenbach (environmental engineer who taught me about land management of waste waters), and Robert LaFleur (geologist who taught me hydrogeology and started my study of karst geology) were especially valuable, sustaining me over the long years of learning and grappling with these materials that I had never studied in graduate school. Two deans of the School of Architecture, Patrick Quinn and David Haviland, gave me many kinds of assistance, for which I formally thank them.

Dr. William Childs of Princeton and Dr. Hugh Allen were former directors of the excavations at Morgantina, Sicily; they opened both the site and Morgantina Room at Princeton to my study, as well as discussing the site with me and supplying photographs and drawings of details of the water system there. With this help, and two lengthy visits to the site, I came to know the water system of Morgantina quite thoroughly, so that it has functioned as my base of comparison with other sites. I must also thank the present excavator, Dr. Malcolm Bell, who by the rigor and exactitude of his standards has forced me to sharpen and improve my understanding and my arguments.

Library research was carried on with the help of the staffs of the libraries of the National Gallery of Art, Library of Congress, and Center for Hellenic Studies (all in Washington, D.C.). Without the patient and clever assistance of the Interlibrary Loan staff of Folsom Library at Rensselaer Polytechnic Institute I could never have continued this study. The collection of the Stanford Geology Library has also assisted my growing understanding of the importance of karst geology in the Mediterranean littoral.

During 1985, thanks to a grant from the American Association of University Women and a sabbatical from Rensselaer, I was able to visit many ancient sites in the Mediterranean, most of them Greek. These were sites about which I had gathered information during the library search.

Most fruitful were the investigations into the water lines of Pergamon, which led to the discovery of the group of hydraulic engineers—led by Professor Dr.-Ing. Günther Garbrecht, former director of the Leichtweiss Institute for Water Research at Braunschweig, Germany—who are passionately interested in the history of their discipline. My most heartfelt thanks go to Professor Garbrecht for sharing with me his great knowledge of Pergamon and for inviting me into the Frontinus Society. I must mention among this group Doctors Hermann Kienast, excavator of the Samos tunnel and Deputy-Director of the German Archaeological Institute in Athens; the late Wolfgang Mueller-Wiener, excavator of Miletus; J. Knauss, from the Technical University in Munich, expert on Mycenaean waterworks in Greece; W. Eck, legal scholar from Munich who works on the economics and management of Roman aqueducts; and K. Grewe of the Landesmuseum in Bonn who studies ancient surveying and the Roman waterlines along the Rhine. These colleagues have not only shared their information generously but also encouraged me by being truly interested in my insights into ancient water management. A leader of this group is Professor Dr.-Ing. Henning Fahlbusch of Lübeck, whose work on Greek and Roman long-distance water supply lines will be frequently cited in these pages, and whose assistance and stimulating interest in my work I can never acknowledge with enough thanks.

Three people have drawn maps and reconstruction views for me: Michael Frachioni, Paula Fish, and Brian Krueger. Working with them has forced me to clarify my thinking and improve my skills of visual presentation. Their maps and views have immeasurably enriched the volume.

I would also like to thank Eric Van Tassel, formerly of Princeton University Press, who convinced me that, by definition, a short book is better than a long one, and William L. MacDonald, who in his great Volume II of *The Architecture of the Roman Empire* showed me how to do it.

In Italy, Greece, and Turkey, I have had the help of local experts. At Agrigento, Sicily (ancient Akragas), Emma and Giovanni Trasatti, who run the sewage disposal plant there, instructed me in the topography of the site as only long-time residents know it, and discussed its water supply with me at great length. They also introduced me to Sr. Arnone, author of the definitive study of waterlines at the site as they were known at the time of World War II. The manager of the Aidone water system near Morgantina, Sr. LaSpina, was equally generous with his time and knowledge. Unsurpassed in professional generosity, however, was Mrs. Eva Touloupa, until recently Director of the Athens Acropolis excavations and museum, and a model of wisdom and helpfulness. For many years, John Camp of the Athenian Agora and the American School of Classical Studies in Athens, an expert on the water system of Athens, has discussed these matters with me and opened to me the facilities of the Agora Museum. This study owes a great deal to him and to his work. During my fall 1988 visit to Athens, Professor Paul G. Marinos of the Deptartment of Civil Engineering of the Technical University, discussed my questions at great length, and single-handedly supplied me with as many answers as all the rest of my informants put together. Finally, a word of thanks to "Mr. John" of the Hotel Nefali in Plaka, and another to Nikki Fintikakis, architect, who knows everyone who knows anything about water at Athens, and made a point to introduce me to them all.

In Turkey one place of domicile stands out in my memory: the excavation house at Pergamon and the kindness of Dr. Wolfgang Radt of the German Archaeological Institute in Istanbul, who made himself and his intelligent staff available to discuss questions of interpretation. Dr. Wolfgang Mueller-Wiener and his staff at Miletus were equally helpful, although our visit was less protracted. In the fall of 1988, Professor A. Trevor Hodge of Carleton University in Ottawa, Canada, offered me the opportunity to spend three weeks jointly studying Greek and Roman water supply in the sites along the western and southern coasts of Turkey; he has my thanks for this trip and for his crucial support of my work.

Contents

List of Figures and Tables

I

Introduction

1

Purposes and Methods

Research that combines geology, archaeology, history, and other disciplines can be successfully applied to . . . providing alternate rationales for interpreting and understanding ancient . . . sites. In many cases obscure historic (and mythologic) references to ancient events and geographies can be resolved with applications of principles of geology and paleography.

—John C. Kraft and George Rapp, Jr.

Geological Reconstruction of Ancient

Coastal Landforms in Greece

Water has been a persistent and consistent factor in urban development and history. One advantage in studying water as it relates to the process of urbanization is that the behavior of water, and therefore to a large extent the management of water, are "culture free." As Mendelssohn (1974) has shown with respect to the physics of pyramid construction and collapse, some aspects of the ancient world—religion, marriage customs—are culture bound but others—behavior of construction materials, water—are much less conditioned by human preferences.

Thus, insights from modern hydraulic engineering can have "chronology-free" validity. We can confidently turn to hydraulic engineers for insight into ancient water management, since water still behaves as it always has and is to be managed as it always was. For instance, modern engineers looking for locations for bridges and dams to be built anew as part of Rome's modern water system, again and again find ancient ruins of bridges and dams just where they have determined are the best locations for new ones. Also, at Pergamon, the long-distance waterlines that supplied the Hellenistic and Roman city have been studied by professional hydraulic engineers, who followed each line through the countryside. When puzzled by a missing segment of the ancient line, they asked, "Where would I put the line next, if I were designing it?" and most often they found fragments of the missing segment just in that place, because the behavior of flowing water and the concepts for controlling it remain constant.[1]

Comprehensive treatment of the topic of ancient Greek water management and its close relation to the process of urbanization in the Greek world of the eighth to first centuries B.C. would involve the work of many scholars. To cite one name only of many for each subtopic, one could mention the following authors who have studied or are currently studying aspects of the question:

Brinker on cisterns
Camp on pipe classification (in progress); Camp has already studied the water system of Athens
Doxiadis et al. on urban location
Eck on legal and administrative aspects (in progress)
Fahlbusch on long-distance water supply lines
Garbrecht on the water supply of Pergamon
Ginouves on baths
Glaser on fountainhouses
Grewe on the surveying of ancient waterlines and tunnels
Günay and his students on karst geology in southern Turkey
Martin on urban form

In all cases, these efforts represent years of work, and yet taken together they do not cover all aspects of the topic. Lacunae such as the lack of specific studies of water distribution within a city still plague the scholar who attempts to write a comprehensive study.

Attempting such a survey of the subject, based on topical studies and on many separate excavation reports as well as on personal investigation of sites, one encounters not only the interdisciplinary problems to be discussed in the next chapter but also the fact that many water system elements have been studied by site only, not comprehensively. These include springs, fountains, and wells; channels and drains; toilets and latrines. Laundry and dish washing have received no study at all, perhaps evidencing a masculine bias in the attention paid to aspects of daily life traditionally classified as "women's work."

Nor have there been studies of urban systems such as defense, food supply, or recreational structures and spaces as a subdivision of urban architecture, let alone studies comparing the urban systems of several ancient cities. Indeed the concept of urban systems has not previously been applied to ancient cities. It would have been infinitely easier to write this book if I could have drawn on numerous case studies as any historian of the modern American city can do. Lacking individual, systemic studies that attempt to arrive at a more complete understanding of how ancient cities actually worked, I have had to forge my questions, methods, and data as best I could. This book is a pioneer attempt to study ancient water management as an urban system, and then to compare such systems in many cities. Undoubtedly the book suffers from its pioneer status.

Since urban systems are made up of subsystems, I have examined and analyzed clusters of water system elements as related to each other, as related to the physical base (geography and geology) of each site, and as related to the social arrangements and historical base of each urban culture. These analyses in turn have been synthesized with the urban design, water resource base, and topography of particular sites to try to understand how the process of urbanization and the developing control of water acted as reciprocal constraints and enablers.

My tasks have been to supply some of the missing information at the subsystem level and to present a thesis about the importance of water in urban growth, in such a form that further research may be stimulated and easily added to this base. I have been dependent on the findings of other scholars about particular water system elements and the water management elements of particular sites, but I have also visited the sites described and made careful note of water system elements not previously reported. Each chapter proceeds by citing examples rather than attempting to give every piece of known data, and exhibits chosen examples in telling juxtaposition. To provide later scholars with a modest exposition, at both the physical and the theoretical levels, of water system elements for further study has seemed to me a useful beginning. My findings on springs and wells, channels and drains, toilets and latrines, and laundry facilities appear in the relevant chapters in sufficient detail to begin to fill in lacunae in the published data. This survey indicates the importance of such elements in urban development. I hope it will inspire the kind of careful treatment of each of these elements that has already been given to baths and fountain houses. Much more classifying and organizing work needs to be done with these elements, analogous to the existing classification schemes for pottery sherds or coins. I hope this book will inspire that additional work, and stimulate the curiosity of specialists and general readers alike.

It has been a major aim of this study to compare and integrate the materials from urban history with those on water management, that each may illuminate the other. My thesis is that increasing knowledge and skill in the management of water related directly to the urbanization of the ancient Greek world. From the accumulated data I have drawn conclusions about relationships between humans and their environment in the ancient Greek cities of the Mediterranean area that may be useful to citizens, planners and policymakers of today. These modest, highly integrated, and economical systems have many lessons for today's planners, operators, and consumers of water. Modern hydraulic engineers and water resources policymakers have been quick to understand that these ancient water systems provide models for modern practice in a field where the complexity of the issues surpasses the ability of mathematics to generate satisfactory models. Hence, they have been generous in accepting these studies in the form of papers contributed to a wide range of professional meetings. I am grateful for the feedback received from these individuals and groups.

METHODS

As part of my doctoral dissertation on Palmyra, I studied the water system of that city, which was founded in 300 B.C. but flourished during the second and third centuries A.D. It was impossible to differentiate Greek from Roman water system elements at that site because no classification scheme existed for water system elements. Yet such a scheme is theoretically possible, because water system elements are frequently or even usually made of terra-cotta, as is the pottery whose chronology has been worked out in detail. A pottery sherd can usually be dated within a twenty-five-year period. Even if pipe patterns do not change as often as dish patterns, it should be possible to work out the sequence of pipe shapes and mortars. This classification would provide a second valuable dating method for archaeologists. With these questions in mind, I turned from Palmyra to the water systems of ancient Greek cities.

This topic was suggested in 1969 by Homer Thompson. He pointed out that although Roman water systems had been studied, at least after a fashion, no one had ever attempted a comprehensive study of Greek water systems. Research began in 1970, investigating the published bibliography. At that point I was a recent Ph.D. with a degree in art history, specializing in the architecture and urbanism of ancient Greece and Rome. Half of my graduate course work had been taken in classical archaeology. It was my intention to make a career as an urban historian, and I began at the historical point where it was easiest for me to accumulate knowledge, considering the resources of faculty and bibliography available to me at UCLA in the late 1960s, and at Berkeley in 1970–71.

Library Research

At Berkeley I won a modest Faculty Research grant in the fall of 1970. With the funds of the grant, I hired a bibliographer and began the search of the literature, first step in the project that was to occupy me for two decades, between and during other studies. My aim was to discover what had been published about ancient Greek water systems. Archaeological journals were most useful sources, together with final publications on the excavations of many sites of the extended Greek world. This initial investigation produced a list of twenty-five sites on which there was published material on their water system elements in 1970, and which were occupied during the Greek era. The sites were then visited during several field trips.

Gradually I came to understand what this water problem consisted of and to realize that asking questions about water supply, usage, and drainage was to demand of the published data answers that they had never been designed to provide. How much easier my task would have been if the excavators had set out to explore the conditions that made human life and society possible at a given site! But this was a new archaeological question, and most of the venerable tomes I was consulting were produced to answer old questions such as, "Where was Homer's Troy?" or "Who painted this black-figure vase?" or "When was this temple built?" If material on water management was included, it was nearly always incidental to the main purpose of the work.

Engineering and Geology Classes

Although each item of collected evidence was precious in itself, and led to further information as I investigated the links between paper and paper, eventually it became apparent that I would need other kinds of information. Since I was unable in several years of diligent search to discover any American hydraulic engineers who were interested in the study of ancient hydraulics, I could not arrange to share the research according to disciplinary expertise. Therefore I enrolled in courses at Rensselaer Polytechnic Institute that seemed germane and read basic texts suggested by my daughter who is a sanitary engineer. By learning the principles of hydrogeology, hydraulic behavior, and land management of waste waters, I was able to position myself at a vantage point similar to that of the ancient Greeks—understanding what happens, and what the possibilities are of controlling water's behavior, but without the mathematical skills of the modern engineer. To this conceptual engineering knowledge, I have added intense study of the geology of the Mediterranean world, paying special attention to the karst phenomena, to clarify my understanding of the physical basis of Greek settlement. Volume II, *Geology and Settlement: Ancient Hellenic Patterns,* will discuss this geological material at length, but enough is included here to make clear the significance of karst geology for the patterns of urbanization observed, and for the history of the process of urbanization (see Part IV).

Field Visits to Ancient Sites and Collections

Basic technical knowledge was not sufficient for my purposes. To begin to understand in depth what the Greek solutions were to problems of management of water in their culture and in their geography, I realized that it would be essential to carry out a series of visits to the sites. My purpose was to inspect the lay of the land, the visible remnants of provisions for water management, and sometimes objects that had been placed in storerooms or on display in local museums. Whenever I could meet and discuss the individual site and its water management problems and solutions with the excavators, curators, and guardians, I invariably learned a great deal not to be found in publications. At some sites there was visible evidence that had escaped the attention of excavators who were seeking to answer other questions. Relations between land forms and the architecture placed on them seem to be the most difficult to photograph, the most nebulous to understand, and thus the most rarely included in standard accounts of ancient sites—yet essential to my attempt to understand the way that urbanization has developed, dependent as it is on the physical setting and on major resources such as water. It has also been useful to observe the sites at different times of the year and in different weathers.

Of the thirty-eight sites visited in 1985, I eventually came to concentrate on Akragas (Agrigento), Argos, Assos, Athens, Corinth, Delos, Delphi, Gela, Gortys in the Peloponnesos, Lindos, Megara, Miletus, Morgantina, Olynthus, Posidonia (Paestum), Pella, Pergamon, Pompeii, Priene, Rhodes, Samos, Selinus, Syracuse, and Thasos. Water system elements from all of these cities had been published to some extent before 1970.

Photos and Sketches

Techniques used during this extensive field trip, and the two shorter trips that followed in 1986 and 1988, included making sketches and notes at the site to depict and comment on observed water system elements. Interviews with curators and other knowledgeable persons were also documented in notes, as were visits to museums and storerooms. Additionally, I made extensive photo documentation of the sites, using both slides and black-and-white photos. Since published photos exhibit only the smallest fraction of known material, it has been essential to have my own more abundant record to study from, particularly as questions of water supply, use, and disposal have rarely been of primary interest to other investigators.

Papers

Since 1987, I have made a policy of speaking on various aspects of this topic to local, national, and international meetings, in order to obtain criticism and other feedback. Rewriting the material for different audiences has forced me to be more precise and specific in my own understanding as well as in the presentation of my understanding. I am grateful to those groups who listened and who published preliminary versions of specific chapters in their proceedings or journals, and to the individuals who took the time to comment and to raise questions I would have overlooked.

NOTES

On measurements: I have left all measurements in the units used by the original sources. The result of translating incommensurable feet and inches into meters, or gallons into cubic meters, and vice versa would be a specious accuracy, which I have eschewed.

1. I am grateful to Professor Henning Fahlbusch, of the Technical University at Lübeck, for guiding me over the long-distance lines that Professor Garbrecht and he and their assistants (both German and Turkish) have traced in some 15 years of work on the site. Their discoveries at Pergamon are reported in many volumes of the *Mittheilungen* of the Technical University of Braunschweig, Germany.

2

A Firm Archaeological Base for Urban History? Difficulties of Cross-Disciplinary Research

If obscurity and provinciality of subject matter proved no obstacle to literature, why should they prove so to history?
—C. Vann Woodward
The Perils of Writing History

For those who posit that cities began in the nineteenth century, an appropriate methodology for studying them is to run insurance data through computers, generating statistics and calling the results history. But if our interest extends deep into the past, to Roman or Greek cities or to the first cities of the Yucatan, Mesopotamia, or China, then we are forced to find ways to deal with quite different sorts of evidence. In the Old World there are deciphered or decipherable written records in many cases; in the New World little written evidence. In both the Old and New Worlds, the chief evidence for ancient urbanism is the physical remains of the city, with the paraphernalia of daily life.

Like other forms of human knowledge, archaeology over the past thirty years has become increasingly conscious of its methodology, goals, biases, and problems. The questions being asked and the solutions being sought today reflect some shifts in consciousness and in method. The identification of one's assumptions and biases is part of the new mode of research. Nowhere is this shift better revealed than at a site like Morgantina, Sicily, where excavation has extended over more than thirty years, as frequently reported in the *American Journal of Archaeology* since 1957. This site represents an opportunity for studying ordinary urban settlements of the Greek world, just as a modern sociologist might prefer to study Dayton, Ohio, rather than Los Angeles, as a typical American city. Morgantina is a fine test case for the use of archaeological data as the basis of urban history. Some general conclusions may be drawn from this evidence about the problems and opportunities of cross-disciplinary investigation.

Since 1977, I have hunted through thirty years of excavation records from Morgantina, looking for the occasional fact about water system elements. Gradually I have come to realize that the data from Morgantina were gathered to verify certain written records from ancient times. The data collected would be very different if at the beginning the excavators had asked more anthropological or geographical questions, such as, "Since water is essential for human settlement, what features of this site provide for that need? And what human interventions were made; that is, what structures were built?"

As an urban historian, I think of cities as sets of systems—"System: an assemblage or combination of things or parts forming a complex or unitary whole." I go to Morgantina or any site to study its urban systems, specifically water supply and drainage. At Morgantina, as elsewhere in the Greek world, the rampart components of defense systems have been studied, perhaps because they are large, overt, and architectural. But street networks or water-and-drainage provisions have received much less attention. Classical archaeologists are neither anthropologists nor sociologists, to whom social networks, reflected in physical arrangements, are their major focus of study. But since I am an urban historian, albeit one trained in the art, architecture, and archaeology of Greece and Rome, contextual and functional history questions seem to me the most interesting we can ask of any site.

To understand a highly complex city requires the insights of many specialists, those who take a broad view as well as those who study the details. Here is another potential conflict with archaeologists who expect to handle the history and topography of the site with no more difficulty than when they deal with terra-cottas or bronzes. The kind of history we can write depends partly on the input of experts and partly on the various "universes" in which a history participates. Not only the insights of numismatists and geologists, but also those of historians of art, technology, engineering, and agriculture could profitably be applied to the material from a site like Morgantina. This concept of "whom do we call in for help" is related to the size and complexity of the mental "universe" into which the archaeologists or urban historians try to fit their discoveries. [Universe: a world or sphere in which something exists or prevails. Also called a universe of discourse. By "mental universe" I mean the cluster of associated facts and ideas that are brought to bear on a discovery, such as the ruler chronologies, material variations, and usage patterns that enable one to identify and evaluate an ancient coin.] A handful of coins or a few red-figure sherds already have their chronological and aesthetic relevance established. They fit into an existing archaeological "universe." A water channel of trapezoidal section belongs to an engineering "universe" to which archaeologists cannot easily relate. Water system elements are seen as fragments of an archaeological complex but usually not simultaneously as fragments of an engineering solution to the problem of water supply and drainage. From the point of view of civil engineers, however, the same fragments are seen as belonging to a classical history universe to which the engineers cannot easily relate. Yet since water still behaves as it always has, contemporary hydraulic engineers have much to offer in interpreting the remains of ancient water systems.

Clearly, objects and contexts are emphasized quite differently in archaeology and in urban history. First, there are different assumptions. To an urban historian, archaeology seems to be strongly object-oriented. Searching for valuable objects affects methods of recording and saving the less-valued objects one was not searching for—such as pipes, which have no intrinsic value except as elements of an elusive urban system for the provision of water and for drainage. Second, since the process of archaeology involves the separation of objects from their contexts, with relatively heavier focus on later study of the objects, there is a resulting mild, but cumulative, deemphasis of context. Third, in archaeology there is the presumption that valuable objects will be displayed in museums—nearly impossible for a street system or a water system. How can the excavator resist the subtle pressure to concentrate on displayable findings and to devalue the nondisplayable?

Despite these caveats, the archaeological method does utilize close interaction between object and context as things are discovered and hypotheses about them verified. The object is validated by its context and the context is dated by the object. It is precisely this grounding in specific physical data that makes an archaeologically based urban history so attractive. Archaeological data have the potential of generating a contextual rather than conceptual urban history. One does not have to suppose or invent; one can know how the city changed over time and how life was lived in it.

Yet because methodological shifts in the study of history are slow in affecting classical archaeology, there are many questions to ask , which as yet have no answers. One unanswered question posed by my study is what percentage of water system elements constitutes a valid sample of the system as distinguished from the objects that compose it? However many coins are found at a site, they constitute a valid sample because their context is not site-specific; they have an extensive mental universe in that their chronology has been exhaustively studied. At this time, pipes and other water-system elements lack any such classification scheme, but are site-specific. Thus when a few pipes, a channel or two, some tubs or washbasins are found, we know neither how they relate to an unimaginable whole water system, nor whether this number of elements is enough to define such a system.

A further complication in the use of archaeological data is the unevenness of the data owing to temperamental differences among excavators, and to the way physical work and analysis/evaluation are divided. Some excavators are more interested in one kind of object and some in another, so that one notebook may have beautiful drawings of coins, another of strata, etc. Such variations in recording are not likely to be any more serious, I think, than other accidents of history that have preserved one set of documents but destroyed another. At some sites, to ensure more uniformity of results, elaborate charts have been developed, and each excavator records his or her findings daily on the same kind of chart.

Season by season and dig by dig, there is another problem. The work of excavation is divided between diggers in the trenches and thinkers who supervise the dig. Such a division of labor contains incipient weaknesses, compounded by the necessity of often having final reports done by still a third set of workers who have not excavated at the site at all. Thus, we can easily see that errors in the data will creep in through the very process of gathering the data. What we usually will not see is how our assumptions skew the data we collect. To illustrate the problem of assumptions with details of the water system of Morgantina, let us consider three pipe questions. First, investigators can be so sure about the function of a pipe that they do not test their assumption. Of the large pipes running in front of the West Stoa, Sjöqvist (1959) thought them to be storm drains, while Stillwell (1963) called them a supply line for the fountains east of the Theater. Since some questions must be left dangling in any research, these are likely to be those assumed less important. The questions about these pipes have not been answered by further excavation.

Second, suppose investigators assume that smaller pipes are for the water supply and larger ones are for drainage. This neat assumption is called into question by the fact that the rate of flow in a pipe depends partly on the size of the pipe. Greek engineers could have learned to manipulate flow by varying pipe sizes. Thus the size–function assumption needs in each case to be checked against the particular circumstances of that line of pipe.

The third assumption relates individual pipes to the whole water system. If the archaeologists asked, "Why is that water system element like that? What is it doing there?" they might, in happening on a pipeline, dig directly along it to see where it goes and to what it connects. Once the archaeologists consider recovery of the water system to be a primary goal of the excavation, they could consciously set out to arrive at contextual dates for one water system element, and then progressively use these dates to evaluate and date other similar water system elements as they are discovered. Any unusual element would be referred at once to a hydraulic engineer. The collaboration between archaeologists and engineers at Pergamon stands as a model for such interdisciplinary cooperation.

Archaeologists who deliberately set out to explore an urban system such as water supply and drainage would provide data for the urban historian much more closely tailored to eventual use in technological and urban history. For example, accurate recording of temporal changes in water supply elements could enable us to chart the urban development of a site. Similarly, the location and number of water sources can help explain housing distribution and building techniques.

Alas, there remain other problems among the disciplines, problems much harder to resolve because they are even more invisible than buried pipelines. These include attitude differences. Archaeological investigation is cumbersome, time consuming, and expensive. Consequently, archaeologists have a "gentlemen's agreement" not to trespass on each other's physical and intellectual territory. An archaeologist who has official permission to dig at a site, and has found the funds to support his or her work, has absolute control over it, deciding who may study the evidence, and who may use the data in writing about this or that feature of the site. This agreement is enforced by sanctions. For example, I am not allowed to publish any findings about Morgantina in an archaeological journal without the explicit permission of the present excavator. If that excavator turns the site over to another excavator, the new one has absolute control over publication of my findings. A new agreement has to be worked out with the new chief. Contrast that with the usual situation in architectural history, where originality, insight, and speed are rewarded, and the scene is set for explosive clashes about intellectual property. If a personality conflict is added to such different ways of handling "truth," the urban historian can find herself barred from using the archaeological data in a general study of urban development. This seems to me a very serious problem if one wishes to construct an urban history firmly based on archaeology.

I will conclude by listing the pluses and minuses of using archaeological data as a basis for urban history. As I see it, the advantages are

1. We can deduce urban history from physical remains in the absence of written documents.
2. We can construct a history of ancient water systems, or other nonverbal aspects of an ancient culture, even though almost no written history of the topic exists, from any era.
3. The complexity of the physical remains corresponds to the complexity of their builders' culture.
4. Though factual knowledge about ancient peoples is partial, it is preferable to mental constructs.
5. We find new questions that cause reexamination of our assumptions and hypotheses.
6. The history of knowledge (e.g., ancient hydraulic traditions and building skills) is expanded.

7. In turn, such expansion induces humility as to our "superior" abilities.
8. We become conscious of value patterns previously unconscious and unexamined, in ourselves and in our disciplines.

The problems or disadvantages of using archaeological data as a basis of urban history are equally significant:

1. Not being allowed to use data.
2. In such fields as water supply, historical method and mental universe are both in their infancy.
3. The urban historian may be overwhelmed by new questions, skimpy data, and rampant assumptions. Thus, a lot of sorting and sifting to obtain the needed information is essential and one must be aware of inventing interpretations unbolstered by facts. I am well aware that I must have inserted into the present work a number of mental constructs lacking real data. If however the work incites others to amplify or disprove my conclusions, it will make a contribution in spite of its flaws.
4. Great humility about X usually goes hand in hand with unrecognized arrogance about Y. I do not see any solution for this—except a sense of humor!
5. Modern physics has taught us that we can't know where a thing is and observe its motion at the same time. A "dead" ancient city is more convenient to study but less comprehensive than one, like Rome, that is still living. The nature of the observation also depends upon the particular observer. An ancient city studied by an urban historian is not the same entity as one observed by an archaeologist.
6. Working with people and data that seem to be in the same frame of reference but are not.
7. Finding ways to publish one's findings.

In sum, I believe that the opportunities of this kind of history outweigh the problems. In looking at the urban environments of the past, historians must consider the documents if any survive, and study personally the physical remains. An urban history worth the price is one firmly based on physical evidence.

II

Modern Questions About Ancient Water Control

3

Water System Evidence of Greek Civilization

Attention to water supply and drainage is the sine qua non for urbanization, and hence for that human condition we call civilization. In fact, development of water supply, waste removal, and drainage made dense settlement possible. (In this book, *drainage* is used to mean the leading away from a site of all sorts of water, whether clean or dirty.) In spite of the importance of this factor for human history, relatively little attention has been paid to the history of water management, more to the histories of food supply and of commerce as determiners of urbanization. To compensate for that deficit, this is a study of the relationship between water management and urbanization. Other factors contributing to urbanization are discussed briefly in Chapter 6.

Many of the "working conclusions" in this chapter and elsewhere are my inferences from the physical data discovered by archaeologists. Very little written evidence has come down to us from the Greek period. We are in the position of reasoning backward from the answers to the questions—always a risky business (Pierce, 1965, 5.590). This is not an uncommon problem in Greek history. Mortimer Chambers has pointed out in a talk on travelers to ancient Greece, given at the American Institute of Archaeology meeting, San Francisco, 1990, that if we had to rely on Greek literature for evidence, we would never know that they had ever painted any vases! Yet no one is suggesting that we desist from the study of vases because the surviving ancient Greek writings do not discuss them. No— we go to the vases themselves for the strongest evidence.

In this chapter the emphasis will be on what had to be discovered and organized so that there could be a complete system of water management for an ancient Greek city. If we try to put ourselves back into pre-Hellenic centuries when the world seemed "new," and look about with curious eyes and that great tool the inquiring mind, what will we see? What did "the water problem" consist of?

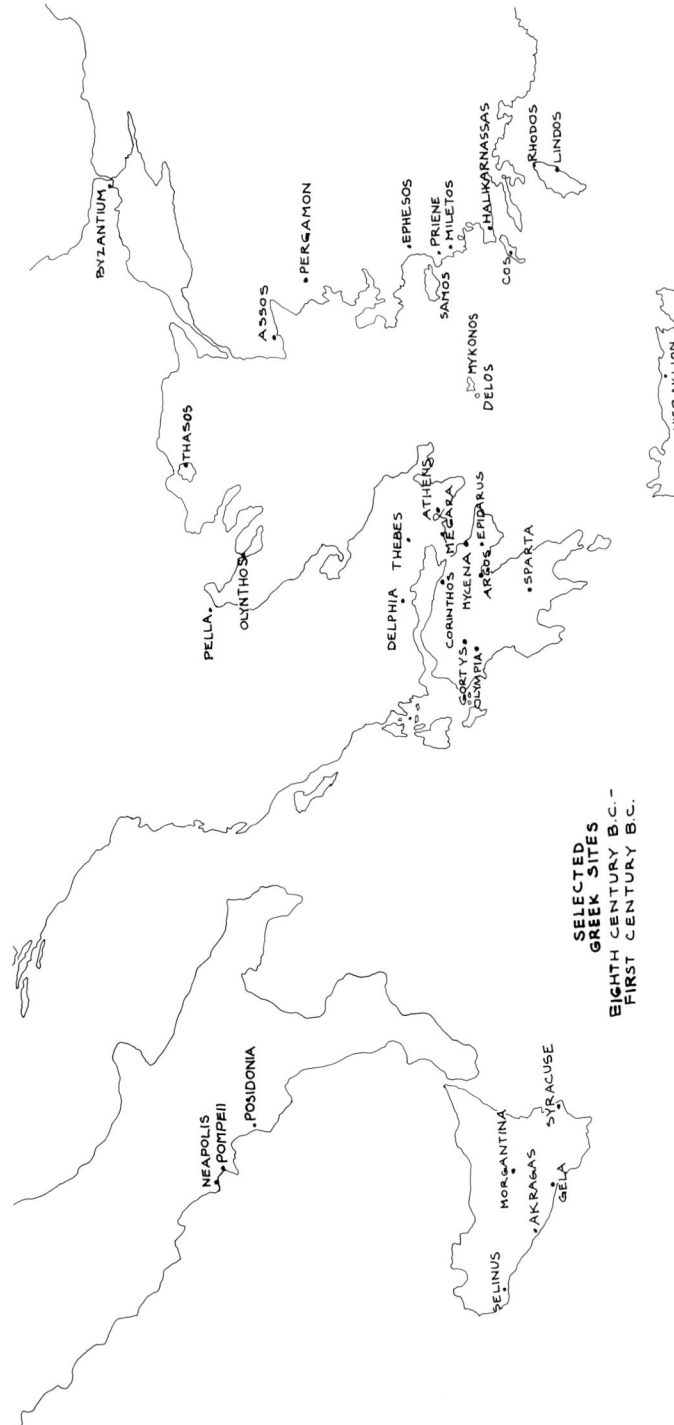

Figure 3.1. Selected Greek sites (chosen for this study because already in 1970 there was published material on their water systems). The Hellenic world comprised southern and western Asia Minor (modern Turkey), the Aegean islands and the northern shore of the Aegean Sea, the peninsulas of modern Greece, all of Sicily except the west coast, most of southern Italy, and some sites (not shown) on the northeast coast of Spain and southern France, and in north Africa.

20

OBSERVATION AND CONTROL

Millennia of observation had enabled the ancient peoples to become expert about many aspects of their environment such as the stars, so that by about 5000 years ago the constellations of the zodiac were recognized and named, and the science of astronomy well begun. During those same millennia, careful observation of other natural phenomena had also revealed much about the behavior of water and led to various patterns of controlling and using it. From the early third millennium B.C. on, the Indus civilization had bathrooms in houses, and sewers in the streets. Their counterparts in Mesopotamia were not far behind (Kahn, 1964; Adams, 1981). In the second millennium B.C. the Minoan civilization on Crete enjoyed running water and flushed latrines of a sophistication quite impressive to their Victorian excavators, themselves just emerging from yet another rediscovery of the joys of indoor plumbing (Evans, 1964, vol. I, 142–43, 226–30).

These two examples serve to demonstrate one important fact about hydraulic knowledge—water's behavior is consistent, but people forget and rediscover information about that behavior, and reinvent how to utilize water for their own purposes. Thus I think it is useful to consider water management as evidence of the state of development of any civilization, Greek or otherwise.

During those dark ages after the fall of Minoan civilization and before the flowering of Greek culture, roughly from 1100 to 700 B.C., Aegean society was in disarray. According to some scenarios, invaders came and went over the peninsulas, islands, and coasts that were to be "Greek"; according to other scenarios, the collapse of the complex Minoan society left a scattered people eking out an existence in a difficult terrain. Little tangible evidence remains of what people built, did, or thought during this time. However, human minds were at work, observing their environment, making "experiments," and accumulating the results, to be passed on to the next generations.

In some parts of the Mediterranean, there was flowing water in the form of lakes or year-round rivers, later to be successfully tapped by the Romans for urban water supply. Never could such water be taken for granted. How rare! How marvelous! Some god must have meant it as a blessing. Was there a spring? Again, a sacred place (J. Rudhardt, 1971). Did the water flow always or intermittently, copiously or feebly? sweet or salty or sulfurous? Was the water therefore good for all purposes, or better for irrigation than drinking? Century by century, the information about water accrued, becoming the basis of a living tradition that informed the decisions and actions of city founders and of engineers.

The rain in the Mediterranean area tends to appear in the winter only, and then in threatening abundance. How to save it for future use? How to dissipate storm waters, easing velocity and volume, so that some could be saved for later use, and some spread out as widely as possible for irrigation (Evanari and Koller, 1956, 39–45; Hammond, 1967, 38–47)? To the north of the Mediterranean, draining away excess water seems to have been a problem equal in magnitude to the necessity of saving water for later use that preoccupied farmers to the south and in the Near East (Shaw, 1984, 121–73 especially p. 137). In each region, water had to be actively managed, not passively accepted.

Individual households could achieve some security for their water supply by building cisterns or excavating wells. The desire to have one's own well or cistern came from the recognition that in a climate with a summer both hot and dry, without rain for more than six months of the year, security and even survival depended on a reliable source of water. Cisterns are known from Minoan and Mycenaean settlements, a thousand years or so before the classical and Hellenistic Greek cities of my study. Judson (1959) has estimated that by capturing even half of the water that fell on the roof of a typical house at Morgantina, Sicily, the inhabitants of that house were assured of the minimum to carry them through the dry season. Many houses had two cisterns, suggesting larger families, a home industry that used water, higher standards of water usage, or simply increased desire to be safe and water-rich for very little additional effort and expense. The domestic cistern was undoubtedly the model for the municipal reservoir, like the rock-hewn tanks at Petra that harvest the runoff from the rocky cliffs of the site rather than from rooftops. Since conditions remained the same, this early solution went on being utilized not for centuries but for millennia. Some cisterns are still operative.

The basic principle of water supply seems to have been to use as many different sources of water as were available and the least necessary physical effort. After choosing a site with an inherently positive geological base (see Part IV), the settlers then developed its various potentials: permanent and intermittent springs, wells, cisterns, and pipelines. All these contributed to the water supply of the town, each reinforcing the other, so that failure of one source had less drastic effects on the residents, because mitigated by continued supply from the others. Some of these sources could be developed by individuals or small groups (cisterns, for example) but drains are likely to have been communal efforts. The people were willing to make this communal effort to improve public spaces by dewatering a low area or carrying away wastes in sewers, not only for reasons of public health but also for aesthetic and social reasons. So much of their social life was lived communally, publicly, that they required the public spaces to be well arranged and cared for. The population of a town was large enough to participate in communal building efforts, and to fund them. They also had technology advanced enough, when added to the knowledge gained through centuries of observation, to make the management and arrangement of water elements enhance urban density.

First came hundreds or thousands of observations about where water was found. From these natural occurrences, it was a logical but bold inference that by digging down from the surface or inward from a slope, one could intersect the seam where water would collect, and have a well or a catchment basin where water was needed. Then came the leap to the generalized principle, then the deliberate search and triumphant finding of water in places suggested by the principle, then codification of such knowledge into a working tradition and passing it down to the next generation. (These issues are discussed in Chapter 10, Natural Models for Water Elements.)

Thus the Greeks had gradually acquired the knowledge of where to look for hidden water. Even today the superstitious think there is something magical about finding water, yet certain physical clues remain helpful in the search. For instance, certain plants prefer to grow with their roots in concentrations of water. In the Mediterranean area, these plants are often the fig tree, the rosemary bush, and the ubiquitous bramble, as well as the more obvious moss (Meinzer, 1927). There are geological clues too. Like the modern archaeological geologist, the ancient settler knew what to look for:

> The striking soft sandiness and bright yellow and orange hues of the marls and flysch [which formed an impenetrable barrier above which water would collect] can often today single out an ancient site before its location is found from a map, and once early farmers became aware of the remarkably favorable properties of these soils, they would encounter no problems in searching out similar exposures. (Bintliff, 1976, 271)

These soils and the rock from which they were formed are usually layered closely with water-bearing carbonate rocks. Whenever impermeable clay lies above or below permeable limestone or sandstone, water collects along the seam, becoming visible as a spring or seep on the face of a hill. If the limestone has been fissured in just the right way, the water might appear at the surface as an artesian well (Steel and McGhee, 1979, Chapter 4 and diagrams 4–14 and 4–15).

Definitions used here for these common water words:

A *well* is a shaft into a water-bearing stratum from which water seeps into the shaft, to be drawn or pumped up by users.

A *cistern* is a water-holder carved or constructed below the ground surface and waterproofed.

I use the word *"tank"* to refer to water-holders built above ground surface.

A *reservoir* is a large (usually municipal) water holder.

A *spring* is a spontaneous flow of water at the surface or in an accessible cave.

An *artesian well* is a place where water flows upward to the surface, under pressure from below; it is thus a kind of vertical spring.

Further, in all the areas studied, underground water carved out *tunnels* in karst formations which could be harnessed to provide copious supplies of water for large cities (LaFleur, 1984, sections 7, 8, 10, 11, 13, 14, 15, and as discussed in Chapter 10).

We are just beginning to realize that the development and ownership of water resources came not by "natural rights" nor a series of accidents, but by conscious decisions of the social group and of individuals. The community organized labor, materials, and money. They worked out the legal aspects of ownership, maintenance, and control. We need to be equally conscious of the engineering advances that made more complex and larger cities possible. What a great shift in attitude and behaviors in bringing the water to the settlement, rather than always having to locate the settlement at the water, or abandoning a settlement if it grew too large for its water supply! Such a change was possible because people gradually developed the technology to transfer water not by carrying it but by means of a water channel or pipeline (see chapter 11, Planning Water Management).

ARCHITECTURAL FEATURES

After the initial period of observation of water came a second of generalization and codification of knowledge. With improved material conditions beginning in the seventh century B.C., the ancient Greeks had the leisure to deal with fine-tuning their water knowledge. With survival assured, they could ask such questions as, How much water did a person need every day? How much for different tasks, and for public functions? Such questions had to be asked and the answers worked out in practice. The answers were closely linked to the way the community was organized and what tasks occupied its members. A place where silver was mined or wool was dyed needed much more water than a village of shepherds or fishermen (Jones, 1982, 169–83). Where the citizens enjoyed public life together, there was likely to be more provision for public display of water to enhance that common life.

As the society matured and became richer, enhancement of the settlement by explicit public facilities for water became the norm, in keeping with the Greek tendency to concretize "ideal form" (Webster, 1973, 8, 267–73). At Corinth, for instance, several fountains marked the Agora. The copious seepage from the seam between impermeable clay and the overlying stone layer was already in the archaic period monumentalized as a fountainhouse (Peirene) with several long basins to catch and hold the water, and with a parapet and screen of columns along the front. Even the less copious Sacred Spring—focus of settlement since Early Helladic times (Mackay, 1967, 193–95)—was as early as the sixth century given a front wall of ashlar masonry with bronze spouts under which water jars could be placed (see Part IX, Amenity and Necessity). Every

Greek city had at least one fountain in the Agora. The hilltown of Morgantina in Sicily, for instance, had at least six fountains scattered about its large Agora (Crouch, 1984, 353–65). Some fountains, whose flowing water was preferred for drinking, were to be found within neighborhoods, as the pattern of corner fountains at Priene and at rebuilt (Roman) Pompeii indicates. (For Priene see Chapter 12; for Pompeii, Chapter 13.)

In addition to fountainhouses, Greek public spaces such as sanctuaries were often enhanced with tanks or very large cisterns, so that the necessary rituals would never want for water. By later Hellenistic times at the latest, reservoirs were set up inside or just outside of settlements. A community then could draw on its wells and cisterns, on fountains within the city supplied by pipelines from springs inside or outside the city, and on reservoirs.

Even such a simple device as a cistern shows increasing sophistication during the fifth through second centuries B.C. Good examples are found at Morgantina. The earliest are irregular in every way, hewn out of sand or loose rock, and lined with stucco to waterproof them. Their wide mouths open at the surface. In the residential quarter on East Hill, such wide-mouthed cisterns of the fifth century were later filled in with third century houses built on top. For the later house, a new cistern was placed under the courtyard, sometimes with a second cistern under the walkway around the courtyard. Water from the roof was led to the cisterns by downspouts. These later cisterns were regular and flask-shaped, with a long neck, and were also waterproofed with a hard plaster coating. The bottoms sloped to a bowl-like depression which collected silt and debris for easy annual cleaning (see Fig. 3.2). The most advanced technical feature of these later cisterns was their long neck, which limited access and evaporation while it placed the body of the cistern—and thus the water that it contained—deep into the earth, mostly below the line of stable temperature, well below that of the ambient, fluctuating air temperature. Ground temperature varies with ambient temperature and soil type but is fairly constant year round at depths determined by these local conditions. In upstate New York, for example, the temperature below 6 feet underground stays at about 55 degrees Fahrenheit. The water stored at this depth would be kept cooler and thus more palatable and purer during the heat of summer. It may very well be from the experience of having to drink such stored water that the custom arose of watering the wine or, more precisely, adding wine to water to kill germs and improve flavor.

There is scarcely a house in Morgantina that lacks a cistern, and even in the later Roman town of Pompeii, with its elaborate water distribution system, all of those "ornamental" atria are the upper surfaces of cisterns, and the holes in the roofs are made to collect the rain water so it can be saved for later domestic use.

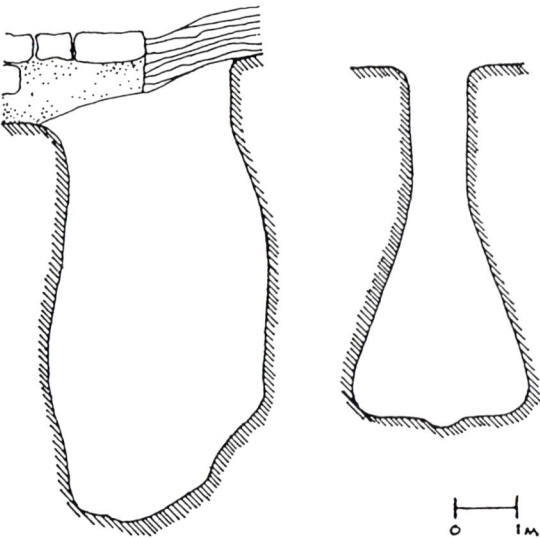

Figure 3.2. Irregular fifth century cistern and bottle-shaped third century cistern from Morgantina. Drawn to the same scale.

Thus the archaeological record points consistently to a plurality of solutions for the problem of water supply. The community learned that it was most effective to allocate some tasks such as building and maintaining cisterns to individuals. Ordinarily cistern water was private but had to be shared when the survival of the group was at stake. It is probable that wells in residential neighborhoods were also shared. We have legal evidence from Athens that people were required to share well water with neighbors whose well or cistern had gone dry (Plutarch, *Lives.* "Solon," XXIII, 6).

At Morgantina there is a well or cistern (the excavation did not reach bottom, so we cannot be sure which) on the western hill, in the House of the Arched Cistern, that is built into the outer wall of the dining room, accessible by a short alleyway from the public street. Thus neighbors could have access to this well without penetrating the private space of the house itself. At another place in Morgantina, northeast of the agora, an apartment building had its own well in the courtyard, for the use of all the residents.

Having found water or stored rain, what uses did these ancient Greeks find for it? How were the uses allocated to the public or private realm? Showers, footbaths, baths in tubs of various shapes were so important a part of Greek life as to be frequently painted on their vases. Excavation has brought to light a number of public bath buildings, some connected with shrines of the healing god Asklepius, and some sited to relate to sports facilities or other public structures (Ginouves, 1962; Delorme, 1960).

This public life was, except at Sparta, restricted to the men and boys of the community, so that the informal gatherings at public fountains played a major part in the social life of women and girls, otherwise confined mostly to the home. Thus even the use of water facilities is highly indicative of the patterns of urban life among the Greeks.

The increasing sophistication of Greek water management during the period studied is well documented in the physical evidence of rooms set aside for ablution and/or excretion in private houses. In fifth century Athens, the modest provision for such functions was a room with a drain into the sewer running in the alley behind the house (Martin, 1956, fig. 40). We assume bathing utilized portable tubs or basins and excretion utilized chamber pots. But by two centuries later, in many Greek settlements, though not all, houses were equipped with bathrooms with bathtubs in a space separate from the toilet. Sometimes, as at Olynthos, there was also a washbasin (louter) in the same room, but at other places such as Delos the louter stood out in the courtyard. That location for the louter facilitated its use for washing dishes as well as hands and faces, as indicated by two small figurines in the National Museum at Athens of women washing dishes. The latrine might be a separate room with a stone or wood bench with the necessary holes cut out, and a drain to the sewer under the street, or it might be a semidefined compartment of the larger bathroom, again drained to the street. At Olynthos, one terra-cotta toilet was found, and a couple of urinals, all three so similar to ours in shape as to prove there is nothing new under the sun (J. W. Graham, 1938, pl. 55) (see Fig. 17.7). Ancient bathtubs, too, have their counterparts in modern Greek hotels: high sides, a seat, a ledge for feet or for a child to sit on, and a lower basin for water to collect in. Few tubs had drains, so that water seems to have been removed with a cup or a sponge. The tub might sit up on a metal stand, or it might be built into the bathroom alcove. Fifth and fourth century tubs were commonly of terra-cotta, while a simpler form made of stone is associated with third and second century remains, either built up of separate slabs or carved out of a block. In either case, the interior was smoothed off with waterproof stucco or sometimes with one-inch cubes of glazed brick, for a comfortable sitting surface. (See Figs. 12.1 for a house plan with bathroom, 20.11A–D for plans of four bathrooms, and Figs. 16.18, 16.19, 17.7, 20.8–10, 22.6, 22.8, and 22.9 for photographs of fittings.)

In public baths, as early as the fifth century B.C., these terra-cotta or stone tubs were arranged in regular patterns, such as radiating wedges around the edge of a rotunda, or in parallel rows, or parallel to the edge of a rectangular space. They could be supplied with running water by a channel at shoulder height for the person seated in the tub. Sometimes the water was even heated (see Figs. 11.8, 16.10, 22.2). Both in the bath buildings and in houses and on vase paintings, we find footbaths (ovoid or more rarely rectangular), shower facilities similar to the high spouts of fountains (Fig. 6.1), and tubs that looked like giant chalices, in which one apparently sat with knees up under the chin (cf. Ginouves, 1962, 183–225) (Fig. 22.9). A very late survival of this type is shown in the Christian mosaics of the eleventh century in the Palatine Chapel in Palermo, where St. Paul sits in such a chalice-tub. Such chalice-tubs were like the very large semispherical pithoi that are found in several courtyards at Morgantina. These are crudely propped up on blocks of stone, and apparently could be filled directly by downspouts from the roof. I think that these were mostly used for washing clothes, which were then hung on lines or poles around the courtyard, humidifying the house as they dried (Fig. 17.5). Lacking a flowing river, some such provision must have been made for doing laundry. Another possibility is that like the farmwomen at Morgantina today, the ancient Greek women gathered at the tank that held the overflow of a spring, scrubbing their clothes on its coping before the water was reused for irrigation (Fig. 15.8).

Thrifty reuse of water seems to have been the norm. Since we know that at public baths in Roman times the water for bathing was reused to flush out the latrines, it is reasonable to infer a Greek origin for so eminently sane a proceeding, a private and domestic origin for such institutional reuse. In the days before soap was invented, nothing would prevent reuse of bath waters for washing the floor, watering potted flowers, or quenching the thirst of the family dog or donkey. In a recent drought in California, people used "gray water" for all of these tasks and more.

DRAINAGE

Eventually, no matter how thrifty the use, there is waste water to dispose of. Especially during the winter rainy season, there are storm waters to channel away from buildings and paved open spaces, toward areas where they are an asset not a menace. Drains were already a notable element of Minoan palaces, and must have been rediscovered as the Greeks began to live in dense settlments. I suspect that community drainage systems were a relatively late development built only when no alternative could be devised for making urban living tolerable. This pessimistic view is derived from the present experience of developing countries such as Nepal. Water systems there have wide popular support, but sanitation even at the simple level of privies is often "too expensive" or "unnecessary." In spite of human inertia and political difficulties, however, Greek cities came to have sewers under the street pavements in residential areas, and great drain channels through the public areas. Drainage elements known within Greek cities include eaves troughs for individual buildings, such as along the steps of the stoas at Cos; drain pipes piercing the walls or foundations of individual houses; collector channels in neighborhoods such as those in the Hellenistic quarter in Akragas; and great drains in public areas such as the Agora at Argos.

A fine example of a neighborhood collector is the channel along the west side of the House of the Official at Morgantina. Built of the same stone as the house foundations and bonded to them, the channel was obviously conceived and built integrally with the house and the street next to it (Fig. 16.14). In the Agora of the same city, the earliest stone drains appear to date from the fifth century B.C., which was the first century of occupation, since they lie under the later North Stoa (Sjöqvist, 1964, 137–47, pl. 41–46, esp. 138–40 and pl. 41; Crouch, 1984, Ill. 5). They are part of the extensive system draining the northwest sector of the public zone and were necessitated by the slope above the stoa. The large size of the stone slabs of these drains was necessary to withstand the force of torrential water after a heavy storm; the size indicates that building drains was a communal effort. The Morgantina drain was similar in form to the great drain along the west side of the Athenian Agora. Waste and storm waters were used to flush the late latrine at the south end of the East Stoa, but possibly because of the diminished flow from the fountain, did so rather imperfectly.[1]

My working hypothesis is that storm waters were used to flush not only latrines but also public sewers, and the combined effluent was used to irrigate crops, especially trees. Modern experiments have shown that a wooded slope can absorb as much as 120 inches of water per year (Shalhevet et al, 1976; Kardos and Soper, 1973, 148–63), grow a fine crop of wood for fuel and for building materials. That the Greeks utilized waste waters in this way was suggested to me by the present custom in Aidone (near Morgantina) where they spread sewage out on what are called sewage farms or sanitary fields. Given the prevalent sunshine, the anaerobic bacteria are quickly killed, and with them the offensive smell—a simple, low-technology solution available also to the ancients.[2] I would like to see an excavation of parts of the south slope at Morgantina, to search for the remains of irrigation channels connected to the evident drainage channels near the city gates.

In any society with a sound ecological balance between man and environment, people have developed the ability to live lightly on the land, contributing to its renewable resources, observing and utilizing natural cycles, harmonizing actions to give as well as take. One such contribution, part of the traditional symbiosis between town and countryside, was the provision of night soil as fertilizer for the crops. Its most important chemical ingredient is ammonia, for which we now spend huge sums in the form of chemicals to apply to the land (Commoner, 1976, 165–72). During the European Middle Ages, it was usual to cart solid human excrement out of town to the fields in special carts or on the backs of donkeys. The same method is still used in Chinese agriculture to achieve impressive yields. There are problems of contamination by transfer of disease-bearing organisms, but again observation would have suggested to the Greeks which risks they were willing to undergo. The Chinese, for example, almost always cook their vegetables, since heat kills many disease organisms. Modern environmental engineers have a rule of thumb, "Human wastes to grow animal food; animal wastes to grow human food." Implementation of this rule, which the Greeks could have learned by observation, curtails the transmission of disease. Constant-drip irrigation/fertilization is especially beneficial in arid areas (Finkel, 1979, 466–70; Shalhevet et al, 1976). We have only recently rediscovered these processes, but no sophisticated technology is required to discover or maintain them, and simple observation could have revealed them to the Greeks. It is easy to imagine such rich fertilizer producing a steady crop of trees on these slopes, renewing the fuel supply, renewing the supply of building materials, stabilizing the slopes against erosion, and recharging the water table. As Lewis Mumford has written about medieval sanitary arrangements in *The City in History* (Chapter 10), crude ways are not necessarily bad ways.

URBANIZATION

Thus the archaeological record clearly reveals the connection between management of water resources and the development of dense human settlement in the ancient Greek world. This society knew how to find water, to save it or drain it away as circumstances required, to transport it by sophisticated long-distance water supply lines, to make public display in fountains and pools that contributed amenity as well as nourishment, to use it both at home, in the public baths, and in sanctuaries, and to drain it away afterward, cleverly reusing it to maintain other necessary resources such as food, fuel, and building materials, and indeed the water table itself.

Greek hydraulic engineering was sophisticated enough to assure the water supply and drainage of a site, to provide what I have called a complete system, and thus to assure that the city could flourish. Like the changing city that it served, the water supply and drainage in an ancient city were constantly breaking down and being repaired, like modern systems. The system was expanded if necessary, even as in our houses and cities. Hydraulic solutions were competent, modest, adaptable to the local situation, and inexpensive because of their modesty.

Traditional knowledge about water management was widespread in the culture, as is evident from the behavior of the Greeks when they left their mother cities to found colonies beginning in the eighth century and continuing into the fourth century, though at a reduced rate. They planted scores of new cities northeastward toward the Black Sea and southwestward into Sicily. A member of an aristocratic family, accompanied by others usually chosen by lot, set out to build a new, independent center for civilized living (A.J. Graham, 1964). Traditional criteria developed for site selection, with the most important factors being defense, abundance of food and water, and beauty of the site (see Chapter 9, Urban Location Determinants). It was the society's previous experience that enabled them to appraise a site's defensive capability, decide what kinds of crops could be grown and how abundantly, and examine a potential site for open and hidden sources of water. That they chose well is evident from the success and long life of many of these colonies; the most striking is perhaps Byzantium-Constantinople-Istanbul, now some 2800 years old.

Cities flourished or died then as well as now. Besides the rather abstract forces of international trade or dynastic ambition, which we acknowledge, ancient urban dwellers were painfully aware of the effects of deforestation and of dewatering. Sometimes the two went together, sometimes dewatering occurred because of earthquake or avalanche. Hence the need for constant upkeep and remodeling of the urban water supply. Rome is only the most well-known example of a city whose history could be explained as a constant search for new water resources and for the funds to pay for them (Frontinus Gesellschaft, 1983). Already in Greek times, the community had recognized the necessity of working together and spending common funds on water supply and drainage for the benefit of all. The development of the water system not only made urban living feasible but also continues to tell us unexpected good news about our Greek predecessors and how they used water resources to improve human living conditions. Perhaps their best idea was to return as much water as possible to the environment near the city, thus perpetuating a balanced mode of existence and preserving the environment for the use of their descendants.

NOTES

1. Dr. Stephen Miller, who excavated this area, said to me, "If you had smelled what I smelled when we excavated it, you'd have had no doubt it was a latrine!"

2. I observed this when Signor La Spina, director of the water and sewage systems at Aidone, showed me their municipal facilities.

4

Modern Insights About
Ancient Water Management

The growth of a city is determined by how much its water supply
can be increased.

—Fun with Facts

Until now no one has studied ancient Greek water supply, use, and disposal as a coherent system. City planners, urban historians, and economic historians today routinely consider the systems that make up cities as well as the networks that cities constitute (Fig. 9.1). Application of their methodologies in analyzing and synthesizing the data from classical Greek cities is highly unusual (Doxiadis, 1972). Yet as an urban historian well acquainted with the cities of ancient Greece and Rome, my task is exactly that—to apply modern methods to the study of ancient urbanization. (Urban systems are discussed more fully in Chapters 3 and 5.)

One could postulate several urban systems for old Greek cities—food supply, defense, residential—each to be considered in itself and in the way it relates to the whole city, as well as how it relates to each of the other systems. This present study concentrates on the basic arrangements for water that made urbanization possible in the Greek world of the eighth to first centuries B.C.; extracts data from the archaeological, geological, hydrological, and literary evidence relevant to water management points to the need for further cross-disciplinary investigations.

The four major points to be examined are how the founders were able to choose a site with water potential; how they determined, developed, and utilized the water resources that were available; how water elements were distributed in the urban landscape; and finally what lessons we can derive for use today from study of the water management techniques of the ancient Greeks—simultaneously modest and sophisticated.

In the early days, in the third millennium on Cyprus, for example, the settlement was placed next to or over the water supply. From the sixth century, however, some impressive engineering works attest to a new determination to bring water from a distance to the settlement. This determination seems to have been the result of expanding population and increased settlement size, both requiring new solutions to the problem of water supply, coupled with new wealth. The knowledge of how to build underground aqueducts was, I believe, transferred to the Greeks from the Persians with whom they came in close contact in Asia Minor and who derived the idea from the Armenians (see Tolman, 1937, 3 and Smith, 1975, 71). Most amazing of the new Greek supply lines was the great tunnel at Samos, which carried water more than a kilometer through a mountain (Kienast, 1970, 97–116; Goodfield, 1964, 104–12). By the end of the sixth century traditional Greek water management included both tunnel and contour-line techniques for long distance transfer of water (Fahlbusch, 1982), setting the scene for urban civilization to flourish during the fifth century. Note that Greek long-distance lines usually ran underground and along contours—modest, durable engineering rather than spectacular architecture (Figs. 4.1, 4.2).

WATER MANAGEMENT

Having selected a site for its generally positive water potential, the founders next faced the specific questions of finding and harnessing that water. Probably they began by grouping their houses around a spring. In small communities the springs would always have remained essential, whether elaborated into fountainhouses or not, while in large centers springs received architectural expression that contributed greatly to the urban design quality of the place. These architectural issues are discussed in Part IX, Amenity and Necessity. The effect on Greek cities and houses of the constraints imposed by the nature of the water supply is discussed in the Part VIII, Physical Constraints on Built Form, where plural, site-specific methods of supply are contrasted with singular and community-wide methods of drainage.

Greek cities had three kinds of water available for three different uses. For drinking, their preference was to carry water from the nearest flowing fountain or spring. Studies of modern urban water usage show that less than six percent of total water supply is used for drinking, as discussed in Chapter 12. Carrying that much of the family supply from the spring or fountain was not an insufferable task for the women and girls, who thereby had a chance to get out of the house and talk with their neighbors. For bathing and cleaning, houseplants and domestic animals, and even for drinking in times of war or shortage, usually each house had a cistern, fed by rainwater. This water was also used for craft activities such as making pottery. The quality of this cistern water was equivalent to the modern category "subpotable." Note that exceptions are known to this pattern of use: At Priene there was so much flowing water that it was used for every purpose in about 75 percent of the houses. But at Pompeii both aqueduct water and well water was contaminated by the

N   S

Schnitt durch den Stadtmauerberg

Figure 4.1. Section of the waterline and tunnel of Eupalinos, at Samos. Published by Kienast (1986/87): Abb. 25b, and reprinted by permission.

Figure 4.2. Interior of the Samos tunnel. At right is the walkway and at left the lower channel in which the water flowed. The tunnel is about 1.75 meters wide and reaches a maximum depth of 8.5 m.

volcano, so that drinking water was drawn from rain-fed cisterns. These examples remind us that the local circumstances affect solutions. They also demonstrate that the principle of multiple sources was flexible enough to allow for variations in water quality.

One further aspect of utilizing water resources was the disposal of waste water and the possible reuse of non-potable water. A ready example is the stone waterbasin of the Athenian Sanctuary of the Twelve Gods. Filled by the overflow from the Southwest Fountainhouse, this basin supplied water for cleansing after sacrifices, and "for watering the trees and shrubs that are attested by planting holes around the shrine" (*Athenian Agora*, 1990, 97; cf. Plato *Laws* 761C and *Kritias* 1176).

In a city, the pavements and roof areas interfere with the absorption of rainwater. The problem is exacerbated in Greek lands because in the Mediterranean climate, the early, heavy rains of autumn fall on ground baked almost as hard as cement. The resulting runoff requires installation of carefully positioned storm drains, with provision for leading the waters out of the city. At Selinus, for example, the ramparts were built with drain slits (some with settling basins as well) at the end of drains from every cross-street, so that runoff could exit (Fig. 12.5a–j),or else the ramparts would behave as dams and be in danger of overthrow by the force of the water (Judson, 1959). This rushing water from storms having flushed out the drains that also received domestic waste waters and (in some places) human excrement could be used to irrigate crops near the city. A useful study would be excavating for irrigation channels and old tree roots on such a slope to verify or disprove this hypothesis. (These issues are discussed at length in Chapter 12, Planning Water Quality.)

The management of water for an ancient Greek city was calibrated to the realities of hydrogeology, of preferred urban form, and of culture. The residents of most cities could afford to prefer fresh, flowing drinking water because it was available at not too great a cost in time or community resources, by means of accessible springs and their associated fountain-houses. The people could store the other water needed for domestic use in cisterns cut into rock or built of stones. When times were good, the domestic cistern allowed for the luxuries of an afternoon bath (in the heat of the day), some pots of flowers, and even domestic animals; when there was a siege or a drought, the cisterns' water meant the difference between survival and death. Wells, cisterns, and springs spaced more or less evenly over the urban landscape (cf. Fig. 4, "Waterworks in the Athenian Agora") not only helped to preserve the physical existence of the people but also signified their democratic equality (see Chapter 11, Planning Water Management).

Modern water resource policymakers and the hydraulic engineers responsible for carrying out public policy on water have in a number of recent international conferences begun to reconsider the use of domestic cisterns. Such cisterns have two advantages: They remove storm waters from the streets to storage, thus reducing the amount of storm water to be controlled and disposed of by the municipality. And in arid or semiarid areas of potential shortage such as Arabia, they provide free water.

DISTRIBUTION OF WATER RESOURCES IN THE CITY PLAN

Let's look at an example of fifth century planning and see where the water system elements are located. If we examine Akragas (modern Agrigento) in Sicily, we see from Schubring's map of 125 years ago (frontispiece) that there had been a highly developed water supply system appropriate to such a large and prosperous city (Schubring, 1870). Akragas was founded in 580 B.C. and first destroyed in 406. Comparing the frontispiece with a modern geological map of the site (Fig. 8.6) we can see that the waterlines that Schubring so laboriously traced depend upon the existence of numerous springs and that Schubring's water lines carry the outflow downwards and spread it out by utilizing karst formations underground. (See discussion in Part IV about karst phenomena.) In turn, we can compare the locations of the springs with the Hellenistic street pattern (Fig. 15.2). The location and form of the city depended on the location and available flow from the springs. (See Chapters 15, 17, and 18 for further discussion of these matters.)

LESSONS LEARNED

These few examples of the relationships between water management and urban form in the Greek city have indicated the sophistication of the traditional knowledge about water, to be expounded in more detail in the rest of the book. This traditional management of water made possible the process of urbanizing the Mediterranean world by Greek colonists during the eighth through fourth centuries B.C., and the process of urbanization made necessary more sophisticated water systems that could support larger populations.

In the absence of documents from Greek times that deal with these topics, we are today in the position of having to reason backward from the answers to the questions. Given that they did locate such successful cities as Byzantium and Akragas, how did they do it? What were their criteria? Could it be accidental that time after time the location chosen was beautiful, easily defended, adjacent to good farm land or a good port or both, and well enough supplied with water to allow for growth to very large agglomerations indeed? I conclude that this result cannot be ascribed to chance (see Part IV, Geography and Geology, especially Chapter 9, Urban Location Determinants). Doxiadis' comparative studies of city location in modern and ancient Greece show that very frequently when the planners ascertained statistically and from survey reconnaissance that a place was logical for a settlement, excavation corroborated that an ancient Greek settlement had been located exactly there. By the best modern standards, then, the ancient Greeks knew what they were doing in choosing urban sites.

The principles behind Greek urbanization were stated succinctly by Aristotle, "Men come together in cities to live safely; they continue together to live well." Safety requires enough water for survival even under difficult circumstances such as war or drought. Living well requires three basic factors in water management. First is the guarantee of long-range security of the water supply. Even though the karst terrain on which many Greek cities were located has the tendency to self-destruct by (among other processes) denuding the surface of vegetation (van Andel et al., 1986, 103–28), human actions can hasten or retard that result. Using runoff and waste waters to grow trees near a city not only provides fuel and building materials, but also has the further beneficial effects of retaining and redirecting water into the water table in the immediate vicinity of the settlement, so that wells and springs continue to make water available. Depending on ground conditions, this process can purify the used water as it percolates slowly through the earth—much more sound ecologically than hasty runoff into streams and the sea.[1]

The second factor in living well is providing suitable water for each use with the least expenditure of community wealth and human labor, a matter of cost-benefit analysis. If every drop of water used in the home or in a small manufactory had to be carried in vases from a spring, the time and labor of women and girls would be available for almost nothing else. But the provision of cisterns reduced the amount of water that had to be carried by over 90 percent. The technology of the cistern is so simple that a family could construct one itself, as well as carry out the obligatory annual cleaning. On the other hand, the benefit of well-designed and well-built drainage channels in public areas and along residential streets, which would transport storm and waste waters outside the settlement and deliver them to irrigation sites, was great enough to warrant public expenditure of time and money on them. Built of large stones beyond the capacity of a single individual or family to handle, the channels suggest a municipal plan for and community wealth devoted to the provision of drains but not cisterns. One of the great intellectual and political questions of today is how to allocate work and decision making for maximum benefit and least cost. This ancient Greek model suggests ways by which we could make similar decisions.

The third factor in living well is embodying a good value system in the physical form of the settlement. Keen realization of the importance of water in a semiarid climate was an appropriate value for these ancient towns, as indeed it is for everyone living under similar water resource constraints. Architectural prominence given to public water works such as fountains makes evident to us that water was a highly valued resource (see Part IX, Amenity and Necessity). The reuse of bath water for washing floors, and of storm water combined with domestic wastes for irrigation, show vivid appreciation of the value of water. Even a detail like washing clothes in the courtyard was an efficient use of human energy as well as of stored water, the clothes humidifying the house as they dried (see Fig. 17.5). Thus the quality of water, the amount of water, and the location of use were all carefully worked out in terms of their architectural form and symbolism, their social cost to the Greek settlement, and their environmental soundness.

It must be admitted, however, that—like their modern successors—few of the ancient Greek settlements achieved total implementation of the best water management that their civilization was capable of. Homer Thompson has reminded me of the "old-fashioned layout and the very inadequate water supply of Athens even in the Hellenistic period" (according to Pseudo-Dicaerchus or Herakleides as cited by J. G. Frazer,

Pausanias, introduction XLii ff, and F. Pfister, *Die Reisenbilder des Herakleides,* Vienna (1956), 72f).

The application of these ancient Greek principles of water management to modern settlements is considered again in Part X, Learning from Greek Experience. At this point in the argument, let us merely quote Robert Frost: "Much of the change we think we see in life is due to truths being in and out of fashion." As has happened so often, we are having to re-learn some water management techniques that were commonplace to our Greek forebears but have since been forgotten. This is not surprising.[2]

NOTES

1. I learned about this process of purification as the water seeps through the ground from Professor Donald Auerbach of Rensselaer Polytechnic Institute whose course in "Land Management of Waste Waters" brought me to understand natural possibilities for management which recycles waters, and who discussed these ancient management possibilities with me at length.

2. One of Crouch's Laws states: *Under the very best circumstances, you can only get across—at most—50 percent of what you are trying to teach, and even then it will be 50 percent chosen completely at random.*

III

Greek Urbanism—
Data and Theories

5

Urban Patterns in the Greek Period: Athens, Paestum, Morgantina, Miletus/Priene, and Pergamon as Formal Types

In order to assess the impact of the delivery and drainage of water on the urban pattern in the ancient Greek world, it is necessary to have clear ideas of what forms their cities took. Thus a brief discussion of urban patterns will be useful.

Traditional descriptions of ancient Greek cities characterize them by typical street patterns, usually two major types: the Hippodamean grid of Miletus of the fifth century, and the terraces like the blades of a fan found at Pergamon of the late third and second centuries, called "scenographic urbanism." Yet a more careful examination of the evidence suggests that for different centuries B.C., there are many more urban types than two. Examples standing for both the repertory of physical patterns and the changes in those patterns over time that we may cite are:

1. 7th century B.C.—Akragas (frontispiece): irregular hill-top site of the archaic period
2. 6th century—Paestum (Fig. 5.1B): "bar and stripes"
3. 5th century—Athens (Fig. 5.1A): organic, focused on central acropolis and agora, similar to Akragas pattern
4. 5th century—Morgantina (Fig. 5.1C): typical West Greek pattern of two flat hills with residential quarters grid platted and lower agora between them
5. 4th and 3rd centuries—Priene (Fig. 51.D): based on prototype grid at Miletus (early 5th century—Fig. 22.4) and refinement of grid as used at Rhodes (mid to late 5th century—Fig. 8.3), an adaption of Hippodamean regularity to a small plateau

6. 3rd and 2nd centuries—Pergamon (Fig. 5.1E): scenographic urbanism, with wedge-shaped terraces

It is difficult to classify urban plans solely by pattern or by century. This is because the changes did not go together in any simple fashion. Inspection of the street patterns of ancient Greek cities, and the relation of those patterns to the sites, allows them to be classified into five basic types, which for easy remembrance I name after representative cities of each type:

1. *Athens-type.* A general rule for cities of a[n ancient] culture states that "the capital city is unlike the others in form." Athens, a seemingly formless, organic city, is quite unlike the well-regulated cities (many of them colonies) of the other types. Although there were particular central areas (the Agora and Acropolis) in Athens that were elegantly organized, the residential areas apparently grew up irregularly before much conscious thought was given to ordering the urban fabric. One can say, however, that the band of private structures bordered the public buildings to produce a centralized, dual focus, settlement. The irregular form of the city seems to be a holdover from Mycenaean times (second millennium B.C.). It is note-worthy that already in antiquity, Athens sent out tentacle-like streets to connect itself to the Lyceum and Academy, and the Long Walls to connect with its port Piraeus. Perhaps Athens is the prototypical octopus city.

2. *Posidonia (Paestum)-type.* In this colonial city of the mid-seventh century B.C., there was one long main street. At the center, perpendicular to the axis street, a wide band of public space was set off, eventually occupied by the agora and the major temples as well as by municipal buildings. Residential streets ran parallel to this band of public space and perpendicular to the main street; there were no cross streets (Bradford, 1957, 225), so the houses formed long strips stretching from the main street toward the enclosing ramparts. This pattern could be described as "axis-with-perpendicular stripes" or bar-and-stripes.

3. *Morgantina-type.* In the fifth century, in western Greek cities of southern Italy and Sicily, a common pattern was two flat-topped hills laid out in grids for houses, flanking a lower open space, which was the Agora.

4. *Miletus/Priene-type* (Figs. 12.4 and 22.4). The city of Miletus in Ionia was rebuilt in the fifth century after the Persian Wars. The zone of public buildings and open space at the center was irregularly adapted to the peninsula's typography, and the rest of the peninsula was laid out in either large blocks of small houses, or small blocks of large houses, but in either case in regular checkerboard grids, while the public spaces were fitted into multiples of a single block. This nuanced regularity was associated with the name of Hippodamus of Miletus, who carried the ideas to other cities that he laid out, such as Rhodes and Piraeus. The checkerboard grid plan went on being used not only during the Hellenistic period, but— with their own variations—by the Romans, especially in connection with

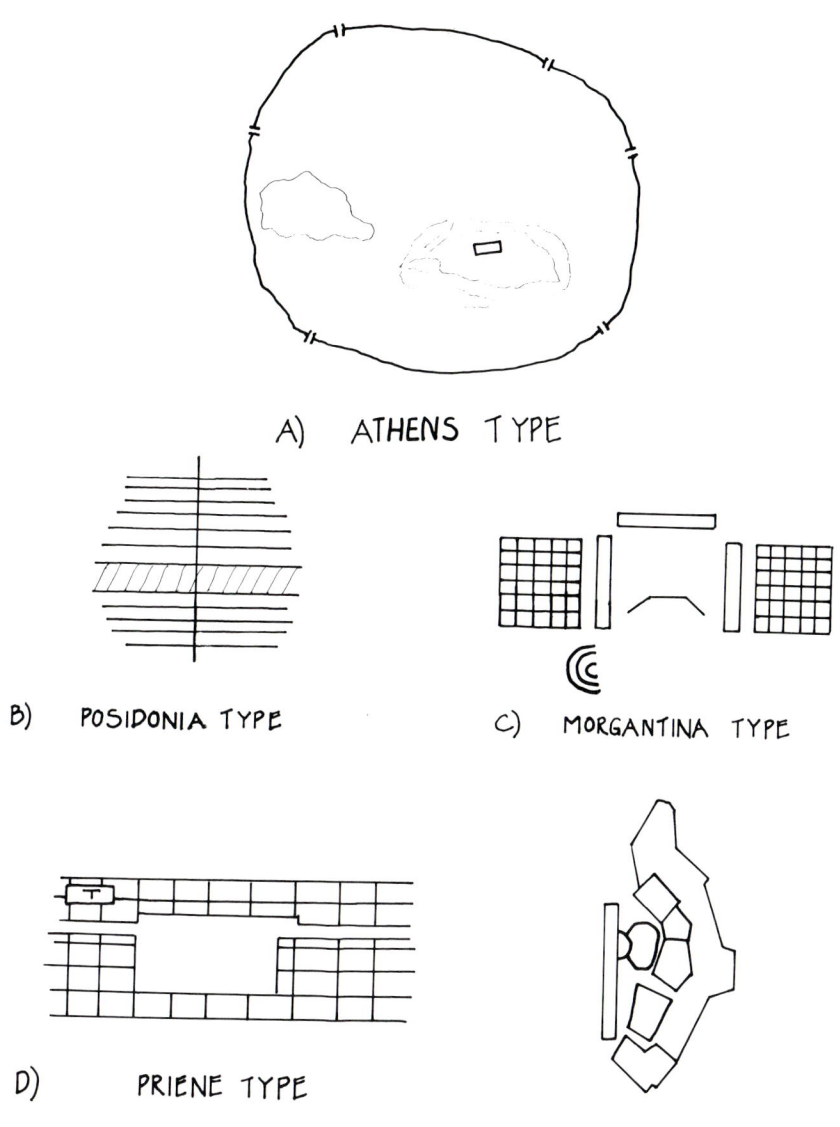

A) ATHENS TYPE

B) POSIDONIA TYPE

C) MORGANTINA TYPE

D) PRIENE TYPE

E) PERGAMON TYPE

Figure 5.1. Urban patterns. A) Athens type—organic plan developed around two nuclei. B) Posidonia type—residential streets and central zone are perpendicular to the main street; central zone was set aside for temples, agora, and other public uses. C) Morgantina type—residential grids on two flat-topped hills flank a lower agora area. D) Priene type—Hippodamean grid—regularized blocks of houses surround rectangular agora lined with porticoes. E) Pergamon type—scenographic urbanism—terraces stepped down like the blades of a fan, focused on the theater.

45

their colonization efforts. However, the Roman version of the grid was more regular and less subtle than the early Greek version. Many early studies of Greek urbanization have fixed on the proliferation of the grid pattern as if the biography of Hippodamus and the variations in the grid were enough to explain Greek city building. That stance is explicitly rejected here, although the influence of both is acknowledged. In Figure 5.1D, Priene is seen as a simple version of this type.

5. *Pergamon-type.* Quite a different effect was achieved by the unknown designer of Pergamon in Ionia, who in the third century B.C. utilized the impressive topography of the hill his patrons had chosen and incorporated existing palaces and ramparts into a dazzling new urban form. The city was laid out on a series of terraces, like the blades of a fan. This type of pattern is termed "scenographic urbanism" (Martin, 1956, 127–51), for it was a conscious effort to build the city as a "theatrical" backdrop for human (and especially princely) activities. The change in scale—towards giantism—is thought to mirror the political changes of the time, through which the citizen/peer became a subject in a much larger national entity.

As a rule of thumb, we can postulate a[t least a potential] gradual increase in both size and complexity during the period studied (eighth to first centuries B.C.). From Argos which seems to still occupy the same medium-sized site [population of 25,000 to 50,000] , and which reached prominence in the archaic period, to Athens which in the fifth century housed perhaps 150,000 people (30,000 citizens) living in close relationship with family farms in the outlying countryside, to Pergamon with its larger size and important role in the cosmopolitan world of the successors of Alexander and new Hellenistic relations of ruler and ruled, to the world-class complexity, density, and size of Alexandria.

A reevaluation of the evidence of urban pattern must consider both the amount of wealth tied up in buildings, streets, fountains, plazas, public buildings, houses, ramparts, and so on, and also the durability of most of these features. Even if the residents of grid-platted Miletus came to prefer the scenographic urbanism of Pergamon, the practical difficulties of remodeling their grid plan into a system of radiating terraces precluded such an alteration of the whole settlement. Thus each city's pattern tended to make physically evident in a permanent way the set of urban concepts that were current when it was being laid out and first built. The city was thus an excellent example of Greek preference for corporealizing ideas.

6

Greek Urbanization—
Theoretical Issues

Urbanization is a process that can be studied both historically and philosophically. The examination by case studies in these pages draws on architectural and art historical insights to illuminate the term "urbanization" as a process. Some theories of great current interest to classicists and ancient history experts are ignored here lest the digression into their arguments impede our concentration on evidence for water management. Rather, we may generalize in very simple terms from accumulated examples.

A family selects a site and builds a house. Their grown sons and daughters form households and settle nearby. Friends come to live there too, and strangers arrive to trade or worship, and stay on. Gradually a small settlement with advantageous resources—human, physical, and cultural—prospers and becomes a town, even a city. It forms ties with other settlements and increases its prosperity by trade and cultural interaction. The city's need for food, raw materials, and population has a strong impact on the countryside, so that other hamlets become towns in response to urban demands for their goods. Thus urbanization may be said to be a process. Growth and decay of urban centers are part of the same process.

Once the process of city building is well underway, the resulting "package" of knowledge and behavior can be exported as a product. Greek colonization of the Mediterranean area was done by means of cities, a group of settlers carrying with them to the new place both the concept of city and the technological and political means to bring it into existence (see Fig. 3.1, selected Greek sites). Colonists were organized in one of several standard ways, to make a new urban place without going through a gradual process of social evolution and physical agglomeration. This set of activities is well described in A. J. Graham, *Colony and Mother-city in Ancient Greece (*1983), and in N. H. Demand, *Urban Relocation in Archaic and Classical Greece* (1990).

In the general field of urban history and theory, we have the works of Vance, Hohenberg and Lees, Wheatley, and Pirenne. From them we learn how urbanization has been understood in the last two centuries. Yet they would be the first to admit that why cities have developed as they have remains still unclear, especially for ancient cities. Is there consensus on the determining factors of urbanization? Since Kraeling and Adams' s *The City Invincible* (1960) it should be commonly accepted that the inception of cities requires certain standard prerequisites, especially variety, and yet many students of urbanization have never heard of this book or idea.

For our purposes, three kinds of literature need to be searched for relevant passages—ancient authors, modern materials on classical cities, and modern technical studies. Chapter 7 deals with the last of these three; here we will examine first the ancient writers and then a few of the modern writers.

ANCIENT AUTHORS

Classicists may expect that this book would begin with detailed citations of all references to the ancient Greek authors' remarks on the water cycle, springs, urban water supply, and so on. When I began this study in 1970, I dutifully went to the ancient authors but found so little that I realized that searching for such references was to look for the proverbial needle in a haystack. Even the useful citations I found did not add up to a comprehensive account of what the ancients knew, believed, or did about water. Sometimes the ancient allusions to water seem correct in their understanding, sometimes merely quaint or farfetched. Only in the cases of Aristotle and Hippocrates do we have what might be called sustained descriptions, but Greek attention to matters of water certainly began before these two writers. The biggest problem I have with the ancient authors, in fact, is that they are not ancient enough, writing four hundred or more years after the foundation and initial watering of Greek cities.[1] I will set out here what I have discovered, in more or less chronological order.

The mythological basis of Greek attitudes toward water is examined by Rudhardt in "Le theme de l'eau primordiale dans la mythologie grecque" (1971). Human attempts to control water in Greek lands seem to go back to mythological times, for the Mycenaean Danaos, who ordered his fifty daughters to kill their fifty cousin-husbands on their wedding night, was also king of Argos, where he supposedly introduced water control, presumably in the second millennium (Bintliff, 1977, 343).

We will turn rather to what the historical record can show us. That "the first clear statement of the hydrology of karst phenomena . . . is in the old Greek and Roman written documents," is recognized by modern hydraulic engineers (e.g., Herak and Stringfield, 1972, 119) who have carefully traced the comments of the ancient writers on ground water. Already by about 1000 B.C., Homer knew that all water came from and returned to the sea.

Theoretical speculation occurred at the same time that engineering knowledge was increasing. The building of underground aqueducts in the seventh century B.C. was attributed by Polybius (*History* X,28) to the Achaemenian kings of Uratu (later Armenia). Recent excavations have verified that qanats or foggaras (underground aqueducts with air shafts to the surface; one term is Persian, the other, Arabic) were in use there (*L.A. Times*, Sept. 29, 1971, 20). Apparently this technology was imported to the Persian Empire in the seventh century and then passed on to the Greeks in the sixth century.

Thales of Miletus (7–6th c. B.C.) thought that the water of springs and streams was derived from the sea, driven from the sea into the earth by the wind, and from pressures of the overlying rocks, driven out again from the mountains. These bits of his theory were preserved for us by Diogenes. Also, Anaxagoras wrote in the archaic period on the connection between the sea and groundwater. Some water ideas of Pythagoras of the sixth century are preserved in the writings of Ovid, who seems to understand water vapor in air, condensing into dew, evaporating again into vapor (*Metamorphoses*, Book 15). Other sixth century ideas are reflected in Plutarch's life of Solon, the law-giver of sixth century Athens ("Solon," *Lives* XXIII,6) about the nature and use of public wells, and the sharing of private supplies (see Chapter 17).

In two of the odes of Pindar of Thebes, we find the claim that "water is the best thing." *Olympian I*, was written in 476 B.C., for Hieron of Syracuse, and performed at his court in the presence of Pindar (translation and commentary of C.M. Bowra, Penguin Books, 1969). This ode begins:

Water is the best thing of all, and gold
Shines like flaming fire at night,
More than all a great man's wealth.

The second, *Olympian III*, was written for Theron of Akragas, also in 476. In the third section of the poem, Pindar writes:

Even as water is best
And gold the most honored of treasures,
So now Theron has come to the verge by his prowess
And reaches from home
To the Pillars of Herakles.

Bowra's only comment on the allusions to water is, "As water, gold, and the sun are each in their spheres supreme, so in athletics is a victory in the Olympian Games" (p.69). He adds in reference to the second citation, "This looks like an echo from the opening lines of *Olympian I* and may well be deliberate" (p.79). More pertinent to our study is the question whether the pressure pipe line at Syracuse, known from anecdotal evidence and thought to have been built in the second quarter of the fifth century (between 491 and 447 B.C. according to Neuberger, 1930, 56), was the reason for Pindar's poetic allusion. At Akragas, we have more detailed verification of the factual basis for Pindar's praise of water and the ruler in the same sentence. At Theron's order, the engineer Phaiax built aqueducts here that drained into an artificial lake he created by damming the valley at the southwestern edge of the city. Forbes dates the work of Phaiax to 489–472 B.C. (Forbes, 1956, 145–89), so the work would have been nearly finished when Pindar wrote. It is tempting to speculate that rivalry between the cities induced Hieron to build similar waterworks for Syracuse, perhaps starting after but finishing before the great system at Akragas. The provision of waterlines had been since the sixth century a favored way that tyrants won the support of the people, the most famous example being the Peisistratid aqueduct at Athens. If the systems at Syracuse and Akragas were already operating or nearly complete in 476, they were well worth celebrating in odes by the foremost poet of the time. Pindar also mentioned the Peirene Fountain at Corinth.

The increase in knowledge of water's behavior is documented in several ancient authors. Herodotus (6.76) in the fifth century B.C., Strabo (6.8.371) at the turn of the millennium, and Pausanias (2.24) in the second century A.D., all report protoscientific experiments of throwing pinecones into a sinkhole to see where they would reappear, and hence trace underground connections between waters (see Chapter 7).

Hippocrates, the Greek physician of the late fifth and early fourth century, wrote of water from a medical point of view (*Airs, Waters, Places*). He distinguished three kinds of water: marshy soft waters, hard waters from rocky heights, and harsh brackish waters, and thought that the influence of water on health was very great (p.71). The worst water for drinking was standing water, which in summer is hot and stinking and in winter is cold and turbid. The next worst is spring water coming directly from rocks, because such water is hard, or from the earth whence it may be hot or may contain minerals such as iron, copper, silver, gold, sulfur, alum, bitumen, or soda. The best water for drinking is that from high places and from earthly hills, because this water is sweet and clear—warm in the winter and cold in summer because it comes from deep springs. Rainwater, although the lightest, sweetest, finest, and clearest water, is the quickest to become foul and bad smelling. For drinking it needs to be boiled and purified. Water from snow and ice is bad because it is muddy and heavy. River and lake waters give people kidney disease and painful urination. If the city uses good flowing water, the people will suffer fewer diseases from the changes of season (pp. 89–103). Hippocrates also discussed the orientation of springs (p. 89) and that of cities. If a city is exposed to the hot winds and sheltered from north winds, water will be plentiful but brackish [like Akragas] (p.73). If this water is near the surface, it will be hot in summer and cold in winter. When the city faces north and is sheltered from the south [like Corinth], the water is hard and cold (p.75). An eastern exposure gives the city clear, sweet-smelling, soft, delightful water, "because the rising sun purifies" the site and its water [like Argos] (p. 81). A western exposure is the most unhealthy since the water is not clear and the site is exposed to rainy winds [like Ephesus] (p. 83). Similarly, he states that the best springs open to the east or eastnortheast. Those of medium quality open to a range of positions from westnorthwest to eastnortheast, slightly worse ones open from the westnorthwest to the westsouthwest, and the worst of all open to the south, in the range from eastsoutheast to westsouthwest. These ratings are adversely affected by prevailing winds from the south. As a doctor, Hippocrates sums up the medical thinking of his time about who can tolerate which waters: "A healthy man can drink any water." The best cooking water loosens the digestive organs, while harsh, hard water is bad for cooking since it dries up and stiffens the digestive organs. If a person has a soft, moist, phlegmatic belly, it is good to drink hard harsh and salty water which will dry up one's complaints. Thus Hippocrates is, of all ancient writers, the most useful for our study.

The historian Thucydides had a few comments to make on water supply. He noted in the fifth century, a century or so after the Peisistratid Aqueduct was built at Athens, that great waterworks such as those require an understanding of human nature and human needs, an understanding of the laws of nature, a great labor policy, and big expenditures (Thucydides, V.i, 54).

Plato was one of several ancient authors who noted deforestation during the fourth century B.C. (*Critias*, iii, D-E). Specific water management problems were cited by many writers, such as Herodotus, the sixth century historian, Aristotle in the fourth century, and Strabo and Pliny in the first century A.D., all of whom commented on the excessive grazing that caused deforestation.

In the fourth century, Aristotle wrote the first book on meteorology, in which he attempted a complete account of the origin of springs and rivers. He wrote that both come from the condensation of moisture, from above and from within the earth, respectively. The sun's rays evaporate the moisture of the sea, making it rise into the air, where it cools, condenses, and falls as rain. Water gathers below the earth in the winter, making the rivers fuller at that time of year, and even making some streams perennial. He also thought that air condensing within the earth formed cold water there. He reflects the lively observational and engineering abilities of the ancient Greeks when he writes:

> In the earth the water at first trickles together little by little, and that the sources of the rivers drip, as it were, out of the earth and then unite. This is proved by facts. When men construct an aqueduct they collect the water in pipes and trenches, as if the earth in the higher ground were sweating the water out. Hence too the headwaters of rivers are found to flow from mountains, and from the greatest mountains there flow the most numer-

ous and greatest rivers. Again, most springs are in the neighborhood of mountains and high ground, whereas if we except rivers, water rarely appears in the plains. For mountains and high ground, suspended over the counry like a saturated sponge, make the water ooze out and trickle together in minute quantities in many places.

In his *Politics* (vii, 1330b) written in the 320s, Aristotle asserts that "cities need cisterns for safety in war." Just at this time, a severe twenty-five-year drought made saving rainwater essential (Camp, 1982, 9–17), and cisterns were built in the Athenian Agora for the first time in centuries (Parsons, 1943, l92).

Another postclassical writer was Diodorus, who described a long-distance waterline at Syracuse (XIV,18), brought from the mountains to the west, whence the "water supply for the city" runs under the north wing of the fortress Euryalus through the suburbs Epipolae and Tyche, with many important branches. Dionysus, ruler of Syracuse, decided to fortify the western approaches to the city and incorporate the aqueduct in the rampart system so that enemies could not ruin the water supply lines. Diodorus also mentions a waterline of the Ortygia quarter (V, 13). Another Hellenistic writer, Demosthenes, describes the Olynthians as having become suddenly rich, and displaying unusual magnificance—quite possibly in their elaborate bathing facilities, featured in almost every house (*De Falsa Legatione*, 426; cf. Thucydides, I, 58).

Lucretius (first half of the first century B.C.) also understood what we now call the meteorological cycle, using it to account for the saltiness of the sea. He describes clouds condensing, gathering more water from the sea, but he thought that seawater itself oozed into the land where it fed springs and streams. Lucretius not only thought the seawater oozed into the land, but also noted the opposite—the submarine spring off the coast at Aradus *(De Rerum Natura)*.

Vitruvius may be thought to sum up Hellenistic ideas on water, at the end of the first century B.C. We read, especially in his introduction to Book IV, of lost treatises written by Greek architects and engineers of the sixth to fourth centuries B.C. I think it is not too rash to assume these lost books included traditional knowledge about hydraulics, as well as site selection in general and the specifics of building temples and other monumental buildings. Vitruvius described evaporation and condensation, correctly tying them to the difference in temperature between day and night. He noted the active role of mountains in interrupting the flight of clouds and forcing them to drop moisture. He realized that rain and especially snow collect on mountainsides and "afterwards in melting, it filters through fissures in the ground and thus reaches the very foot of the mountains, from which gushing springs come belching out," while rivers and springs in the hot plains furnish water full of the "hard and unpleasant parts" left behind by evaporation. Interestingly, Vitruvius thinks that hot springs are brought by the force of the air in them to the summits of hills via narrow channels.

Vitruvius's slightly younger contemporary, Strabo, wrote that the Peirene Fountain in the Agora at Corinth was fed by a spring named Upper Peirene near the top of the acropolis, from which water flowed underground to the lower fountain (Strabo, 8.6.21).

The great Roman traveler Pausanius made some note of Greek water arrangements as well as Greek architecture and sculpture. Pausanias (I,14,1) describes a fountainhouse in Athens called Enneakrounos (Fig. 20.7). From his description, it sounds like the simple sixth or fifth century plan found in several fountains: a rectangle with a shallow basin at each end of the room, fed by a terra-cotta pipeline and drained by another terra-cotta pipeline running to the northeast (see Fig. 20.7).

Several modern hydrogeologists or geohydrologists have taken the trouble to ascertain what the ancient writers had to say on their topic. Baker and Horton (1936, 395–400) have conscientiously gathered up the fragments lest anything be lost, and my account has benefitted from their work. For instance, they cite Seneca who wrote the first review of the subject of the origin of springs, in about A.D. 60 in "On the forms of water," book 3. Other authors cited by Baker and Horton come well after the Roman period, and hence are not of interest for this study. Herak and Stringfield include a few additional citations (1972, 19–24).

The brevity of this exposition will probably not allay the concerns of classicists, but my own anxiety about such summary treatment was re-

Figure 6.1. Women at showerbath, from a sixth century vase. Reprinted from Neuburger, 1919, 1930, 1931, by permission from Macmillan Co.

lieved when I learned that the ancient authors had never discussed vase painting either. Thus I hope I will be excused for seeking the evidence of how the ancient Greeks managed water where it is to be found, on the sites and in the archaeological and geological literature, rather than in the ancient authors where it is for the most part not to be found.

MODERN AUTHORS

In the standard readings on Greek urbanization, the books that deal comparatively with Greek cities, are von Gerkan, *Griechische Staedteanlagen* (1924); Doxiadis, *The Method for the Study of Ancient Greek Settlements* (1972); Metraux, *Western Greek Land Use and City Planning in the Archaic Period* (1978); Cook, *The Greeks in Ionia and the East* (1965); Woodhead, *The Greeks in the West* (1962); Lavendan, *Histoire de l'urbanisme* (1926); Martin, *L'urbanisme dans la grece antique* (1956); and now Demand, *Urban Location in Archaic and Classical Greece: Flight and Consolidation* (1990). While valuable studies, these in general reflect more interest in documentary evidence and classical history than in technical arrangements, or social structures. For Greek cities, we do have Rostovtzeff's *Social and Economic History of the Hellenistic World* (1941), technical studies like Scranton, *Greek Walls* (1941), and F.E. Winter, *Greek Fortifications* (1971). The technological histories written before 1980 tend to generalize on the basis of very little specific data, often repeating opinion as if it were fact. The two most often cited histories of technology are Neuberger, *The Technical Arts and Sciences of the Ancients* (1930), and Forbes and Dijksterhuis, *History of Science and Technology* (1963), neither of which is strong on documentation of their assertations about ancient water management. Renate Tölle-Kastenbein's *Antike Wasserkulter* (1990) is a more recent object-oriented contribution.

Studies that correlate geography, geology, and settlement history are just beginning to be done; Van Andel and Jamison's team study of the Argolid from 1987 on (not yet published) is a stellar example, although it involves only villages and no urban sites. Yet as early as 1963, in "The Waters of Ancient Hellas" (a lecture given at Athens on March 19, 1963), W. K. Pritchett had noted that through study of their waters, "one might arrive at some conclusion about why the Greeks located their towns where they did . . . many of the springs were used for medical and healing purposes and it would be interesting to find these and have their waters analyzed" (see Part IV).

The types of evidence currently available to us for studying ancient Greek cities are:

- Traveler's reports, particularly when they describe and illustrate now-vanished structures. (See, for example, Fig. 18.4.)
- Archaeological excavation reports. Some, such as the exemplary

volume on *The Springs* from the Corinth series (Hill, 1964), point toward the complex interaction of water management and urbanization which is the topic here, but never actually pose the question in terms of "how much water, how much city?"

- Histories based on ancient documents such as Rostovtzeff, and those that compare ancient circumstances with more recent data, such as the Ekistics studies of Greek sites.
- Comparisons of selected features of a number of Greek sites, such as the fortification and social-and-economic studies mentioned before. Scully's controversial building-type study of temples in *The Earth, the Temple and the Gods* (1962) might be placed in this category.
- Insights from hydraulic engineering and groundwater hydrology which have "chronology-free" validity, such as the studies of karst/water potential of Greece done for the Greek government by Leo Picard of UN/FAO (1964). The modern demand for water has spurred many geological and climatic studies of the Mediterranean. See Part IV for general remarks on the Mediterranean climate, with its variations north and south, and the influence of the land mass of Asia to the east; problems of concentration of rainfall in winter months; and contrast with general climatic and geological situations of Iraq and Egypt, each quite different from the Greek circumstances.

The freshest recent approach to ancient urbanism is William MacDonald's second volume of *The Architecture of Imperial Rome* (1986), but for our purposes this book has two drawbacks: It deals exclusively with Mediterranean cities during the Roman era (even though many of them had been Greek and retained Greek features), and it concentrates on the *visible* built form of the city, ignoring such crucial but invisible constructed features as the sewers. His excellent book is the best modern scholarship has produced, but there is wide room for new studies of ancient Greek cities in all their four-dimensional reality.

As Lindh and Berthelot (1979, 4) have pointed out in their seminal paper, "Socio-economic Aspects of Urban Hydrology," "the field of urban history is almost devoid of modern research investment . . . [there is] little study . . . of the effect of human settlement upon natural hydrological conditions"—or vice versa, we may add, of hydrological conditions on human settlement. Lindh and Berthelot were drawing on McPherson (1974, 13), who complains, "Although water is a necessity, an economic reality, an amenity, and an aesthetic component in urban settlements, research on urban water resources has lagged behind large catchment research in nearly every nation." McPherson was reporting on the situation among engineers and policymakers, but that among historians and archaeologists is hardly different. One may well ask, Do we know enough about the water-urbanization interaction, and is it the right kind of information? According to McPherson, "An overall, integrated, interdisciplinary approach should be adapted to the study of settlements and their water provisions, including research in the social organization of water resources and research on the effects of water system elements on society." He adds, "Social organization is a critical factor in water-resource development" (pp. 28,38). The interface between social organization, resource base, and architectural manifestation of the society is the focus of this work.

Although all of my examples and data are selected from the ancient Greek world, by implication the role of water is equally important for other cultures, notably those in hot, dry climates. At the outset of this study, in 1970, a rough listing of places in the Greek world as to the degree of understanding about their water resources would have found most places listed in the "imperfectly known" column, a few in the "well known," and still others as "question never came up." "Known" means here that the hydrogeology of a site was understood and related to its archeology and urban history at least in preliminary form as evident from existing travelers' reports or excavation reports in 1970.

THEORETICAL ISSUES

Where to begin on the interaction between water management and the process of urbanization for these ancient cities? By amassing thousands of facts? By developing an elegant theory? "Without theory or generalization of the problem, it is hard to know which data to collect. Without data, it is hard to gain precise knowledge about the overall system or the important relations which may exist among aspects . . . A rough model can be delineated to act as a guiding scheme for data collection, through successive processes of repetition, refinement, or elaboration [of] the conceptual approach as well as the required data" (Lindh and Berthelot, 1979, 4). Knowledge is thus inter-active between data and theories. Of the twenty years I have already devoted to this study, the first fourteen were devoted to finding out what the problem was and where to look for answers.

The kinds of facts needed to build credible urban history are archaeological, economic, geological and geographic, sociological and psychological, and historical including architectural, intellectual, economic, military, and technological history. Many, many case histories must accumulate before one can generalize in the sense of drawing compelling conclusions. For the modern era, since about the thirteenth century, those facts have been accumulated and deductions drawn from them that make urban histories of postmedieval Europe and of the United States fairly credible. For other parts of the world and for other eras, we are lacking both a critical number of basic studies of particular sites and comparative studies of aspects of groups of sites.

In the absence of such particular studies, we are not yet ready for binding generalizations in the sense of deductions, although we may offer some tentative conclusions as postulates. Thus if we find several sites with circumstance X, we may begin to suspect that X is not accidental, and begin to look for it at other sites, sometimes finding it and sometimes not. X may be The Rule or may be just one version of The Way Things Are. In Chapter 9 on Urban Location Determinants, "beauty of site" is treated as one of these nonaccidental circumstances.

The notion of taking a systems approach to urbanization has been confined entirely too strictly to economists and to analytical planners, whereas it is an approach that could help many students of urban complexity to order their data. That cities are made up of things or parts is not in question. Rather, the question is whether the parts bear a "complex or unitary" relationship to each other, and thus the whole qualifies as a system. Do the found or noticed elements relate systematically, and how does this happen? What proportion of materials, in what arrangement, need to be discovered before we can understand them as a system rather than as fragments? (See also discussion of clusters in Chapter 16.)

Suppose two different scenarios, A and B. In A, one could find a lot of fragments of information and never get beyond understanding them as fragments, because in fact they were originally parts of piecemeal solutions and not parts of a system. An example could be a garbage dump. Or, in B, one could find a lot of fragments and at some point realize that one is dealing with a system. Here an example could be the mosaic tessera of a floor, which become—when enough are seen in place—a picture. We can diagram the idea as in Table 6.1.

An interesting philosophical question is, "At what point does one have enough data to cry, 'Eureka! A system!!' " Perhaps the new discoveries in

Table 6.1
Fragments and Systems

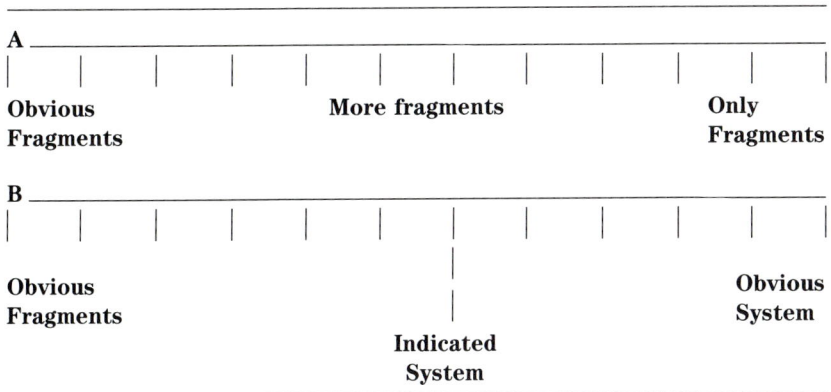

chaos theory or fuzzy sets will enable someone to deal mathematically with this question.

As Lindh and Berthelot have shown, systems do not fit into clear boundaries or hierarchies (1979, 14; cf. Lindh, 1987, 191–200). All the cities of a nation, for instance, form an interactive system, but also the urban nucleus and its associated elements form an individual urban system. There is a necessary link between the area concept of city and the system concept, so that modern cities are social-spatial units with complex socioeconomic and hydrological problems. The urban ecosystem is open-ended and dynamic, including machines, materials, processes (such as hydrological processes) as well as the population by means of which the (socio-mental?) culture affects the (material-technical?) system.

In fact, the urban area incorporates both physical and nonphysical systems (Lindh and Berthelot, 1979, 15–16). A perfect example is the defense system of an ancient Greek city, which included

- Walls, towers, and gates
- Diplomatic activities of statesmen
- Generals and other officers
- Trained soldiers and possibly a navy
- Morale of the people
- Stored food, water, and arms

In short, the defense of a city was inconceivable without both physical and intangible factors that together constituted the defense system. Another of these urban subsystems is the hydrological system, which is structured by the social system and, in turn, channels and conditions human behavior. So complicated are the interactions of these subsystems that it is necessary to use verbal models to study them—mathematical models are unworkable (Lindh and Berthelot, 1979, 23). Perhaps for this reason, engineers and water policymakers have been quick to perceive ancient Greek water systems as models for simple and economical water systems in the modern world.

There has been no comparative study of ancient urban patterns that takes into consideration water management as an urban system. In this volume we begin to analyze clusters of water system elements as related to each other, as related to the physical base, and as related to the social base. These analyses in turn must be synthesized with the urban history, geography, and geology of particular sites. In a subsequent volume I expect to deal specifically with the relationship of geology and geography of particular Greek cities to their urban form, but in this volume I undertake the more general task of relating Greek water management to the process of urbanization. The evidence now available indicates, as I will show, that there is a definite correlation between complexity of the city and ecological sophistication of the water system.

URBAN LOCATION

The ancient Greeks chose urban location with these factors in mind:

- Location in either an area of good, relatively flat, land for agriculture, or near high grazing land, and/or with access to fishing areas— a combination of two of these three was essential
- Water available all year long
- Defensible site
- Surplus wealth for trade
- Landscape beauty within the site and visible from it

Experience had taught them that a balanced rural economy of herding, farming, and fishing would ensure the food supply and probably a surplus when added to the production of craftsmen and miners. Therefore a site on a "seam" between hills for grazing and flat land for fields, or between fields and sea, or between sea and grazing, was optimal. Some cities, like Argos, could draw on all three sources of food and wealth, hence her early rise to power among the Greek city-states.

A modern person, inured to urban poverty and ugliness, might think that surplus wealth and beauty were optional extras, but in fact I have never come across a Greek site without them. As (possibly unwitting) neo-Marxists, we can assimilate the importance of surplus wealth for the viability of these cities but we have trouble recognizing the significance of the last factor listed, beauty. The beauty is, however, so striking a feature as to be unmistakable, and I postulate that the beauty contributed strongly to the initial selection of the site and to the longevity of the settlement. To the argument that "all Greek sites are equally beautiful" I reply that within a generally positive terrain, aesthetically speaking, the founders selected and then developed the micro-site where maximum beauty resulted from subtle manipulation of sight lines, natural features, and architectural forms (see Doxiadis, *Architectural Space in Ancient Greece* (1972).

It is well known that from the eighth through the fourth centuries B.C. the Greeks founded colonies all over the Mediterranean but especially along the northeastern parts of the Aegean extending up to the Black Sea, in southern Italy, and in most of Sicily, with a few in eastern and southern Spain, southern France, and northern Africa. The sites that I have visited (perhaps 50 by now) are alike in being beautiful, but also alike in being almost exclusively located on karst geology. Like the beauty, this feature might be termed an accident, until we realize that such karst geology provides a recognizable and manageable supply of water (factor 2). I have come to suspect that Greek colonizers went looking for rock formations that "looked like home," because their tradition taught that if it had the physical features of "home" it would also have the necessary water as well as being manageable by the technological traditions they brought with them from the mother-city.

In the chapters that follow, we will consider selected examples that illustrate facets of the general problem of the relationship between urbanization and water management. In all of these places, much is known about the urban form, but the connections between that form and water as a determinant have not previously been described and analyzed. My research has shown that the physical form or pattern of a large city such as Syracuse contrasts with that of a small one like Morgantina, not only in street pattern and extent of built-up area, but specifically in number and distribution of water system elements. Similarly, the distribution of water system elements contributes to the regularity of a large city like Miletus or Rhodes (Figs. 22.4 and 8.3), and to the irregularity of Athens. Supply, usage, and drainage all contribute to urban patterns. See for instance Chapters 11 on Corinth and her colony Syracuse, 18 on the Acropolis at Athens, and 13 on the early site Olynthus compared with later Pompeii. But even these case studies leave us with questions: Are the patterns different for each era? each region? Does the size of the city determine the patterns? To what extent? Tentative answers to these questions may become evident as we weigh the evidence from many sites.

Urban theories that have been most useful as research tools for this study have been sketched here. The challenge of "infolding" old and new concepts, old and new data, is one that urban history has in common with all expanding fields of knowledge today.[2] This chapter presents both a new look at some old theories, and some new theories with which to study old cities.

NOTES

1. Classicists desiring a more complete survey of the ancient literature will find it in Renate Tölle-Kastenbein, *Antike Wasserkultur* (Munich: Verlag D. H. Beck, 1990), which appeared after this book was written.

2. The concept of infolding arose in a seminar on teaching at Rensselaer Polytechnic Institute, led by Professor Jonathan Newell, ca. 1987.

IV

Geography and Geology

7

Karst: The Hydrogeological Basis of Civilization

Because water is so vital to life, the distribution of natural water resources should be a clue to past settlements.

—W. S. Loy
The Land of Nestor

A whole series of questions flows from Loy's general understanding, such as: Was there a particular sort of land form associated with ancient Greek settlements? Were settlements always located at springs, and did springs always have settlements? Why were there springs in some places and not in others, in what seemed to be the same sort of terrain? How much have the typography and the water resources changed since antiquity? How much did they change in the last 800 years B.C.? What can we tell about the water resources of antiquity from observing the modern situation? What were the relationships between ancient Greek settlements and the occurrence of karst phenomena? Was karst a geological form that had special relevance to water resource management in ancient Greece? Answers to some of these questions will become apparent as we discuss the geological aspects of ancient Greek urban history.

ECOLOGY

Man-environment relations, in the ancient Greek world as elsewhere, were complex interactions of mode, duration, and intensity of human interference with the initial site conditions and with the climatic and biotic flux, affected by the resilience of the ecosystem. To understand these human communities in their physical setting, we need to study a range of features, many complex interactions, and man's impact on the setting, realizing that our research goals and those of other experts may be widely divergent. Such complex interactions are called socionatural systems by J. W. Bennett (1976, 22). The condition of the watersheds of the hinterlands, in good times and bad, is directly pertinent to the ability of cities to extract water and transport it to municipal users. Hence the problems of erosion are not irrelevant to our topic—the management of water and the process of urbanization (Thrower and Bradbury, 1973, 59–78; Aschmann, 1973, 362–66). The thin, barren soil of these rocky peninsulas and islands is the result of climate not man. At the least, the currently observable extensive and permanent deforestation of uplands is locally a *very recent* phenomena (after the Younger Fill, to be discussed later) and therefore not a cause but a result of existing conditions. Bintliff (1977, 537) even thinks that since erosion creates new arable land in valleys, it may in the long run be beneficial to man!

Fundamental research remains to be done on the nature of geological timescales (Rapp and Gifford, 1985; Cullingford, Davidson, and Lewis, 1980; Thornes and Brunsden, 1977). The very slow pace of geological change is usually thought of as unrelated to historical change. Although we would like to know, for instance, precisely how fast the process of the physical change called downcutting has been through a given limestone strata, we can today at best approximate the rate, and guess how long it has taken a spring to arrive at the level where we see it today (See Dreybrodt, 1990). More accurately subdivided geological timescales within the historical period would be of inestimable value to the historian who attempts to use geological information.

Ideally, archaeologists and urban historians would always have the help of geologists in their attempts to understand the nature and geographical constraints of human settlement. "A geomorphologist ought to be an integral member of any archaeological project, as he or she can tackle a range of problems from environmental reconstruction and change, site distribution, and site development to conservation evaluation." In this imperfect world, however, we must instead lament the "lack of consistent methodology for analysis and evaluation of environmental conditions relevant to archaeology" (Rapp and Gifford, 1985).

Of all the available physical science, karst geology is of special importance for the understanding of Mediterranean water management (compare Fig. 7.1 with Fig. 7.6). Karst is defined as an area of limestone terrane—a special geological spelling of the general word "terrain"—having surface openings, pinnacles, blind valleys, and underground drainage channels (see Fig. 7.3). In the Mediterranean areas that were Greek during the eighth to first centuries B.C., karst phenomena are widely distributed. Karst dominates the geology of continental Greece, including the Peloponnesos and northeastern Greece, of Crete and the Aegean islands, and it is a significant landform in several areas of Italy that were of major importance for colonization in Greek times, such as the "heel" area, and the east and south coasts of Sicily (Belloni, Martinis, and Orombelli, 1972). The southern one-third to one-half of Turkey and more than one-third of its water potential is karstic, as Özis has pointed out, with one-third to two-thirds of the river flow originating in karst springs (Özis, 1985, 95).

Figure 7.1. Map of karst areas of the ancient Greek lands in modern Turkey, Greece, and Italy, after two maps by P.T. Milanovic, 1981. Reprinted by permission.

One of the hypotheses of this book is that, having learned to manage water in the karst terranes of their homelands, the Greek colonizers of the eighth to fourth centuries B.C. deliberately went looking for similar-looking rock formations.[1] By so doing, they could be confident both that they would find water and that their water technology would be adequate to manage that resource. As a corollary, in doing the research, I have followed Picard and Burdon's pattern of consulting with local people who still preserve traces of that traditional knowledge: "The shepherds, farmers and villagers of Greece have contributed not a little to the success of [this research] by their readiness to guide [us] to little known springs and seepages and to recount their observations on the hydrological phenomena of the countryside they know so well" (Burdon, 1964, 84).

Some problems of the area have been recurrent since archaic times, namely deforestation and drought. Ancient deforestation may be partially attributed to recurrent dry spells such as the twenty-five-year drought in the third quarter of the fourth century (Camp, 1982). Although modern writers have tended to blame the goat, Bintliff (1977, 75) asserts that the goat was not a significant agent: The goat has been domesticated (with the sheep) for 7000 years in Greece, but many areas have been deforested only in the last 200 years. Note, however, that Homer Thompson reports that with the demise of goat farming in the past fifty years, the hillsides of Attica are green once again (personal communication).

The literature has preserved evidence of ancient attempts to understand the geological setting of Greek civilization. Ancient tracer experiments took place near Argos, with fir cones being thrown into sinkholes on the plateau to the west, to ascertain which hole was the source of which spring near or in the city. Herodotus (6.76), Strabo (6.8.371), and Pausanias (2.24), all report these experiments. The pinecones were thrown into the Stymphalos kathvothros (sinkhole) and reappeared at the Kephalari resurgence, source of the Erasinos River, just south of Argos. Such experiments—repeated by Burdon (1964, 53–55; 1967, 308–17)—would have increased the engineer's and government's ability to protect the sources of municipal water from pollution (Stringfield and Rapp, 1977, 2).

Summing up the understanding of the Greco-Roman world of the first century B.C., Virtuvius wrote in Book 8 Chapters 1 and 2:

> In clay the supply is poor, meagre, and at no great depth. It will not have the best taste. In fine gravel the supply is also poor, but it will be found at a greater depth. It will be muddy and not sweet. In black earth some slight drippings and drops are found that gather from the storms of winter and settle down in compact, hard places. They have the best taste. Among pebbles the veins found are moderate, and not to be depended upon. These, too, are extremely sweet. In course grained gravel and carbunbcular sand the supply is surer and more lasting, and it has a good taste. *In red tufa it is copious and good, if it does not run down through the fissures and*

escape. At the foot of the mountains and in lava it is more plentiful and abundant, and here it is also colder and more wholesome. In flat countries the springs are salt, heavy-bodied, tepid, and ill-flavored, excepting those which run underground from mountains, and burst forth in the middle of a plain, where, if protected by the shade of trees, their taste is equal to that of mountain springs.

In the kinds of soil described above, signs will be found growing, such as slender rushes, wild willows, alders, agnus castus trees, reeds, ivy, and other plants of the same sort that cannot spring up of themselves without moisture . . . The valleys among the mountains receive the rains most abundantly, and on account of the thick woods the snow is kept in them longer by the shade of the trees and mountains. Afterwards, on melting, *it filters through the fissures in the ground, and thus reaches the very foot of the mountains, from which gushing springs come belching out.* (Emphasis added)

GEOLOGY—DESCRIPTION

Karst is a geological area in which the terrane—usually limestone—interacts with water to form characteristic surface features (sinks, ravines, etc.) and underground water channels (Quinlin, 1978). Karst terranes have dolines, disappearing streams, karren (repetitive patterns such as flutings, eroded by water on the rock surface), and subsurface flow in conduits created by solution. Karst is divided into covered and exposed, with the most pertinent catagories for Greek study being the covered karst: the less common interstratal karst (covered by rock) and subaqueous karst (such as submarine karst). These features readily develop in areas of one-season rainfall. Among the exposed karsts, denuded karst from which the cover has been eroded is the most important and most widely found, especially in Greek lands. Karst occurs in ten kinds of rock, nine being carbonate.

Much of the land bordering the Mediterranean is made of carbonate rocks, laid down and uplifted in the long eons when the sea was alternately dry land. These rocks are seen today as layers of limestone, dolomite, or marble, depending on their exact chemical composition and their subsequent history of pressure and heat. Coarse crystalline limestone has less karst than fine crystalline limestone, especially in areas where limestone overlies impermeable rock (Bogli, 1980, 8). Karst is most common where soluble rock lies under a permeable but insoluble rock such as sandstone, or the extremely hard marble cap I noted on the hills at Miletus (White, 1977, 176–87).

Most of the water in karst comes from the weather cycle or from the sea, but some hydrothermal karst is known, from heated waters deep within the earth. Karst is a 10,000 to 100,000 year process, dissolving the stone at approximately 0.5 to1 mm per year, or 500 mm in 500 years. The rate is both chemically and hydrologically dynamic (Sweeting, 1964, 92–

95). The rate of change in dolomite is somewhat slower than limestone. The process seems to alternate slower and faster intervals of change. Quinlan (1978) notes aquifers (water flowing underground through rocks) as being confined (having fixed boundaries), partially confined, unconfined, or leaky. The flow may be diffuse (seeping along and through joints, bedding surfaces, small caves, and pores) or concentrated through conduits (flowing in cave systems). Circulation depth may vary from superficial to extremely deep; Bogli notes karst as deep as 3000 meters and as high as 2000 meters (Bogli, 1980, 103, 110). Both shallow and deep karst is revealed by surface springs. The simple assumption of one water table per region is frequently void in karst, where an irregular and discontinuous water table interacts with the strata of limestone, forming karst at many levels, and hence multiple water tables in hills and mountains which are known as perched karst or perched water tables (Loy, 1965–6, 65; Bogli, 1980, 82; Burdon, 1964, 21; Palmer, 1976).

The topographic setting (especially relief and hardness of rocks,) controls placement of recharge and discharge. The topography of Ionia in western Turkey was described poetically in the nineteenth century as:

> A hand of which the back represents the plateau, while the fingers represent lines of mountains sticking out 100 or 200 miles between valleys whose west ends have been depressed beneath the sea and form gulfs. The south rim is the highest. Its limestone heights often tower 10,000 feet above the sea . . . the seaward slope is quite moist and well forested . . . On the west the wind flows up the valleys between the fingers, and brings rain and fertility in its train. (Huntington, 1911, 103)

In sandstone (not common in Greece) water moves at an even pace (since the rock is porous but nonsoluble) but in limestone it moves unevenly (since the solubility of the rock leads in time to enlargement of the conduits), flowing faster at the end of the cycle (Davis, 1981, 136–59). The direction of flow can be horizontal, nearly vertical, or ascending (artesian), and the flow can be thick or thin, with either single or multiple aquifers in one karst system. Recharge of the system can be either concentrated or diffuse, with the water coming from infiltration of rainwater, other aquifers, lakes, or rivers. Discharge is the symmetrical reflection of recharge.

Like other landforms, karst is subject to geological transformation which can range from almost no modification, through burial and abandonment, to rejuvenation. The dominant land formations associated with karst in the Mediterranean area are dolines (also called sinkholes, poljes, or katavothres depending on their size), crevices or ravines, and cave systems. Since, however, so much of karst is subterranean, it is not all that easy to look at a landscape and be certain that it is or is not karstic. Karst can have "no, slight, moderate, or pronounced surface expression" (Quinlin, 1978, 10).

The bare karst of high mountains behaves differently from forest-covered (silvan) karst where the groundwater is rich in dissolved CO_2 and $CaCO_3$ which produces sinter deposits in the conduits (Bogli, 1980, 41–42). The more forest cover, the more active the karst system below because of increased acid in the water (Loy, 1966, 32). The rate at which the water flows through a karst system varies from a few meters to half a kilometer per hour, depending on the chemistry of the water, and results in corrosion when the water is low in limestone and passes over a slight incline, erosion when the water is high in limestone, or incasion when the passage collapses (i.e., the gradual solidification of the collapse debris, cemented together by the calcium carbonate in the flowing water) (Bogli, 1980, 78, 44, 144 and pl. 8.2). The major solvent in carbonate rocks is carbonic acid (A.N. Palmer, 1984, 182), but the corrosion process is largely caused by mixing waters, especially by the air bubbles in the water. This capacity of mixed water to corrode is especially notable when there are large temperature differentials daily or seasonally, and most notably when the waters are near the ground surface, accessible to both temperature change and acid from decaying vegetation. The Burdon FAO report (1964) suggests that it may be possible to speed up the karstification of fissured rocks by using strong hydrochloric acid in them. It does not seem to matter whether the water is pressurized or flowing freely, so far as its corrosive ability is concerned (Sweeting, 1964, 92–95), but "the same water that can corrode limestone when it enters a flooded passage, in a dry passage produces concretions" (Bogli, 1980, 186–7). These concretions are variously called *sinter* or *flowstone*, with sinter appearing white and floury because it is either calcium carbonate or a silicate deposited by springs, while flowstone is calcium carbonate only, and is deposited in many colors depending on the exact solution of stone and water, although in much of the literature, "sinter" is used for all deposited concretions in karst. In this work, I have eschewed such fine distinctions and called all deposits from limestone-bearing water "sinter." Sinter is a basic by-product when large dissolution and large precipitation take place, especially near the surface. (Bogli, 1980, 187.) When velocity increases, laminar flow becomes turbulent flow, and eddies in the turbulent flow cause mixing, which in turn can lead to increased solution rate (J. Palmer, 1976, 11), so that in a sense the process feeds on itself. Thus in the disused Roman aqueducts east of the city of Rome, more deposit of sinter is seen where the flowing water had to change direction, as when it went around a corner. In the fountainhouse at Megara, more sinter is found on the front sides of the front piers, where the water was continually stirred by people drawing water (Fig. 7.2). Sintering is significant to this study because its tendency to fill up channels and pipes constituted a severe challenge to the ancient technicians. Because so much of the flowing water in Greek lands was heavily laden with calcium carbonate, and because of the preference for limestone-flavored drinking

Figure 7.2. Detail of sinter (deposits of calcium carbonate) on the front (only) of a pier near the front of the fountainhouse at Megara. Piers nearest the front were subjected to maximum turbulence, hence developed the most sinter. At the top, a much weathered column drum; below it, the front and side of an octagonal column originally finished with plaster but now covered toward the bottom with irregular layers of sinter. One of the dividing walls of the reservoir is visible behind the column. These piers supported the roof, keeping the water from evaporating and from being polluted.

water, the ancient builders and their clients were forced to contend with the sinter deposits made by this water in their pipes. Sinter made their maintenance of the urban water supply a more difficult task. Surviving today in those ancient pipes, sinter provides mute evidence that ancient Greek cities consistently used calcium-carbonate laden waters. I argue that two factors determined this choice: preference for the taste of such water—a preference we share today—and convenience of using the most readily available waters.

In Greece, Turkey, and Italy, the limestone occurs as a rocky mantle with possible block faults (Huntington, 1911, 91–106, esp. 104). The Greek natural pattern is steep slopes bare or with few trees, but densely wooded on terraces and plateaus (LeGrand, 1977, 10–18). The steep slopes concentrate runoff into dolines and hence into underground shaft-and-channel systems, with the water appearing again downhill in surface springs, or flowing underground as aquifers. In Attica, for example, permeable limestone or dolomite with or without marble, plus travertine from an ancient spring near Kifissia, and crystalline marble at Mt. Ymettos together constitute a "three-fold complex of limestone, marble, and dolomite, each thick enough to form a good reservoir and each separated from the other by a thick series of water-retaining schists," according to Picard, who was asked by the UN soon after World War II to do a survey of karst water potential in Greece, a report in which he comments repeatedly on the excellent "producer quality" of the limestones and marbles of the country. Yet the yield of water from the carbonate rocks, and the degrees of fertility in the soil formed by breakdown of the same rock, vary greatly from place to place in the Greek world. In the islands, whose bare rocky surfaces excite photographers and poets but make settlement difficult, "most of the island soils are barren from structural causes, while

Figure 7.3. General scheme of water/limestone interaction in karst terrane. *1.* Caprock impermeable strata. *2.* Limestones. *3.* Swallet, where water enters the rock. *4.* Shaft. *5.* Collapse sink, one of a series. *6.* Resurgence. Water cannot easily penetrate the impermeable rock (1), but finds ways to enter and enlarge fissures in the underlying limestone (3). Shaft formation (4) in karst terrane results in spaces like the domed chapel and spring of the Asklepion at Athens. Resurgences (6) are typical Greek springs. Retreating escarpments like this are visible along many of the coasts of Greece, as well as inland. Based on diagrams by Pohl (1955: 23, Fig. 5, by permission of the National Speleological Society); and Crawford (1984, reprinted by Chapman and Hall, 1991: Fig. 13.3, by permission of Chapman and Hall).

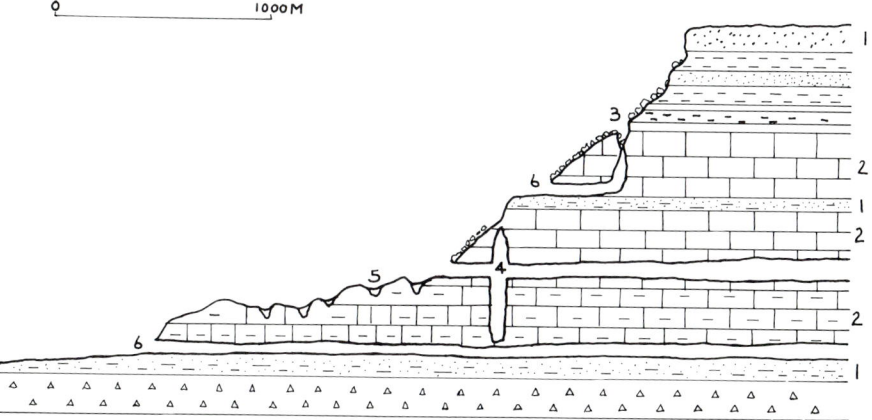

the sediment systems seem also to have led a fairly independent life. The best areas of land were so before man's arrival and in most respects have continued to be so until the present . . . The present dangers for the islands from human misuse are palpable but it is anachronistic to transfer present conditions of human ecology . . . uncritically into the past" (Bintliff, 1977, 537). The dangers referred to are exacerbated because of scarce rainfall, intense evaporation, and infertile soil—none under human control. We will return later to this issue of human impact on the environment.

In Italy and Sicily, "a more or less intensive development of karst phenomena is present in all regions," most notably the foothills northwest of Venice, and the region of Apulia in the "heel." In Sicily, karst is locally developed in the Madonie mountains of the interior, at Palermo, in the hills above Syracuse, and in the southcentral area; other karsts depend upon gypsum outcroppings (Belloni et al., 1972, 85,112), as at Akragas (see Fig. 8.5)

The shafts and channels of karst behave as natural pipelines, with direct conduits enlarging and indirect ones being abandoned (Fekete, 1977, 35). Sinkholes or dolines are places where surface drainage has found a fissure leading into the limestone rock, and has over time enlarged it. Then the water can more readily flow at this place, and the increased amount of water further enlarges the hole. Vertical shafts might be considered a special case of doline (Quinlin, 1978, 160), since like dolines, shafts are vertically enlarged by solution at 1 millimeter per year (J. Palmer, 1976, 54; Pohl, 1955, 5–24; Baker, 1977, 333–39). Yet the difference between them is significant: while dolines enlarge from the top downward, shafts enlarge upward from the action of water flowing quasi-horizontally, along the bedding planes (Bogli, 1967, 17–18). Vertical shafts are especially found where sandstone or other impermeable rock lies above the limestone (Quinlin, 1978, 35; Bogli, 1980, 156), and they may extend not only upward to the ground surface but also downward like a cased well. An example is found above the North Demeter Sanctuary at Morgantina where a spring appears at the top of the hill along the seam at the surface between sandstone and sandy-clay.

A larger form of doline, the *polje*, is found extensively in Greece and in Italy especially east of Rome in the Apennines (Bogli, 1980, 71), although karst in Greece can occur without poljes (Dufaure, 1977, 27–58). A polje differs from a lake in its drainage pattern, since not only can all the water drain out abruptly, like pulling a plug, but also water can under some circumstances flood up into the polje from its shaft. Another name for this kind of feature is an *estavelle* (Bogli, 1980, 124). The former Lake Kopais north of Athens, for instance, is a large standard polje with Younger Fill at the bottom. Recent studies of Lake Kopias have been done by J. Knauss and his collegues of the Technical University at Munich *(Kopais I-III)*. Other poljes in mainland Greece are known at Tripolis, Feneos, Stymphalos/Climendi, and Alea/Skotini.

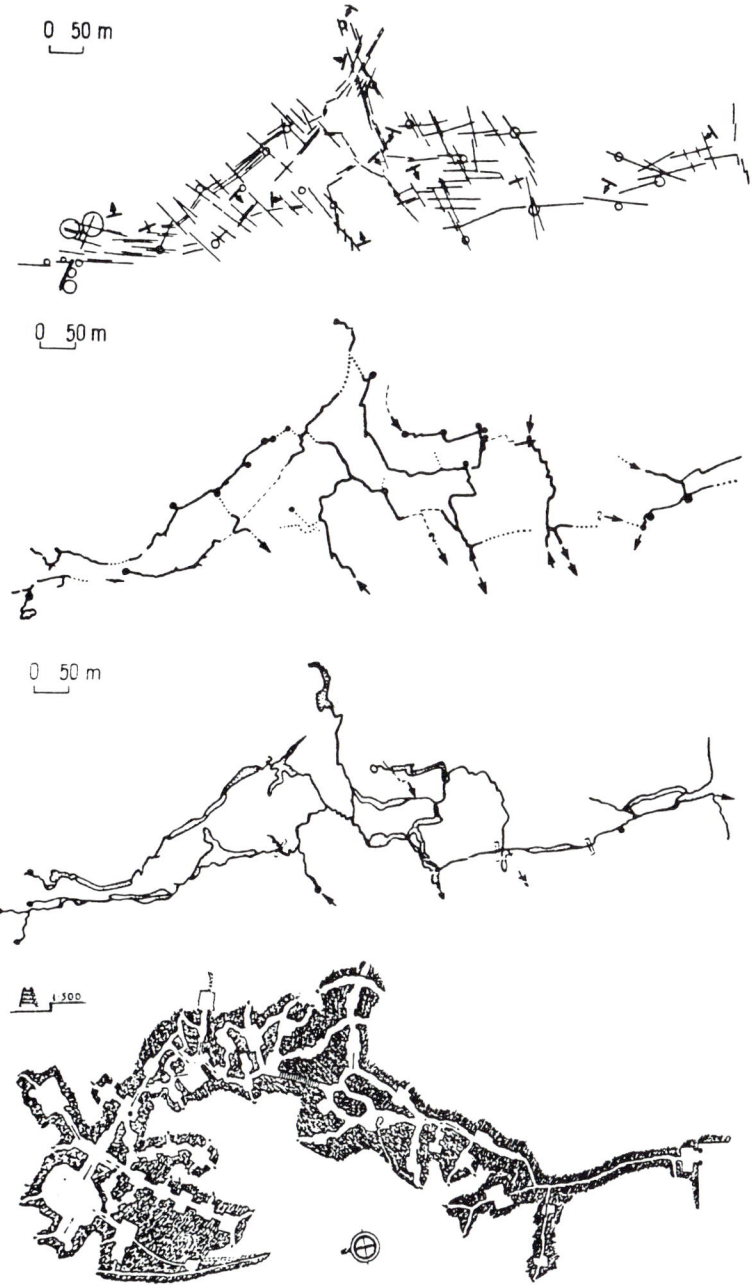

Figure 7.4. Three phases of karst cave development in Italy, compared with plan of the Purgatorio ipogeum in Akragas (bottom). The three plans of karst caves have a scale of 0–50 m while the ipogeum below is drawn at 1:500. The three cave phases were reprinted by Jakucs 1977 (from Pasa, 1961) and are reprinted by permission of Adam Hilger Publishing, Ltd. The plan of the ipogeum at Akragas is from B. Pace, *Arte e civilita della Sicilia antica* (Milano, 1938, reprinted by permission of the Scocietà Editrice Dante Aleghieri, Rome).

Caves in karst are formed by corrosion by much the same physical and chemical processes as dolines, but are horizontally oriented. Because much of this action takes place underground, it is possible to have a large difference between surface and subsurface drainage in karst areas (Le-Grand, 1977,11). By studying caves we have valuable clues to the hydrological network, as we shall see in Chapter 18 (The Well-watered Acropolis at Athens). Higgins (1962) was the first to study the caves of the Athenian Acropolis as a group. Caves with tunnels extend along gently sloping planar surfaces, growing through maximum dissolution of the stone (Burdon, 1967, 313). Depending on their configuration, caves may be considered as natural pipelines (Fekete, 1977, 35; Quinlin, 1978, 108; Mijatovic, 1977, 279). Some caves open to the ground surface, and some are hidden within or below it. Frequently, springs are located within caves, such as the springs associated with the church and monastery of Panayia Spiliani on Samos, above Pithagorio.

Reservoirs and Springs

Karst serves as an excellent reservoir for drinking water, owing to its joint network, caves, shafts, and dolines (Jennings, 1971; Picard, report 3, 1957). Karst is noted for the springs that appear at the base of a mountain, where the soluble layer of limestone abuts an impermeable layer of stone or clay (Bogli, 1980, 81). It is these springs that made karst so useful to Greek city builders, and we will come back to them. In Greek lands, much karst is connected to the sea by underground drainage (Maurin and Zoetl, 1967; Kashot, 1977, 311), which can wastefully empty the fresh water into the sea or can contaminate fresh with salt water by means of a siphon (J. Palmer, 1976, 107; Bogli, 1980, 127–28). The form of the underground conduit system is typically that of upright shafts or steep canyons upstream, with low-gradient "tubes" (channel and cave systems) downstream. Since the underground drainage tends to concentrate if the rock conditions permit it, larger horizontal and vertical openings develop at the expense of smaller ones. One may think of the mountains as gigantic water towers (Mijatovic, 1977, 262–78, esp. 271), an example being Mt. Parnis in Attica, with "ideal geohydrological conditions for the storage of groundwater" (Burdon, 1964, I). These conditions include high infiltration and low runoff, with karst waters forming perched water tables even at high altitudes (Burdon, 1964,36). Siphons above the water table use and widen vertical passages. Under pressure from upstream, the water in any particular shaft or cavern follows the shortest hydrological connection to outflow in a karst spring, keeping to the constraints of local geology (Bogli, 1980, 117). Flow from a low spring ordinarily puts a high spring above it out of action.

Output of these karst systems is most useful to humans in the forms of springs and perennial rivers, which could either be used directly or tapped for long-distance waterlines. Perennial springs are particularly ap-

Figure 7.5. View of a quarry at Syracuse, the famous "Ear of Dionysius" where the Athenian prisoners worked as slaves in the late fifth century. This is the outlet of a karst water system.

preciated in Mediterranean lands where rainfall is mostly confined to one season, the winter, while need for water is greatest in summer. Springs may be located in permeable strata above impermeable materials, especially along the boundary between limestone, sandstone, or clay (Jennings, 1971, 78; Kastning, 1977, 193–201, esp. 199); at the outfall of widened joint fractures; as an overflow spring draining the waters of the phreatic (below groundwater level) zone; as an ascending spring draining along joints or strata, or rising in alluvium (Figs. 7.7–7.9). These ascending springs include artesian wells. Emergent springs include the spring "at the foot of barren limestone hills" of Mt. Ida from which flows the Scamander River of the plain of Troy in Ionia (Diller, 1881,634), and the spring that supplies the river at Gortys in the Peloponnesos. Most common in Greek lands are resurgences from swallets or dolines (openings through which streams descend underground), such as those mentioned earlier that flow out near Argos, supplied by dolines on the high plateau to the west. Exsurgences are the result of local seepage, and in many cases are seasonal only, flowing at the end of winter and into the spring season.

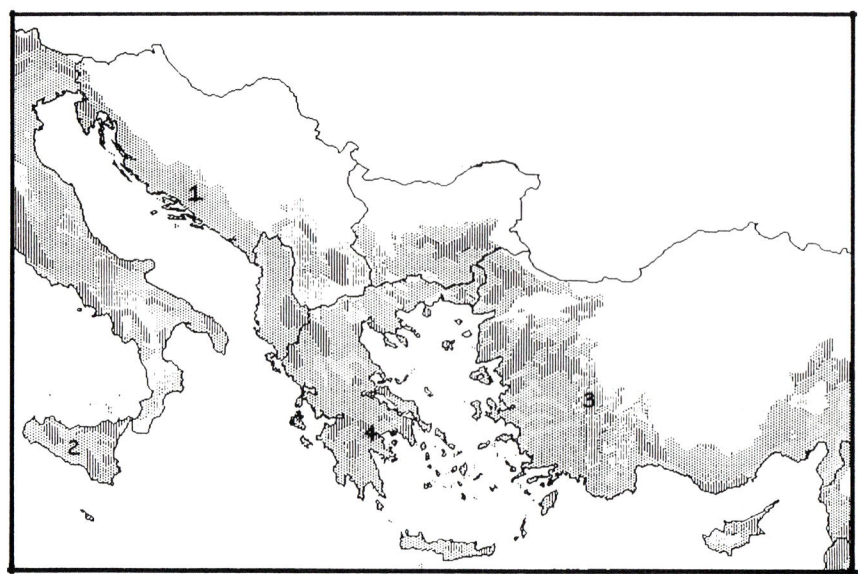

Figure 7.6. Groundwater resources in the Greek world. 1. Limestone. 2. Alluvium. 3. Poor groundwater resources. 4. Moderate water potential. Map suplied by R. Brinkman, Land and Water Development Division, U.N. Food and Agriculture Organization, Rome, and reprinted by permission.

Figure 7.7. Diagram of contact spring, at the ground surface where limestone and an impermeable stratum come together. Reprinted by permission of Springer Verlag, from Bogli, 1980:122, Fig. 9.2.

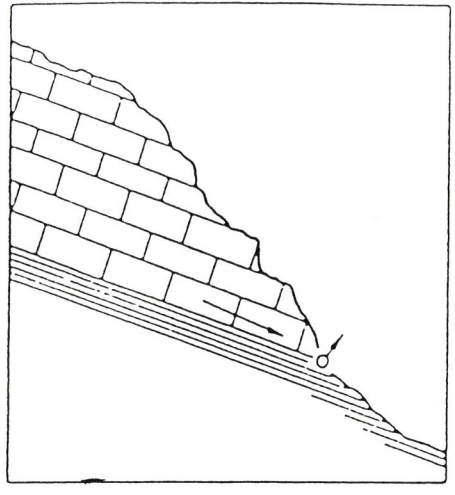

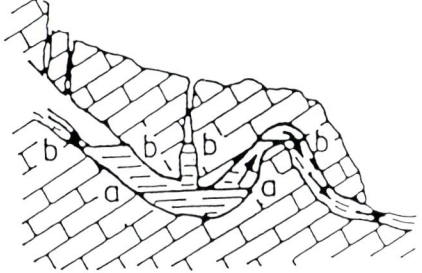

Figure 7.8. Diagram of a siphon causing an intermittent spring. The flow of the spring depends upon there being enough water upstream that the water level is at *b* or higher. At *a* or any other level lower than *b* no water is flowing from the spring. Jennings (1971): 75, reprinted by permission of M.I.T. Press.

Most fascinating and, until recently, mysterious are the submarine springs of the coastal waters (see Figs. 7.9, 7.10). Those in the great harbor at Syracuse and the Almiros spring just west of Iraklion in Crete are perhaps the most famous. Such springs pour their water out through open joints, caves, or Y-shaped openings in the sea floor. These submarine springs adjoin karst areas, and are located in relatively impervious parts of aquifers (Jennings, 1971, 78; Stringfield and Le Grand, 1969, 387–404; Milanovic, 1981,105). Their flow can be steady (from land to sea) or can be reversible, as at Tarpon Springs in Florida. In many cases, a widened U siphon has one leg in fresh water and one in salty. The fresh water is lighter and the sea water denser. If the flow were constant, the interface between the two types of water would behave as an impermeable barrier, but because of tides and other fluctuations, there is a zone of transition. The sinkhole (one leg of the U) acts as a cased well down to the mixing zone. If the fresh water head (pressure exerted by a body or column of fluid) is large, dynamic equilibrium results and there can be a spring of fresh water erupting in the sea. Five feet of head is enough, as at the Sea Mills of Cephallonia. It is satisfying to know that the mysterious harbor springs at Syracuse have so elegant an explanation.

Similarly, springs may occur underground or in caves. Karst springs have been found in many areas of Greece. Most springs are found in complex geological areas, according to Loy (ca. 1965, 67). He reports that

Figure 7.9. Submarine spring, diagram. Q marks the spot where the fresh water erupts in the sea, forced out by the pressure (head) of the water. Reprinted by permission of Springer Verlag, from J. Stiny, 1933, Abb. 121.

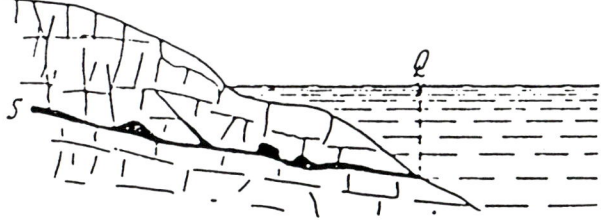

Figure 7.10.   Photo of a freshwater spring in the sea near Kiveri, Greece, south of Argos. The ancient-to-18th century harbor springs at Syracuse were of this type.

in the southwest Peloponnesos there are 2 major and 118 minor springs, 26 rivers, and a type of irrigation system "so simple it should be considered as part of the natural water resources." (We will definitely not so consider it, but give credit to the "simple" farmers who have learned to work so cooperatively with nature.) A list of locations of karst springs is given by M. Komatina (1977, 289); and a more complete account is *Inventory of Karstic Springs of Greece, I-III*, published by the Institute of Geology and Mineral Exploration, Athens (1978–80).

Climate

The Mediterranean climate, though markedly different from the continental climate north of the Alps and from the very dry Middle Eastern climate of Mesopotamia and neighboring lands, has its own variations between north and south of the Mediterranean Sea. The influence of the land mass of Asia to the east is mitigated by the prevailing westerly winds. If the winds blew regularly from the east, the whole Mediterranean area would have a climate decidedly different from the present one. As it is, the concentration of rainfall in winter months, not mitigated by annual flooding as in Egypt, is a constraint for farmers and municipal water officers alike. Evidence for climatic change since antiquity—although often postulated—is not strong enough to convince most experts. Major changes since the Bronze Age in the location of springs and in rainfall in the Peloponnesos (Loy, ca. 1965, 140) cannot really be extrapolated to the entire Mediterranean area. Rather, a fragile equilibrium between climate and vegetation has persisted (di Castri and Mooney, 1973, 59; *pace* R. Carpenter, *Discontinuity in Greek Civilization* and M. Cary, *Geographic Background to Greek and Roman History*). Normal fluctuation of the climate is recognized, but since classical times the changes have been non-catastrophic, that is, no new Ice Age, although a cool period during the last half of the first millenium B.C. is noted by some volcanologists (*Changes of Climate*, 1963, 127).

Yet the erratic quality of the climate has been a major factor in the way karst has developed here, and consequently in how people manage the resulting water supply. Irregular precipitation and high runoff result in infiltration and retention (di Castri and Mooney, 1973, 53–56), which shows seasonal variation (Mijatovic, 1977, 263). According to Burdon (1964, 36), almost half of the rain becomes infiltration in the Parnassos-Ghiona area where Delphi is located in the midst of heavily wooded mountains. Collecting water from a large watershed, a karst system is often out of phase with local rain events, and karst springs therefore exhibit a dampened curve in their outflow, which is to the advantage of humans who need water year round. The amount of water can be big enough for rivers, such as the biggest spring in the Peloponnesos, Ayios Flores, which has such a large catchment that it flows during several dry years when lesser springs dry up, in contrast with the thousands of seeps that are gone by August (Burdon,1964, 36–38; Loy, 65). In the Peloponnesos region, probably two-thirds of rain evaporates, and about 5 percent is wasted in submarine springs, leaving only about one quarter for runoff infiltration which eventually feeds springs (Loy, 63).

Landscape

Trees were grown as crops very early in Greek agricultural history, no later than the middle of the second millennium B.C. (Aschmann, 1973, 364). Which came first, the trees or the rain? "Erosion and karst favor each other," writes Dufaure (1977, 336; cf. Sweeting, 1964, 92–3). The delicate balance in karst terranes, where the upland is in most danger because it is the most fragile (Naveh and Dan, 1973, 373–90, esp. 387), can be destabilized by careless land clearing or short-fallow in prosperous times, or because of no soil conservation and pastoralism in bad times (van Andel et al., 1986, 125). Wars and unrest lead to the destruction of forests and of agricultural terraces. The most threatening failure is lack of maintenance of terraces. The destruction of such resources was probably accompanied by the extension of pasturage (Aschmann, 1973, 365). In the Early Bronze Age, there was severe erosion possibly combined with population growth and a climatic disaster. For the later Bronze Age fewer sites have been found, suggesting a smaller population and less stress on the land. After 1000 B.C. the landscape was stable through the fourth century B.C., apparently because the farmers had learned the difficult lesson from the earlier erosion and had turned to the use of terraces. Yet the lesson had to be learned again and again: A depressed rural economy in which shepherds allow sheep and goats to clamber at will over the terraces and eventually break them down, so that severe erosion follows, is worse than total economic collapse. Political fragmentation and disaster during the Hellenistic period in Greece accompanied rural collapse and renewed severe erosion, the latter now thought by some to be the origin of the Younger Fill. It is extremely difficult to say whether the rural collapse caused the political instability, or vice versa. Additionally, volcanic eruptions seem to have brought about a long period of colder than normal weather during the Hellenistic period, to about 100 B.C. (van Andel et al., 1986,177–225).

Probably to be associated with the earlier Younger Fill was the creation of deltas after 10,000–7000 B.C. but before A.D. 300—highly significant for many port cities from Miletus in the east to Ostia in the west. Mediterranean rivers are limited in length but their transport of huge amounts of suspended material led to landlocked cities. Ancient ports such as Ephesus became separated from their coasts beginning in the fourth century A.D. (Furon, 1952–3, 90; Meiggs, 1960). At the same time, the sea has risen or the land has sunk in many coastal areas, slightly but constantly in the last 2000 to 5000 years, about 2 meters as an average: Ionia: 1.75 meters; Leptis Magna 2 meters; Attica 1–3 meters; Delos 1–3 meters; but at Syracuse, there is no evidence of change. At Pylos, Mycenaean ruins on Older Fill are 3 meters underwater, while Hellenistic ruins are under 1.5 meters (Bintliff, 1977, 25). The difficulty of managing the water supply and drainage of a city undergoing such drastic change to its physical setting can well be imagined.

Even though 1500 years is but the twinkling of an eye in geological terms, we are probably dealing here with at least two separate erosion cycles, visible in different parts of the Mediterranean region. Maximum erosion in Sicily was dated by Butzer (1974, 134) to two periods: 700–325 B.C.[2] and to the Middle Ages; and a deforestation of the fourth century B.C. was noted by several ancient authors. Still, "soil erosion has been relatively unimportant during the last 5000 years," in a central part of the Greek world, the Southern Argolid, according to van Andel et al. (1986, 110–11; cf. Davidson, 1980, 143–58). That area has had relatively little erosion even without conservation. Conversely, Melos in the Cyclades is barren of trees now and seems likely to always have been so (Davidson, 1980, 150–51) because of violent seasonal rains and steep topography. Gage reports stream terraces being formed very rapidly (months or decades, not millennia) in areas of strong relief, steep gradients, and high precipitation (such as the west coast of Asia Minor), where the amount of energy available allows rapid change. He comments: "Slow continuous change is clearly not a characteristic of this geomorphological process" (1978, 621).

The modern population explosion, resulting pressure on the land, and— even more crucial—heedless use of technology such as construction of railroads and highways without regard to the ecological system, have resulted in extremes of deforestation in Greece during the past 200 years. We have inconclusive evidence, at most, to justify attributing equal and similar heedlessness to ancient peoples (van Andel et al, 1986, 125–26).

Stability of landscape is a most complex issue, and it is an unsatisfying argument that overemphasizes one factor as the major or only cause of instability. It is important to remember that denuding is a natural process in karst terranes, and will take place without human aggravation— although human misuse of land can exacerbate the effects of denudation. In addition to the sheet erosion that pulls topsoil into karst dolines and fissures, other factors such as natural fires and organisms that damage or exterminate species have had major impact on geomorphology quite independent of human actions.

Waste

Within karst terrane all waters, whether pure or polluted, are more or less equal in their rates of circulation. Karst is therefore a less reliable waste-disposal environment than soil because it is easily polluted. Treatment of waste through soil is good when site factors such as topography, soils, geology, and hydrology all are positive (Belson,1977, 175; Tennyson and Settergren, 1977, 411–18). A fifty-day minimum is thought necessary for purification of wastes fed into the groundwater system in soil, but in the stone channels of karst, circulation may be faster, and certainly the amount of filtering done by the soil cannot be expected in bare rock.

URBANIZATION

Given the positive physical base for water supply that karst terranes offer, were there direct relations between karst and urbanization in ancient Greek times? The number of archaeological sites shows that people lived in twice as many places then as now, but not (contra Furon, 1952–53, 102) that the population was twice as numerous in antiquity. This was possible because already by the second millennium B.C., the Greeks had a water technology that widened their choices among, and control over, local environments.

Another aspect of the relationship between karst and cities would not have become apparent in one or even several human lifetimes. That is, urbanization itself has the effect of greatly increasing runoff, proportionate to the amount of pavement, and thus of displacing the point of entry of the groundwater into the ground. Instead of generalized and gradual seepage of water through tree and plant roots into the soil, the urbanized area pours torrents of waters gathered from roofs and pavements onto the immediately surrounding unpaved surfaces, overloading their capacity to absorb, and promoting flooding. Conversely, the action of karst waters in gradually cutting deeper and deeper into the limestone may eventually leave high and dry a city that was depending upon them for its water supply (Melhorn and Flemal, 1975, 230. Dissolution rates have been studied in 1990 by W. Dreybrodt.) The ancient engineers[3] had need of every ounce of cleverness they possessed to keep their cities appropriately watered.

We may conclude that the interaction of karst geology, human management of water, and the process of urbanization was complex. As the experience of the last 200 years has shown, changes induced by human activity, combined with minor climatic fluctuations, can cause local ecological systems to cross the threshold of permanent danger (Gage, 1978, 623). Learning to control water in the karst terrane, beginning in the archaic period, was a significant accomplishment of the Greeks. The famous tunnel at Samos and fountainhouse at Megara, of the sixth and seventh centuries, respectively, are evidence that long distance water supply lines and their associated fittings and structures were well within the competence of these engineers (see Figs. 4.1, 4.2, 22.14, 20.6).

NOTES

1. The ancient Greeks did not, of course, call their geological environment "karst terrane," nor did they manage its water supply in the consciously mathematical way that a modern hydraulic engineer does. However, the sophistication of their water management indicates a high conceptual understanding of the constraints and potential of their resource base.

2. I am sceptical of this dating since this time period marked the years of greatest Greek wealth in the island.

3. Although modern persons who do this work are engineers, it is an anachronism to call the ancient builders by this term. Yet since L. Sprague de Camp's book *The Ancient Engineers* (M.I.T. Press, 1960), the term has been widely used for the ancient builders.

8

Greek Settlements and Karst Phenomena: Corinth and Syracuse

The further back in time the historical geographer proceeds, the more difficult becomes the task of reconstruction, but the more important it is for him to understand the nature of the land from which its past occupants wrested a livelilhood. With each step back in time, history becomes more geographical, until, in the beginning, it is all geography.

—Michelet
The History of France

To get a sense of the relationship between karst geology and Greek settlement, we will look at examples from the Greek mainland, the islands of the Aegean, and Sicily. There is no attempt here to be comprehensive, as the necessary field work has not been done to make that possible, but rather these examples are selected to suggest the way that karst water potential played an important role in site selection and development. The major examples selected are Athens and Corinth for mainland Greece, Rhodes for the Aegean Islands, Assos and Priene for Ionia, and Syracuse and Akragas for Sicily. Other places will be cited briefly if the details from those sites are particularly illuminating.

Karst phenomena, as we have seen, are found throughout the Greek world. Since Athens is perhaps the best documented Greek city, and has in addition a phenomenal karst system as its monumental focus, it receives here a section of its own, Chapter 18, The Well-Watered Acropolis. In Chapter 11, Planning Water Management, we discuss Corinth's water system in comparison with that of her daughter city Syracuse. Here, however, we will consider the aspects of water at Corinth that derive from the karst geology of the area.

CORINTH

This city is an excellent example of the adaptation of urban requirements to karst terrane, the siting of an ancient Greek city to take advantage of this natural resource. Ancient Corinth was built on gradually sloping terraces below the isolated protuberance of Acrocorinth, which acts as a reservoir, with the flow of waters through it resulting in springs (Fig. 8.1). That karst waters are to be found in perched nappes even at high altitudes accounts for the spring of Upper Peirene not far below the summit of Acrocorinth, as well as the two fountains half-way down the road from its citadel, and the fountain called Hadji Mustapha, at the immediate foot of the citadel (as reported by the late seventeenth century traveler, E. Celebi, cited in Mackay, 1967, 193–95.)

The aquifers also supply the aqueduct (probably ancient) from Penteskouphia southwest of Acrocorinth. The form of such an underground conduit system is typically that of steep "canyons" or shafts upstream, with low-gradient "tubes" downstream (J. Palmer, 1976, 94,144). Although the channels at Corinth have not been studied by a geologist, we know that at least one stretch of tunnel at Corinth had a slope of 1:200 (Hill, 1964, 54).

Tubes and channels have been reported again and again in the excavations at Corinth, some recognized as being in use at least by the fifth century B.C. (Wiseman, 1978, 82), others flowing until at least A.D. 400 and others such as the West Tunnel serving as reservoirs for at least 1800 years, and holding up to 120,000 gallons (Hill, 1964, 57). These tubes varied in length from 50 to 3000 meters (Wiseman, 1978, 202; Hill, 1964, fig.4, p. 16; Robinson, 1969, 1–35), collecting water from several small "streams" that they intersected. The walls of these tunnels were impervious clay, but sometimes the ancient engineers had to cut up into the roofing of conglomerate, in which case the rocky part might be stuccoed for water retention. Occasionally, as at Lerna, the clay walls of the tunnel were also stuccoed. Some changes in the levels of the clay-cut channels may be attributed to natural changes as the flowing water downcut its bed, but others were probably man-made. Even today, with very little repair, this system could be made to supply a good-sized modern city.

Careful comparison of the patterns of tunnels at Corinth in the Agora area and at the Asklepion-Lerna complex with the patterns of Italian karst tunnels suggests strongly that the ancient Corinthian engineers were utilizing existing but irregular karst tunnels, carved out during long eons in the permeable limestone and conglomerate lying just above the impermeable clay. At first, sixth century or earlier, they would only have formalized the outlet of the resurgence into a fountainhouse, such as the Sacred Spring or the Cyclopean Fountain, but later—though still in the fifth century—to balance supply and demand, reservoirs were dug adjacent to the outlets, by digging in the clay and supporting the overhanging conglom-

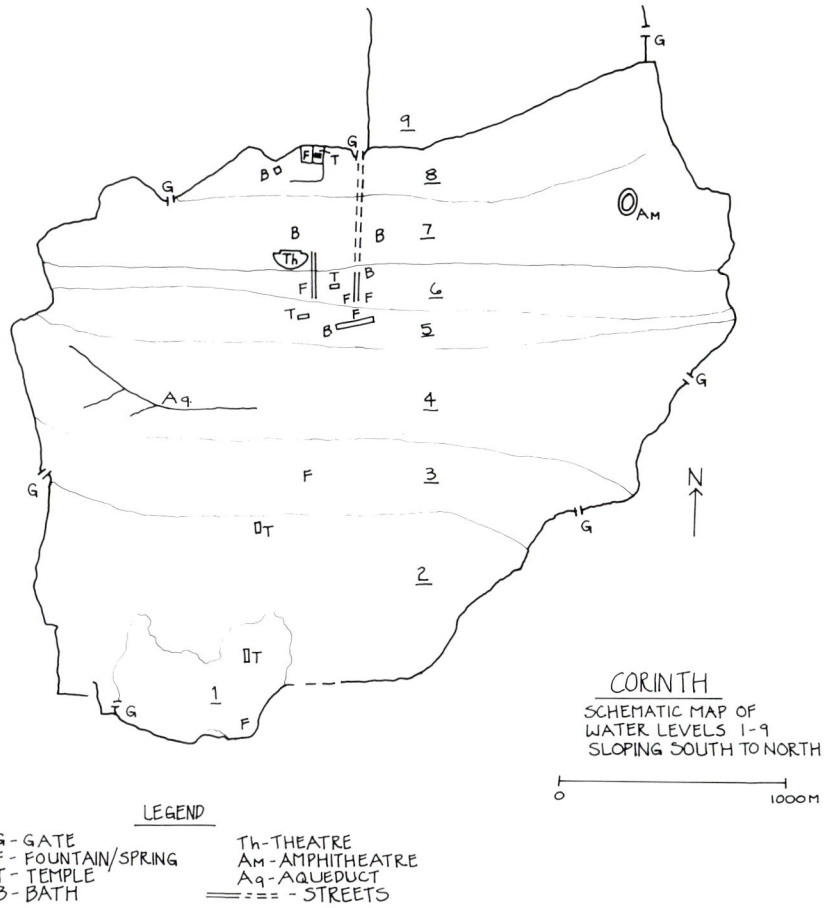

Figure 8.1. Corinth, geological relief. The site steps down in a series of terraces from the top of Acrocorinth at the south (bottom of the plan) to the north, the plain near the sea, at the top of the plan. Water collected in the mountains had many opportunities to come to the surface at places where the Corinthians built fountains, baths, etc.

erate with walls, piers, and columns. Early reservoirs at Corinth effectively prove that the Greeks preceded the Romans in building reservoirs on the principle of filling up at night and drawing down in the daytime (cf. Glasser on Greek fountainhouses, [1983], and Fahlbusch on reservoirs [1982, 111–13, 121]).

An important piece of evidence for the natural karst origin of the tunnels and springs is their intermittent flow. Peirene Fountain, for example, has been called "a copious natural spring of immemorial antiquity" (*Ancient Corinth*, 1954, 35), and certainly maintained its importance over many centuries, requiring at least two major rebuildings and embellishments (see Fig. 11.2). Still, the original small spring that fed both Peirene and the Cyclopean Fountain was amplified no later than classical times by flow from uphill through a series of tunnels leading back to the mountain and a series of reservoir chambers that follow the natural layout of the contours in clay and stone. These interventions tell us that the flow of the small natural spring there was insufficient for the classical city. The Sacred Spring which like Peirene lay one level below the Agora, tucked under the conglomerate shelf, was monumentalized in the sixth and fifth centuries but gradually went out of use in the fourth century, being replaced by a conduit and basin above the shelf, as the water deserted its natural channel, probably for a lower one. I wonder whether the construction of the elaborate water system of the South Stoa toward the end of the fourth century could have cut off the supply to the Sacred Spring? Farther to the west, the Glauke Fountain (Fig. 11.3) seems never to have been a natural spring, being located in a layer of limestone above the conglomerate, and yet was given the shape of a crude grotto. It held 14,400 gallons and was fed by conduit from the Hadji Mustapha source mentioned before. It may be that the common occurrence of veins of water in limestone quarries had suggested that this relic from the quarrying for the archaic Apollo Temple be adapted as a fountain for its neighborhood. There was a venerable association of Temples of Apollo with springs, such as those that cluster around his temple at Delphi, so it may be that this fountain reinforced the sacredness of the precinct here at Corinth. Certainly it was a convenient source of water for visitors to the temple and its district.

Further evidence for the karstic nature of the channels in the Corinthian Agora are the depth and ample supply of the line serving the South Stoa (Broneer,1954, 59ff; Williams and Zervos, 1981, 118). Each of the shops of the stoa has a well about 12 meters deep, each set in a line at the same distance from the entrance, and each separately connected by spur channels to the water line in which the water still runs so cold that the excavators referred to it as "refrigerated." This description of the water supply of the South Stoa seems to me somewhat mistaken in its geology:

> From the point of view of construction it would have been far more convenient to dig the channel directly in line with the shop wells so as to make each well a manhole for the removal of the earth. Instead of this simple procedure, the channel and the wells were dug independently and when the proper depth was reached in each well a small hole was punched connecting the spur channel with the well shaft. In some instances, when the well was used as a manhole connecting with the tunnel, the large opening was walled up later except for a small hole through which water could circulate. (Broneer, 1954, 59)

Rather, I suppose that the irregular channel preexisted the stoa and its wells, being a natural karst channel. This source was tapped by the wells of the sixth century houses that preceeded the South Stoa. Having observed the seasonal variation in the flow of this channel, the engineers hesitated to either tap directly into it, or to interrupt it with their construction any more than was absolutely necessary. Therefore they set the stoa foundations forward of the line of water and designed the water supply of the stoa as separate from but tapping into the natural flow. Plate III of *Corinth*, Vol. I, Part VI, shows both the South Stoa and the west and east waterlines that cross the Agora. The surface drainage in stone channels now easily observable in the Agora is Roman, much later than the supply lines flowing at -12 meters or thereabouts. The early karst channels at depth, and the Roman surface drains are shown in Figure 11.1.

The South Stoa is probably from the second half of the fourth century B.C. Already in the fifth century, there was enough water supply in the southwest corner of the Agora to warrant construction of the Centaur Baths (ca. 425–400 B.C.) (Williams, 1976, 100–15). On the next lower terrace, at the northern edge of the city, another bath was built and rebuilt in connection with both the gymnasium and the Asklepion. Both of these baths are sited next to obvious changes in ground level. Whenever I see a bath that snuggles into a rocky shelf, I suspect that a vein of water came to the surface at that spot, and a bath was built to take advantage of it, such as the gymnasium baths at Priene in Ionia (Figs. 12.6, 16.10). In the case of many sanctuaries of Asklepios, the vein of water seems often to have been thermal or sulfurous, or distinctive in some other way that made people attribute health-giving qualities to it. Such uncommon waters may still be karstic in origin, as we have seen, their unique flavors resulting from the strata they flow through.

How much water would this tunnel system have supplied to Corinth? The west tunnel was giving 3000 to 3500 gallons per hour at the time of excavation, and could hold 120,000 gallons, but other lines brought the total to possibly 8000 gallons per hour even in summer. The southeast branch gave 11,460 liters per hour, or half as much as the west branch (Hill, 1964, 57). In a karst system, seasonal variation would not be nearly as marked as the observable differences in flow in rivers or alluvial wells. Glauke's reservoirs could hold another 14,400 gallons. How much more was added by the aqueduct in the western part of the city? (Robinson, 1969, 1–35) How much more to supply the Roman baths at the eastern edge of the city? The fact that there is no ready answer for this question of total water supply for the city indicates the different goals of the excavators from those of the urban historian.

Besides running water, the populace relied on cisterns. Most noticeable today are the large number of cisterns on Acrocorinth, within the circuit of walls. It is regrettable that excavators do not clearly distinguish between wells and cisterns. Upper Peirene, the source near the mountaintop, might be either based on verbal descriptions. Yet when we learn that 3 or 4 feet of water stand in it, even in June, and that at the bottom are three separate passages back into the rock, we suspect that a natural spring has been amplified by man's handiwork, so that additional veins of water will collect here. I first met this technique of enlarging water-bearing strata in several directions leading to a collection basin when I studied the water supply of Palmyra, Syria (see Crouch, 1969, and 1975). Compare this with the fountainhouse at Pergamon, on the south slope of the citadel, as reported in *Altertumer von Pergamon* (I, 3, 410ff). Upper Peirene is about 300 meters lower than the summit of the mountain, low enough to benefit from infiltration and to tap into a perched nappe of karst water. (Similarly situated fountainhouses are known at Pergamon, one 250 meters and one 300 meters below the summit, according to H. Fahlbusch, personal communication.) Possibly confused by the duplication of names, Strabo said that the Peirene Fountain in the Agora was fed by this spring near the top of the Acropolis, from which water flowed underground to the lower fountain (Strabo, 8.6.21). He must be given credit for understanding that the mountain was the origin of the channeled waters that supplied the town below.

To conclude this account of karst in mainland Greece, we will examine briefly the role of water from karst formations at a major and a minor shrine, Delphi and Gortys. The central pivot of the sanctuary of Delphi was the Kastalian Fountain, which gushes out of the ravine between the two Phaedriades peaks, tapping karst water at a little over 500 meters altitude (Fig. 8.2). Already in archaic times there was a fountainhouse built here next to the road. In Hellenistic times the fountain was enlarged, moved uphill, and given an elaborate facade with seven marble pilasters and four niches cut into the mountain, above a narrow reservoir from which the water overflowed into a lower court. This spring was probably the source of the water for the gymnasium and its bath just below in the ravine. Other springs and associated fountainhouses may still be found in the main sanctuary farther west along the road, stretching toward the top of the hill. From above the theater level, water was led to supply a large bath immediately east of the Temple of Apollo, and fountain basins survive above, beside, and below the temple. This group of springs surrounding the temple was associated with the Pythian oracle. All in all, the abundant water served to make this dramatically beautiful site also a practical one for a pilgrimage center and games location.

Similarly, at Gortys in Arcadia, a Temple of Asklepios was copiously supplied with water for the ritual and healing baths that took place there in the specially provided building (5th–3rd c. B.C.). As we have seen, this part of the Peloponnesos is well watered. The River Gortynios flows from karst springs, and well into the dry season, in June, there is water in the

Figure 8.2. Kastalian (Castalli) Fountain above the highway at Delphi, showing niches for dedications and horizontal lines for pipelines or for affixing architectural members. Overflow from the spring-fed fountain basin, cut into the living rock of the karst system, supplied the gymnasium on the terrace below the road.

river at least 4 feet deep and 10 feet wide—cool, refreshing water, amidst parched and rocky hills. This secluded sanctuary came to have at least two temples as well as the sophisticated baths. The baths were sited to take maximum advantage not only of the water from the river but also of solar heating. (See Ginouves, 1959, 38 and his Figs. 46–53, and compare with Thatcher, "Solar and Radiant Heating—Roman Style: The Open Rooms of the Terme del Foro at Ostia," 1958. I can testify to the calming and healing atmosphere of Gortys.)

The importance of karst in the Aegean islands may be seen clearly at Thasos, an island of marble covered with forest, where the karst development has been extensive. The marble is accompanied in the mainland territory that belonged to Thasos, by igneous rocks, granites, gneisses, schists, conglomerates, limestones, actites, poros, and sandstone, as well as gold and silver (Lazaridis, 1972). So much water is available that brooks are formed, especially on the north and east of the island. Most noted were the springs of Hagia Marina, which still supply water to the present town, through the gates of Heracles and Dionysos. There were also an-

cient wells and cisterns (still in use). Abundance of groundwater and of
rain made necessary the building of sewers and storm drains; the earliest
found is from the fifth century B.C., with some—such as the drains of the
Agora—still in use (Lazaridis, 73–4).

Karst water supply on Rhodes (which has a variety of karst named
after it) can be seen not only in the complete water supply and drainage
system that underlies the main city of Rhodes but also in the provisions
for watering the very ancient sanctuary of Lindos and its associated town
(Renz, 1929, 308–14; Meulenkamp, de Mulder, and van de Weerd, 1972,
541–53 and 4 maps). Meulenkamp et al. refer to the "bioclastic limestones of the Rhodos Formation dipping west [from Paradision on the
northeast coast] with intercalation and displaced boulders of bluish clays
or marls" (p. 551)—a combination that would permit karstic activity, especially as the authors go on to say (p. 552) that "limestones of the Rhodos Formation are found at more than 200 meters above sea level."

At Rhodes City, the Acropolis is noted for its grottoes that supplied
the city through a series of aqueducts (Fig. 8.3). These grottoes are cut
"in the [aforementioned] bioclastic limestones of the Rhodos formation,
with, in some cases, the floor cut down into clayey and marly units that
correspond to a line of seepage" (personal communication, Professor El-
len Rice of Oxford University, quoting an unnamed geologist with whom
she has inspected these formations). The waterlines that lead away from
the grottoes tap into the karst channel and gather its water for delivery
from the Acropolis to the monuments of the city below. As Professor
Rice suggests, it is quite likely that additional water was brought to the
acropolis and on to the city from the karst formations in the higher ground
to the south. These formations have also been studied by Professor Paul
G. Marinos, engineering geologist of the Technical University in Athens,
who assures me that his studies prove the karstic nature of some Rhodian terrane (personal communication).

The town and sanctuary of Lindos on Rhodes also was provided with
several waterlines, feeding fountains in the town, as well as having an
elaborate system of some eighty cisterns on the Acropolis (Kinch, cited
by Dyggve, 1960, Vol. II, 375, n.2). Dyggve reports the earlier descriptions
of water lines from the hill immediately west of Lindos and from farther
away, towards the center of the island, at Kampana (Dyggve, *Lindos*, 49–
50). The lines were both carved and built, some being equipped with air
shafts. The workmanship was similar to the ramparts of the Lindian
Acropolis and therefore possibly like them dates to the third century B.C.

Given the importance of Rhodes as a trading center, especially in the
second and third centuries B.C., and of Lindos as a pilgrimage center, it
stands to reason that it would need a reliable water supply, and would
have the means to pay for it. Yet we know that the importance of Rhodes
City began in the fifth century, when Hippodamus of Miletus was called
upon to lay out the new town in the best "modern" fashion. It is signifi-

cant, I think, that our knowledge of the most ancient street pattern of Rhodes comes from discoveries of its water pipelines and sewer pipes, as published most recently in Hoepfner and Schwandner, *Haus und Stadt in klassischen Griechenland* (1985), where the section on Rhodes is the work of Gregorios Konstantinopoulos, formerly in charge of archaeology at Rhodes City.[1] Thanks to these undervalued bits of evidence from antiquity, we know that the city plan of Rhodes was a grid subtly adjusted to produce smaller blocks bounded by more frequently occurring streets in the districts near the port, and larger blocks with more widely spaced streets farther out (Fig. 8.3). (This point is made and discussed convincingly in G. Konstantinopoulos, 1968, 115–23. Also see the recent study by P. Pedersen, 1988, 98–103.)

Figure 8.3. Plan of the city of Rhodes. Aqueducts are shown by rows of circles; sometimes these coincide with the lines of streets. The ancient streets are known by the water supply and sewer pipes, also found under the streets. Since medieval times, the street pattern in the old town nearest the harbors is much less regular than this. Map based on the work of G. Konstantinedes, former ephor of Rhodes.

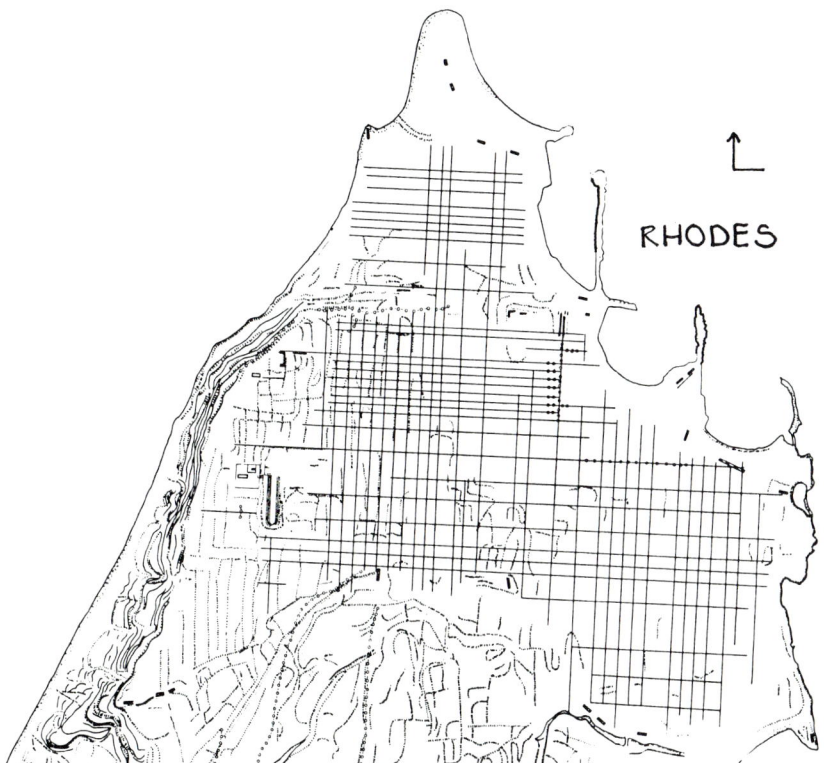

KARST AT GREEK SITES IN ASIA MINOR

Since the same geological features continue from Greece through the Aegean islands and into Asia Minor, ignoring modern national boundaries, we find karst features equally in the western and southern coasts of modern Turkey which were home to Greek peoples since at least 1000 B.C. (In 1988, Vit Klemes, then president of the International Association of Hydrological Sciences, told me that there was no Greek city that was not built on or next to karst, and cited as proof the Greek cities of Asia Minor.) Karst in these areas is distinguished by carbonate rocks, subsurface streams in the upland areas, and karst springs that contribute significantly to surface flow in the lower elevations (Özis, 1985, 95). Major karst basins are located at Sardis, Dalaman, and along the south coast of Anatolia, according to Özis's map (Özis, 1984, fig 1, p. 96) (see Fig. 7.1).

Karst is found in Ionia as far north as Troy, where the presence of limestone results in springs at the foot of Mt. Ida—seemingly dry and barren—that supply the Scamander River and flow in an arc south to west to north around the hill of Troy. In addition, smaller springs closer to Troy have been tapped in ancient and modern times for drinking water. From Assos, slightly south of Troy, to the center of the coast at Priene, and on to the south and southeast, the hills store and release groundwater, via karst mechanisms, in sufficient abundance to have made settlement possible and even comfortable. After describing the geology of these two cities, I will pose some questions about the water supply of Priene's neighbor, Miletus.

The site of Assos has alternate layers of limestone and other carbonates with volcanic rocks (nine layers, of which five are carbonates and one is a mixture of conglomerate, sandstone, and shale). It was the presence of the water trapped in the carbonate rocks that made settlement here plausible, while the volcanic rock (the Acropolis may once have been a volcano, according to Diller, 1881, 166–77) is well known to disintegrate into fertile soil. Thus the geology provided for food and water. The fact that limestone forms the lowest strata, at sea level, explains the spring at that level on the beach to the east of the tiny modern settlement at the ancient port of Assos. A major thermal spring is also located somewhat to the west in this corner of western Anatolia, its waters reaching over 100 degrees Centigrade (Brinkmann, 1976, 105, map of thermal springs). Such thermal springs were often the locus of pilgrimages in the ancient world, and functioned as medical centers.

Farther south on the coast, at Priene, the geology is a mountain range of marble, well wooded, and supplying ample water for settlement and for agriculture. So much water was available from the mountain, that no more than 20 or 25 percent of the houses at Priene had cisterns, most being supplied by pipelines directly tapping the hill, or delivering water from a reservoir on the Acropolis to storage chambers just inside the eastern rampart but above most of the settlement, to the fountains below. Even in the summer, there is so much water here that the tourist restaurant at the foot of the site can afford to have a constant waterfall splashing into a tank making a pool for their dining terrace. This is only the overflow from the supply to the modern village tapping, as did ancient Priene, the veins of water in the massif behind the town.

Across the valley of the Meander River, Priene's neighbor Miletus provides a very stimulating example of a city watered by karst formations. The archaic city was binodal, with a residential area and Acropolis relatively higher and closer to the coastal range of hills and a port quarter with temples and bath on the lower peninsula, closer to the sea. Like a textbook example of karst, the hills step down toward the river, the flat cap of each a very hard limestone in a thin layer, over more soluble layers of softer limestone. The archaic Acropolis with its residential district has recently been excavated: a relatively tall hill at the neck of the peninsula on which the fifth-century-and-later city was built (Mueller-Wiener, 1987). The archaic city was destroyed during the Persian Wars, which may also have damaged the earliest port and temples on the left side of the peninsula. When the city was rebuilt in the second half of the fifth century and later, most of the classical and Hellenistic buildings stood on the peninsula. I suggest that one reason for the apparent transfer of residential concentration was that the karst water system of the mountains may have been tapped at this time for delivery to lower levels in the rebuilt city (see Fig. 22.3). However, it must be noted that the evidence for the residential pattern is both old (early twentieth century excavations) and sketchy; the original excavators (Wiegand, 1908) made little effort to dig beneath the classical level, and the residential quarters have not been restudied subsequently, so that the best we can do in the present state of knowledge is make educated guesses about the process of urbanization of the site.

With the help of Frau Karin Weber of the German archaeological staff, I was able to climb into the hills and find one source of water that today supplies the village of Cimarlarin Totontarlasi near Miletus, and in Roman times supplied several baths along the right edge of the central monumental district of the city. It would have been equally easy to tap other springs for the bath of Faustina on the other side of the city near the theater, and for the residential areas of the city. Although there are many visible pipelines at Miletus, as well as drainage channels, the present excavators have been studying questions other than the water supply.[2]

KARST IN SICILY

It was precisely the karst areas of the Italian peninsula and of Sicily that drew the Greek colonists in the archaic period. Italian karst has been studied by Belloni, Martinis, and Orombelli (1972, 85–128) who show the major areas near the Alps, in the Central Apennines, around Bari, and through the whole heel area. For Sicilian karst one must turn to Dall' Aglio and Tedesco's work (1968, 171–210) (see Fig. 8.6). Sicilian karst has been studied perhaps the least of all, but is known in the vicinity of Palermo, at Syracuse, and at Akragas where it occurs in conjunction with gypsum. Since Palermo has very few Greek remains, we will confine our examinations to Syracuse and Akragas.

SYRACUSE

Syracuse is located on a corner of the southeast coast of Sicily, in an area where two major layers of limestone are interstriated with narrow terraces of marl and conglomerate (Fig. 8.4). The site tips upward as it goes inland to the northwest. Within these terraces, the karst process over many millennia has cut channels that slope gently toward the sea, channels that, as we will see in Chapter 11, were used to deliver water to the growing city in Greek times. Rather than a single source for the water supply of the city, Syracusan water comes from many surface and subsurface openings in the limestone, particularly where this stone lies above impermeable strata such as marl. Already in Hellenistic times, the karst process (and possibly a large increase in population) seems to have left the important fountains above the theater with insufficient water, for a 25-kilometer-long aqueduct—Galermi—was built to bring water from mountains farther to the west (Figs. 11.6, 11.7). Later, in Roman and Byzantine times, when the many channels at the level of the theater went dry, they were reused as catacombs (Figs. 11.5 and 15.5; cf. Figs. 15.4 and 15.6). The karst origins of these catacomb passages are evident in the irregular twists and turns that they take. Equally plausible is a karst origin for the submarine and coastal springs that Syracuse is famous for (as mentioned in Chapter 7). At the very edge of the water on the west side of the original island site of Ortygia, the spring of Arethusa still bubbles up. Other outlets of fresh water in the Great and Little Harbors have been part of travelers' tales since Greek times. Travelers were amazed to see smooth circles of fresh water in the choppy salt water of these bays. Fantastic tales were invented to explain these phenomena, such as the myth of the nymph Arethusa who escaped an unwelcome suitor by swimming away to Sicily and becoming a spring at the edge of the sea. Modern studies of similar springs off the Greek and Yugoslavian coasts have helped us realize that karst waters have been cutting shafts upward through limestone, and under the pressure of the head from the inland mountains, driving the fresh or brackish waters out into the sea whenever the sea floor came to be pierced by a fissure or collapsed as a doline. Since Syracuse is essentially a great dish of limestone, the inland waters flow down the dip as the strata become the sea floor, only to escape upward in wells on Ortygia and springs at the edge of the island, and become

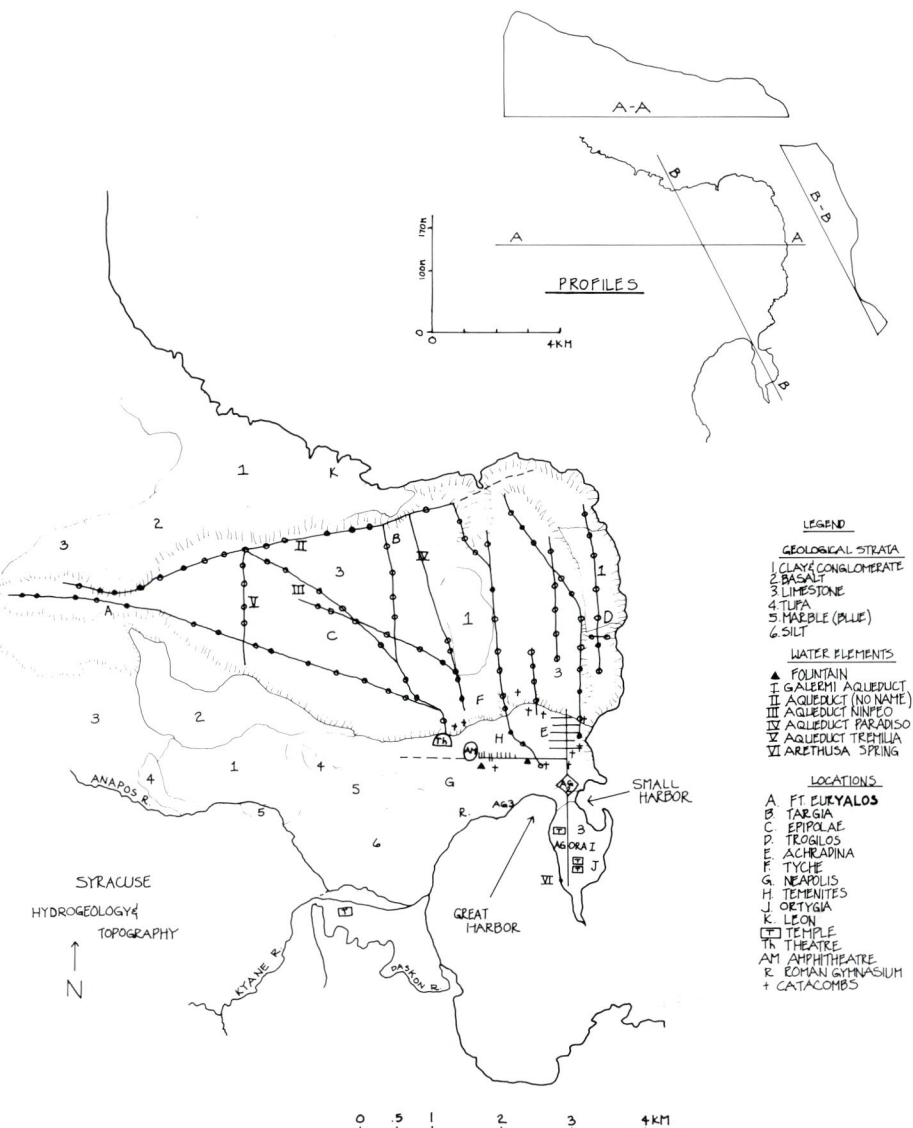

Figure 8.4. Hydrogeology of Syracuse. The great and small harbors of the ancient coastline are shown; between them is the peninsula or island of Ortygia (J) where the original Greek settlement was located. Later suburbs which still later became the city proper are at B through H. Catacombs, once karst resurgences, are at +. In addition to the fountains and spring shown here, there were for many centuries fresh-water springs in the midst of the great harbor, and the two rivers seem to have had spring origins. The outer defenses of the city, at Fort Euryalos (A) were cut into the limestone of the neck of the high ridge above the city. East-west and northwest-southeast site profiles are shown at upper right (note different scale). Redrawn from Drögemüller, Schubring, and others.

95

wasted in submarine springs within the harbors (Figs. 7.9, 7.10). The karst origin of Arethusa is indicated by the citations in ancient authors that the spring's water turns cloudy after heavy rains in the Arcadia suburb (Burns, 1974, 391; references to Pindar *Nemean* 1, 1; Ovid *Metamorphosis* 570–343; Vergil *Aeneid* 3.692–97; Pausanias 5.7.3) It seems likely that both the Anapos and Kyane Rivers in the plain beyond the Temple of Zeus have their origin in similar karst springs.

It is significant that eighth century Corinthian settlers, who brought with them a basic water technology from their mother city, would select the site of Syracuse which had geological features analogous to Corinth. Thus the technology they already had could be easily adjusted to operate on the new terrain. The pattern is clear. Just as Syracuse enjoyed the latest philosophy and drama from mainland Greece, so also it imported the latest water technology (if it had not developed), and thus kept abreast of engineering developments that made possible the continuing growth of the city. (See the maps of Syracuse [Figs. 8.4, 11.4], Selinus [Figs. 12.3, 12.5], and Akragas [frontispiece and Fig. 15.2]).

Equally favored by its karst setting was the city of Akragas (Agrigento). This region has a base of blue clay or marl over which lies a 10-meter thick strata of shell limestone, one of three kinds of limestone visible here. The shallow depth of the limestone over the clay meant easy access to water, since "the rainwater filters down through the limestone and then runs down the impermeable surface of the blue clay layer" (de Waele, 1971, 3–4). Marinelli (1917) described Upper Miocene gypsum in the Agrigento area. The gypsum is found as hills on marly clay and in blind valleys where swallow holes form when the gypsum and clay meet. The softness of the stone meant that neither the karst waters nor humans had any difficulty in cutting channels or wells through it, so that the hill became honeycombed with shafts and passages. Just as at Corinth and Syracuse, the ancient engineers undoubtedly utilized existing shafts and channels for the magnificent fifth century B.C. water system that the ancient writers attribute to Phiax. Where the soft stone showed a tendency to collapse, as at the mouths of channels, it was reinforced with ashlar masonry which still existed in the eighteenth century but which I was unable to find in the 1980s, except possibly at the opening to the Purgatorio Hypogeum. In the late twentieth century expansion of the city, these ancient ashlars seem to have been robbed out or covered up.

The softness of the stone and continued karst activity have combined to produce a sponge-like effect in the hill. Although the municipal water supply today is officially 80 liters per second, the sewage treatment plant processes 200–250 liters per second, which can only be explained if the hill itself is contributing to the runoff (Crouch, 1989, 155–74). Severe earthquakes during the same postwar period have also contributed to the disruption of the sewer system. In ancient times, the storm runoff and probably the sewage were fed to an artificial lake where fish and water

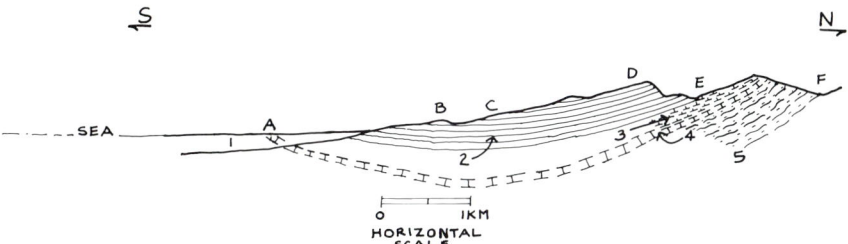

Figure 8.5. Geological Section of Akragas (Agrigento). Letters: A. Asklepieion. B. Ridge of temples. C. Hellenistic quarter and present museum (former church of S. Marco). D. The modern town, site also of the archaic and medieval towns that preceded it. E. Level of modern railroad station. Numbers refer to geological strata: 1. Quarternary deposits along the shore. The limestone units underlying the site are indicated by 2, 3, and 5. If the sulfur series at (4) were projected to the left in the same arc, it would come to the surface again in the plain to the south of the ridge of temples, at A—just where the Asklepieion is located. Asklepieia usually are sited to take advantage of special waters like this, sulfurous or thermal, and indeed a spring was a feature of this Asklepieion. Redrawn from a section published in Petroleum Society of Libya, *Guide to the Geology and Culture of Greece*. P. Norton, editor, 1965.

fowl were cultivated (see map, Fig. 15.2). One further curiosity of the water supply is the Temple of Asklepios in the coastal plain below the ridge of temples. Many Asklepia were watered with sulfurous or other distinctive water, a possibility here because of the gypsum strata. A spring, described by some ancient authors, is noted at this Asklepeion. Figure 8.5, a section of the Agrigento syncline, shows the sulfurous gypsum strata clearly (Petroleum Exploration Society of Libya 1960, Fig. 12). The downhill extension of the gypsum strata comes to the surface on the sloping plain that leads to the sea, just about where the Asklepion is located. (It would be interesting to examine the whole site with a hydrogeologist, for the resolution of many questions about the water supply and drainage of this site.)

We might expect that the geology of Akragas would be similar to that of Gela and/or Rhodes, joint founders of the city. And indeed, de Waele calls Gela "a comparable landscape" to Rhodes. The abruptly rising peaks of soft stone of both Rhodian Lindos and Akragas held sanctuaries dedicated to Athena and Zeus Atabyrios (Polybius *History* 9, 27). Large swallow holes, few in number, and large horizontal caves are typical of the karst formations of both areas. Just as at Corinth, there were vertical shafts in the peaks and tubes in the form of caves in the lower terraces.

It is apparent that much additional study is needed, not only for clear archaeological understanding of these sites, but also to make available to modern policymakers and engineers the accomplishments of their pre-

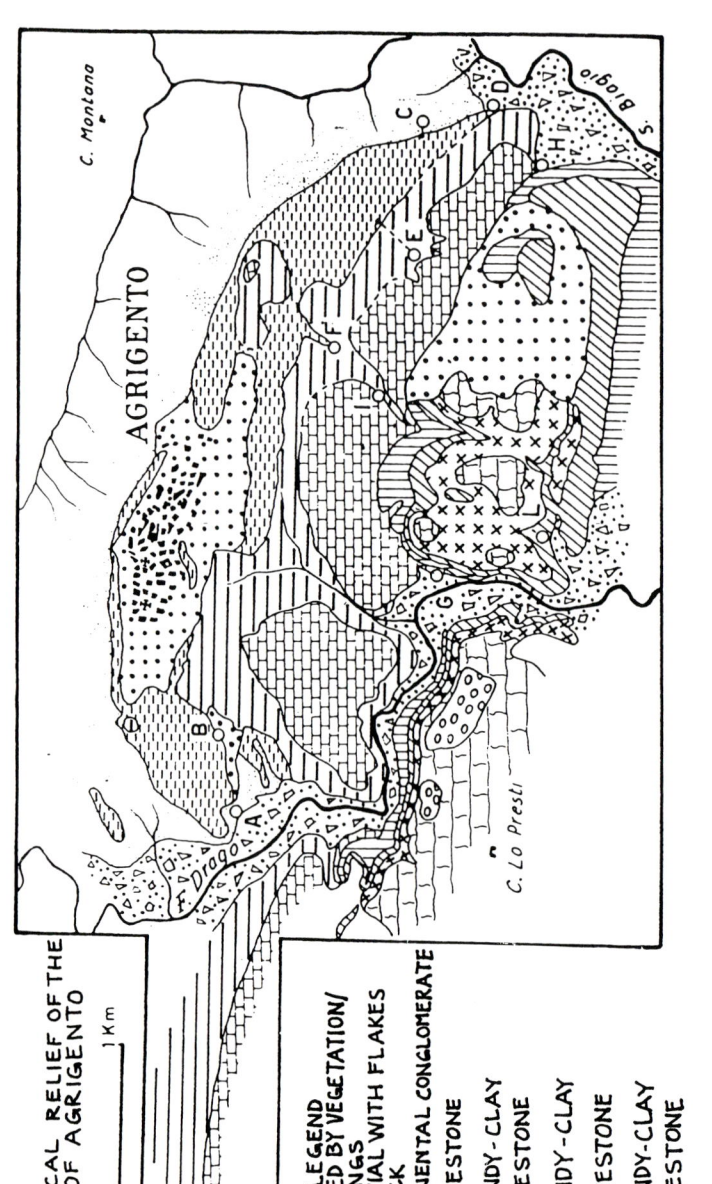

Figure 8.6. Map of the geology of Agrigento (ancient Akragas), published by Dall'Aglio and Tedesco (1968): 208 and reprinted by permission from Professor Dall'Aglio.

98

decessors in maximizing use of the natural water potential of their urban sites. Some ancient Greek sites have substantial modern populations: Argos, Gela, Lindos and Rhodes City, Megara, Pergamon, and Samos, while Athens, Corinth, and especially Agrigento, have such large populations that their problems of modern water supply and drainage cry out for every available solution. The present day applicability of these ancient Greek methods of supplying and draining water has been insisted upon by modern engineers, geologists, and water policy planners.

NOTES

1. Mr. Konstantinopoulos has been outstandingly generous in sharing with me his understanding of his city, and also in putting me in touch with the excavator of the mines at Laurion in Attica, Mr. Petrakos.

2. I am more grateful than I can say to Dr. Mueller-Wiener of the D.A.I. in Istanbul, who arranged for my visit to the site in October 1988, at considerable personal inconvenience to himself, and who answered innumerable questions. He also supplied some photographs and drawings of pipes, etc., that he had discovered at the site (Fig. 16.6), and encouraged his knowledgeable and intelligent assistants to help me.

9

Urban Location Determinants: Argos, Gela, and Pergamon

Examples are cited as pertinent illustrations rather than as "type localities"; they have been selected because they are either best documented, most representative of a particular type, or unique. No attempt has been made to discuss all known examples of a given type . . .

—F. Quinlan
Types of Karst

A city is the locus of both sociocultural and physical-technical elements in a society. To begin to understand the importance of both kinds of factors, ancient cities are convenient examples to study, especially dead ones that do not "wiggle" under the microscope. By isolating one urban system (water management) we can begin to understand the complication and variability that characterize these early cities, and hence gain insight into the development of other urban systems, as well as the role that water management plays in the evolution of all cities.

The received wisdom about the placement of cities usually rates defense as the primary factor, with access to arable land and concentration of trade activities being the other two important factors. A hill top, a protruding ridge, a peninsula or an isthmus between two rivers—all were sites easily defended by walls and hand weapons. Even a broad plain could be utilized if there were a slight rise that could be fortified, such as at the Mycenaean city of Tiryns in Greece. A city on a slight rise in the midst of broad fields of arable and irrigable soil was ideal.

Such a formulation leaves out the possibility of deliberately choosing as a site a port city that tapped directly into grazing lands, or the importance of a balance of either fish or meat complementing cereals in the diet. It is more accurate to say that two kinds of food were necessary, either crops and fish or crops and meat. This concept broadens the number and kinds of "ideal" sites.

Trade routes, the third factor, also are more complex in form and have more varied effects on urban location than early theories would admit. There are at least three kinds:

1. Overland routes (e.g., the Santa Fe Trail, with its two terminals at Independence, Mo., and Santa Fe., N.M., with Santa Fe being a crossroads where routes from Los Angeles and Mexico City also converged)
2. Land and water interchanges (the north-south land route through France crossing at Paris the east-west river route along the Seine)
3. Water-water interchanges such as New Orleans (Gulf of Mexico and Mississippi River) or Amsterdam (Rhine River and Atlantic Ocean)

Whether the account of cities was based on geography, history, or economics, the confluence of the three factors of defense, trade, and arable land has in the past seemed enough to determine the matter. A few revisionists have nudged us to rethink this. It may have been Jane Jacobs who first turned our attention to the probability that the impact of cities on the countryside has been far greater than that of the countryside on cities (Jacobs, 1969). Jacobs suggested that the excess wealth generated in cities stimulated the increase of production in the rural areas, rather than the other way around.

More recently, as other disciplines have turned their attentions to cities, some additional factors have been noticed as contributing to location decisions. Political and military histories have shown that time and again national governments have "artificially" placed towns so that they dominated and controlled their territories for the central government. The artificiality of the cities founded according to this principle during the Roman Empire, distinguished (by us) from some hypothetical norm of organic growth, has been cited to account for the waning of so many late Roman towns and for the reruralization of Europe after the fall of the western Roman Empire (Pirenne, 1934).

In a more sophisticated manner, the economist Hohenberg and the historian Lees (Hohenberg and Lees, 1985) have shown that central place theory, traditional among economic historians, fails to account for the patterns between and among cities during the past 1000 years in Europe. They have developed a richer theory that incorporates both central place and network concepts, thereby far more completely explaining the origin and persistence of cities for the period studied. They define a "central place system" as "more or less even spatial distribution of cities around a central capital, with regional boundaries typically falling in zones of weak interaction," and emphasizing local production and administration. A network city functions in long-distance trade, as part of an extensive but irregular linkage (see their chart, p.65) (Fig. 9.1). A detailed study of networks and central places, based on many examples, is lacking for the Greek period. Unfortunately, no one since Rostovtzeff (1941) has made a

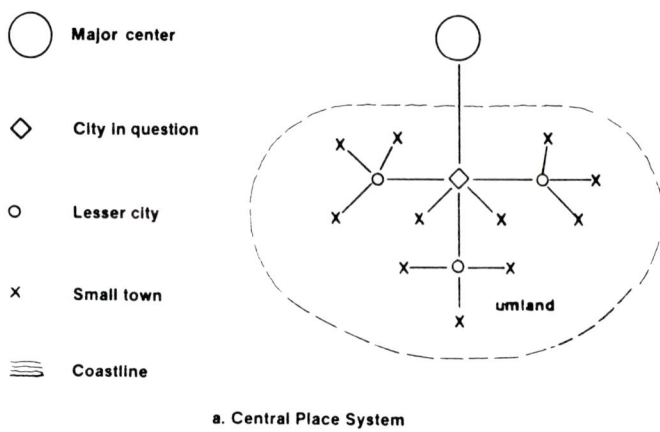

a. Central Place System

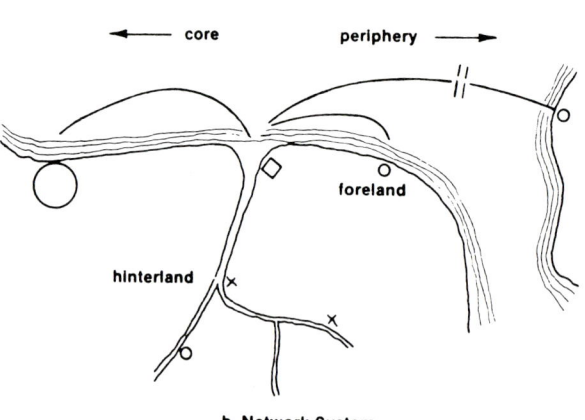

b. Network System

Figure 9.1. Graphic presentation of two basic theories of the interconnections between cities, a. central place system and b. network system. Reprinted by permission of the publishers from *The Making of Urban Europe 1000–1950* by P.M. Hohenberg and L.H. Lees, Cambridge, Mass.: Harvard University Press, copyright 1985 by the President and Fellows of Harvard College.

general comparison of the particular economic situations of Greek cities, and it has been entirely too long since the Doxiadis organization began their investigation from a modern planning perspective of the locations of ancient Greek cities (Doxiadis, 1972; Wagstaff, 1975, 163–68). Neither of these studies has spawned descendants.

In their seminal book, *The City Invincible*, Kraeling and Adams (1960) published papers from a conference of leading anthropologists, archaeologists, geographers, etc., concluding that the single most important factor essential for the origin of cities in every area of the world is variety. The more differences at a particular location in relief, rock and soil; natural cover; food plants and animals for farming, grazing, and hunting, or fish for catching; climate; and ethnic diversity, the more likely a city is to develop there.

GREEK SETTLEMENTS

Greek settlers had more leeway in choice of settlement location than one might at first think, given their ubiquitous cistern technology that freed them from total reliance on running water. Some geographers assert that sites adjacent to springs, rivers, and lakes were the urban locations of choice. Soil scientists counterclaim, with some justice, that water can, after all, be transported, and therefore soil, which cannot easily be moved and which must be of good quality for farming, is the ultimate determinant of settlement location. Ideally an ancient Greek town was located amid the area of best soil where the most work was done, while farthest away was the worst soil, to be allotted the least work. The ideal pattern of ancient settlement favored springs but only where good land was also available. That is, the ancient settlers chose fertile soil if they could not have water and fertile soil at the same spot. Springs might be as much as twenty minutes away from the major focus of settlement (Bintliff, 1977, 115). I argue that several developments made this preference a logical choice—the cistern for storing rainwater at the point of use; wells in the torrent beds, in alluvial fans and into perched water tables; and long-distance waterlines that made moving water feasible in a way that moving soil could never be. Ancient cities had waterlines both above and below ground—and here I refer not to classical cities but to their Bronze Age predecessors, Mycenae, Pylos, and Melos. This connection is evident, for example, on Cyprus where Porphyrios Dikaios has shown (*Sotira*, University Museum, Philadelphia, 1961) that neolithic settlements were associated with perennial springs and could be located by modern excavators who searched near such springs.

Available technology must also have played a role in urbanization, but it is difficult to be specific about this factor in the present state of knowledge. To date, for ancient times we lack the studies of the impact of technological innovation on the quality of life in urban areas that Joel A. Tarr has called for (1979, 276). In the present study of water management as it relates to urbanization in the Greek world, we see how these ancient people "made divisions between private and public control of urban technologies," and "how efficiently this service was delivered" to the community—exactly as Tarr demands. It is my contention that ancient Greek settlements were originally sited where such services could be delivered efficiently.

The studies of Van Andel et al. (1986), Pope and Van Andel (1984), and Vita-Finzi (1969) have begun to help us understand the limits placed on settlements by geology. Their analyses suggest that details of the geographical situation such as the amount of rainfall and extent of karstification together with the amount and quality of arable land at a particular site were more significant for urban development than was simply being in east Greece (Ionia), west Greece (southern Italy and Sicily), mainland Greece, or the islands. Because the amount and accessibility of water resources vary, the relation to water differs by region and even from place to place within a region, and can be seen in localized architectural features. Also, when the topography varies—seaside or inland, plain or mountain, standing alone or in a cluster of cities—the relation to water can differ.

The effect of shore location on physical pattern is most clearly seen in the contrast between a port city like Halicarnassus and an inland city like Athens. In the port city, major plazas and public buildings focused on the water, in a linear or semicircular pattern, while in a city like Athens, surrounded on all sides by its rural territory, the central buildings and spaces were more or less evenly surrounded by, first, a band of urban density, then the walls, and then the rural areas. The effect of hill location can be seen in a town like Morgantina located at the "seam" between forested land to the west and northwest and lower agricultural land to the south and east. Morgantina occupied a fairly narrow ridge and had all its public buildings and spaces grouped at the center in immediate proximity to the ramparts and to the access road to the valley below. In this case the defensibility of the site was more important than any ideal distribution of density or balance in the plan (see Fig. 15.1).

A fortunate combination of site, resources, and human energy (often ethnically hybrid vigor) was essential to enable maximum growth in the few cities as large and powerful as Pergamon. Expansion was based on exploitable resources of all kinds and on technological developments such as increasingly sophisticated water management skills.

There are a number of unknown factors that involve both water management and urbanization, such as the relationship between ownership of land (whether rural or urban), on the one hand, and implied or explicit rights to water, on the other. Technological and social history would benefit from studies of irrigation practices among the Greeks in different regions. Our ideas on their use of military force as related to colonization or the building of long-distance water supply lines or the control of water resources amount at this time to more questions than answers—questions which are beyond the scope of this study.

Water was not the only resource that limited urban growth. Constraints on supplies of food, fuel, and building materials relative to how the resource was used; constraints on population size, growth and age distribution; and proximity to sources made great differences in the resulting city. Modest agricultural surpluses have already been mentioned as resource constraints. These were strongly affected by the amount of arable land near a city. Megara, for instance, is situated on a narrow isthmus with a range of mountains behind the city. Its agricultural base was marginal for a city that aspired to prominence. Outgrowing its food base in the coastal plain, Megara turned to trade and colonization for survival. The citizens spent great amounts of energy and wealth in a long but eventually futile attempt to stave off second- or third-class status. If they had been able to concentrate on trade and colonization in an era of peace, they might have survived with high status, but their resource base near the urban core was too narrow to permit them to withstand the damages of the incessant wars of the fifth century. Yet readers of twentieth century science fiction will recognize a classic plot situation in the fact that one of Megara's colonies was Byzantium—a brilliant success by any standards. We can imagine the realists of ancient Megara cutting their losses by emigrating to the colony, leaving the mother city to become a backwater. Urban relocation has recently been studied anew by Nancy Demand (1990) who begins her study before Homer and ends after Alexander, but does not explicitly consider water as a major determinant.

Some ancient authors, such as Plato (*Laws* V, 745; VI, 778; VIII, 848), Aristotle (*Politics*, VII, 12, 2–3), and Vitruvius (I, 2, 7), set forth principles for locating cities—but it must be remembered that the earliest of these was written half a millennium or more after the foundation of the settlements referred to. Hence, I think we are historically more accurate in examining the cities themselves to determine the principles on which they were founded.

The data currently available suggest for ancient Greek cities the following series of urban location determinants:

A. On defensible site
B. Amid arable land
C. On trade route
D. Where needed by superior government
E. Where appropriate for central place or network urban function
F. At focus of maximum variations
G. At juncture of best water and soil resources

(to be designated respectively by their letters in the tables that follow). We will add Jacobs' postulate that

H. The city was founded before the hinterland was developed

although strictly speaking it is not a determinant but rather a factor in the city's history and we will also add

I. Beauty of site

to Table 9.2, since it appears in all Greek sites to a greater or lesser degree, and was far from being a neutral factor in site selection.

Suppose we consider these factors in relation to the twenty-four sites studied in this book—Akragas, Argos, Assos, Athens, Corinth, Delos, Delphi, Gela, Gortys, Lindos, Megara, Miletus, Morgantina, Olynthus, Paestum, Pella, Pergamon, Pompeii, Priene, Rhodes, Samos, Selinus, Syracuse, and Thasos. (The reader will remember that these cities were selected because in 1970 there was published material on their water systems.) Let us then construct a chart that makes the relation of each factor to each settlement apparent (Table 9.1).

A few comments on Table 9.1 are in order. First, it is apparent that Gortys is an anomaly, being even more than Delphi a religious site only and not a true city. Nevertheless it is included in my water research because of its very fine bath building supplied by a pipeline. Survey reconnaissance and early excavations have suggested an acropolis and a residential area, so it may be that future archaeology may reveal a true settlement here.

Defensibility (factor A) was a major factor in 20 or even 22 of the 24

Table 9.1
Urbanization Factors

Sites	Factors							
	A	B	C	D	E	F	G	H
Akragas	*	*	*	*	N		*	*
Argos	*	*	*		C		*	
Assos	*	*	*		N		*	
Athens	*	*	*+		N & C	*	*	
Corinth	*	*	*+		N	*	*	
Delos	*		*+		N	*	*−	*
Delphi	*	*			N	*		*
Gela	*	*	*	*	N		*	*
Gortys				*			*+	
Lindos	*	*?	*		N	*	*	
Megara	*	*	*		N	*−		
Miletus	*	*	*		N	*−	*	*?
Morgantina	*	*	*−	*	N (&C?)	*	*	*
Olynthos	*	*	*−		N	*−	*	
Paestum	*?	*	*?	*	N	*−	*	*
Pella		*	*?		C?	*−	*	*
Pergamon	*	*	*+	*	C	*+	*	*
Pompeii	*	*	*	*?	N	*	*	*
Priene	*	*	*	*	N	*+	*+	*
Rhodes	*?	*?	*+	*+	N & C	*+	*	*
Samos	*	*	*+		N	*		
Selinus	*	*	*	*	N	*	*	*
Syracuse	*	*	*+	*	C & N	*+	*+	*
Thasos	*		*+		N	*	*+	*

An asterisk indicates the presence of the factor and question marks indicate that I am unsure of the magnitude of this factor. Plus (+) = abundance of factor; minus (−) = less than average. N = Network; C = Central place.

settlements. The defensive features were superb at 8 of them, while 2 had below-average strength.

Being at the center of an area of arable land (factor B) was important at 19 to 21 of the sites.

Having a trade crossroads (factor C) was significant to some extent at 20 to 22 of the settlements, and for 8 of them trade was a major reason for existence. Two others of the 22 were not major traders but undoubtedly had some trade, namely Paestum and Pella.

At least 10 of these settlements were clearly founded as colonies (factor D), plus ancient Corinth which was refounded after the mid-second century B.C. as a Roman colony, Pompeii, which went through several periods of conquest and recolonization, and Rhodes which was the product of deliberate union of several small towns in the late fifth century B.C.

Only about Gortys do we lack all information about its role as central place or network city (factor E). Since, however, it was a religious pilgrimage site, it functioned in a modest way as both. For the cities listed, I have intuitively assigned an N (network) or C (central place) designation, except in the 4 to 6 cases where the city seems to have played both roles. These assignments should not be taken to mean that the point has been proved, but rather that it has been indicated.

Factor F, variety, is noticeable at 19 of the sites, in varying degrees. Outstanding are Pergamon, Priene, Rhodes, and Syracuse, where the variety contributed to growth to metropolitan status at three sites, with only Priene remaining a small town. Priene, hampered by its narrow site, was eclipsed by its large neighbor, Miletus.

All of the settlements studied had water resources (factor G) as a major feature, as one would expect from their inclusion in this study. Further examination has shown that they are not unusual or exceptional as Greek sites go, except perhaps in their success as urban centers. Of the 24, only Delos had meager water supplies, but this deficiency was overcome by use of cisterns, a standard technology for the Greek culture. Contrariwise, 5 of the sites—Akragas, Gortys, Priene, Syracuse, and Thasos—had excellent water reserves, easily accessible. Pergamon came very quickly to rely on a combination of cisterns and long-distance water supply lines that together made up the very good supply system of this site. Both technologies were well developed by the third century when this site was developing.

Some 14 or 15 of the settlements are known as deliberately founded places (factor H) rather than organic growths. If the time period of this study were pushed back to the third millennium, we would no doubt find that many more of the settlements were deliberate foundations of that age, possibly of the eponymous heroes associated with each site. (The reader will note that I favor the theory that some historical truth underlies most myths.) That the history of nearly 60 percent of the archaic and classical settlements has preserved knowledge of a deliberate founding in the late second or more likely the early first millennium B.C. suggests that this procedure was the norm for ancient Greek settlements.

Suppose we simplify our findings by summing them up in Table 9.2.

Factors D and H, nonorganic inception and the existence of a city before development of the countryside, may be two aspects of the same story of urban origin. Ten of the settlements in category H exhibit factor D as well (two-thirds of the 15). In the case of the other places, we lack the data to determine how the city originated.

More interestingly, factors A, B, C, E, F, G, and I seem to correlate strongly. That is, sites well placed on good soil, with an ample water supply, with a good variety of other resources including human ones, easily defensible, and participating in trade have left enough remnants of their material arrangements to be discovered by modern archaeologists,

Table 9.2
Urbanization Factors Abstract

| | Factors | | | | | | | | |
Sites	A	B	C	D	E	F	G	H	I
1	*	*	+	*	*	+	+	*	*
2	*	*	+	*	*	+	+	*	*
3	*	*	+	*	*	+	+	*	*
4	*	*	+	*	*	+	+	*	*
5	*	*	+	*	*	*	*	*	*
6	*	*	+	*	*	*	*	*	*
7	*	*	+	*	*	*	*	*	*
8	*	*	+	*	*	*	*	*	*
9	*	*	*	*	*	*	*	*	*
10	*	*	*	*	*	*	*	*	*
11	*	*	*	−	*	*	*	*	*
12	*	*	*	−	*	*	*	*	*
13	*	*	*	−	*	*	*	*	*
14	*	*	*		*	*	*	*	*
15	*	*	*		*	*	*	−	*
16	*	*	*		*	*	*		*
17	*	*	*		*	*	*		*
18	*	*	*		*	*	*		*
19	*	*	*		*	*	*		*
20	*	−	−		*		*		*
21	−	−	−		*		*		*
22	−		−		*		*		*
23					*		*		−
24							−		−

* = factor is present; + = strongly present; − = factor may be present.

analyzed and described by urban historians, and very often visited by tourists who want to experience their beauty. Of the twenty-four sites listed, only Megara and Pella are not overwhelmingly beautiful in their modern form, and even they are pleasant enough. Neither of those two has been excavated extensively enough to reveal the pattern of the settlement as a whole, although excavations are proceeding at Pella.

In the present state of knowledge, we can say very little about the roles of individuals in the founding and subsequent history of most of these places. A few individuals have been associated with the founding or rebuilding of specific cities, such as semimythical Byzas who is said to have founded Byzantium in the seventh century with the blessing of his father, Poseidon, or the historical Gelon and Hieron I who rebuilt Syracuse in the fifth century. The role of individuals in urban failures is less well documented. Who was the Gothic commander who ordered the aqueducts cut outside Rome in A.D. 405 and thus doomed the city? Yet from our knowledge of later human history, it seems likely that the decisions and actions of individuals had strong impact on the choice of site and the pattern of development and demise for these cities as well as for their successors.

The accessibility of water was highly significant. During the period studied, the Greeks learned how to extend their reach for water farther and farther into each city's hinterland, so that the city could house a larger population with its water-using activities. We suspect that changes in water resources were major factors in changing economic bases. For instance, water and food shortages may have necessitated colonization—as John Camp (1979, 1982) has demonstrated as a result of the eighth and fourth century B.C. droughts at Athens. Other kinds of resources were also limiting in particular situations, such as shortages of wood for building houses and ships and for fuel, ample supplies of silver for money and lead for pipes (Athens and Pergamon both benefited from such assets), or wool or clay as raw materials for exportable manufactured goods. A city with ample trade goods could buy any food not supplied by the local area but still had to find water within its own territory in order to survive and prosper.

Future comprehensive studies of what effect these cities have had on their natural surroundings are essential. Changnon (1973, 27–41), for instance, asserts that urban effects on weather are both obvious and subtle. In his conclusion he gives these figures:

- Increased rain over the town and downwind: 5 to 30%
- Increased thunderstorms: 15 to 30%
- Days with 2 or more inches of rain increased: 20 to 40%
- Runoff increased: 15 to 29%
- Groundwater more polluted downwind, probably from atmospheric pollution
- Increased amount and therefore value of principal crop (corn)

The city used as a chief example in Changnon's article is St. Louis, Missouri. Among the obvious urban effects on weather, he lists decreased visibility from smoke, fog, and smog; less wind near the surface but increased turbulence aloft; and increased temperature. Among the subtle effects, he lists alterations in the previous patterns of fog, cloud, rain and snow, solar radiation, humidity, increased electricity in the atmosphere, and more severe weather. Although such interpretation of data cannot be applied uncritically to ancient cities, in the absence of modern climatological study of ancient cities, one must extrapolate from what is available. The resulting questions will be useful even if the answers are imprecise.

McPherson (1974,14ff), too, has noted the hydrological impacts of urbanization, adding to Changnon's list the effect of the built-up area on disposal of waste and surplus waters, as well as on the water supply itself, both amounting to a change in the water balance. McPherson's Table 1 shows average changes in climate, and figures 1 and 2 are charts that contrast the preurban and urban hydrological cycles. If only 20 percent of a natural catchment is converted to urbanization, peak runoff is increased 200 percent, and there is reduced infiltration into the ground, as well as changes in the local microclimates. Specifically, the local microclimate changes, since natural radiation and wind are altered by the buildings; urban heat, water vapor, and pollution rise into the atmosphere; and urban traffic contributes to local turbulence. The water vapor content of the air is different from that in the rural areas, since the temperature is up but the relative humidity is down and the precipitation is quicker. Higher temperatures in turn generate more fog in more polluted cities, both at low levels and higher as clouds.

These findings of modern hydraulic engineers and scientists, if routinely applied to the sites of ancient Greek cities, could help us understand more clearly the mutually interactive effects of city and setting. Having observed during several centuries many of these effects of urbanization, it was not beyond the Greeks to deliberately plan for them, and to site their towns according to the desired and obtainable end result rather than the original situation. In a colonization effort extending from the eleventh to the third century B.C., there was time to observe and plan better for the future. The careful principles under which a city was sited in Greco-Roman times are set out in Vitruvius, Book I Chapter IV, and examined in Crouch et al., *Spanish City Planning in North America* (1982, 32–33): attention to prevailing winds and to sun angles, fertile and resource-full hinterland, and so on. Although modern American culture assumes the normality of moving away if a place does not please, European cultures still maintain the mind-set of building well where one is, because one's great-grandchildren and their great-grandchildren will be living there too.[1]

THREE EXAMPLES

To bring this discussion of urban location determinants to an increased level of specificity, let us consider three examples, one from each major sector of the Greek world, and one from each important era. These will be the mainland city of Argos, whose foundation dates from legendary times (early second millennium at the latest); Gela, a Sicilian city of the early archaic period (eighth or seventh century B.C.); and Pergamon, founded in western Anatolia in the late fourth century B.C. by a general of Alexander the Great. Each will be examined in terms of the location determinants listed earlier. These cities have been selected because they span both the breadth of geography and the depth of time of the Greek world.

Argos (Figs. 3.1, 16.2).

The city state of Argos was founded by the Pelasgians, probably in the third millennium. The urban core was placed on a terrace between the north-south running limestone ridge that supplied both water and building stone, and the Argolid plain to east and northeast, with the sea to the southeast and south. Let us apply to the analysis of Argos the urban location factors listed previously:

A: on defensible site. So excellent were the defensive capabilities of Larisa Mountain behind Argos that the fortress there was reused by Romans, Byzantines, and Venetians. The lower hill of Aspis to the north of the city proper was fortified as early as the Early Helladic period, since it was placed to guard the inland route to the north.

B: amid arable land. Argos controls the Argolid plain, a plain that according to most geologists was in ancient times steadily being increased as a delta. Additionally, the Argives drew upon the fish in the bay and the hillsides for grazing their flocks.

C: on trade route. Trade routes to the north towards Corinth, Megara, and Athens met at Argos with local routes to the villages of the Argolid plain and the Tripoli plateau. Pottery from Argos was particularly important during the late Geometric period.

E: where appropriate for central place theory of urban function. The trade routes described above indicate Argos' role as a central place in its city-state. There was also some networking with colonies and other cities of the wider Greek world.

G: at juncture of best water and soil resources. A series of major springs are still to be found along the north-south ridge mentioned above. To the north of Argos, the waters are available for farming. To the south, much of the water is wasted in marine springs that open in the sea. Argos is sited where there is plenty of water, but close enough to the sea to make seafaring trade a major industry and ships an important element in defense of the city. The delta, being renewed by frequent floods and deposits of silt, was good agricultural land.

Gela (Figs. 3.1, 22.2).

This city was founded jointly by Rhodes and Crete, on a site carefully selected to maximize the potential success of the colony. The first Greek settlement at Gela seems to have been in 689 B.C. (i.e., shortly after the eighth century drought), on the acropolis part of the site toward the east.

A: on a defensible site. To this day, Gela sits on a long ridge high above the sea. The earliest city occupied the eastern part of the site, but after destruction and depopulation, a new fourth century city spread out along the entire ridge. In the later fourth century B.C. a new rampart was built by Timoleon, a segment of which is today the major tourist attraction of the site, located in a public park in the western part of the town.

B: amid arable land. Behind the ridge was the rich hinterland, stretching northward towards the interior highlands. Although trade had drawn the Greeks to Sicily in Mycenaean times, it was the fertile land that enticed them there in the archaic period, plains where they could grow the grain so urgently needed in the mother cities of the Greek homeland.

C: on trade route. Eventually Gela became a major city of the Greek world, largely on account of its grain trade. To a lesser extent, there was also trade with the interior, which in turn fostered the Hellenization of the island.

D: where needed by superior government. In the case of Gela, we know that it was deliberately founded as a joint venture by colonizers from the Aegean island of Rhodes, cooperatively with a group of colonists from Crete. Rather than superior government, a phrase that does not fit the circumstances of the loose cultural hegemony and political arrangement of competitive polities of the Greek world, let us say, "previously existing government."

E: where appropriate for network theory of urban function. Gela was most important as a transmitter from one part of the Greek world to another. It is well known, for instance, that the tyrant of Gela donated the famous bronze Charioteer of Delphi to that sanctuary to celebrate his victory in the Olympic games. Gela was an artistic and cultural center of the classical world of the fifth century, a position it could afford because of its wealth from the grain trade.

G: at juncture of best water and soil resources. The wealth of the city came from the rich agricultural land behind and beside it. That the site was amply watered is evident from the only other major surviving classical monument, the bath complex near the present hospital, dating from the fourth century B.C.

H: the city was founded before the hinterland was developed. This point has been amply discussed above.

I: beauty of site. The views from the site and the pleasant variation of elevation and orientation within and along the ridge are basic features in the beauty of the place. Also important is the light. The local stone is not attractive, but structures made from it seem likely to have been stuccoed with a plaster of marble dust as were the buildings at both Akragas and Selinus. If the modern enthusiasm for parks at Gela is a local tradition as strong as locating the buildings of the city along the ridge, then ancient Gela also would have had public areas set aside for enjoyment of the site.

Pergamon (Figs. 3.1, 5.1, 16.5, 16.13, 17.10, 20.1, 22.1, 22.10–13)

Latest of the three to be founded was Pergamon, which is also farthest east. After Alexander the Great had conquered the Persians, he needed a place to store the loot. The citadel of Pergamon was selected, and the treasure deposited there in the care of Philetairos and 5000 Macedonian troops. One story has it that after Alexander's untimely death, his widow and baby son were also deposited there, meeting untimely ends. Philetairos and his successors, the Attalid dynasty, used the treasure and soldiers to exploit the considerable resources of the province, and deliberately built a city as a work of art, perhaps the first in history.

A: on a defensible site. First settlement at Pergamon was on top of the high hill. Even as the city expanded, this area remained the location of the ruler's palaces, with stores of food and military equipment enclosed within strong walls that were enlarged as needed. A multitude of cisterns increased the defensive strength of the hill which was also supplied by a long-distance aqueduct that utilized a series of siphons.

B: amid arable land. Pergamon dominates a wide valley that stretches far inland and three kilometers to the sea. The ancient city-state incorporated other hills and plains also.

C: on important trade route. Major international trade from Asia and Mesopotamia was funneled through Pergamon to Greece and Rome (east-west), while an important north-south route from Byzantium (present Istanbul) southward to Ionia passed through Pergamene territory. The city was ideally placed for trade and could dominate much of that commerce with the money coined from its silver mines.

D: where needed by superior government. In the case of Pergamon, the action of the superior government in founding the city is preserved in its foundation story. From all the possible hill fortresses of Anatolia, Alexander chose the one that had all the other advantages we have mentioned, thus indicating yet another facet of his genius—the selection of sites for successful cities.

E: where appropriate for central place and network theory of urban function. Pergamon functioned as the central place of its own city-state, and as an important node in the network of Hellenistic cities. Through cities like Alexandria, Pergamon, Rhodes, and Syracuse, the active intellectual and commercial life of the Greek world was carried on and was extended beyond the immediate coasts of the Mediterranean into their hinterlands as well as into Egypt, Persia, and other neighboring states.

F: at focus of maximum variations. Local and Macedonian population groups, together with the stimulus of foreign traders, visiting scholars, and artists, created the Hellenistic civilization that flourished at Pergamon. The city-state included seashore, plains, hills, and mountains, with the varieties of flora this suggests, and with the industries of fishing, farming, grazing, lumbering, and mining, plus the full range of urban crafts.

H: the city was founded before the hinterland was developed. Here at Pergamon we see a prime example of the city stimulating the hinterland to produce both agricultural products, silver from the mines, exportable craft items, and long-distance trade.

I: beauty of site, to the highest degree. Although there are sites with more intimate charm (one thinks of Priene, Pinara, and Phaselis), none has a grander beauty than Pergamon. The builders of the city took full advantage of the site both in situating particular structures and in arranging vista points for travelers, in a fashion that cannot be improved upon.

For all three of these Greek cities, the criteria of site selection that we have inferred from the resulting settlement pattern are thought-provoking. Particularly in the United States, where so many towns seem to have "just happened" or been located mainly to profit one person or a small group, these ancient Greek criteria for urbanization stimulate us to reconsider what it is that we do when we build cities, and for whose benefit. For purposes of this study, it is significant that at all three, provision of water was carefully considered at the beginning, and carefully managed during the active history of the settlement.

NOTE

1. Issues of the relationship between geology and urban location will be examined more fully in a companion volume, *Geology and Settlement: Ancient Hellenic Patterns.*

10

Natural Models
for Water Elements

The Greek builders developed their control over water by careful observation coupled with trial and error, to determine where there would be ample water supply. They could amass the same kind of knowledge as modern engineers, although on a different (nonmathematical) basis. They were adept at utilizing observation but not at complicated technical manipulation of data, at least partly because of the defects in their mathematical system. They also were adept at utilizing discoveries made by their neighbors, such as the qanats of Persia. Unfortunately we do not know how much of the highly developed Mycenaean and Minoan water technology survived the "Dark Ages" of the first third of the first millennium B.C.

The features of a karst landscape that tell modern engineers where to drill would have spoken equally strongly to their predecessors:

1. In limestone gaps between vertical or steeply dipping aquicludes (strata that hold water but do not transmit it)
2. In open faults or at fault intersections, especially in younger faults not resealed by precipitated calcite
3. At the noses of limestone spurs jutting into alluvium, places that are often the location of springs, but even if no spring is visible, one can find water at depth
4. On the peak of an anticline where tension opens the aquifer (cf. artesian wells)
5. Below surface drainage—especially in places with large solution openings (FAO, Vols. 4 and 5, pt. 1, p. 24)

Thus, inspection of the karst terrane would have enabled the ancient water specialists to find and utilize springs, and also to know where to dig for wells. Such knowledge contributed directly to the success of ancient Greek cities.

Inspection of and meditation on the natural environment over many centuries gave the Greeks the necessary models to develop highly sophisticated water systems. In what follows I am speculating, but in no case do these suggestions go beyond what would be possible given both time, intelligence, and necessity.

SHAFTS

In the case of either dolines/sinkholes or the kind of shaft that grows gradually upward, the lower end of the shaft is always or seasonally filled with water (see Fig. 7.3). One day a small child flipping pebbles into such a shaft would have heard the resulting splash and realized what it was— water down below. If it were a time of shortage, or if it were her task to walk a long distance for drinking water, the child would urge using the more readily available source. All that was needed was to tie a rope to a pail, let it down, and pull it carefully upward.

From this fortuitous use of found water, it was only a step to thinking about where and how to dig a shaft in another place, for the convenience of settlers. We know that already by the sixth century B.C. wells of 60 feet (Athens) or 45 feet (Morgantina) were common in Greek cities. This tells us that the first experiments in well digging came much earlier, and that in cases of necessity, even greater depth could be achieved.

Various sorts of barriers were experimented with to keep people and objects from accidently falling into the well, resulting in the standard late-classical and Hellenistic form of the cylindrical wellhead made of stone or terracotta, placed over the openings of wells and cisterns alike.

In light of the fact that modern Greek cities are testing sinkholes for possible use as places to dispose of municipal sewage (Marinos, 1978), it is fascinating to see the ancients utilizing the same natural cavities. At Priene, for instance, at the western end of the long main street of the town, the large drain that runs all along the edge of the street dives into the tangle of stones from the ruined entrance gateway and completely disappears. Outside the gate there is no trace of erosion or any other form of runoff. The only explanation that I have been able to think of is that a natural vertical shaft, connecting to horizontal channels far below, was utilized by the ancient engineers to receive drainage. When the gutters were relaid by the excavators earlier in this century, they could do no better than utilize the same shaft. Karst literature is full of cautions about contaminating the water table by such polluted water (Le Grand, 1973, 861). But ancient cities rarely generated as much chemical and heavy metal pollution as modern industry. In our times, such contaminants often amount to 50 percent of the waters needing treatment at a sewage plant, and prove to be the difficult half to cleanse (personal communication from an environmental engineer).

AQUEDUCT MODELS

The natural occurrence of shafts in karst terrane may have suggested the combination of underground channel and air shafts evenly spaced that characterize the qanat of the Middle East and many Greek aqueducts of the sixth century B.C. (Fig. 10.1). Notable are the tunnel at Samos (Figs. 4.1, 4.2, 22.14) where the shafts are irregularly spaced, and the Peisistratid Aqueduct at Athens, where more regular spacing has beeen noted. In addition, some sections of the Galermi Aqueduct at Syracuse have air shafts (Fig.11.6).

Further, it is my contention that aqueducts began as natural channels harnessed for municipal use. Later, the outfall of the water may have been manipulated for human purposes—moved or dammed or the output saved in reservoirs. The careful inspection of natural models would have prodded the early technicians to duplicate or even improve upon what they could see.

Cisterns and Reservoirs

Suppose one were building a house in a Greek village of the seventh century, making the walls of adobe from clay found on the site, and possibly even baking roof tiles from the same clay. When you were through, just before the winter rainy season, there would be a large hole on your property from which the clay had been extracted. During winter the hole would fill up with rainwater. During the following dry season, it was convenient to have extra water on hand to wash clothes, water the donkey, and even irrigate the garden. But the mess of mud from everyone walking in and out of the pond would be considerable. Perhaps the first farmer just suffered from the mess, glad to have the extra water. But eventually

Figure 10.1. Plan and section of qanat, traditional underground aqueduct of the Middle East. Air shafts connect the water channel to the ground surface. Such qanats could be up to 100 kilometers long, and are still built and maintained in the Middle East. Reprinted by permission from I. Kobori (1979):8, Fig. 4.

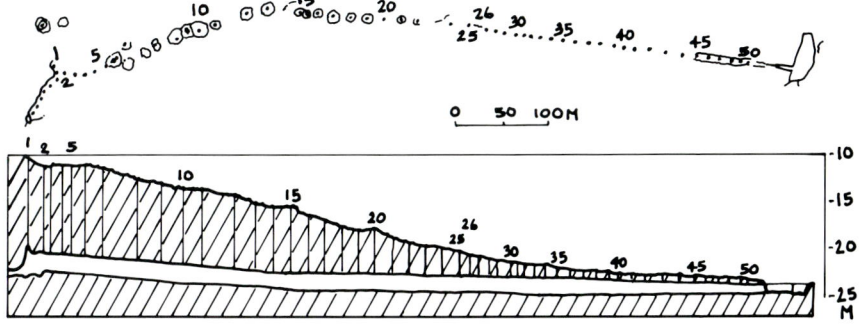

someone hit on deliberately carving a storage place for water under the courtyard of the house, filling it by funneling water there from the roofs. To keep down the mess, the new cistern was covered by the paving of the courtyard. Eventually the cistern's shape changed from a wide irregular mouth—the result of that initial excavation of clay for other purposes—to a circle or oval just big enough for a person to climb down for the annual cleaning out. Wellheads proved ideal for topping cisterns also (Figs. 20.8–10).

Reservoirs are larger and more public than cisterns. Perhaps they developed in two ways: (1) by extension of the idea of a cistern to a larger size for a larger number of people to use, such as a holding tank behind a public fountain. A good example is the famous fountainhouse at Megara, of the sixth century (Figs. 20.2, 20.6). (2) From inspection of caverns, where the water tends to collect in small natural lakes. It would be easy to decide to tap such a natural lake for a municipal water supply or for water to be used in a religious precinct (Fig.15.7), or to emulate the natural cavern by carving a reservoir where it was needed along the course of a natural stream.

It seems that the network of channels running under the agora at Corinth, for example, are karst channels that have been enlarged, directed, and blocked at certain places to serve as reservoirs for the South Stoa and for Peirene Fountain, to name only two (Fig.11.1).

Natural Channels as Conduits

The channels at Corinth are excellent examples of natural channels harnessed as underground aqueducts. (They are discussed in Chapter 8.) It is only a step, but a large one, from manipulation of an existing water network, to the realization that channels could be dug to divert water from where it was being wasted to where it was needed. Such a decision would be likely when, for instance, the natural flow of a karst system terminated in a submarine spring. If nearby farm land or a settlement had need of the water, there would be strong incentive to interfere and divert the water before it could reach the sea. That the Greeks were well aware of the possibilities of diverting water is obvious from the story of two warring cities in the Peloponnesos, where one diverted the flow of a spring-fed river from its usual swallowhole in order to flood the enemy town (Pritchett, 1965, 124–28; Burdon, 1964, 53–55, based on Herodotus 66.76, Pausanius 2.24, and Strabo 6.8.371).

Blockage as Dams

Observation of the blockages caused by earthquakes or by the process of doline collapse could easily suggest to the Greek engineers that water be diverted by man-made obstacles. In some of these cases, the cavern system would be large enough for human investigation, and a plan could be made to at least temporarily divert the water where human need was greatest. Just after World War II, the copious flow of a karst-filled mountain was wastefully pouring into a brackish marsh on one side of the mountain on the island of Lemnos, while the city on the other side suffered from lack of water. Picard, in his FAO report (no. 3, 1957), suggested damming the flow before it reached the marsh, and diverting it to the town. It is worth noting that Lemnos was the site of the first known Greek aqueduct, built by Theodorus of Samos in 575 B.C. (Feldhaus, 1931, 122). If dammed, the water would probably try to regain its own path; preventing this possibility would be a constant struggle. But if the need were great, it would be worth the effort.

Natural and Artificial Siphons

We have seen that karst formations frequently involve siphons that operate at least during the winter and early spring, and in some cases at all times of the year, depending on the amount of water, the topography, and the water pressure. Since this activity takes place within the channels in the rock and is not readily visible, I think that it would be hard to understand directly from the hydrological evidence. But once an ancient Greek had stumbled on the idea of the siphon in another context, this new idea could be used to understand and explain intermittent springs. From understanding, it is a short step to attempting to duplicate the perceived behavior of the water.

For a modern engineer, the distinction between a siphon, which leads water over an obstacle, and an inverted siphon, which leads water through a valley, is clear and important. We have physical evidence for the use of siphons by Greek engineers in the third century B.C. at Pergamon (Giebeler and Graber, 1897, 185–86), in the line from the north that brings the water from the mountains, down into the valley, over a hill, down into a second valley, and up to the citadel. The segments in the valleys are inverted siphons, and the segment over the intervening hill is a siphon. Siphons are associated with pressure lines. In Syracuse the aqueduct built between 491 and 447 B.C. is said to have been a pressure line (Neuberger, 1930, 56), but terra-cotta or stone pressure pipes seem not to have survived. However, the 25-mile stretch of Galermi Aqueduct originates high on a mountain, producing enough head to require management as a pressure system. Once again we can reason backward from the observed end-product to the necessary knowledge and reasoning that made the end-product possible.

Some of these systems were very sophisticated, apparently requiring persistent maintenance and fine-tuning, appropriate for the Greek technology that relied on individual intelligence, but considered not cost-effective by the Romans, who did use siphons but not to the limits of the technology as had the Greeks (see Fahlbusch, 1982, 133–37, on cost estimates for Greek versus Roman long-distance water supply lines).

Springs as Resurgences

We have noted before that stories have come down in the ancient literature about experiments to determine the connection between sinkhole
and spring. The most famous example is that concerning the sinkhole on
the Tripoli plain above Argos. It took careful observation and thoughtful
meditation to perceive this connection. Once the specific connection had
been made both intellectually and physically, it could be extrapolated to
the hundreds of other springs in Greek lands. Encouraged by the proof
of connection, the ancient engineers could begin to apply their inventive-
ness to manipulation of the available water supply, which in turn made
possible larger and more complex cities.

CONCLUSION

Throughout this study of ancient Greek water management, I have had
to consider how tools, elements, and practices were invented or developed that would make urban concentrations not only possible but preferable—and preferable not merely for cultural advantages but even more
basically for sheer survival. Gradually I have come to realize that the
Greeks picked up many clues from their environment and transformed
them by the application of their renowned mental powers. Those great
minds were not confined to producing sculpture or drama, but reached
out to the natural world, for understanding and control. Eventually they
were able to manage water so simply and elegantly as to make later
students (ourselves) almost blind to the accomplishment involved. We
are so accustomed to turning on the tap and finding water of the right
temperature and flavor that we do not question how or why. Yet someone
had to discover, invent, and develop the water system, just as they did
the coinage and the religious ritual. It is not easy for us to learn not to
take for granted those arrangements that seem obvious, but we can at
least try to make ourselves more conscious of the achievements of our
predecessors. We need to remember Teilhard de Chardin's dictum: The
beginnings are always lost. The suggestions of this chapter as to what
some of those beginnings may have been are an attempt to redress that
balance.

V
Planning

11

Planning Water Management: Corinth and Syracuse

Where water is in short supply—in El Paso—it costs 53 cents per gallon. Where it's plentiful—in Philadelphia—it costs $1.78 per gallon.

—*Fun with Facts*

The ancient Greeks could not afford inefficient and impractical cities. This one insight has guided my research ever since I attended the International Water Resources Association conference in Rome in 1986 and learned how concerned modern water engineers and policymakers are about careful utilization of water resources. We twentieth century Americans can afford waste, because we are both rich and spendthrift. But the ancients were living very close to the edge in an ecosystem that sustains human life only if it is carefully, respectfully managed. How successful they were in city site selection and in city building is evident from the fact that so many of their cities survived for such long times—Athens nearly 5000 years; the great capital Byzantium-Constantinople-Istanbul since the eighth century B.C., a lifespan of about 2800 years; and even obscure towns like Morgantina, Sicily, for 450 years.

Given a hot and semiarid Mediterranean climate with rain only in the winter months, careful attention to water supply and distribution was essential for a Greek city. As long ago as the second millennium B.C., the Mycenaeans who lived in mainland Greece and the Minoans of Crete took great care of the water supply and drainage of their sites, using cisterns, wells, pipelines, rock-cut channels, and so on (Evans, 1964 reprint, vol. I, 103–05, 141–43, 333–36, 378–84, 389–98; Broneer,1939, 317–433; Mylonas 1966; Knaus, Heinrich, and Kalcyk, 1980). Because of the gap in the archaeological record, we cannot be sure whether any of their knowledge about water management survived the collapse of these civilizations and the 400 years or so of the "Dark Ages" that followed. Some ideas such as cisterns seem to be both so basic and so easy for a single family to execute, that it is likely their use persisted no matter how primitive conditions became. Others, such as the use of pressure pipes, seem to require a fairly sophisticated society and probably the existence of a group of architect-engineers to carry out the building process, and therefore we would not expect them to survive but to be independently re-invented when later Greek society reached technological sophistication.

Highly developed urban water systems of classical and Hellenistic times were based on careful study of the behavior of water integrated with equally knowledgeable manipulation of human economic and political behavior. It is no accident that we look back to the Greeks who brought political interaction, discussion, and writing to a superior level, since in many ways they are still our models. The political maneuvering necessary to build a modern water system cannot be very different from the problems that surfaced when an ancient Greek town needed a water system, and similar negotiations were necessary to resolve the issues. During the eighth to first centuries B.C., the Greeks were building cities that were increasingly complicated. The water management system—that complex of physical objects, technological development, and human behaviors that supplied, used, and discarded waters—was one of the subsystems that made up a Greek city, ranking with the food supply system, the defense system, the municipal government system, and so on. The food system and the water system were the two basics that made urban life possible, and it is curious that until now the water management system has frequently been ignored completely in trying to understand the Greeks, or at best has been only partially acknowledged.[1]

When Greek society reappears as an organized and expanding entity, in the eighth century B.C., Corinth was a leader of the colonization process that was to characterize the next four centuries. [Corinth itself dates from the fourth millennium (H.S. Robinson,1965, 4).] As a city began to press too heavily on its economic base (particularly agriculture), a group of citizens, under the leadership usually of a younger son of an aristocratic family, set off to found a new city in the relatively empty lands adjacent to the Aegean region, either northeast toward the Black Sea or southwest to southern Italy and Sicily. Not until Alexander the Great, 400 years later, was there any attempt to unite all Greeks into one political entity, but during that whole time there were close cultural and often economic relations between mother cities and their colonies, as well as between the various unrelated polities of the Greek world. Frequently the sites chosen for new colonies had earlier been trading outposts (for details of locating sites for cities, see Chapter 9, Urban Location Determinants). Only those settlements survived that were endowed with the water they needed—a great success story in the history of the relationship between water management and Greek urbanization.

In the founding of Syracuse as a colony of Corinth, in 734 B.C., there was the usual transfer of culture—language, religion, governmental organization, customs of daily life, and traditional knowledge such as crafts, farming, and water management. In this chapter, I suggest that whatever elements of water system Corinth and Syracuse have in common after the eighth century are owing to three factors: their common culture with its backlog of traditional technological knowledge and openness to new technical developments; the fact that water is amazingly consistent in its behavior, thus calling for consistent solutions to the problems of managing it; and finally that the settlers deliberately chose sites where their water technology would work. The transfer of traditional knowledge about managing water was facilitated by the similarity of geology and climate between the two sites.

Traditional knowledge of finding and collecting water was coupled in the Greek world with increasing sophistication in the transport of both fresh and used water during the period studied (eighth to first century B.C.). (See Chapter 3 on traditional knowledge of finding water.) Fahlbusch (1982, 131–39) has studied the transport of water in long-distance water supply lines, noting that socioeconomic arrangements changed in parallel with other societal changes, and with the development of increasingly sophisticated technology. In the seventh century, for instance, the tyrant Theagenes at Megara kept firmly in his own hands the power to erect water system elements such as his famous fountainhouse. In sixth century Athens, Peisistratos gave this power to a board of commissioners, and in the fifth century, such individual engineers as Eupalinos of Megara took charge of the work and were held responsible for it. Eupalinos also built the tunnel at Samos. In the fourth century, we hear of building commissioners approving of the alignments for waterlines. At the same time, in Rome, the architect-engineer delegated responsibility for actual construction of the line to a businessman/contractor, as was the custom for other major construction projects. In the present state of knowledge, it is not possible to declare firmly that each of these examples stands for a consensus at that time on how water should be managed; rather, we may use them as illustrations of the possibilities at any given time. In general, it seems to me that newer ways of managing water were added to older ways rather than substituting for them.

These changes in who was responsible are paralleled by changes in what was built. The wondrous tunnel at Samos had clay pipes laid in a channel that sloped separately from the bed of the tunnel. Later, and at other places, cut and built channels followed the contours of the hills, while in major cities with a strong economic base and demographic demand there could be—as early as the third or perhaps even the fifth century—pressure pipe lines and siphons. Pressure pipelines at Syracuse, Akragas, and Pergamon, are discussed by Nerberger (1930, 422), and Forbes (1955, 151), but their documentation is weak. It could be a reflection of the wealth and sophistication of Syracuse that pressure pipelines are ascribed to it as early as the fifth century B.C. Greek cities were by the fifth century commonly supplied from waterlines based on gravity flow and on the natural geological pattern of the site. In Roman imperial times the engineers used a combination of tunnels, contour channels, bridges, and siphons, all developed in the preceding era.

CORINTH AND SYRACUSE (FIGS. 8.1, 8.4, 11.1, 11.2, 11.3, 11.4, 11.5. 11.6, 11.7, 11.8, 11.9)

Corinth and its very successful colony, Syracuse, may be compared as to natural resources, elements of water management—springs, fountains, cisterns, wells, pipes, and channels—and water use. For each aspect of the water system , we will examine first the example from Corinth and then that from Syracuse if there is a comparable one. This section continues by describing each water system as a whole and evaluating its effectiveness, and concludes by suggesting which elements of the Syracusan water system seem to take their intellectual or technological origin from Corinth. This comparison will be fairly easy for the major quasi-architectural features such as fountains, but difficult for pipes and channels, because of extreme differences in the way the different elements have or have not been published.

When we see how much water was available at both of these sites, and in what wide distribution, we can recognize that the abundance of water was a prime reason for selection of each for settlement, as it was for continued growth of the settlement. Water contributed markedly to the economic success of each site. The fact that each site was easily defensible was the other major factor in its choice.

Corinth

As H.S. Robinson (1965, 4–6) has written of Corinth:

> The ancient city grew up on the slopes of Acrocorinth because of the importance of the hill . . . on the north slope of the hill . . . there were good supplies of water combined with gently sloping terraces of fertile fields . . . Graves and some household deposits of the 10th, 9th and 8th centuries have appeared at isolated points throughout the central area of the later city, but we have no means as yet of estimating the size or economic status of the city in these years. That very period during which the city was achieving its greatest growth and when the Bacchiad kings were sending out colonies to Magna Graecia . . . is almost unknown to us from archaeological evidence.

That the archaeological evidence from the earliest period is scanty forces us to examine very carefully whatever evidence is available. Robinson continues: "Wells of the late 8th and 7th centuries which have been found in and around the area of the later market-place indicate the presence of houses or civic buildings . . . the Potters' Quarter, west of the town, . . . flourished from the late 8th through the 4th century B.C.

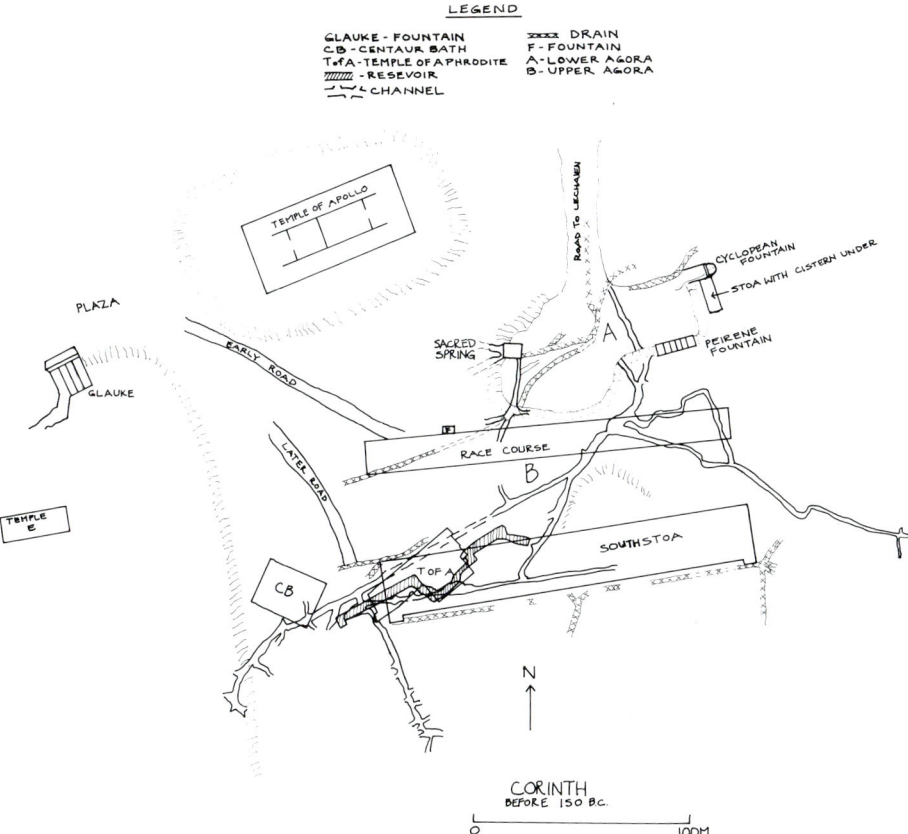

Figure 11.1. Corinth. Central district in Greek times, before 150 B.C., with special reference to the water system elements.

. . . produced the pottery carried in Corinthian ships all around the Mediterranean world."

In appearance, the site of Syracuse is somewhat different from that of Corinth. The latter is some 3 to 5 kilometers inland but had ports at Lechaeum and Isthmia (to the west and east of the Isthmus, respectively), while Syracuse was founded as a port of trade on the island/peninsula of Ortygia and grew gradually inland and uphill. Corinth lay at the foot of the abrupt peak of Acrocorinth, while Syracuse's uphill termination was the fortress of Euryalus, perhaps as tall as Acrocorinth, but reached by gradually sloping land on the east, southeast, and south, where the city lay. The climate in both is essentially Mediterranean, although one must allow for the differences that occur because one city (Corinth) slopes downward to the north and lies near a large bay (the Gulf of

Corinth) and the other (Syracuse) slopes downward to the southeast, and lies on the open sea. Hydrogeologically, the sites are similar in that layers of permeable rock and impervious clay collected water in quite similar fashions and made it available to human use. Natural channels through the rock seem at both sites to have been amplified and directed to behave as underground aqueducts.

We will better understand these features by examining details of the water system in each place, beginning with the fountains at Corinth. The "compact, whitish clay—the typical light-colored clay used in the archaic period by the famed potters of Corinth" (H.S. Robinson, 1965, 9) was a crucial stratum in the layers of rock that collected the rainfall and made it available for human needs. Under a 1.5 or 2 meter thick layer of porous conglomerate lay the impervious clay. Water trickled down through the rock and spread out along the surface of the clay, from whence it could easily be collected. At least by the sixth century, the Corinthians had learned to improve upon nature, making a spring house by cutting back the clay so that an outlet was shielded from the sun by overhanging conglomerate, and then cutting tunnels back into the clay just under the stone, to tap the water-bearing seam.

Three fountains are known in the Corinthian agora area that date from the earliest period—the Cyclopean Spring, Peirene, and the Sacred Spring. There is question as to whether the Glauke Fountain (not a spring), set apart from the others at the opposite end of the archaic temple, belongs to this early period also. Let us consider them in that order.

The Cyclopean Spring was located to the east of the road that led from the coast and the agricultural terraces up to the area of the Agora and the early race track. This spring stood at right angles to the fountain of Peirene, both located on the left as one mounts the street. As its name suggests, the appearance of the Cyclopean Spring alluded to great antiquity with its masonry of rough-hewn stones forming the walls of a "natural" grotto of irregular hexagonal shape, its street-side end a parapet toward the user. Thus in appearance this fountain was an enhanced natural object reminding users of a very early period in Corinthian history (Mycenaean times). Both the Cyclopean Spring and Peirene were tucked in under the conglomerate that formed the surface of the upper agora. Originally, a natural spring just to the east of Peirene may have supplied both fountains, with the water stored in two holding tanks immediately south of Peirene and in a cistern immediately south of the Cyclopean fountain. Probably by the end of the fifth century B.C. the flow of this spring was supplemented by a common water supply tunnel for the two fountains. The chronology may have been:

- Discovery of a group of springs at the head of the valley leading up from the coast to Acrocorinth—major reason for locating the center of Corinth where the agora still is

Figure 11.2. View into Peirene Spring at Corinth, past one bay of the Hellenistic colonnaded facade to the collection basin behind. This facade was pierced by the hole at lower right, probably in Roman times, to allow the waters to fill a new series of collection basins between the later outer facade and the one shown here. The Hellenistic columns, about 1.6 meters tall, stand on the outer wall of one of four reservoir basins of that period.

- Formalization of Cyclopean and other springs as fountainhouses
  - Cyclopean fountain in "natural" grotto fed by water from spring that also fed Peirene
  - Cistern built to hold water for Cyclopean Spring
  - Earliest monumentalization of Peirene fountain
  - The two fountains and their holding tanks supplied later (fifth to fourth centuries B.C.) from the long channels that tapped the karst channels from Acrocorinth
  - In the Hellenistic era, Peirene was developed further and at the

same time, new construction began to squeeze against the site
of the Cyclopean Spring
- Destruction of the city ca. 150 B.C.
- City rebuilt as a Roman town
- Refurbishing and expansion of Peirene completely concealed old
  Cyclopean Spring
- In Byzantine times, the Cyclopean Spring was opened up again (Hill,
  1964, 47 n.1) perhaps because constriction of the channels else-
  where had caused the water to erupt here again

Most famous and long-lived of the Corinthian springs was Peirene,
first mentioned by Herodotus in the sixth century B.C., and by Pindar in
the fifth century; Euripides also alluded to the spring in *Medea*, agreeing
with the other two authors that Peirene was the center of Corinthian life
(cited in Hill, 1964, 1). If the fountain was so famous in the sixth century,
it is likely to have been already in place even earlier, by the seventh
century at least. The Roman author Pausanias said that Peirene was just
outside the agora of his day (Hill, 1964, 23); actually it is located at the
lower level where the main road entered the agora (Figs. 11.1 and 11.2).
(See Part IX, Amenity and Necessity, for fuller discussion of the locations
of public fountains.)

Like the Cyclopean and Sacred Springs, Peirene began as a point of
natural outflow of waters collected along the seam between conglomerate and clay. In appearance, it was probably a cave (Hill, 1964, 23). Several building periods are in evidence, from the earliest channels barely
0.25 meters below the conglomerate surface, through many deepenings
and extensions of the channels back toward Acrocorinth. Some tunnels
eventually ran more than 3000 meters back into the rock (Hill, 1964, Fig.
4, p.16 ; H.S. Robinson, 1969,1–35). Remodelings in the levels of the early
spouts and in the parapets for the later drawbasins culminated in the
Roman period in the elaboration of the courtyard into one with a central
pool flanked laterally by two large semicircular exedrae and entered on
either side of a third exedra of the same pattern, set opposite the new
colonnaded facade that stood in front of the large old drawbasins. Behind
the Roman columns, the inner facade was the old Hellenistic one with
small Ionic columns and well-worn parapets. Farther in were the four
long basins of the archaic reservoir, filled from the channels leading back
into the hill. Hill states that the system was essentially unchanged
throughout the Greek era (Hill, 1964, 15–45). However, it seems that to
keep the spring flowing copiously it was necessary from time to time to
extend and deepen the channels corresponding to the natural tendency
of the water to cut deeper beds for itself. So, also, the facade of the
fountain was refurbished or rebuilt every few centuries.

The Sacred Spring, third of these very early fountains, stood on the
west side of the main street, near the southeast corner of the hill on
which stood the archaic temple. The relationship between that temple,

the Sacred Spring, Peirene, and the Cyclopean Fountain (called simply Fountain House) is shown in figure 5 of Williams and Fisher (1971, 12). Beginning as a natural grotto-like spring, this fountain had to be rebuilt later after the conglomerate roof collapsed. Today one unlocks the iron gate and goes down several steps below the present ground level, where can still be seen the fine ashlar wall of the rebuilding, screening the channels cut in clay and rock that brought water to this place. Bronze lion heads were found in situ on the wall, and the gutter into which their water poured lay at the base of the wall—a small gutter, indicating that the flow of the spring by the time of the sixth century rebuilding was meager. The water came originally from a small natural spring. Because of the sacred nature of this spring, it was worth amplifying that source later and supplying the spring from deeper channels. However, as the level of the agora became higher, this spring was entered less and less frequently, and the final phase of water use at this spot (end of third to middle of second century B.C.) directed the water from the channels to a square basin on the agora surface above the old reservoir, which had been carefully buried (Hill, 1964, 116–96).

The last fountain we will look at is Glauke, which stands 80 meters southwest of the archaic temple, and is of the same rough native rock as the temple (Hill, 1964, 200–24). It is evident that an adjacent hill was quarried for blocks to build the temple and possibly other buildings, and that this 15 by 14 meter cube was left in place. Someone had the inspiration to use the quarry trenches as reservoirs, and to fit the big block as a fountainhouse, with draw-basins, access stairs, and supply pipes. At first the excavators assumed that the fountain block dated to the sixth century B.C. like the temple (H.S. Robinson, 1965, 11), but more recent studies have disclosed the Roman type of terra-cotta pipes bringing the water to the fountain and other evidence to indicate that the whole fountain may date from the later period (Williams and Zervos, 1984, 97–101). One of the arguments for the Roman date of the fountain is the vaulting cut into the rock; however, Williams and Fisher write (1971,12; cf. Wiseman, 1970, p.13 n.43), that the Greeks had used vaults since the sixth century B.C. It is very difficult to date rock cuttings.

This careful reading of the evidence, however, fails to solve the question of what the cube of stone was used for if it were not a fountain? Why was it left there—in a very busy part of the city center—from archaic times until after the middle of the second century B.C. when the Romans rebuilt the area, and then through the Roman period until today, if it were not a useful object? What was its function during this interval? Because Glauke stands on top of the layer of conglomerate rather than under it like the three fountains discussed previously, it could not tap into the underground karst network. Rather, it was supplied by pipelines that were perforce at a higher level than the channels that fed the other fountains. The pipelines were liable to accidents and deliberate attack, and would therefore have needed replacement in a more overt and easily

Figure 11.3. Glauke Fountainhouse, Corinth. Sculpted from a huge block of stone that remained after the Temple of Apollo was constructed in archaic times, this fountainhouse seems never to have been a spring, but rather to have been supplied by pipes bringing water from uphill. The arched openings cut in the rock are approximately 4 meters tall.

dateable fashion than the underground clay-cut channels. Therefore I speculate that the fountain is indeed archaic, but refitted with pipes, possibly "modernized" with rock-cut vaults, and given a newly paved setting in Roman times. This scenario accounts for the fact that its cubic mass has always occupied the same location in what was a very congested part of the city. As suggested in Chapter 8, temples of Apollo are associated with springs, so that a functioning fountain near the entry to this precinct of Apollo would be appropriate and worth the trouble of fitting Glauke with a long-distance supply line.

Although this account by no means exhausts the list of fountains at Corinth, it is sufficient to give a sense of the provision of water in copious amounts at the center of the commercial, political, and religious focus of the city. Would that it were as easy to describe the fountains at the center of Syracuse!

Syracuse

City founders and architect-engineers, as was customary, selected the site of Syracuse for its inherently positive base, including water supply, and then located public buildings and private shops and houses according to the customs of daily life. Because of the geology of the site, with its earlier and later limestone layers above clay, there was an abundance of water. Many of the same processes were at work here as at home in Corinth, with the water cutting its own channels through the rock and even etching out access shafts, so that the ancient engineers had rather to manage the water than to find or even import it, and this for many years (eighth to fifth centuries B.C.).

Archaeological knowledge of the site of Syracuse has been hampered by the fact that the medieval and baroque city overlies the most ancient settlement on the island of Ortygia, while the Hellenistic city, long rural, now feels the forces of modern urban development. Still, we can make a few comparisons with Corinth that may be illuminating.

The most diligent scholar of the water lines of Syracuse was J. Schubring, who published his detailed account in 1865. Schubring also wrote on the water channels of Akragas.[2] He followed every trace of every line, both within and outside of the city, counting the shaft openings (pozzi) as he did so, and examining reservoirs, as well as the remains of fountains, wells, and so forth. More recently, Alfred Burns (who had the advantage of being an industrial engineer as well as a classicist) has examined the water supplies of Syracuse and of Akragas, and published a sketch map (1974). One would give a great deal for a unified map that displayed all the currently known features of ancient Syracuse superimposed on the faint traces of the modern city and well captioned, but it does not apparently exist. Maps 14 and 15 of the Hellenistic quarters of Syracuse and of Ortygia, respectively, in *Storia della Sicilia* (1979) were useful sources for Figures 8.4 and 11.4 here, which attempt to bring together what is known from many sources about the geography and urban plan of ancient Syracuse.

A notable source of water on Ortygia, the first site of settlement at Syracuse, was the spring named after the nymph Arethusa. Located just at the edge of the sea, this pool has since baroque times been framed with an architectural setting, but seems always to have had wild papyrus plants growing in it, giving rise to the myth that the fleeing nymph, after whom the spring was named, was trying to escape from the amorous attentions of the god of the River Nile—since papyrus grows wild elsewhere only in Egypt. The nymph dove into the Mediterranean, and came up here on Ortygia. Actually, this spring is one of a series that used to be visible in both the Great and Little Harbors flanking the island, originally fresh water but of salty taste since an earthquake in the twelfth century (Schubring, 1865; Sweeting, 1973, 212). In the traditional literature, these fresh intrusions into the salt water are variously explained as natural springs or as breaks in an undersea aqueduct. When I visited Syracuse in 1985, I looked in vain for them. Since then, I have searched in the literature and found the answer to the mysteries of their appearance and disappearance with the other material on karst phenomena: The water-bearing karstified limestone formation is overlaid by an imperme-

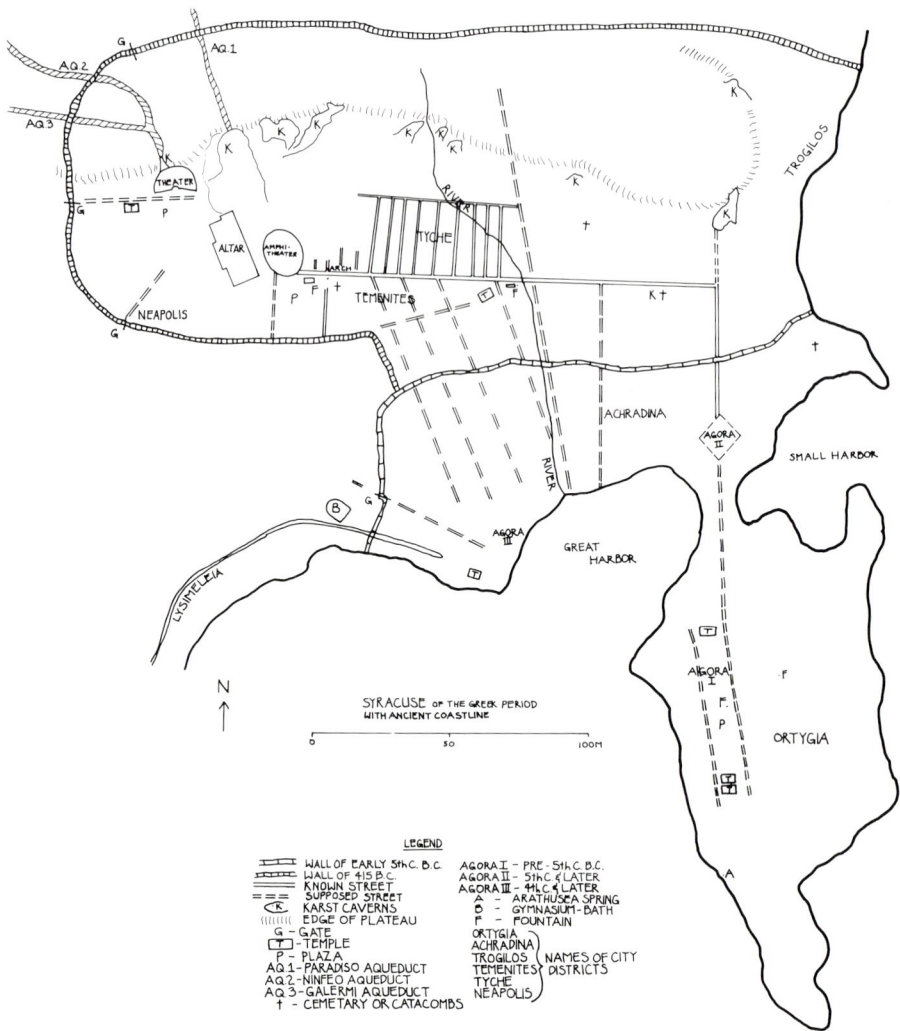

Figure 11.4. Map of Syracuse in Greek times. The shoreline is that of Greek and Roman times. Note numerous karst caverns, today known as quarries or latomia. All streets and public spaces shown are taken from archaeological reports on the site.

able layer, together sloping downward in a great disk shape from the fortress of Euryalus northwest of the city, down and under the city, coming to the surface again on the island. The water seeps along the bedding planes in the limestone, but tries to come up to the surface through shafts that form along upright cracks in the rock. From time to time, the top of one of these shafts collapses, allowing the fresh water to flow out under pressure, and forming an artesian spring on land or in the sea as the case may be. So much for the appearance of springs in the sea. That these springs are not now flowing may be due to two separate factors, or to a combination of them. The easiest explanation is that the shaft collapsed and was plugged up, preventing the water from flowing out. Given the recent surge of urban development at Syracuse, an equally likely explanation is that the groundwater table on the slope went down because of many uphill demands, reducing the pressure (head) that had previously forced the spring water out to the surface of the harbor.

Since the earliest temples of the city have been found on Ortygia, and the area is still the focus of urban life, we can deduce that the earliest agora and other municipal functions were there. They would have needed the usual complements of public fountains, drains, etc., but these have not been systematically located, and may prove irrecoverable because of the density and persistence of later use of the site. To tap for public use the water flowing in bedding planes but fairly near the surface of the island, there were three or four water lines crossing it, as reported by Schubring. He lists one waterline as opening near the cathedral, one in the cloister of S. Lucia, two near the spring of Arethusa, and one line on the coast of the Great Harbor. One plaza on Ortygia is called "Ronco del Pozzo"(area around the well).

Other visible features of the water system at Syracuse are located on the mainland, in what became first the suburbs and then intrinsic parts of the city: Acradina, Neapolis, Tyche, and Epipolae. A major focus of development in this region was the series of grottoes above the theater, where water still collects and is disbursed for further use (Fig. 11.5). Water naturally forms caverns in limestone, and it is common for the pressure of water farther uphill to drive springs out into the open wherever such caverns intersect the surface. Thus the early Greeks found water naturally flowing here. Over time (two or three centuries), two things happened: The water found a new path, farther down the hill, and the increase of population increased demand for water. Since settlement had originally taken place in this immediate area because of the springs, it was reasonable to continue to use these outlets, but to re-supply them with long-distance lines bringing additional water from farther uphill and from the west. Both the Ninfeo Aqueduct from the northwest (uphill) and the Galermi Aqueduct from the west converge at these grottoes. (We will discuss these supply lines later.) The grottoes make a handsome frame for the theater, lying in a gentle arc along the uphill side of the street that edges the top of the cavea. They were a favorite site for burials during later centuries, so that both the face of the rock and the walls of each cave are pocked with niches now. The dates for all of this activity are hard to ascertain, but I will hazard the following chronology:

- Water with CO_2 in solution carves out channels in the limestone, a process beginning eons ago and still continuing
- Natural springs in caves draw settlers

Figure 11.5. Reconstruction of fountain grottoes above theater, Syracuse. A series of natural grottoes that received the outfall of karst channels were amplified over time, receiving waters from the Galermi aqueduct and other long-distance water supply lines. The area also served as a cemetery or sanctuary during some times in its history, as is indicated by the many niches and inscriptions cut into the face of the stone, at left.

- Greeks of the archaic and classical periods utilize these little caves and channels to serve as aqueducts, enlarging them as necessary, no later than early fifth century

Schubring suggests that old cemetery areas near the quarries and springs, for a long time outside the city, were in Gelon's time incorporated into the expanded urban fabric. In this scenario, the widening of channels for catacombs would already have begun in the fifth century or earlier. During the reign of Gelon, in the first quarter of the fifth century, settlers were brought in from Kamarina, Gela, Megara Hyblea, and Euboia. To provide for these new settlers, he built aqueducts for the Tyche, Achradina, and Ortygia areas (Schubring, 1865, 618–20, 625).

- The earliest aqueduct here dates from 491 to 477 B.C.
- The theater is built, in the quarry area below the road and springs, late fifth century, after the war with Athens, using Athenian prisoners as quarry slaves. It has the normal drainage system for a classical theater.

- To maintain fountains and waterlines at uphill locations, water must be brought in from farther away and from higher sources (late classical and Hellenistic eras), necessitating the construction of long-distance water supply lines, possibly including pressure pipe lines, and quite possibly tapping karst channels.
- Water table drops because of large demand; Greeks increase supply (as would modern engineers) by waterproofing tunnels, diverting streams, and using parts of old tunnels as reservoirs
- Dwindling flow of water at the grottoes and other outlets while the population increases requiring long-distance water supply so the Aqueduct of the Nymphs and the Galermi Aqueduct are built to supply grottoes, etc., no later than third century B.C.

In *Storia della Sicilia*, (1979) plate LXXXIX, figures 92 and 93 show the interior of Galermi, and date it as "classical" which should mean fifth to fourth centuries, in contrast to the Tindari line which is termed "Hellenistic."

- Romans conquer Sicily in late third century, bringing into existence an early Greco-Roman society.
- Gradual reduction of population parallels gradual down-cutting of

Figure 11.6. View down into stone shaft of Galermi Aqueduct at Syracuse, towards water still flowing in a channel at the bottom. The narrow dimension of the shaft is .5 to .7 meter.

underground water, and population moves downhill to utilize lower outlets, and to be closer to continuing commercial center.

- During the Roman period, new water system elements are added to compensate for old ones going out of use, and to provide for normal Roman activities such as bath-gymnasiums and other needs of the new and possibly enlarged population.
- After centuries of use as waterlines, abandoned grottoes and underground tunnels are pressed into service as tomb sites perhaps as early as the last century B.C., but increasingly in the third and fourth centuries A.D. The Greeks and Romans rarely buried their dead within the city limits, but often reused cemetery areas after a lapse of time. The reuse and probable enlargement of the aqueduct channels as catacombs speaks strongly of an era when no water flowed in the tunnels. They certainly would not have contaminated an active and important water source with dead bodies.
- By the second or third century A.D., the water system had continued to change as maintenance had been deferred or nonexistent.
- After a gap of centuries, the modern population finds new sources of water (e.g., deep pumping in the plains west and especially southwest of the city), and renovates the old Galermi aqueduct.[3] Professor Aurelio Aureli of the Geology Department of the University of Catania (personal communication) reports that the springs in the harbor were fed from the west, by the same aquifer that gave rise to the Rivers Kyane and Anapos; the disappearance of the harbor springs may be due to massive pumping in this western plain.

Thus in the case of the grottoes above the theater and the lines that supplied them, the continuum spring-fountain-waterline exhibits all the complexity that is possible, given centuries of change in both the location of the vein of water and the preferences of the human users.

There are other fountains from ancient times in the Hellenistic parts of Syracuse, but none are ancient enough to be relevant to our investigation of Corinthian influence in the development of the water system of Syracuse. Largest of these later fountains is one to the immediate southeast of the amphitheater, at the west end of the major east-west street. It stands on a level 10 or 15 feet below the arch that terminated the street, suggesting that it predates the arch and that its location depended upon where a vein of water came to the surface. At least one of the water lines that honeycomb this hill was made to supply this fountain in Roman times, but I think (because of its awkward relationship to the street system here and to the amphitheater) that the water line is much earlier than the amphitheater.[4] It is interesting to note that one practice described by Fahlbusch (1982, Abb. 4), that of stuffing an ooze gallery with stones to facilitate the collection of the water, is visible in the third and fourth niches from the right end of this fountain.

Turning from fountains to the waterlines that supplied them, we must admit that we have no evidence for long-distance supply lines in the Greek world as early as the eighth century when the colonization of Syracuse was taking place from Corinth; however, by the seventh century or early sixth, the line supplying the Megara Fountainhouse was built. If we find similar waterlines in Syracuse and Corinth, it must be the result of two factors coinciding: First, both cities seem to have imported the water technology that had been developed originally in the kingdom of Urartu (modern Armenia), then adopted and promulgated by the Persians, and used in Greek lands initially on islands like Samos and Lemnos very near to the Persian possessions in western Asia Minor (discussed in Chapter 6). Second, the geology of the two sites was similar enough that the same technology worked well at both places. This new long-distance waterline technology was easily adapted to their own purposes by a people who had centuries of observation and experimentation behind them, as well as a pressing need for ample water supply for growing urban centers. Here I would like to add that the colonists from Corinth were, it seems likely, explicitly looking for a site on which it would be possible to apply what they knew of water management, farming, trade, and so on. Similarly, it was the Scandinavians who found it possible to colonize Iceland and Greenland, as well as Vineland on the North American continent, and it was the Spanish from Mexico and their Indian allies who found it possible to colonize New Mexico. In each of these three cases, the similarities of terrain and climate between base and colony are not accidental (Tuan, 1974, 66–70).[5] With these caveats in mind, let us consider the evidence for long-distance water supply at Corinth and then at Syracuse (Figs. 8.4, 11.1, 11.6, 11.7, 15.5, 15.6).

In Corinth, Peirene deserved its name of perennial spring since it still (in the early 1960s) gave 4.2 to 8.1 cubic meters per hour depending on the season and the year (Hill, 1964, 29). The water arrived at Reservoir 4 and from there filled the other three reservoirs and three draw basins. This reservoir was filled by the east tunnel, tall enough to walk in and with its ceiling formed by the bottom of the conglomerate level. The east tunnel was followed by the excavators for 175 meters and the west one for 260 meters. The west tunnel was "used for 1800 years as a reservoir, filled up to within .75 m[eters] of the top" (Hill, 1964, 57). Hill's theory is that the west tunnel was begun "to strengthen and direct the flow, [to] collect water from several small streams [i.e., karst channels] as its line crossed theirs." In order to collect the waters from the seam between clay and rock, the west tunnel branches many times; two branches, for instance, serving the water system of the South Stoa, upstream from which was an underground reservoir. This tunnel is typical of those used at Corinth, in that each channel has short branches for collecting water, tapping not only those important flows that we call springs, but also seeps and various sorts of oozing. The west tunnel taps two springs nearest Acrocorinth, as well as the small spring only 8 meters north of Peirene—this one finished with very carefully cut masonry, as if to call attention to its role as a shrine (Hill, 1964, 61, and fig. 31d). Apparently this spring was the original supply for the Cyclopean Spring and Peirene. The tunnel system is furnished throughout with well-shafts, which facilitated both cutting the tunnel and maintaining it. Twenty of them are visible from below, four from above. One row of openings lies about 15 meters away from the foundations of the South Stoa, spaced at regular intervals to serve the shops; the shafts seem to have been built at the same time as the South Stoa. Others date from as early as the sixth century B.C. to as late as the Byzantine period (ca. sixth century A.D.), judging from their fill—all of which tells us that maintenance of this system was a constant requirement, and change in the system inevitable as the human population changed its habits and needs. In the agora area, cross tunnels ran between the major lines, which followed the slope of the agora from up in the southwest corner to down in the northeast corner (Morgan, 1939, 256) (see Fig. 11.1). The ultimate extent of the channels may have been 2200 or even 3500 meters back toward the great "sponge" that was Acrocorinth.

A second set of important water tunnels and cisterns was found in 1962 about 1000 meters southwest of the old agora (Robinson, 1969, fig. 1) The main tunnel was traced for more than 600 meters and seemed to run in the general direction of a spring at the foot of Acrocorinth (now called by its Turkish name, Hadji Mustapha). The water seemed destined to supply a small valley west of the city, and on the way there to serve both the domestic and the industrial needs of the persons living and working in this quarter. As usual, the tunnel was interrupted every 60 meters or so by manholes, many of them oval, which is not uncommon at Corinth. Already in the fourth century B.C. part of the system went out of use. Almost 200 meters of the tunnel (the branch to the southeast) was used in Roman times, if not before, as a reservoir.

The length of 3500 meters of channels attested for Corinth was far outstripped by the longest of the waterlines at Syracuse: the Galermi Aqueduct, which ran some 25 kilometers from the west into the city, and which still flows although its waters are no longer serious contributors to the water supply of the city. It was extremely interesting, however, to see in 1985 that a modern waterline of large size is being built that runs from very near the source of Galermi, on Crimiti Mountain, and follows much of the course of the ancient line. Schubring traced the entire line of Galermi (ca. 1860), reporting that in some places it was visible by the line of pozzi and in others by the line of brambles growing with their roots in the leakage from the line. Both kinds of evidence are still appar-

Figure 11.7. Galermi Aqueduct at Syracuse. Line of aqueduct channel, covered here by pointed roof, and leading to stone shaft in middle distance.

ent (1985), as well as stretches where one sees the line's arched or gabled roof rising through the grass and brush (Fig. 11.7). As it approaches the city, the waterline branches many times. Within Syracuse, Galermi is less easy to trace, but eventually it filled a large reservoir somewhat northwest (uphill) of the theater grotto area. A line led southeast that fed the grottoes, then in turn branched left and right past the theater and downhill to the sea in both easterly and south-southeasterly directions. Cavallari reported that Galermi surfaced above the theater, between the Ninfeo and Paradiso Aqueducts, at the height of 60 to 70 meters above sea level, having originated at about 187 meters on the mountain above Belevedere (Cavallari, 1887, esp. pl. 15).

Without attempting to describe the remaining waterlines of the city in the exhaustive detail of Schubring, let me list them here and then go on to some general remarks about the method of supplying the city with water in this way.

GROUP ONE

1. From the mountains to the west, the "water supply for the city" runs under the north wing of the fortress Euryalus through Epipolae and Tyche, with many important branches (Schubring, 1865, 586). Schubring states (p. 629) that because the Athenians had attacked the city from this area, Dionysus decided to fortify it and incorporate the aqueduct in the rampart system so that enemies could not ruin the water supply lines of the city (Diodorus, 14,18).

2. One branch, which is built in a different fashion and so may not be Greek, crosses under the Anapos River to the west of the city and runs at a lower level through Neapolis.

3. Another line, found a few steps from the "prison of Dionysus" was set in a fold of the city wall, was made of "beautiful early stonework," and had many lead channels associated with it (Schrubring, 1965, 588). Lead should indicate Roman intervention into an earlier Greek system. Roman lead pipes are known at Morgantina, for instance, in the late second and first centuries B.C. (Crouch, 1984, 358).

4. From the waterline nearest the top of the hill in Epipolae and Tyche, at the right in Schubring's "Plan von Syrakus," branched off the aqueduct called Tremiglia because of its destination; from this juncture it may have run approximately parallel to the main line much farther uphill, until it turned and ran into the bay of Trigilos, part of the Great Harbor (Schrubring, 1865, 599–600).

5. Ninfeo.

6. Targietta.

7. Paradiso, which ran on to the amphitheater area.

8. Zappala.

9. And finally the high line turned south and ran through Achradina, although today the link between the two lines is missing [because of the continued erosion of the valley head above the bay called Tonnara?]

10. Aqueduct under the sea of the Little Harbor. [I am highly skeptical of this as a built waterline, but can easily imagine a karst channel in this area.]

11. Waterlines on Ortygia, near temples, and near spring of Arethusa (Schrubring, p. 608, quoting Diodorus V,13, who writes that Arethusa was the end point of the Crimiti aqueduct, serving as a reservoir for it in the Greek times. This would mean that the present baroque walling around Arethusa replaces much older reservoir walls).

GROUP TWO

12. A line that taps mountain springs and feeds the Anapos River.[6] This line runs for part of its way perpendicular to the river and part of the way parallel to the river (Schubring, 1965, 611). These channels may be a complicated system for handling flood waters and providing for irrigation. (They need modern study by hydraulic engineers and archaeologists together.)

13. Part of this line runs parallel to the Ninfeo line and appears between the theater and the Ear of Dionysus (one of the quarries), as a new arrangement in a district that had earlier been served by Crimiti water only. Schubring comments several times on the bitter taste of the Crimiti water so the provision of an alternate supply may have been to overcome this drawback (see, e.g., p.594). Note that there may have been a deliberate decision to import waters of different tastes and hence of different chemical compositions, in order to mix them and thereby remove sinter deposits from pipes and channels. I suggest that the well-known but hard-to-explain importation of bitter waters in an aqueduct of Rome could have been to achieve the same effect. If so, this is another example of Sicilian ideas influencing the Romans.

14. A pond and river fed from the spring Kyane and called by its name. [Although there may originally have been a spring here in the plain west of the city, this place seems now to be fed from the same Anapos line that comes from the mountains, and to be part of the same effort to control flooding, etc. (personal observation, 1985.)]

Schubring also gives his estimates of dates for each of the lines (pp. 617–38). Burns (1974, 390) does not always agree with Schubring on number or dates of lines, but he urges the particular usefulness of studying Syracuse as a typical case for many Greek cities in the matter of water management. I would say that Syracuse is a model rather than a typical case.

Thus for the springs and fountains of Syracuse, we have some evidence, and for the long-distance water supply lines a great deal more. From the evidence of the extensive development of long-distance water supply lines—even if there were no references in the ancient literature— we can see that Syracuse was a very large and wealthy city. Money was frequently reinvested here in the water supply system so that it could continue to function well to provide for the needs of residents and visitors.

Comparison of Water Elements

Other elements of the water system contributed equally, although not so dramatically, to the supply and use of this vital liquid. In both Syracuse and Corinth there are archaeological data to support a brief discussion of the other water system elements. In both cities, public bath buildings served the large population. At Corinth (Figs. 8.1, 11.1), these were from the Greek period:

- The Centaur Bath west of the South Stoa, 425–400 B.C., rebuilt and then abandoned in 325–300. Buildings and water were heated (Williams, l976, 109–15; 1977, 40–53).
- The possible Greek bath between the North Market and the archaic temple, from no later than 300 B.C.[7]
- The bath at the Asklepion. It was customary for sanctuaries of Asklepios to be equipped with baths. This sanctuary at Corinth was located where it could tap extensive water channels, and included its own formal bath. This location enabled it to appeal to the foot traffic climbing up to Corinth from the port below.
- The underground bath west of the Lerna area, adjacent to the Asklepion. This structure was published as the Fountain of the Lamps.
- It should be noted also that the Roman gymnasium just south of the Asklepion replaced the Hellenistic and earlier Greek gymnasium on the same site, and is assumed to have included bathing facilities (*Wiseman*, 1972, 9).
- Perhaps further investigation will reveal a Greek bath under the Roman one on the Lechaion Road that was recently reported by Biers (1985). There was also another Roman bath north of the new excavations near the theater, dating from the Hadrianic period. Both of these baths are located where I would expect Hellenistic baths to have preceded them, and possibly classical era baths as well.

Thus by archaeological evidence we know of five major bathing facilities within the Greek city, and tradition adds another at the "Baths of Aphrodite" on the scarp just above the coast, directly north of the city (see the map "Water Sources," fig. 43, in Sakellariou and Faraklas, 1972). (Williams is also skeptical of this water outlet as a bath.) Their map also notes several "sources" (numbers 3–8, 10, 15, 16) with Greek and Turkish names that I take to be outlets of underground water lines.

At Syracuse, a population of nearly a quarter of a million needed to be provided with bathing facilities. Pace (1935–38, II, 463) says there were 240,000 people in 4800 square kilometers, thus a density of 50 per kilometer. It seems likely, then, that further excavations will uncover more bathing facilities. Those that can be listed today are of varying degrees of visibility:

- One in Tyche.
- One in Achradina with a large rectangular cistern, part of a gymnasium in this area (both in Orsi, 1900, 207–08).
- One near the present railroad station, which Schubring said had a

Greek plan but Roman workmanship (Schrubring, 1865). Excavation has been hampered by the very high water table so that trenches and other declivities immediately fill up with water. This bath was also part of a gymnasium in Roman times. It seems likely that an earlier Greek bath stood here.

- One described by Ginouves as having two rotundas and a sauna, and dating from no later than the third century B.C. One rotunda had basins on stands, and the other had columns. Water was supplied by both wells and an aqueduct. Lines from the aqueduct came into the building under the vestibule. This bath was located just north of the Paradiso Latomia (quarry/karst outfall). One would like to know where the waste waters went from this bath, and why if it was as late as the third century it was so primitive as to have only three rooms (Ginouves,1959; Delorme, 1960)? (Fig. 11.8).

Even though this list is incomplete, we can assert that both the locations and the variations in the types of baths known at Syracuse indicate that new and up-to-date baths were added as the city grew. These were supplied by the same waterlines that supplied the fountains, although we would expect that special spur lines had to be constructed to divert the necessary water supply from the main aqueduct line to the bathing establishment. For economy, we would expect that baths were located as close as possible to the waterlines. Certainly the close connection between

Figure 11.8. Greek bath found north of the Paradiso Latomia, Syracuse. Reprinted by permission from G. Cutrera, "Rovine di un antice stabilimento idraulico in contrada Zappala," *Notiizie degli Scavi di Antichicta*, 16(1938), plate XXI.

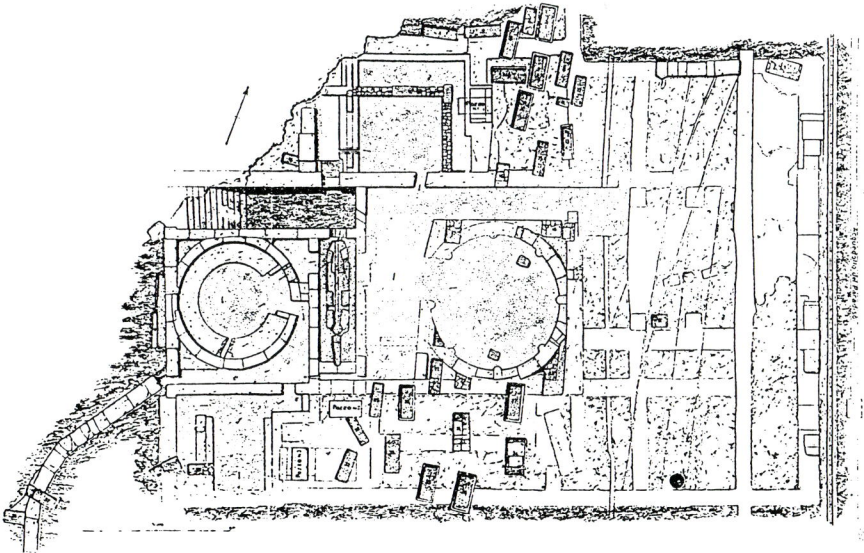

waterlines and baths has been proved at Pergamon, where the West and East Baths of the Gymnasium were located directly below the Roman Madradag channel which probably replaced the Hellenistic twin pipeline (Fahlbusch, personal communication). It would be interesting to check the bath locations at Syracuse with this in mind.

Domestically and strategically, the importance of wells and cisterns for assuring the water supply for residences and industry is demonstrated at both Corinth and Syracuse, even though the evidence was not gathered in order to prove this point. In Corinth, for example, wells and cisterns in the area of the Asklepion and gymnasium show that these edifices replaced houses of the sixth and fifth centuries (Roebuck, 1951, 14, 26, 46, 74–76, 96, 102–06), while the wells and cisterns east of the theater give evidence of occupation since Early Neolithic times (Williams and Zervos, 1982, 116–22, pl. 37) We have already mentioned the wells and cisterns of the Agora from the tenth to the eighth centuries, and can note here those of the fifth and fourth centuries west of the Agora (H.S. Robinson, 1969, 2, 38) and the sixth and fifth century ones under and around the South Stoa (Broneer, 1954, 95), as well as the same date for wells and channels from houses south of the Sacred Spring. Perhaps the most interesting shaft near the Sacred Spring is the one with a rectangular well head over a circular well later enlarged to an oval shaft, which was used during the sixth and fifth century and then went out of use. From inspection of the shaft, I suggest that these differences in form indicate at least three periods of use. The area immediately east of the museum at Corinth has wells and cisterns whose contents give a capsule history of the area, wherein one can read the construction, use, filling, clearing out and reuse, and refilling of both wells and cisterns for domestic and industrial use, as the fortunes of the city changed (Weinberg, 1948, 198–241).

One unchanging feature in the life of Corinth from very early through Late Roman times was the worship ("participatory ritual"?) of Aphrodite on the top of Acrocorinth. To accommodate throngs of worshippers and to safeguard the garrison in time of siege, the Acropolis was supplied with many cisterns as well as having its own spring (Upper Peirene). There is one cistern only 20 or 30 meters from the peak, still containing water in 1985. I counted 16 along the path from the top to the level of the spring, which is 350 meters lower than the crest. Additional cisterns are scattered over the Acropolis in many places. Larger public reservoirs were noted in sections of the channel system under the Agora, remodeled as reservoirs, such as the long reservoir of the fifth century under the South Stoa, that went out of use in the fourth century (Broneer, 1954, 95).

Only a few cisterns have been described in the archaeological literature from Syracuse, and these are entirely from the late Hellenistic period, with some early imperial Roman examples also. Largest of these is a tank 6 meters long, placed between the walls of two neighboring houses

(Gentile, 1951, 285–87, 294). The size of this does not begin to compare with the 200–foot-long cistern related to the South Stoa in Corinth. The paucity of domestic data here suggests that excavators have been unable to look for residential quarters because they had to concentrate on saving and understanding the major monuments threatened by modern urban expansion, a problem the site of ancient Corinth is fortunately free from. Although a few house walls from the eighth and seventh centuries have been found at both sites, there are not enough examples to allow us to get a sense of what was common provision for domestic water use in the centuries when Corinth founded Syracuse.

The evidence does enable us, however, to assert that both mother city and colony had mixed systems of water supply, in which the oldest methods of wells and cisterns and tapping natural springs were gradually supplemented by methods relying on more advanced technology. Thus in classical and Hellenistic times, the engineers of the city could provide the amplification of the waters of a spring by directing to it flows and seepages from farther uphill, and by erecting completely artificial fountains such as Glauke or its small neighborhood equivalents. Enough water was available for ordinary domestic use, for industry, for ritual ablutions, and for the public baths that were so important an amenity of everyday life.

Pipes, channels, and drains cannot be described at either Corinth or Syracuse, because they have not been explicitly published. Still, we can conclude on the basis of the information available that every feature of the fully developed water system contributed to both survival and amenity, from the "insurance" of private wells and cisterns multiplied by the public water lines, to the sophistication of reusing waste waters for irrigation to ensure a continuous crop of trees (for fuel and building materials) near the city. (See Chapter 15 on the variety of elements making up the typical water system; the issue of water as amenity is discussed further in Part IX.) Greek tradition emphasized the prudence of having a multiplicity of supply sources, each a safeguard against failure of the others. The water management tradition evolved in response to the real risks of urbanization in this climatological niche. Weighed in the ancient cost-benefit analysis was the prudence of reuse and extended use (also discussed in Chapters 3 and 4). Every potential water decision was evaluated as to its cost in human effort and in community wealth. I have mentioned already the decisions to locate bathing establishments near waterlines with ample flow. Fahlbusch (1982, 131–39) has discussed the general question of cost-benefit analysis, reading the ancient decisions from the waterlines as built, by a modern hydraulic engineer trained to make exactly the same kinds of analyses.

It is not coincidental that Gelon, who moved the populations of several towns to Syracuse, also built several aqueducts for them in the newly settled quarters. One can interpolate a public works program that con-

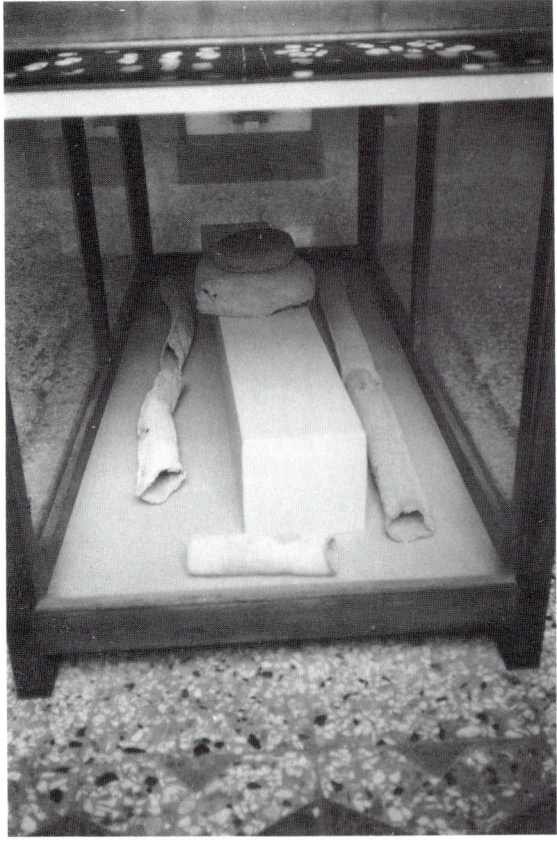

Figure 11.9.   Lead pipe in Syracuse Museum, probably from after 200 B.C. These pipes are 5 to 7 centimeters in diameter.

structed not only aqueducts but also roads, houses, and public buildings, redistributing some of the wealth that Gelon had won in taking over Syracuse, and binding the new residents to him as their patron and benefactor so that they sided with him in any altercations with the earlier residents of the city. Similarly, some Roman governmental money must have gone into refurbishing the water system when it was decided to rebuild the city of Corinth and turn it over to army veterans. That story takes us beyond the period of this study, however.

These two cities provide powerful examples of water in the urban landscape and water as the sine qua non of urban ecosystems. Colonists from Corinth were aware of how important water was in the flourishing condition of their home city, and I believe that they deliberately sought not only a new site with a positive resource base, but specifically a site where the customary technical knowledge that they carried with them was appropriate to handle the new situation: same geology, same climate, so that the same flora and fauna could flourish, and especially humans and all their works. Those who settled Syracuse seem also to have carried a mind-set that accepted new ideas and mechanisms for water management, so that as water technology changed at home in Corinth, the same new ideas found acceptance in Syracuse. We know that Plato, for instance, was equally at home in Syracuse as in Athens, which is an indication of the level of intellectual life in Syracuse in the fourth century.

PLANNING

The kinds of information and political processes necessary to plan and implement such an ancient water system are clarified for us by comparative data from modern water planning. In both cases, interactions between humans, their culture, and their environment can lead to misuse or abuse that affect hydrology (adapted from Lindh and Berthelot, 1979, 4–5):

1. Alteration or destruction of the natural hydrological balance
2. Modification of the runoff pattern
3. Degradation of the environment
4. Failure to know or understand the interrelations between people and the environment
5. Unfair allocation of costs and benefits at least partly because it is hard to tell who benefits
6. Inadequate allocation of money to hydrological problems
7. Conflicts of interest between user or supplier groups, and between them and the government
8. Selfishness about contributions to solutions
9. Lack of planning and fragmented services

Not only hydraulic engineering factors but also social and economic factors must be considered in water management planning. Planning for water management, involving multiple objectives and expert input from several disciplines, is complicated. Because of the constraints of multiple objectives (both then and now!) and the need for many kinds of expert input, the study of water management among the ancient Greeks is far from being straightforward, simple, and clear. Even the term *water management* needs clarification. Lindh points out that water management is a loose term, used on two levels: the formulation of strategic goals and policies, and the tactical administration of the chosen means of implementation (Lindh and Berthelot, 1979, 6). The term is used here precisely because of this double level of meaning.

In the next chapter, I turn to one aspect of water management, the use of waters of different qualities, as an example of the careful thought that went into ancient Greek water management.

NOTES

1. My articles on "The Water System of Palmyra" (1975) and "The Hellenistic Water System of Morgantina, Sicily" (1984) remain highly unusual attempts in the literature of classical archeology to portray complete water systems.

2. I have felt a true camaraderie with this 19th-century German whose work encouraged me in the lonely years when I could find no one else to share my fascination with the topic of ancient water supply.

3. Modern aqueduct construction and repair I learned about in an interview with Mr. Davi of the Ufficio Technico of Syracuse, facilitated by V. Castanza of the Archaeological Service in Syracuse; they both have my thanks.

4. I am grateful to Mr. A. LaMesa, head gardener of the archaeological park that contains the Theater and the Latomia at Syracuse, who showed me the water system elements of his domain and shared both his knowledge and his enthusiasm with me.

5. I expect to deal with colonization in the Old and New Worlds, specifically comparing Roman and Spanish practices, in a future work. Meanwhile, see Crouch, 1991.

6. I saw this connection, thanks to G. Aresco, who showed me the Galermi line.

7. I could never "read" these ruins as a bath, and was relieved when Dr. Williams told me in 1988 that it is not a bath, although it was so published.

12

Planning Water Quality: Potable and Subpotable Water at Selinus and Priene

Nothing can make water better.

—Ursula Le Guin
Always Coming Home

PRINCIPLES

Today when the rigors of an arid climate (Arabia) or other constraints on water resources press the limits of water supply, hydraulic engineers have to reconsider the nineteenth century answer of one quality of water for all uses. In places where population density far exceeds the supply of potable water—Hong Kong—or where the scanty spring water is not enough to support the massive tourist industry—Bermuda—(Deb, 1987, 222) there is no choice but to use subpotable or nonpotable water whenever feasible. Absolute scarcity of drinking-quality water is the strongest reason for water managers today to consider alternate procedures, but in some situations the quality not quantity of water is the issue. Heavy metals, long-lasting pesticides, or other carcinogens may require separation of the purest supply for drinking and cooking from the less pure supply for other uses, lest the water itself cause disease during a lifetime of use. Since potable water amounts to a small fraction of use in a modern city—6 percent or less (J. Thapa, personal communication)—alternative delivery systems for that small amount may be feasible, with the main systems delivering subpotable water for bathing, cleaning, watering lawns, and so on, and nonpotable water for industry or irrigation.

It is easier to contemplate in theory these logical divisions than to make actual plans for altering the delivery system in metropolitan water districts. Political and economic realities restrict change in built-up areas unless the danger is severe, but in some new suburbs in Florida dual pipelines are laid for potable water inside the house and subpotable outside. Drinking bottled water is becoming more common. Many municipal water systems now supply partially purified (nonpotable) water to industry for cooling or other processes. Still, these new ideas have not been widely implemented to date.

It is unexpected, then, to find that the ancient Greeks had just such a triple system of water supply and reuse. Each Greek city had both public fountains and springs supplying flowing water of the best quality, and private cisterns in houses and public buildings to supply still water of good quality, plus a drain system that led used water outside the city. Wells were also used; those in the Athenian agora are typical for Greek technology, "ranging from two and one-half to thirty-seven meters, and averaging about 10 meters (32 feet)," whereas Solon's law said the digger could give up if he had not struck water at at 60 feet (M. Lang, 1968). When I first gathered the data, it made no sense to me that the Greeks would want spring water if they already had cistern water at home, or that each house had a cistern when there was running water at the corner fountain. Yet carrying water is laborious, especially if that supply is for all domestic use as well as for any artisan activities taking place in the courtyard of the house. Gradually I became conscious of how much work would be involved in hand-carrying all water. Still, it was not until I learned of the "6 percent" figure that I began to realize that it was worth the effort to carry enough fresh water for each meal, just as today people in small towns like Troy, New York, go to the local spring for water to make coffee or to dilute frozen juice concentrate. Friendly conversation at the fountain, while the modern plastic container or the ancient amphora filled up, could be a pleasant part of the daily routine. In the ancient cities, neighborhood wells served similar functions.

For most domestic and light industrial tasks, the cistern under each courtyard was the normal source of water. The rainwater that fell on the roof of an average house, if collected and stored in a cistern, was enough to supply all family needs for at least six months, even without special conservation measures, and without calculating the alternate supply of drinking water from fountains, springs, or wells (Judson, 1959, 27). During the wet months, the supply of water in the cistern would be alternately depleted and refilled; if the cistern were full when the rainy season ended, its six months' supply ordinarily carried the family through until the rains began again the following autumn. Some houses, such as the House of the Doric Capital at Morgantina, had two cisterns, effectively guaranteeing a full year's supply. Since the cisterns were cleaned out annually, the water in them was essentially clean and could be used for drinking and cooking if necessary. Placement deep in the earth kept the cistern water cool, and thus more palatable, but for most families the

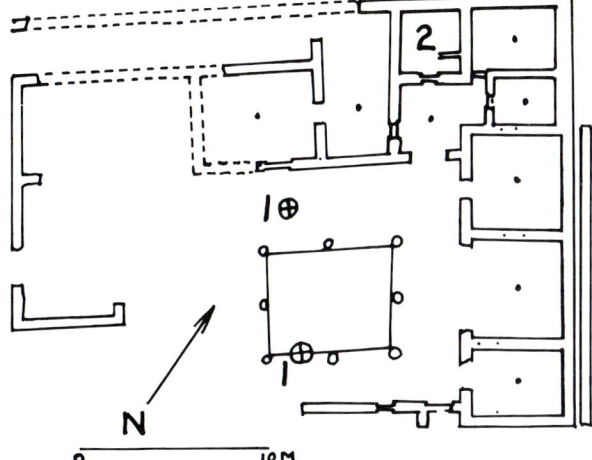

Figure 12.1. Plan of House of Doric Capital, Morgantina, with its two cisterns (1) and bathroom (2). Reprinted by permission of the present excavator, Malcolm Bell.

taste of spring water was preferred for drinking. "Subpotable" cistern water could be used for domestic cleansing and watering animals, and plants. If the family industry, such as making pottery, required water, the cistern could be tapped for that also. It seems likely that bathing, cooking, or laundry water was reused to flush the latrine or for some small-scale industrial processes. Such reuse would be somewhat more feasible for them than for us, as neither soap nor detergent was then in use.

USE OF WATER

There was an efficient grouping of water-use features of the house. Locating the cistern in the courtyard meant that this was also an alternate, logical place for the basin for washing hands, faces, and dishes. In Morgantina (as well as a number of other places) laundry also was done in the courtyard. Several houses there have a large hemispherical pithos located under a downspout that automatically filled the pithos with rainwater in the winter, and at Delos several low tub-with-scrub-boards lie in the courtyards where they would have been used (see Figs. 16.18, 22.9).

Used water and storm runoff were collected in sewers, to drain out through either slits in the ramparts or channels under the streets leading through the gates of the city. A letter from Hermann Kienast, excavator of the Samos tunnel and author of the study of the walls of ancient Samos, reminds me that thick stone or clay pipes were incorporated into the curtain walls to release water otherwise trapped inside the walls, and thus prevent collapse of the walls (Kienast, 1978, S.45 and Abb. 21). Nonpotable water, whether wastes or storm runoff, could be reused outside

Figure 12.2. Slit in ramparts near the postern below the House of the Official, Morgantina. Such slits permited runoff from inside the city to escape, possibly into an irrigation system outside, rather than build up behind the walls and endanger their stability. The slit is too small for anyone but a small child to penetrate, being approximately .3 by .6 meters.

the city all year long for irrigation. Growing wood for fuel and for building material would have been a high priority in the immediate vicinity of the town. The drainage system was completely gravity-fed, but some human manipulation of the water would have been necessary to allocate it for industry or in the fields for irrigation.

This system achieved high efficiency. For the provision and use of each quality of water, the minimum in human energy and economic resources was required, because for each arrangement maximum thought had been given. Fetching water from the fountain was in its way a social interaction, like buying and selling or exchanging views, and thus appropriate in or at the edge of the marketplace. Both the product—water— and the activity—fetching it—were refreshing and contributed to the quality of life that the Greeks valued. Between the domestic cistern and the public fountain, women as well as men could live pleasantly.

An unusual feature of these arrangements is that the time and effort of women and girls were considered valuable to the whole society, and worth utilizing efficiently. The cistern, an extremely cost-effective source of water in terms of human labor, was built integrally with the houses and maintained by the family. Water for the cistern was captured directly from the roofs without human effort, once the drainspouts were set in place.

However, for activities requiring larger amounts of water, efficient placement of the supply was the norm, just as we saw in the grouping of activities around the domestic cistern. The locations of springs and their associated fountainhouses determined the placement of the agora, the sanctuaries, and other nodes of activity—the ancient equivalent of the central business district.

As a modern person, my standards for sophistication and elegance in urbanization include provision of water supply and drainage. When we see that even small towns like Morgantina made the necessary expenditures of thought and money to provide drains from every house into the sewers of the street, it is reasonable to infer that constructed drainage was the norm in this culture. From the neighboorhood street drains, larger channels led to the nearest exit from the city, rather than allowing liquid wastes to accumulate close to the houses. If this latter pattern had been the norm—as has all too often been the case, in nineteenth century London or twentieth century Calcutta, for example—it would be evident centuries later during excavation or urban renewal, as when the stinking moats of Istanbul were cleared out during the 1980s and were made into a public park.

EXAMPLES

Two ancient cities that had water systems that allocated different qualities of water to different uses may be examined to make our study more vivid and more specific. They are Selinus on the south coast of Sicily, and Priene, an Ionian Greek city on the west coast of Asia Minor (see maps, Figs. 3.1, 12.3, 12.4).

Selinus flourished on the agricultural wealth of the surrounding plains and on trade with Greece, Carthage, and Rome as well as with natives of the interior. Before we examine the water management of Selinus, let us make a rapid survey of the topography and chronology of the city (Martin, 1975, 54–67; Theodorescu, 1975, 108–20). Selinus was a very large city of several districts, although this fact is not easy to grasp when visiting the site. At the site's center lies a headland, running perpendicular to the sea between two rivers. The only part extensively excavated is the Acropolis with its group of temples, agora, and residential area (Fig. 12.5).

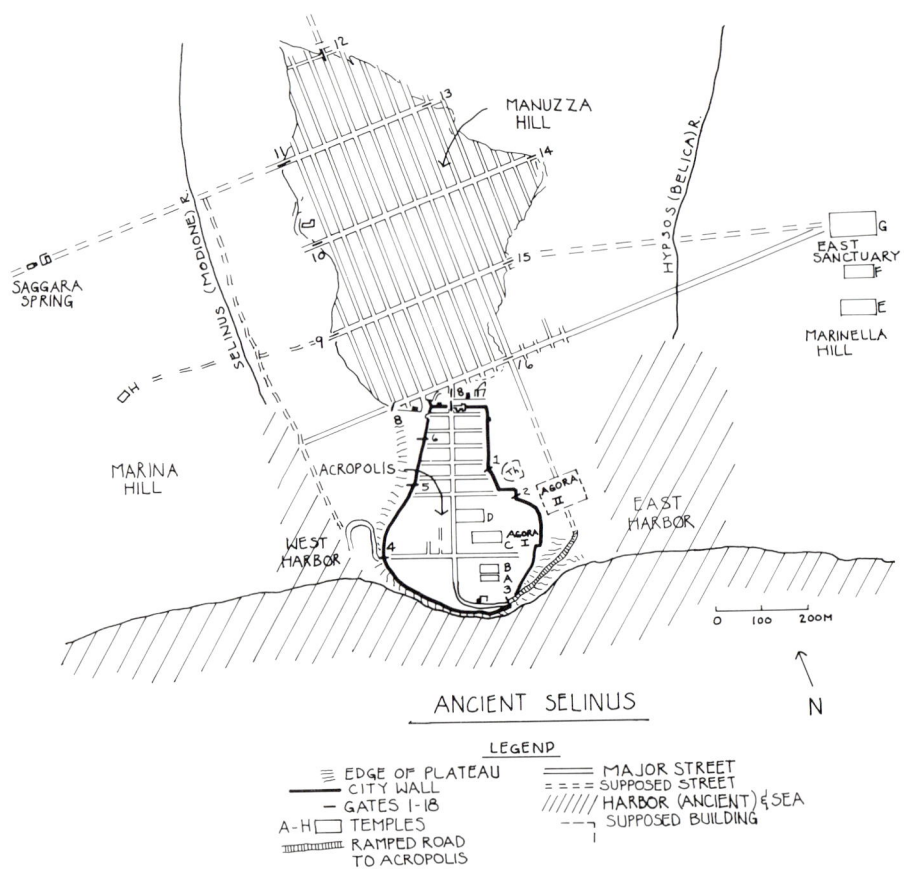

Figure 12.3. Map of Selinus area, with ancient coastline and built-up areas.

Figure 12.4. Plan of Priene, by Kummer and Wilberg, 1885–89. From top to bottom: *A.* Acropolis where a reservoir was fed by lead pipes from an aqueduct tapping karst springs in the marble mountain. *B.* Waterline crossing the city rampart on the east. *C.* Series of tanks and reservoirs for the town, supplied by aqueduct B. *D.* Demeter Temple, supplied with water from a vein in the mountain here, with additional water from roofs and from spring overflow, held in large and small cisterns. *E.* Roman bath, just below the theater. There are fountains, cisterns, and other water system elements along the street between the bath and theater. *F.* Houses at the left, on the same street, were supplied by pipes that tapped directly into the slope behind them, and also had street fountains to draw on. *G.* Lower than the terrace of the Athena Temple but higher than the North Stoa of the Agora, the Prytaneion had its own fountain and cistern (see Fig. 12.6) *H.* The Agora is discussed and shown in detail in Fig. 14.1. *I.* Houses to the west of the Agora were mostly supplied with water in pipes, but about 25 percent of them had cisterns. Their toilets and stables sometimes shared one space. *J.* The waste water channel at the edge of the main street of the town terminated in a

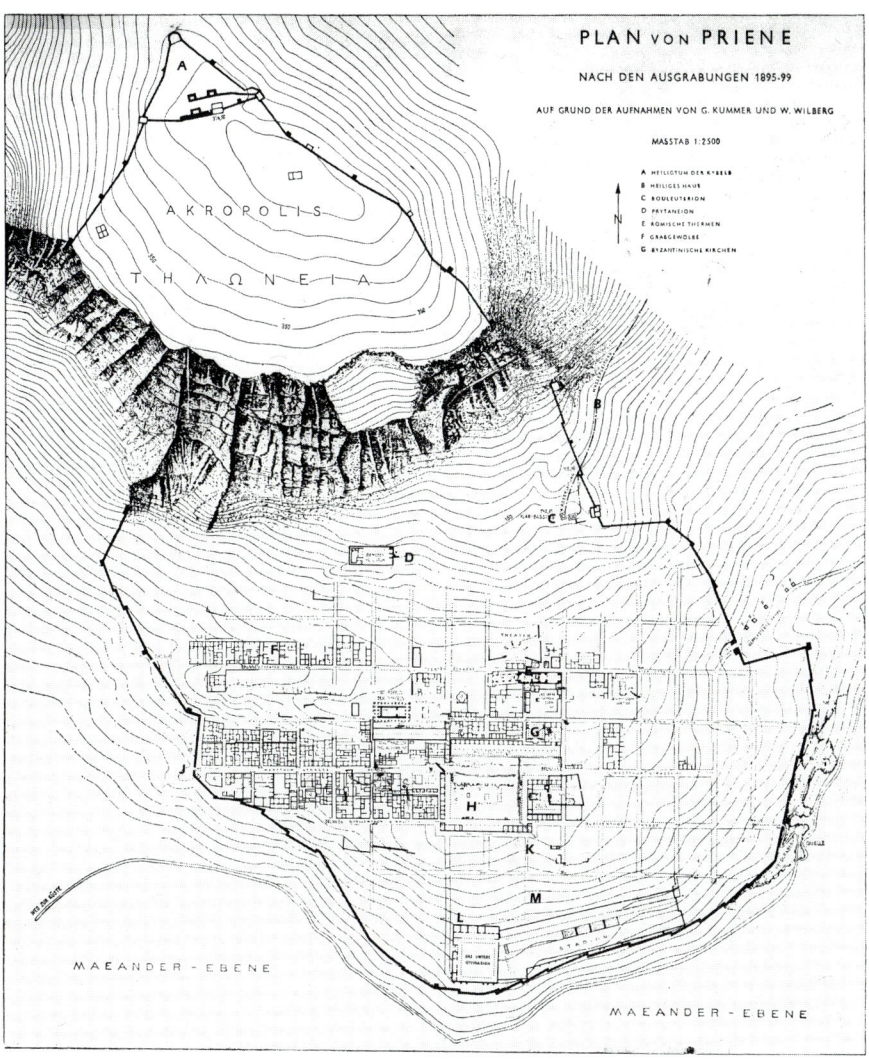

PLAN VON PRIENE

NACH DEN AUSGRABUNGEN 1895-99

AUF GRUND DER AUFNAHMEN VON G. KUMMER UND W. WILBERG

MASSTAB 1:2500

A HEILIGTUM DER KYBELE
B HEILIGES HAUS
C BOULEUTERION
D PRYTANEION
E RÖMISCHE THERMEN
F GRABGEWÖLBE
G BYZANTINISCHE KIRCHEN

gate at J, where it poured into a karst shaft (indicated as Sump on figures 12.6 and 12.7), as it still does, and was led away underground. *K,K.* Drains from the Agora and its neighboring streets were led down the steep slope between the agora and the stadium below. *L,M.* At L the palestra with school rooms and bathing room, and at M the stadium below a cave-spring. Like the stadium at Delphi, this one was located to take advantage of an ancient spring. When I was there in 1988, the spring had been newly cleared. Water from this spring supplied the bathing room in the palestra to the left of the stadium; the bathing room is located in the northwest corner of this complex, and is marvelously well preserved. (See Fig. 16.10.) *N.* Spring outside East Gate, connected with the Agora by a stepped street. At the bottom of the plan, the word Meander appears twice, showing the bed of the present river; in classical times, an arm of the sea separated Priene from its neighbor Miletus to the south and justified the placement of Priene high on its terrace, above storms and sea-borne attack. Reprinted by permission of the German Archaeological Institute, Istanbul.

157

Colonists from Megara built the acropolis sanctuary (planned not later than 570–560 B.C.). They laid out a wide north-south street and the two east-west streets perpendicular to it, flanking the acropolis sanctuary, a band of public space across the widest part of the headland. Selinus is an example of the most common urban plan of the seventh and sixth centuries: one long straight street as the axis of the site, with cross-streets perpendicular to it, which we have called the Posedionia (Paestum) plan (see Chapter 5 and Fig. 5.1).

To the east, across the river, stood three more large temples and some houses. Pre-Greek occupation of Selinus is known only on this hill. Wharfs, warehouses, and residential quarters occupied the banks of the eastern river. A similar pattern prevailed on the slopes of the river to the west of the acropolis, though for sanctuaries there were only two small temples built on the far side of this river. To the north of the acropolis, a narrow neck of land connected that headland with a plateau today called Manuzza, stretching to the northwest; this was the prime residential area of the city, and some excavation has been done here. The cross streets of this sector terminate at the points of easy access to the plateau, and align with the axis from Temple M on the west hill, which was a very early focus of settlement, probably because of a major spring, to be discussed later.

After 408 B.C. the population changed from predominantly Greek to more strongly Punic—but the Hellenic influence in this part of the Mediterranean had been so strong for more than 300 years that the new settlers were Greco-Punic in culture. For about a century and a half they enjoyed the natural and commercial advantages of the site, probably utilizing the same sources of water. Then in 252 B.C. the Romans conquered Sicily but did not occupy Selinus; in fact, there is little evidence of any later occupation, which undoubtedly has been the chief factor in the preservation of the site.

In our other example, Priene, we find many contrasts of date, plan, scale, location, ethnicity, topography, geology, and position in the sequence of city planning history, as compared with Selinus. The original site of Priene is unknown, though it supposedly was founded from Thebes, perhaps during the wave of migration from the Greek mainland around 1000 B.C. (Stillwell, MacDonald, and McAllister, 1976, 737–38). The citizens of Priene fought in the Persian Wars of the early fifth century, but the city's small contribution in ships and men indicates that it was never a large place. Apparently the original city suffered severely in these wars, possibly to the extent of being razed and depopulated. (I suggest looking for the earlier Priene somewhere uphill and inland from the present site.) It is possible that changes in the water supply may have contributed to the decision to move downhill, if the water naturally cut itself lower and lower channels. Priene was in classical times a seaport, but the silting up and delta-building of the Meander River gradually changed the terrain and altered the available resources of the city. The city, north of Miletus, across the Meander River, was rebuilt on a plateau between the plain of the Meander and a nearly perpendicular cliff upon which stood a fortress and acropolis for the city. The plateau sits safely above the flooding of the Meander, which still troubles Miletus, and consequently well above the early arm of the sea which was both the opportunity and the danger for this small community. Today the site is about 12 kilometers inland and has no harbor. In the fourth century Priene was refounded on its present location—"the most spectacular [site] in Ionia" (Stillwell, Mac-Donald, and McAllister, 1976, 737–38)—where earlier Naulochos, the harbor of Priene, seems to have been located. This happened just as the Carthaginians were taking over Selinus, but Priene survived almost half a millennium longer. In plan, the fourth century city was a checkerboard with Agora at the center. Our maps (Figs. 12.6, 12.7) show how the water supply and sewers of the city conform to the checkerboard plan.

A word on the geology of the two cities. Selinus lies in a zone of calcerous rocks, layered with sandy-clay, good for the collection and availability of potable water. The most notable spring at the site is Gaggera on the west hill, near Temple M (which had so much impact on the street pattern of the Manuzza plateau). This spring, when measured in 1965 and 1966, gave between 1.6 and 2 liters per second, depending on the season (Dall'Aglio and Tedesco,1968,171–210). Since such a flow would not be enough to supply the very large city that Selinus became, we need to look inland for additional sources, possibly the spring near Castelvetrano. The pressure line that can be inferred from the lockstones found at various places on the Selinus acropolis, but not as far as I know reported in the literature, probably took its origin from this spring.

Priene's geology, though quite different, was equally amenable to exploitation for human settlement. The geomorphology of northern Ionia is characterized by a series of river deltas cut through crystalline rock structure, while from Izmir south there are varieties of karst in the mountains of limestone and marble. At Priene in the southern region, the massif is of marble above schist. Enough water percolates through fractures in the marble and comes to the surface as springs to ensure the greenness of Priene even in August. The absence of cisterns in the ancient houses suggests that the supply of flowing water was sufficient for all uses. A pressure pipeline (lead) supplied the acropolis. From it the water went to the collection tanks just inside the eastern wall of the city, above the houses, and the water was distributed by gravity flow. At the foot of the site today, water from a line that comes around the right shoulder of the hill supplies the small village before gushing into the pool in front of the tourist restaurant.

In spite of the striking differences between the two cities, we find in them many of the same water system elements that were everywhere characteristic of the Greek world: fountains; pipes, channels, and drains;

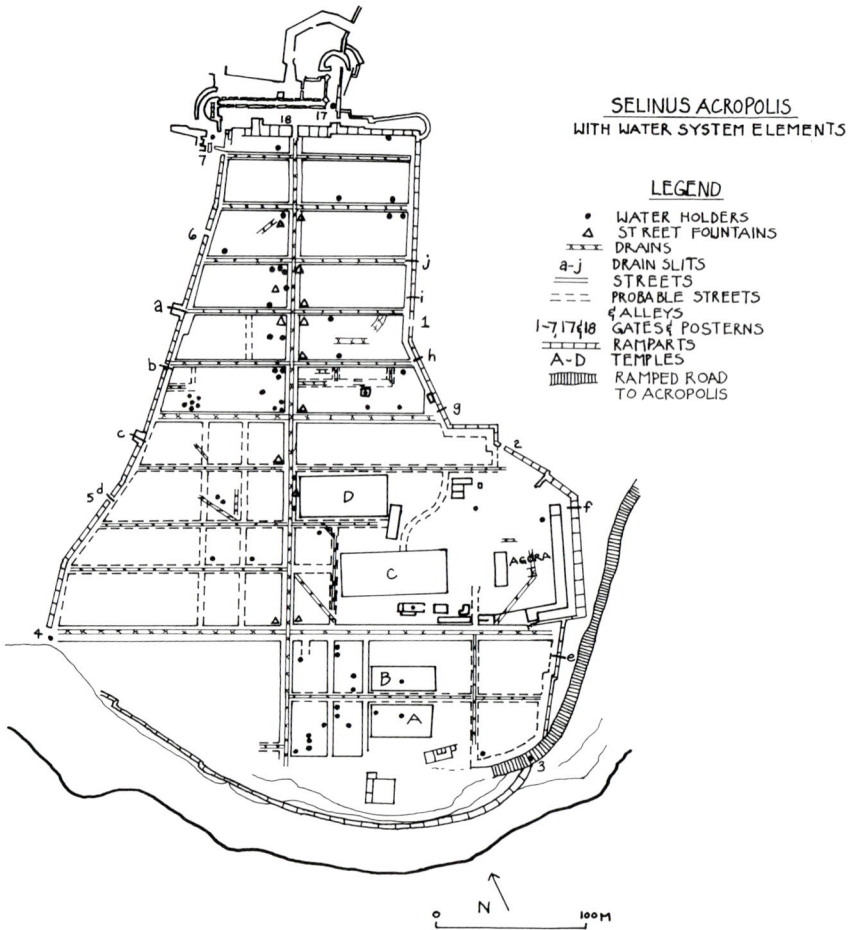

SELINUS ACROPOLIS
WITH WATER SYSTEM ELEMENTS

LEGEND
• WATER HOLDERS
△ STREET FOUNTAINS
DRAINS
a-j DRAIN SLITS
STREETS
PROBABLE STREETS
& ALLEYS
1-7 17&18 GATES & POSTERNS
RAMPARTS
A-D TEMPLES
RAMPED ROAD
TO ACROPOLIS

Figure 12.5. Map of Selinus Acropolis with water system elements. Water holders may be wells or cisterns, and are distinguished from fountains, which received flowing water from pipes.

bathrooms and their fittings; water storage. The elements are physical manifestations of the traditional knowledge and social behavior for finding, transporting, and using water, for distinguishing between different

Figure 12.6. Plan of pipes of drinking water system, Priene. Springs, fountains, and sump added by the author. Based on a study by Sekil, a graduate student of Professor U. Özis at the Dokuz Iylul Technical University of Izmir, Turkey; in turn based on earlier work of Wiegand. As published by Reimer Verlag, Berlin, in Wiegand et al, *Priene*, and reprinted by permission of the German Archaeological Institute, Istanbul.

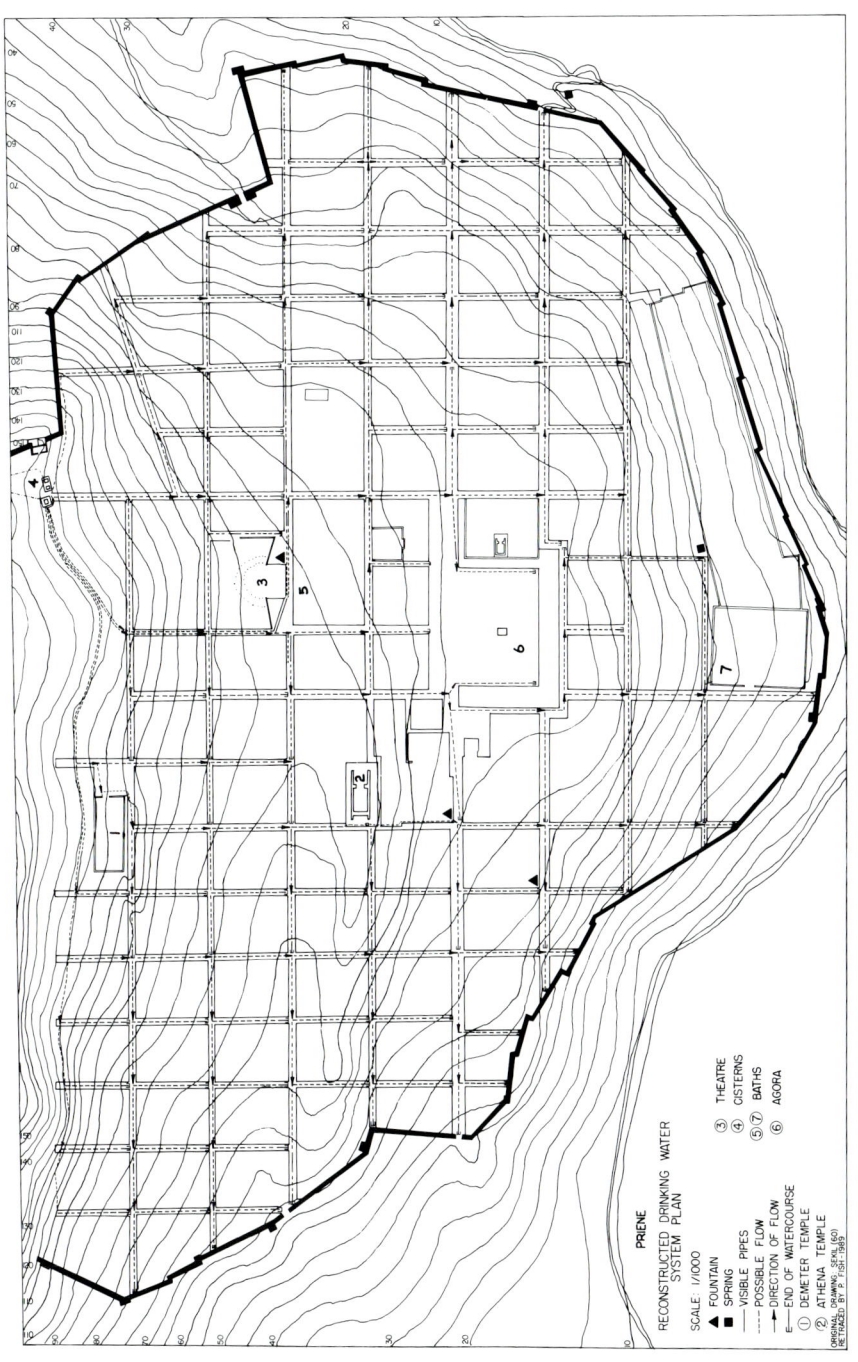

PRIENE
RECONSTRUCTED DRINKING WATER SYSTEM PLAN

SCALE: 1/1000

▲ FOUNTAIN
■ SPRING
— VISIBLE PIPES
--- POSSIBLE FLOW
→ DIRECTION OF FLOW
⊢ END OF WATERCOURSE
① DEMETER TEMPLE
② ATHENA TEMPLE
③ THEATRE
④ CISTERNS
⑤⑦ BATHS
⑥ AGORA

ORIGINAL DRAWING: SEKIL (60)
RETRACED BY P. FISH-1989

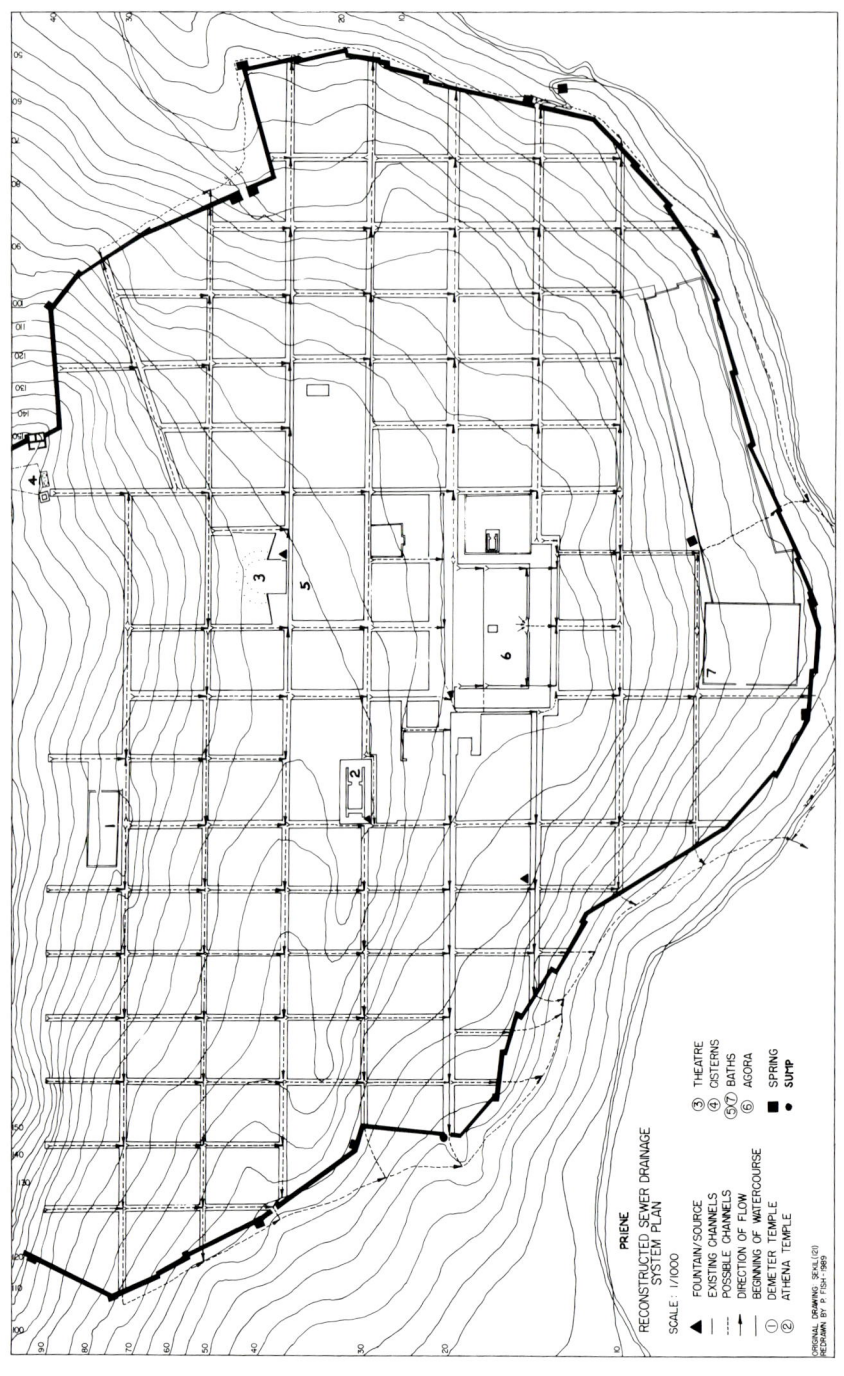

PRIENE
RECONSTRUCTED SEWER DRAINAGE
SYSTEM PLAN

SCALE : 1/1000

▲ FOUNTAIN/SOURCE
———— EXISTING CHANNELS
------- POSSIBLE CHANNELS
——→ DIRECTION OF FLOW
——→ BEGINNING OF WATERCOURSE
① DEMETER TEMPLE
② ATHENA TEMPLE

③ THEATRE
④ CISTERNS
⑤⑦ BATHS
⑥ AGORA
■ SPRING
● SUMP

ORIGINAL DRAWING: SCHULI(2?)
REDRAWN BY P. FISH -1989

grades of water, and for reusing and disposing of water economically and prudently. To enumerate the water system elements of each city and set them in relationship with one another, we are forced to use inaccurate and incomplete data since neither site has been excavated for the purpose of understanding the whole water system. Nevertheless, by bringing the available evidence into juxtaposition, we can glean from it some useful insights (table 12.1).

It may be easier to comprehend these water system elements if we classify them according to their functions, dividing them into public amenities, infrastructure, and domestic use (tables 12.2–12.4).

A few comments on these entries will help to put the data in perspective. Both cities relied more than other places on piped water; Delos, for instance, relied much more on cisterns and wells for domestic water than either of these cities did. Wells and cisterns are known at Selinus, but not evenly distributed across the site, so far as we now know. Since the excavated acropolis at Selinus was not as heavily settled as the north plateau which is almost unexcavated, the pattern of distribution of water system elements will undoubtedly seem quite different once excavation has revealed more of the prime residential area. Both Priene and Selinus utilized holding tanks, reservoirs or surge chambers. Three springs are known at Priene, but only one at Selinus. At least one formal public fountain was found at Selinus and perhaps as many as three, while sixteen waterbasins were placed along exterior house walls on the cross streets of the acropolis area. At Priene we know of six public fountains and three basins. Although pipes have been found in at least eight locations at Priene, including 20 or 30–foot runs of pipes under Spring Gate Street (Wiegand and Schrader, 1904, 68–80), I saw only two individual pipes at Selinus. However, the presence of four lockstones there suggests that one long-distance water supply line had been a pressure pipe of metal now robbed out. Priene had a pressure pipeline connected with the water chamber high on the acropolis, with at least one lead pipe found there (Wiegand and Schrader, 1904, 72). Both sites have numerous channels and gutters, but Selinus has manholes for access to underground lines. Since the two cities flourished at different times, it is not surprising that their washbasins and tubs were of different shapes. Such shapes changed every century and a half or two centuries during Greek times (Ginouves, 1962). It is interesting that in the late Greco-Punic houses that invade the

---

Figure 12.7. Plan of channels of sewer system, Priene. Note sump at west end of main street, which was probably a karst shaft utilized for drainage. Springs, fountains, and sump added by the author. Based on a study by Sekil, a graduate student of Professor Özis at the Dokuz Iylul Technical University of Izmir, Turkey; in turn based on earlier work of Wiegand et al., *Priene* (ibid.). Reprinted by permission.

Table 12.1
Water System Elements at Selinus and Priene

Element	Selinus	Priene
Cistern	16	4
Tank	2	3 "surge chambers"*
Well	1	1
Spring	1	3
Fountain	1	6
Waterbasin	16	3
Pipe	1	8
Pressure pipe	possible	1
Stone pipe	4 lockstones	2
Lead pipe	possible**	1
Drain	35	9
Channel gutter	19	yes, not counted
Manhole	2	unknown
Bathroom	several	2
Public bath	unknown	2
Tub	6	3
Washbasin	2 types	1
Latrine	1	3
Slabs over drain	yes	yes
Well/cistern head	3	1
Spout	unknown	1
Drain slit	10	3
Settling basin	1	1
Laundry basin	unknown	unknown

*Surge chambers are tanks that receive water from a pressure pipeline, allowing the pressure to escape harmlessly into the air before the water is drained into another line of pipes (see Hodge, 1990).

**I saw a doorsill with a 2 inch hole, just the right size for a lead pipe.

"Unknown" means that I did not see them and have not found them in the literature.

Table 12.2
Public Amenities

Element	Selinus	Priene
Fountain	1	6
Water basin	16	3
Public bath	unknown	2
Public latrine	1?	3?

Table 12.3
Infrastructure

Element	Selinus	Priene
Spring	1	3
Pipe (terra-cotta)	1	8
Pressure pipe	possible	1
Lead pipe	possible	1
Stone pipe	4 lockstones	2
Drain	35	9
Slabs over drain	yes	yes
Drain slit	10	3
Channel, gutter	19	yes
Manhole	2	unknown

Table 12.4
Domestic Fittings

Element	Selinus	Priene
Cistern	16	4
Tank	2?	3?
Well	1	1
Bathroom	several	2
Tub	6	3
Washbasin	2 types	1
Latrine	1?	3?
Well/cistern head	3	1
Settling basin	1	1

sanctuary area at Selinus there are standard Hellenistic bathtubs, and yet no evidence of typical stemmed washbasins.

Few recognizable latrines survive from either city, although that may be explained at least at Selinus by the fact that domestic bathrooms included a space separated from the rest by a half-wall, and drained to the sewer in the street (Fig. 20.11D). I think that people urinated here, using dirty bath water to flush the floor through the drain, and that excrement was deposited in portable chamber pots, for collection and distribution as fertilizer on the farms outside the city walls. In other words, we see that not every human activity has a corresponding *architectural* solution. In both cities, channels at one edge of the street carried waste and rainwater toward the gates or toward slits in the ramparts, and thence out to the fields or nearby rivers (Fig. 12.7).

RESOURCE CONSTRAINTS

Priene and Selinus have representative, not identical, examples of the standard water system elements known in the Greek world, employed prudently because of their resource constraints. What constraints did these ancients have to consider? Was there any similarity in their situation to those that impel us to experiment with three-tiered water systems? To put the Greek situation as simply as possible: First, in their climate the heat of summer makes ample water supply essential, just at the time of year when there is no precipitation. Water must be saved and carefully managed to last through the summer. Second, they relied on human and animal rather than mechanical or fossil fuel energy for the execution of work. Third, the gradual deforestation of the land resulted in scarcity of fuel for cooking and heating and of building materials. Some of this deforestation was integral to the karst process (Bintliff, 1977, 50ff; Chapter 7 here), but deforestation could be aggravated or ameliorated by human behavior such as over harvesting wood close to a city or, on the contrary, carefully reforesting.

In response to these constraints, the Greeks had learned to locate water sources and to place their settlements nearby, as we have seen in the case of the Gaggera Spring at Selinus. Later they conveyed water from distant sources to existing cities (Fahlbusch, 1982, 34–41) to supplement springs, wells and cisterns at the site, as was the pattern at Priene. Thus they developed a plurality of supply, ensuring the security of the community by not relying on only one source for so crucial a resource as water. To complete the ecological loop, they learned to drain waste and storm waters away from the city for use in fertilizing and irrigating crops, whether food or trees. Reuse of waste waters immediately produced more food and also replenished the water table so that the wells and springs continued to flow for their children and grandchildren. This is resource management—inferred from the resulting duration of urban life— on a fifty to one hundred year cycle, as is the growing of trees, and speaks to us profoundly—if we will listen—about the values of their culture. When we see that the cities endured upwards of four hundred and fifty years, we ask, How was it done, given the constraints of the geography and of human nature? What would we have to do to sustain a settlement here? The constraints, as we have seen, dictate the solutions. The Greeks knew how to conserve water for both public and private use, by storing it as close as possible to the point of use, covering channels, and diverting the excess from their ever-flowing fountains to the reuses mentioned earlier.

The crux between supply and discharge was usage. Here the ancient Greeks differentiated as a matter of course between three qualities of water. First-quality water was available in both Selinus and Priene for drinking. The subpotable water of cisterns was used at Selinus for noningestive domestic activities. At Priene, because of abundant flow of water from the mountain, there was no need to distinguish so clearly between potable and subpotable water uses, so that at least some of the subpotable activities were handled by public installations such as the two large bathing establishments, and some were supplied by drinking-quality water from pipelines, as we do today. Cooking, laundry, and bath water could be reused to clean floors and then to flush latrines. Reused water and the runoff from storms was collected in drainage channels and pipes, to be used for irrigation—the ancient equivalent of the nonpotable water that our systems supply for industrial use and irrigation. Even here, however, the 25 percent of the houses that were placed at the outer edge of the plateau are those where cisterns are found; separated from the abundant resurgences of the cliff face, this group of houses had to rely on saved rainwater for many domestic uses.

Thus the evidence from two ancient Mediterranean sites verifies the insights of modern hydraulic engineering, and these insights in turn explain the otherwise contradictory evidence from Greek water management. Given the principle of allocating three appropriate qualities of water, the ancient Greek evidence falls into a coherent pattern, parallel to the most modern ideas. What grim necessity forces certain modern cities to arrange for their survival, similar pressing necessity induced the ancients to organize some 2500 years ago. We had forgotten a great deal that we now rediscover with difficulty. The nineteenth century cost-benefit analysis that decreed one kind of water—potable—for all uses is now being seriously questioned on both economic and medical grounds. It is time to rethink the best uses of our resources, time to look again to our predecessors the ancient Greeks.

VI

Supply, Distribution, Drainage

13

Early and Late Examples:
A New Look at Olynthos
and Pompeii

The arrangements made in ancient cities for the management and use of water varied over the extent of the Greek world, depending on local topography and geology. They also varied by time period. In the absence of detailed whole-site studies, we can no more than suggest some of those differences. Our method will be to examine one early city and one late, looking for similarities and differences. The chosen examples share the useful (for us) feature of having been destroyed, so that their ruins preserve a set of arrangements not diluted by later habitation. The examples chosen are Olynthos in northeast Greece, destroyed at the end of the fourth century B.C., and Pompeii near Naples in southern Italy, destroyed in A.D. 79. A description of each will point out features that are typical for that time period, and we will conclude with a direct comparison of the two water management systems.

OLYNTHOS

Olynthos (Fig. 13.1) is located in northeastern Greece, at the base of the left peninsula of the set of three which also includes Mount Athos. Geological maps of the area (Institute of Geology and Mineral Exploration, "Geology of Greece" series (1:50,000), Athens, Greece, ca. 1984) show that a large limestone massif terminates just to the north of the site, and could be tapped for its karst waters. Indeed, a pipeline was found coming southward for five miles (D.M. Robinson, 1935, 219 ff and fig. 12; Robinson and Clement, 1938), from the springs near Polygyros and from northeast of the church of Hagios Nicolas. More traces of the line were observed in the plain. In Volume II of the Olynthos excavation reports (Robinson, 1930, 12), the line is thought to be sixth century because of some fragments of black-figure vases found with it in the dig, yet in Volume XII this aqueduct was declared fifth or fourth century because of its

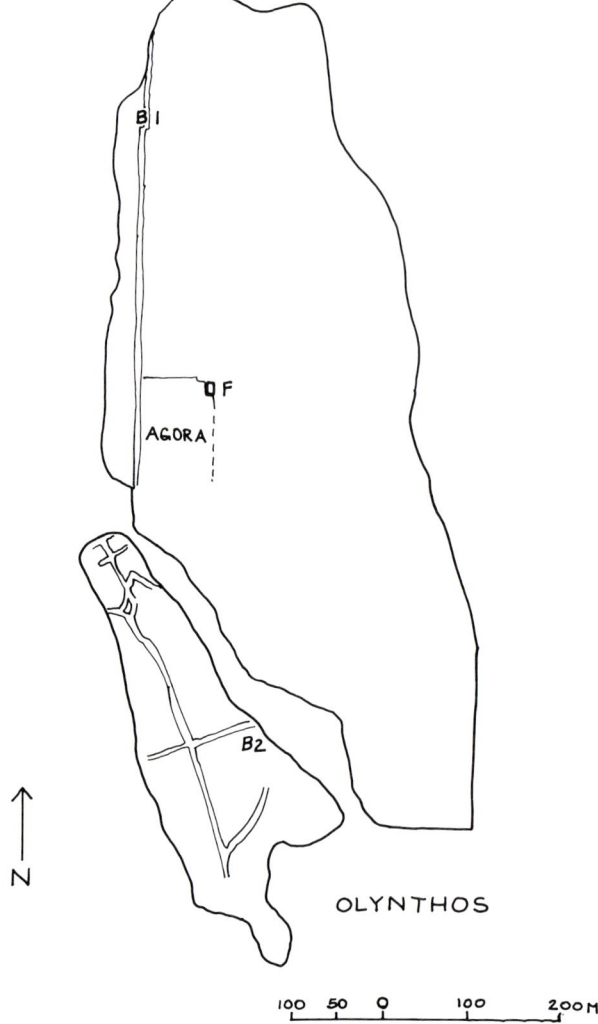

Figure 13.1.   Plan of Olynthos. South Hill settlement dating from the sixth century is shown at the bottom of the plan, a typical bar-and-stripes street pattern. Then in the very early fourth century, the North Hill was laid out in a modified Hippodamean grid. The bath at North Gate is at *B1*, the fountain house (Fig. 20.3) at *F*, and the earlier bath at *B2*. Redrawn from Robinson, 1946 and used by permission of Johns Hopkins University Press.

beautifully cemented joints with mortar of pure lime with a little silica (Robinson, 1946, 107). The line is described as having pipes about 3 inches thick (.45 centimeters), and therefore is probably a pressure pipe. A siphon arrangement requiring the water to travel under pressure was necessary because the pipeline had to rise to the site of the city after crossing a lower valley immediately to the north (Hoepfner and Schwandner, 1985,41). If, as I suspect, the aqueduct was carried also to South Hill, another pressure pipe would have been necessary to overcome the additional rise in elevation. The single pipe from Olynthos that I saw at the Old Museum (now a storage area) in Thessalonike was an elbow pipe, with walls nearly 2 inches thick. It had one opening on top, about 6 inches in diameter, and one at the end, about 7 inches clear. Both openings were fitted with complicated ridges to join them to the next segment of pipe. At the time, the pipe impressed me as being probably fourth century. It seems to be from a group found in the road at the south end of North Hill (Robinson and Clement,1938, 110). However, an elbow pipe of similar form was part of the discovered aqueduct, where it turned east from Avenue A, as seen in Figure 1 of plate 96 of Volume XII; in this context, the excavators considered it sixth century. This aqueduct makes it possible to date the use of siphons to the sixth century B.C., and probably the development of a true pressure system must therefore belong to the sixth or early fifth century.

Since the South Hill at Olynthos seems to have been settled in the sixth century B.C.,[1] several factors suggest that the line may originally date from that time:

- Water available in the hills to the north could have been brought to the settlement, which was placed near broad plains perfect for growing wheat, so badly needed in the mother city of Athens.
- During the sixth century, long-distance waterlines were built in Athens by the Peisistratid tyrants, as elsewhere in the Greek world. This technology would have been available to the colonists as well. Compare this with Thebes, where a classical aqueduct from the higher hills to the south replaced the Mycenaean one (Symeonoglou, 1985,141–44). The Theban aqueduct also tapped karst waters.
- One need not accept one set of evidence about the pipeline's date and exclude the other, since it is most common for waterlines to need repair. If the sixth century aqueduct did not need repair until the fifth or fourth century, the original builders had done very well indeed!
- Even if the aqueduct is as late as the fourth century, which I doubt, it still may retain the title of "alteste Druckwasserleitung der griechischen Zivilisation" bestowed on it by Hoepfner and Schwandner (1985, 41). We will need more definite proof of the date of the Syracusan line to give it the first date. For purposes of this book, I consider Minoan and Mycenaean civilizations as distinct from the Greek culture studied here, so I ignore the well-known pressure pipeline at Knossos on Crete.

The water was brought to Olynthos through the North Gate of North Hill where provision was made for those entering the city to at least wash their feet, and possibly to take a shower (Robinson and Clement,1938, 12). The North Hill is roughly the shape of a left hand, palm down; the north gate was, as it were, at the tip of the little finger. There was a second bathing establishment at the East Gate of South Hill. This one is described as being of the sixth century or before (Robinson,1930, 25).

Once inside the North Gate, the aqueduct ran underneath Avenue A at a depth of 6 meters near the gate, to 3.1 meters at the elbow, where the line turned east-southeast under the Agora and towards the fountain-house in Block Biii of Avenue B (Fig. 20.3). Although badly preserved because the stones of its walls were robbed by later settlers, enough remains of the fountain house for our purposes. It stood immediately south of a ramp leading up from the Assembly Hall to the Agora; both structures were located at a lower level than the Agora to their west. The aqueduct brought water to a three-chambered reservoir some 5.7 by 4.3 meters in area, west of the fountain house (Robinson and Clement, 1938, figs. 2, 96). The front wall of the reservoir seems to have had a series of spouts under which amphoras could be placed, and to the left a watering trough for animals was tucked against the retaining wall, against the hill. The trough and spouts were covered by a roof supported by a pair of columns (likely, wooden posts) and two antae (ends of flanking walls, decorated like columns), making a hall about 1.4 meters deep; a larger paved area separated the hall from the cobbled street. Excess water was led away in pipes under the street to the east, possibly to supply a lower fountainhouse in the eastern part of the city. (J.W. Graham, 1938, 307–11 and Robinson and Clement, 1938, 116). There were also drains leading from the fountainhouse, which seem to pertain to its latest period of use (Hoepfner and Schwandner, 1985, 41; Robinson and Mylonas, 1946, plates 89–96, 233.) The dates of the fountainhouse—built in the sixth century, but possibly rebuilt as late as 479, and again partially rebuilt after the Spartan destruction of 379 (Robinson and Clement, 1938, 26)—reinforce the idea that the aqueduct that supplied it belongs to the sixth century but underwent many rebuildings. These early dates also suggest that we revise backward to the sixth century the use of pressure pipelines in Greek aqueducts.

Altogether, the excavators have published details on nineteen different runs of pipelines, in a chart called "Principal Pipes and Pipe Lines" (Robinson and Graham, 1938, 311). Given the customary silence about pipelines, one is grateful for so much information, while still regretting that they were not able to explore the entire aqueduct system both within and outside the settlement.

Flowing water from the pipelines brought fresh drinking water within easy reach of every household at Olynthos. The rest of the water supply for the settlement was available in the customary cisterns, although not all houses had them. Usually they were located in the courtyards of houses, although they could be placed in the pastas (veranda). Just as later at Delos, the cisterns were filled by pipes from the roofs; one such pipe was found. Cisterns were cut in the hardpan, lined with plaster, and the mouth was set into the cement floor of the courtyard. Each cistern could hold 6000 to 7000 gallons or 23,000–26,000 liters. One was double-chambered, a type known also from Athens and Morgantina. Those published range in depth from 4 to 6 meters, and are of the bottle-shaped variety, known at Morgantina from third century houses but here found in fourth century houses (Robinson and Graham, 1938, 204; cf. Robinson and Mylonas, 1946, 101).[2]

On South Hill there are an amazing array of pre-Persian War cisterns (before 479 B.C.), some 20 of them. They were roughly made, and filled with fifth century rubbish when discovered, having fifth century buildings erected over them (see plan in Robinson and Mylonas, 1946, 242). Some of this group had been waterproofed. I will grant the use of the water-proof ones as cisterns, but, in my opinion, the others are likely to have been storage granaries enabling the early citadel to withstand siege. Certainly today their haphazard relationship to the sixth century plan of South Hill is not only curious but also dangerous for the unwary tourist, since the cisterns are located in the middle of the main street and within the open agora area of the early city. South Hill was dug early (1928), when archaeological technique was in its awkward adolescence.[3]

Although we lack a chart of the incidence and dimensions of cisterns, the excavators have provided one about the dimensions of bathrooms, and the find-spots of bathtubs (Robinson and Graham, 1938, 204). Largest of the bathrooms was 3.2 by 2.4 meters, in house A ll c. Thirteen bathrooms opened from the kitchen, two from the courtyard, one possibly from a shop, and eight occupied corners of larger rooms. One house had two bathrooms (Robinson and Graham, 201). Much is made in Volume VIII (1938) of the location of the bathroom in the so-called flue, a two-story space next to the kitchen which served also to evacuate smoke and heat from the hearth to outdoors. Later accounts of the bathrooms at Olynthos downplay the concept of flue. Where the bathroom occupied a space next to the kitchen, it was convenient to heat bath water at the common hearth, and the warm air from cooking made winter bathing more comfortable. The typical bathroom was 2.25 by 1.5 meters, with plastered, painted walls and a cement, mosaic, or tile floor (Robinson and Graham, 1938, 204). Twenty-two bathrooms are listed, of which three definitely did not have built-in bathtubs. This does not, of course, exclude the possibility of tubs with metal stands, placed on the floor, and thus leaving no physical clues. Five of the tubs are described as well-preserved. None are today visible at the site. The one found in trench 7 (which had been set on the floor rather than fastened to it), is now at the Johns Hopkins University Museum (Robinson, 1930, 97 and fig. 248). Tubs are shown in Robinson and Graham (1938, pl. 53 and 54), they were usually 1 to 1.25 meters long by .70 to .75 meters wide, by .40 meters high. (p. 200) Several of the tubs are to be seen in the Old Museum at Thessalonike. One is noteworthy for the drainhole that was broken into its lowest point, and for the very low raised seat that elevated the bather above the collecting dirty water; the seat is not visible on the exterior, although most tubs from Hellenistic times do show their change in interior levels by corresponding changes in the exterior profile. This tub was 50 by 25.5 by 11 inches deep.

Other bathroom fittings were toilets, which were usually portable at Olynthos, as we know from the fact that only one (that looked exactly like our toilets, save for its rough terra-cotta finish) was found at the site—the rest vanished into probable reuse by later residents of the area (Fig. 17.7). Several vessels that look like urinals were found fixed in latrine walls, leading to the sewer in the street or alley (Robinson and Graham, 1938, 205, pl. 55).

When the houses of North Hill were built, no later than early fourth century B.C., careful provision for drainage was made in the narrow alleys that bisected each block of ten houses. Many alleys still retain their cobblestone paving, and in a few places the white stone slabs that covered the drains were found in situ. Sometimes the stable and latrine were one space, as in house 2, where they occupied a narrow corridor paved with cobblestones and utilizing a terra-cotta pipe as a drain (Robinson and Clement, 1938, 51–52). This pattern became the dominant one at Priene, where most houses date to the third and second centuries B.C.

Finally, water usage was facilitated by basins on pedestals, called *louters* by German archaeologists, *washbasins* in American English. These were made of terra-cotta or marble, and resembled our birdbaths, having a pedestal and a wide shallow basin. Although they could be found in the bathroom, they were most frequently placed in the court or kitchen. One house (IV 9) had four of them, in court, kitchen, pastas, and an inner room, while house A5, the home of a stonemason, had five of these basins that he had been working on (Robinson and Graham, 1938, 317).

From these physical remnants of the water supply system at Olynthos, we must agree with Demosthenes, who describes the Olynthians as having become suddenly rich, and displaying unusual magnificance (Demosthenes, *De Falsa Legatione*, 426; cf. Thucydides, I, 58; both cited in Robinson, 1930, 97). In many ways, their settlement seems like a reaction against the cluttered organic character of earlier cities such as Athens. Not for them the Athenian boast, "We wished to live richly rather than be rich."

POMPEII

When we turn to the Greco-Roman city of Pompeii (Fig. 13.2), we are faced with greater complexity in both the city itself and accounts of its

Figure 13.2. Plan showing all the known water system elements of Pompeii. (Compiled from maps published by Escherbach, Larsen, and Richardson.)

excavated features. Partly, I think, this is the result of the destruction of Pompeii being closer in time to us by 400 years, and partly the result of the life at Pompeii being more rich and complicated. Pompeii was located, not at the fringe of culture as in Olynthos, but right in the midst of the densest Greco-Roman area. Souvenirs from Pompeii fill our museums and discussions of Pompeii our bookshelves, since its rediscovery in the second half of the eighteenth century; whereas Olynthos was rediscovered only in the the 1920s and the material remains from it are much less rich and compelling. Since it is a thesis of this book that increasing sophistication of water management went hand in hand with the ability to construct larger and more complex settlements, these two cities have been chosen to demonstrate an earlier and a later stage in that process. Note that I believe that Greek society in many parts of the Mediterranean area shaded imperceptibly into Greco-Roman and thus into Roman, so I deem it reasonable to select Pompeii as the later example, a city typical enough of that history.

Pompeii is located on the Bay of Naples, south-southeast of Mt. Vesuvius. The earliest remains that have come to light here are Greek—a Doric temple at the south edge of the site, traces of a fortification wall buried in the later agger, some Attic black-figure sherds, and a set of bathing chambers with their supporting well and cistern. Probably these remains are from a Greek trading colony, possibly an outpost by which Poseidonia (Paestum) traded with the Etruscan city of Cumae to the north. The temple is the one in the Triangular Forum, set on a height next to the small palestra and the large Greek-style theater. The temple is archaic, though altered later; the theater, dating from the second century B.C. may well replace an earlier use of the slope for informal seating at performances. These structures occupy a part of the site closest to the River Sarno, which gave easy access to the hinterland. According to Strabo, the site was held by Oscans, then Tyrrhenians, and then Pelasgians, before the Samnites took it over in the late fifth century B.C. All of these tribes were hellenized through the same process of trade in goods and in cultural ideas that also hellenized Sicily and other parts of Magna Graecia.

Immediately to the west of the Triangular Forum lies the oldest residential and commercial district of the existing town, centered on a long rectangular Forum and bounded by a ring of streets (Vico dei Soprastanti, Via degli Augustali, Vicolo del Lupanare, and Via dei Teatri) which may mark the place of a very early fortification wall. Houses and shops and public buildings occupy blocks that are relatively small and square, contrasting with the outlying quarters of the city where the blocks are long and narrow.

Sources of water for Pompeii were wells, cisterns and other reservoirs, and a long-distance water supply line. There were no springs within the city (Richardson, 1988, 51), and yet the Villa of the Mysteries, outside the Herculaneum Gate, had neither cistern nor connections to the aqueduct system (Robinson, 1988, 176), so this house must have depended on a nearby extra-mural spring.

Wells within Pompeii tapped the water table as deep as 38.25 meters below the surface (Maiuri, 1931, 546–57). Surviving wells include the very early and large one immediately south of the Doric Temple, dating probably from the sixth century, since the temple is from 555 to 500 B.C. However, the tholos (circular building) over this well is later—third or second century. The water table here was found at 20 meters (Eschebach, 1977, 3).

The city was also served by a long-distance supply line from the hills to the east and northeast, subject to the usual repair and rebuilding of any line located in earthquake and volcano country, and in service for several centuries. A good map of the aqueducts of the area from the Appenines to the coast, and from Pompeii to Naples can be found in H. Escheback (1977, 3). Two are identified in the legend but three are shown; the longest goes to Naples, and a branch of this one may have supplied Pompeii in Samnite times, no later than the second century B.C. and possibly as early as the fifth century (Murano, 1894, 128). Mau (1982) thought the Pompeii aqueduct was built between the two Punic Wars (235f), and the line he describes seems to be the one on Eschebach's map running from Nola to Pompeii but not recognized in the legend. More likely, as Eschebach's map (first figure, 1977, 3) shows, the sources of the Sarno River, which lie near the Serino aqueduct, were tapped to supply Pompeii directly. A profile of the whole 110 kilometers of the Serino Aqueduct is shown as Abb. 7 of Esherbach (1977).

Eschebach's and Larsen's (1983) separate studies of the physical fabric of the water towers of Pompeii have made clear that the *castellum aquae* (main water distribution tower at the highest point in the town), water towers, and lead pipe distribution system must be dated to the time of Augustus. In many places in the town, pipes of lead are evident on the exterior of houses, attached to the wall with iron clamps. But this does not prove that the erection of a long-distance water supply line for the town waited until so late in its history. (Now that Fahlbusch has taught us to look for the kinds of line the Greeks knew how to build, someone may wish to restudy the evidence and look for new evidence for water management before the town became a Roman colony.) Already, Eschebach has found evidence of Greek-period water management at the later Stabian Baths, deeply buried under what he thinks is the material from a volcanic eruption of the mid-Hellenistic era.

The routes of the later aqueduct (Augustan with Claudian repairs) within Pompeii are shown on another H. Eschebach map [(1979, 48, Abb. 14 "Plan der Wasserfuhrenden offentlichen Gebaude (Strang II der Wasserleitung) mit moglich Zuleitung")], of interest to us because these lines and their corresponding drainage channels take full advantage of the terrain, as any earlier Greek-period lines would also have had to do. The high line from the reservoir at Porta Vesuvio (through which flowed 6500 cubic meters per day) supplied the Central Bath, Stabian Bath, Isis Temple, Samnite Palestra, both theaters, the Gladiators' House, the Triangular Forum, and the Sarno Bath at the lower gate. The west branch supplied the Forum Bath (a high reservoir here had a capacity of 72 cubic meters), the Arch of Caligula and Arch of Germanicus at the Forum (both were equipped with fountains and reservoirs), and the marketplace. The east branch along Via Dell'Abbondanza served this residential quarter, running to the house of Julia Felix, the Grand Palestra, and the Amphitheater. Capacity of the large open-air tank at the Grand Palestra was 1340 cubic meters.

The experts differ in how many people they think lived at Pompeii and in how much water they (a) would have needed or (b) were supplied with. Eschebach estimated that the population may have been as little as only 8000, utilizing 800 liters per day each for a total of 6.4 million liters per day (the 6500 cubic meters mentioned above)—in spite of the fact that people at Rome are thought to have had 600 liters per day each (H. Eschbach, 1977, 22). Murano estimated 12,000 people using 3 million liters per day (quoted in n.10 of L. Eschebach, 1987) while Stillwell, MacDonald, and McAllister (1976, 724–26) set 20,000 as the maximum population. At any rate, all the scholars seem to understand that the residents utilized both well, cistern, and aqueduct water, in a system that was "well thought out, efficient, copious, even wasteful" (L. Eschebach, 1987, 205). Some of this redundancy was due to the usual precautions against drought and war, but at Pompeii an additional stimulus was that the well-water was often bitter or sulfurous from the volcano, and hence not fit for drinking (H. Eschebach, 1977, 28). Maiuri (1931, 556) had the water of the well near Porta Vesuvio analyzed by S.E. Del Blasi (director of civil engineering at the Unversity of Naples), who reported:

> L'acqua del pozzo presso Porta Vesuvio, per l'esiguo numero di germi apparententi ad una medesima specie volgare; per l'assenza di germi anaerobi del *B. coli* e di alteri forme batteriche di significato indiziario; per l'assenza di qualunque elemento organizzato, microscopicamente accertabile; per i risultati delle indagini chimiche, presenta i requisiti di un'acqua *chimicamente e microbioligicamente pura.* Tuttavia non solo per il residuo fisso (a 110 degrees C.: gr. 0.975 per litro) che è circa il limite massimo consentito per le comuni acque da bere, ma anche per l'eccessiva durezza totale (gradi francesi 56,4), l'acqua esaminata non può essere dichiarata potabile ai fini di un continuato consumo: sebbene in vista del basso grado di durezza permanente (gradi francesi 5,2), possa essere temporaneamente bevuta senza danno, quando difetti altra acqua meno ricca di sali. In ogni modo, l'acqua può essere adoperata a qualunque altro uso, senza inconvenienti igienico-sanitari.

> [The water in the well near Porta Vesuvio, because of the small number of germs belonging to the same common species; because of the absence

of anaerobic B. coli and of other bacteria of noted significance; because of the absence of any elements traceable by microscope; and because of the results of chemical analysis, the water is chemically and microbiologically pure. Its fixed residue (at 100 degrees C. = 0.975 gr. per liter) is within the higher limits set by common law for drinking water, but because of its excessive total hardness (French measure 56.4), the water examined cannot be declared potable for continuous or permanent consumption. However, in view of the low grade of permanent hardness (French measure 5.2) it can be drunk temporarily without danger, given the lack of other waters less rich in salts. In any case, the waters can be used for many uses, without any health risk.]

Maiuri comments on this report and the water in question:

Dall'analisi adunque risulterebbe che l'acqua che i pompeiani erano riusciti a captare a costo di cosi grave lavoro, nelle piu ascose porfondita del sottosuolo della città, non può ascriversi, per la sua eccessiva ricchezza di sali, fra le acque che l'igiene moderna prescrive di uso potabile continuativo e permanente. Nè tale sua qualità poteva sfuggire agli antichi abitanti della città, perchè a parte il caratteristico sapore e gusto dell'acqua leggermente acidula, la sua durezza era chiaramente rivelata dalle spesse incrostazioni che se osservano lungo le pareti dei pozzi dell'"Terme Stabiane" (No. 5) e della "Casa della Regina d'Inghilterra" (No. 6), dove per il funzionamento degli apparecchi di sollevamento a ruota, l'acqua scorrendo dalle secchie lungo le pareti, ha formato un cosi spesso strato d'incrostazione da nascondere el tutto le strutture murarie. Ma non v'era per i pompeiani, prima dela canalizzazione della acque da piu lontane sorgenti, altor mezzo per assicurare l'alimentazione idrica della città con sorgive permanenti captate nel suolo stesso della città; e, d'altro canto, agli inconvenienti sanitari che potevano esser prodotti da un'acqua troppo dura di sali, si rimediava con l'uso pormiscuo delle acque pluviale raccolte dal tetto compluviato degli atri e dei peristili nelle capaci cisterne di cui era provvista ogni abitzione ed edificio pubblico.

[From the analysis, therefore, it seems that the water that the Pompeians succeeded in obtaining with such difficult work, from the deepest subsoils of the city, cannot be considered, because of excessive salts, as potable for continuous and permanent use. But even these ancients were aware of its true nature, partly because of its lightly acidic taste and partly because of the encrustations along the walls of the Stabian Bath and the House of the Queen of England [sic], where, because of the pumping action, water gushes out from openings along the walls; the encrustation is so great that it has entirely covered the original wall. But the Pompeians before channeling these far-away sources, had other means like natural springs. Also, to offset the dangers to health from such hard water, they collected rain water from the roofs into cisterns, and almost every house and public building was provided with this set-up.[4]

Cistern water was thus more palatable than water from wells, but aqueduct water the best tasting of all.

A useful study of the water towers that distributed the aqueduct water within Pompeii is that of J. D. Larsen (1983, 411–67). He understands well that the towers are a series of linked siphons, which the Greeks had been managing with increasing sophistication since the fifth century. There is some evidence for pressure pipes of different materials as part of this aqueduct system. (We will return to this later when we discuss pipes.) Larsen published a map (fig. 2) with the locations of the water towers and the *castellum aquae* or *castellum publicum,* but he omitted the fountains of the two arches at the Forum. Since most of this distribution system as it has been recovered dates from Roman times, we will turn now to the two more ancient contributors, well and cisterns.

Already in 1931, Maiuri knew about eleven wells at Pompeii, one at the Porta Vesivius, two on the V. Consolare on the front of block I of Region VI, one in a tavern on the Via del Foro, three in baths [the Stabian Bath, Forum Bath, and the House of the Queen of England (block 14 no. 6 of region 7) (but not listed by this name in later literature)], plus four in private houses. Richardson (1988), summing up the research of fifty years, reports that there are as many wells as public fountains, which means somewhere between forty and fifty. The earliest two recovered are in the Triangular Forum, and in the Stabian Bath. Wells are concentrated in the area around the main Forum and along the main streets. Four wells in the Forum went dry in the first century and were filled in— a problem that may have speeded construction of the Augustan Aqueduct. In houses, wells are usually placed just off the entrance passageway, so that water could be shared with a neighbor without disturbing the household (Richardson, 1988, 53).

Both public and private buildings had elaborate arrangements for capturing rainwater and storing it in cisterns. If a building had a peaked roof, water was captured in gutters along the eaves line, or led by downspouts from the point where two sets of eaves came together above the party wall. The downspout pipes of terra-cotta were often set into the wall. The pipes emptied into a cistern under the building, and if the flow from two roofs were mingled, one would find that the cistern was held in common, and had one access shaft set in the thickness of the party wall. In houses with courtyards or atria, the roofs sloped inward and drainage from them collected at the the edge of the eave and funnelled by means of a spout at each corner so that the water shot out and fell into the *impluvium* (a flat basin at the center of an atrium) below. From the impluvium, the water first filled the cistern and then overflowed into a channel that led outside to the street. A *puteal* (cistern head) set at the edge of the impluvium made it easy to dip up water as needed. There is some question as to the date of the oldest surviving impluvium house at Pompeii, but it may have been either the House of the Surgeon of the fourth to third century (Robertson, 1964, 303), or the House of the Faun of the third century (Richardson, 1988, 53). The venerable pattern of the Greek courtyard house with cistern below the main courtyard was thus incorporated into the Roman atrium house (Fig. 13.3). "The value of portico roofs as rain collectors seems to have been an important factor in the spread of peristyles in Pompeii in the second century" (Richardson, 1988, 394 n. 8).

The early garden cistern of the House of Sallust was typical of the Samnite era. Ancient examples for a public building are the cisterns of the Temple of Apollo next to the main Forum, accessed by two drawshafts in the open area in front of the third intercolumniation from each end of the south portico. In the north portico of the same precinct what seems to be a different cistern is accessed by a large lava manhole in the third intercolumniation from the west.

In public buildings of the Roman era, the management of water meant saving roof drainage via gutters, settling basins, channels leading to cis-

Figure 13.3. Courtyard at Pompeii with opening to cistern (wellhead is gone) and behind it a washbasin at the edge of the impluvium. The washbasin is approximately .6 m. tall. Compare with the cistern system of Fig. 16.16.

terns under the portico floors, and recovering it through drawshafts (puteals) or lids usually placed in the line of the colonnade for minimal obstruction. Unlike the flask-shaped cisterns that we have noted in Greek private houses, these Pompeiian examples tend to be rectangular and roofed with either flat paving stones or vaults. In this they resemble the cisterns of Delos, which date mainly from the second century B.C. Stored nearer the surface, this water would have been warmer and more likely to fill subpotable uses such as cleaning, bathing, watering plants and animals, while drinking needs were filled at Pompeii by the fountains of the aqueduct system.

Earliest of the roofed cisterns at Pompeii was the one cut into the clay under what would become the Stabian Bath, at the level of the foot basins of the earliest period. H. Eschebach dates it ca. 425 (Samnite period). It measured 8.5 by 1.7 by 1.9 meters deep, and was probably made to supplement the waters of the deep well (13 meters) in the same corner of the bath. Since volcanic waters are often hot and/or strongly flavored, it is tempting to think that, in its first version at least, the Stabian Bath was a health spa utilizing these waters for special cures. Additional cisterns of this bath were found to the northeast of its palestra and to the east of the women's dressing room. Other public reservoir-cisterns were those under public buildings in the main Forum, the Triangular Forum, the Basilica, the Venus Temple, the peristyle of the Large Theater, the House of the Gladiators (H. Eschebach, 1977, 3,6), the west side of the palestra of the Central Bath (Richardson, 1988, 286), and just south of the Temple of Zeus Meilchios.

Since the reservoir northwest of the Large Theater supplied the fountains of the scaena frons (Richardson, 1988, 218), it is appropriate to turn now to the question of fountains at Pompeii. Between forty and fifty are thought to have served the city, grouped in threes or fours depending upon one of the water towers, so that no one had to walk more than two or three blocks for drinking water. Forty are known with certainty, and the other ten are likely to have served the as-yet-unexcavated northeast section of the city. Thirty-two fountains were placed at street corners, out of the traffic, six along Via Consolare and its extension Via di Nola, six along Via di Stabia, seven along Via Dell'Abbondanza, and two in unpaved back streets of the northwest and northeast quarters. Another four in the main Forum were out of order at the time of the volcanic eruption (presumably from an earlier earthquake). Supplementing the well in the Triangular Forum described earlier, there was a fountain at the north end of the precinct, in the form of a very large shallow basin of large-crystal Greek marble, filled by a small jet from a pipe. It is tempting to think that this basin is the "missing" washbasin from the fifth century palestra across the street, moved to the Triangular Forum when the palestra no longer functioned as such and when the forum was rebuilt as a public park during the Augustan period. Another fountain basin and pedestal, somewhat smaller, were found in the 1797 excavation of the north portico of the palestra, just west of the major entranceway, presumably fed from the pipe found embedded in a column of the portico. This later basin fountain has an Oscan inscription that dates it to the third or second century. Other fountains used the piers of arches instead of a column of a portico as their structure. It was customary to fit triumphal arches with holding tanks and fountains, as we see here in both the Arch of Germanicus and the Arch of Caligula at the main Forum. As for reservoirs, only the fountain between towers 1 and 2 along the Via di Stabia had a visible reservoir nearby; the others seem to have depended on the constant flow of aqueduct waters. We have seen that neighborhood fountains were a feature of Hellenistic cities, but until Pompeii we have not seen a city where the fountains were distributed so evenly and conveniently.

In addition to public fountains, there were many fountains in private houses, the ultimate collection being possibly the House of the Vettii where there are twelve fountains around the edges of the peristyle garden, plus two set in the midst of the garden. Besides their ornamental and psychological functions, fountains in the home fed garden pools and fish ponds, and runoff from them supplied cooking water, bath water, and latrine flushing. Unfortunately, we have less data about private water arrangements than we would like because many private houses were poorly excavated during 1940–60, and were not published (H. Eschebach, 1977, 17).

Terra-cotta and lead were the usual materials for pipes at Pompeii but some villas had pipes and taps and other fittings of bronze (Material on pipes is from Larsen, 1983, 53–59; Richardson, 1988, 61–63, 109; L. Eschebach, 1987, 202–205; H. Eschebach, 1979, 38, 49; H. Eschebach, 1977, 16–20. esp. n.73 which refers to a deposit of pipes and other water system elements in the women's section of the Forum Baths).

Metal water heaters are also known from private houses such as the House of Loreius Tibertinus, which had its own bath, ornamental fountain, and extensive garden with a complex of fountains. Most houses had taps, especially middle class houses, where the taps controlled the water for nymphaea, fountain niches and cascades, fountains with jets of water, baths, washbasins, fishponds, and reservoirs. Some examples are the House of the Vettii (the entrance and atrium of the early house on the site survive in the late house now visible here, according to a letter from W. E. Jashemski) with taps in kitchen and peristyle, and the House of the Silver Wedding, with an elaborate atrium fountain and in the latrine a pipe with a nozzle. These domestic fountains were often tiny jets or streams, even in houses with elaborate displays such as the House of Julia Felix, where clever manipulation of reservoir ponds and gravity meant that little additional piping was necessary to distribute the water purchased from the aqueduct. Such lavish use of water implies a dependable supply (Jashemski, 1979, 327). It also implies a clever use of resources. Jashemski describes two gardens that used gravity flow to direct street drainage into the highest part, slowing down the flow with steps and shallow channels, and at the low point piercing the wall so that the water continued to flow into the next garden. After filling jars set in the ground and flowing through channels made of roof tiles, with the overflow sheeting across the ground surface as it had in the first area, the water again pierced the lowest wall and entered the third garden area where a double cistern "typical of the old Samnite houses" received the water. These sets of channels and tanks conserved the water of downpours, making ingenious use of street waters and topography (Jashemski, 1974, 249–50).

Pompeii was watered, then, by a triple system: wells and cisterns tapping groundwater or saving rainwater; gutters and channels directing rain water where it could be best used; and lead pipes carrying water from the water towers to fountains and to individual buildings both public and private. The water towers, in turn, were fed by the aqueduct which tapped distant springs. The standardization of pipe sizes (approximately 1 inch, 2 inch, 3 inch) suggests that water was purchased by pipe size, the size regulating the flow (Larsen, 1983, 53; see G. Kuhne's translation and commentary on Frontinus, 1983, 81–128, with a lengthy discussion of standard pipe sizes). In many houses the lead pipes are exposed, running in the gutters below the eaves of the peristyle, or climbing the walls with the help of heavy iron staples; such pipes may also be seen on the exterior walls of houses, and laid along the seam between house wall and sidewalk.

Since, as we have seen, storm runoff was harnessed to water gardens within the city, I consider it unlikely that all such waters from the city were poured into the Sarno River with no attempt to use them for irrigation. Both surface drainage in gutters and underground sewers (channels or large pipes) were engineered to maintain health and beauty within the town. The two levels of drainage were integrated. A good example is the overflow of the Fountain of Mercury at the northeast corner of block VI viii, which cleaned the street gutters as it ran south down the street of the same name to the Arch of Caligula. There it turned east along the Via della Fortuna, then south along the Strada Stabiana to the Tetrapylon of Holconii at the southwest corner of VII i. At that point the drainage went underground to a drain that joined the great sewer running south from the Stabian Bath. This sewer, having collected waste water from the bath and surface drainage from the center of the city, emptied out through a great box drain in the west flank of the Porta di Stabia. Meanwhile, surface drainage from west of the Forum was emptied out near Porta Marina to a canal that ran along the west side of the city. Drainage of the Forum itself was "the most sophisticated hydrological engineering of Pompeii" (Maiuri, 1931, 63–70, as quoted in Richardson, 1988, 62). All around the plaza, "mouths" (arcs of circles) were cut in the base of the lowest step. Through these mouths the waters drained into two large channels along the east and west sides and across the south—in other words, at the downhill ends of the drainage. The so-called well in the southeast corner of the Basilica is likely to have been an access shaft to this system. In a recent article, G.C.M. Jansen (1991) refers to "wells" at Herculaneum as serving to direct rainwater into the groundwater, similar to the shaft at Priene (already discussed). The large holding tanks found at each extremity of the southern end of the Forum were fed by the channels. Since the south end of the Forum is closest to a major slope, at this point the sewers under Via della Marina (west) and Via della Scuolo (south) drained downwards. The one along the Via della Marina turned south between the Basilica and the Temple of Venus rather than running directly under the Marina Gate as we would expect—parallel, in other words, to the branch from the southeast corner of the Forum. The cant of the streets outside the Forum and also the height of the stepping stones in the street were calibrated to allow for the behavior of water after heavy rain. No stepping stones have been found in the northeast sector, but many were found in the central area near the Forum (Richardson, 1988, 60).

In the eastern part of the city, surface drainage emptied out via the Porta di Nola and the Porta di Sarno. Interestingly enough, the drainage of Region IX went to Porta di Nola even though the ground in that region sloped toward the Porta di Sarno, and the drainage of Region II east of Via di Norcera all went to Porta de Sarno, although Via di Nocera itself led to a southern gate of the same name. Thus the engineers had made deliberate decisions about how much drainage could be accommodated at each gate, and built gutters, channels, and sewers accordingly. At the Porta di Nola, I saw what I take to be a collection chamber for the impounding of such drainage.

A sewer network of many branches has been found in the excavated portion of Pompeii, and may be inferred for the rest. It was Mygind who first published an article about the sewers of Pompeii (1977, 77–157). Although the sewers receive surface drainage from street gutters "at significant points" they do not attempt to duplicate the pattern of that surface net, rather being located under the alleys and side streets. Richardson (1988, 61) thinks this was to avoid the possibility of heavily loaded wagons crushing the vaulted roofs of the sewer channels. A more compelling reason might be that necessary repairs to and cleaning of the sewers would not interfere with street traffic if the sewers were placed in the alleys. We have seen at Athens, Olynthos, and Akragas of the Hellenistic period that Greek cities commonly had their sewers running in the alleys. The sewers drained the private houses and the side streets, as well as the public buildings and spaces, and the major streets of the town. The sophisticated drainage pattern here at Pompeii was a logical development from the network that we saw at Priene which does duplicate the surface pattern. Since I have postulated that drainage was a community necessity as soon as the settlement reached even minor density, it is satisfying to read that H. Eschebach (1979, 39) thinks the sewer along the Via Dell' Abbondanza is Samnite work, and that the ditch along the agger (earthern rampart), running along the west side of the Stabian Bath (as shown in his plan of the earliest period of that structure), was likely used as a sewer.

The excavators have published relatively few free-standing latrines in Pompeii, although of course each of the baths was so equipped. There was a large public latrine at the northwest corner of the Forum, possibly two small ones at the south, and an equally large one at the Grand Palestra. Houses had their own latrines, such at the one at the Villa of the Mysteries placed on a jutting corner half-way along one side, accessible from the exterior but also from the nearby kitchen and bath suite (Richardson, 1988, 172–73, 172). Many of these domestic latrines did not drain into the sewers but rather into cesspools, as they did also at classical Athens. Since the Romans were generally lavish with running water, this decision to use cesspools was not, I think, based on water shortage, but rather on thrifty attitudes about reuse of cesspool contents for fertilizer.

Although there is plenty of published material on the public baths of Pompeii, we will not discuss it here since most of what survives is from the latest period. Let us only mention again the fifth century elements found under the Stabian Baths. Unfortunately a comparative study of the bath suites found in private houses has never been done. Houses of the middle and upper classes made architectural provision for excreting and bathing at home, while members of all classes of society used the public baths and latrines. The architectural remnants of bathrooms but not latrines are more elaborate than many of their Greek predecessors, occupying several rooms, yet we must remember that such suites are not unknown elsewhere, such as that in the third century House of the Official at Morgantina. One did not need to live at the center of Greco-Roman life to benefit from the current technologies of water management.

CONCLUSION

The water supply, usage, and drainage system at Pompeii comes down to us as markedly more complex than that at Olynthos. Not just two rudimentary baths at the gates, but three large elaborate baths at the edges of the Forum district plus the Suburban Bath just outside the Porta Marina, plus the Republican Baths (out of commission at the time of the final destruction), and the Sarno Baths at a lower level. Not just one or two fountain houses supplied by an underground aqueduct, but a series of nearly fifty fountains supplied by visible water towers connected in a series of siphons to a larger tower that received the water of an aqueduct and divided it to supply the different districts of the town—a larger and more subtly engineered system than the surface drainage and sewer system. Building on the pioneer work of their Greek-influenced predecessors, the Roman residents of Pompeii had a very high hydraulic standard of living. Roman water management technology and political processes enabled them to build cities of over a million population, perhaps ten times the size of Athens at its antique maximum, but also enabled them to supply small towns like Pompeii with the normal accoutrements of water usage for a high standard of living.

NOTES

1. For references to Olynthus as a colony of Athens see A.J. Graham, *Colony and Mother-city in Ancient Greece.* Manchester University Press, 1964; Chicago: Ares Publications, 1983; or J.M. Carter, "Athens, Euobea and Olynthus," *Historia* 20 (1971) 418–29.

2. Compare this with the definitive work on cisterns at Pergamon by Werner Brinker, a dissertation under the direction of G. Garbrecht, Braunschweig, 1990. Unfortunately, this was not available to me when this book was being written.

3. This according to Nicholas Cahill, whose Berkeley Ph.D. dissertation reexamines the details of the city plan with reference to how the settlement worked. I am grateful to him for a long discussion of the nuances of the Olynthos plan.

4. Translation of the Italian provided by Fred Fracccioni.

14

Morgantina's Agora—
Design and Drains

The agora fulfilled a complex role in the life of Greek cities. In Greek agoras, nearly the whole range of public activities was accommodated: governmental, religious, commercial, military, and social. The market function of the agora was essential to the survival of the city, with the availabilty of everything from imported grain to locally grown lettuce. Services, from haircutting to the teaching of Stoic philosophy, were available. Government offices and officers were readily at hand. Temples, shrines, and monuments to heroes iterated religious, cultural, and moral values from every corner.

The agora at Athens is probably the most thoroughly studied of the early ones. In shape it is an irregular quadrilateral, eventually monumentalized with stoas and other public buildings along all four sides. The buildings were placed at the edges of the large open space which therefore was available for many activities. Cisterns and wells of the pre- and postclassical periods were scattered over the surface. Only one well is known, however, from the classical period, that in the shrine in the northwest corner (*Athenian Agora Guide,3*) suggesting that the sixth century aqueduct was supplying enough water for the population during the fifth and early fourth centuries. Fountains marked important points of entry, and drains led the excess water northwestward toward the city gates (Figs. 16.15, 17.11). As the agora changed over time, being filled in with additional structures, the sources of water and the drains were continually adapted to the new demands.

The organic form at Athens contrasts with the more regular but even earlier surviving form—eighth or seventh century B.C.—at Posidonia (Paestum), where a broad strip of public space for temples and agora was set aside at the center of the town (Fig. 5.1B). On this flat site, two sacred precincts flanked the agora (later Forum). The long and varied history of the site precludes our easy understanding of the design of the Greek agora here. Regularity at Posidonia is a function of its status as a colonial city—a city that was planned and laid out all at one time. Careful attention was given to the provision and use of water. An imposing gymnasium of Greek times, which included a pool large enough for swimming, was later remodeled to meet Roman tastes. The inclusion of such a pool strongly indicates that the site was abundantly supplied with water. Numerous fountains also testify to this fact, as do the cisterns and wells in the houses. Gutters, drains, and a great drain in the public areas complete the necessary provision of water system elements.

A later agora pattern, and one more fully worked out architecturally, is seen at Ionian Priene, of the third century (Fig. 14.1). Situated at the center of the main terrace of the city, this agora was rectangular in form, its upper edge parallel to the main street of the town. Above the street, and at a slightly higher level, ran a long stoa. Below the street was the main open space of the town, framed by additional stoas on the east, south, and west sides of the space. The streets outside the agora wall were supplied with stone drains, and a major outfall—still visible on the face of the slope down to the stadium below—was located at the end of the eastern side street.

Some agora uses required buildings, some open spaces. For instance, assembling the citizens, as well as market activities, required that open space be permanently maintained at the center of the city. This traditional connection between open space and citizenship may be precisely the reason why the Romans filled the Athenian agora with miscellaneous buildings, and provided an alternate market area (the Roman agora) to emphasize that the Athenians were no longer an independent people.

Another use of the open space was the early open air theater with removable bleachers. Eventually this function received a structure of its own. Temples to civic gods and shrines to civic heroes accumulated over time at the edges of the agora space. The housing of governmental records and meetings of councils and other governmental committees required other buildings such as the *bouleterion*, frequently added adjacent to the agora, as at Priene and Miletus. The most typical agora building was the stoa, equipped with small fountains and latrines for public use, and therefore needing drains attached to the public sewers. In the stoas were located small stores for buying and selling small precious items that needed to be locked up at night, with small offices behind or above them, and with a portico that provided a covered but open area for walking.

The agora belonged to the city as a whole, though residential lots were private property. For maximum benefit to all the residents, it was located at the center of the settlement, this location resulting either from the city growing up naturally around its focus, as at Athens, or from deliberate planning as at Miletus. The agora was delimited by boundary stones, as we know from Athenian examples. As urban heart, the agora flourished in proportion as it provided the most necessary aspects of life, in particular, water. The Morgantina agora, for instance, was equipped with no fewer than six fountains (see Chapter 20).

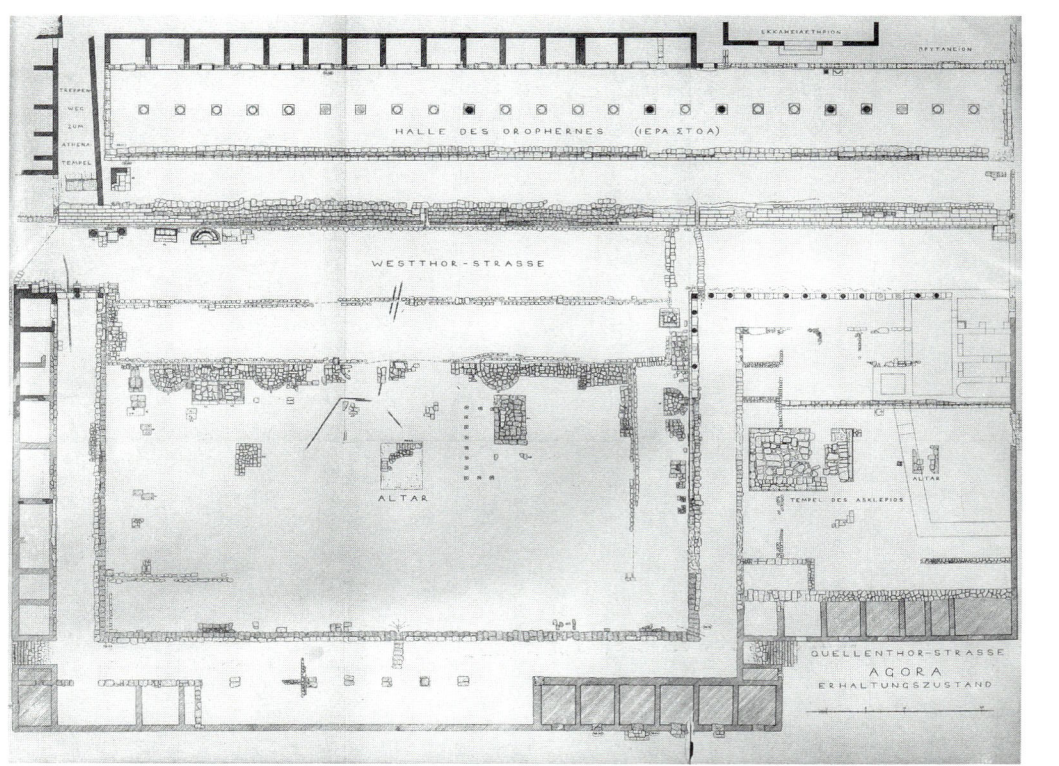

Figure 14.1. Agora of the Ionian type at Priene, with regular porticoes bordering three sides, and a fourth across the main street. A fountain stands at the angle formed by the left end of that last stoa and the step street leading up to the Athena Temple on the next higher terrace. Three pipelines are shown entering the Agora from the top of the plan and several others lie above and to the left of the large altar in the middle of the Agora. The white slabs that cover drain channels are shown to the left and bottom of the wall framing the open space of the Agora; similar drains enter the agora at upper right and can be followed most of the way to the lower edge. At lower right, "Quellenthor Strasse"(Springgate Street) leads off (via a step street) to the spring outside the eastern gate. As published by Reimer Verlag, Berlin, in Wiegand et al, *Priene*, and reprinted by permission of the German Archaeological Institute, Istanbul.

The provision of fresh water and the drainage of waste water are taken for granted nowadays. In the ancient world, hydraulic engineering played a major role in urban design and politics. In Athens during the sixth century B.C., the Peisistratid tyrants built an underground waterline that won them lasting popularity. The fountainhouse at Megara (seventh century) and tunnel at Samos (sixth or fifth century) exhibit the same motivation: to win the favor of the people by supplying a basic necessity as one of the benefits of urban living.

As Fahlbusch has shown in *Vergleich antiker griechischer und romischer Wasserversorgungsanlagen* (1982), the Greeks gradually learned to control both water supply and drainage. When the settlement site was initially selected, it undoubtedly had a spring or other water source that was sufficient for not only the first people but also for the increased population as the settlement became a town. At that point the spring was usually dignified with a fountain house whose nymph guarded the water from casual pollution. As the town grew, one spring or fountainhouse was no longer enough. Sometime in the seventh century B.C., the Greeks were building long-distance water supply lines and complementing them with drainage channels. By means of this technology, the town could grow to quite a large city with many fountains. Attention to both fountains and drains characterizes the agoras of all sizes and periods, from provincial Morgantina to Athens and the imperial Fora of Rome.

At Morgantina, attention to drainage is evident from the earliest version of the agora in the fifth century, and continued through the construction of the Great Steps in the third century (Fig. 14.2). Indeed, modern excavators have found it necessary to clear out the old drains for current use, in order to complete their digging and make the site attractive for tourism.

The increasing mastery of hydraulic technology during the sixth to second centuries B.C. made possible larger cities, with larger or multiple agoras. Athens is a good example, for the earliest location of the agora was either immediately northwest of the Acropolis, conveniently near to Klepsydra Spring (older theory) or to the east of the Acropolis (newer theory suggested by the Aglaurion inscription, *Athenian agora*, 1990, 210). In the seventh century the technology of water supply was sufficiently developed to allow the agora to be moved to a larger site farther northwest (its present location), supplied by pipelines from Klepsydra. In the sixth century increased population and increased industrial demand made necessary the importing of more water from eastern hills, via the Peisistratid Aqueduct.

Sophisticated observation and analysis of geological potential for water supply enabled the Armenians, then the Persians and Greeks of the archaic period, to tap and use natural flow in karst terrane, as we have seen at Corinth. By the fifth century B.C., water from a network of tunnels was impounded in a series of reservoirs that supplied the Peirene Foun-

Figure 14.2. Plan of the Morgantina Agora. Key to the plan: *Stoas* framing the upper open space are *x*(West), *v*(Doric), *w*(Northwest), *y*(North), *q*(East). Southwest of *v*, at a higher level on West Hill, is the large *cave-spring* of Fig. 17.2. The *Bouleterion* is at *u*. The public space of the Agora is divided by the *Great Steps* at *o*, with the higher level being to the north. *Grannaries* bracketing the lower open space are at *g* and *d*. *Fountains* are at *p* (Northeast—but the cave-spring behind it (Fig. 17.1) is not shown), *h*(Southwest), *r*(at south end of East Stoa), one in the corner of the Macellum (*z*, shown as a small rectangle above the circular wall), an unlabled one at the eastern side of the theater shown on the

194

tain, Sacred Spring, and Cyclopean fountain—all located in the Corinthian agora. To become a very large city, it was essential to be located on terrain with multiple sources of water. An example of a city with multiple agoras is Akragas (modern Agrigento) in Sicily, which had not only a lower agora located between the famous ridge of temples and the artificial lake, but also seems likely to have had at much higher elevation an upper agora on or near the present city plaza, where even today at one corner a major spring erupts so strongly as to require the main road to be rebuilt every few years (see chapter 15).

Western Greek cities of the sixth and fifth centuries B.C. frequently situated the agora on a lower flat area between two flat hills where, according to Metraux (1978), houses were built. Morgantina is a rare example of a Western Greek agora that was not rebuilt later as a Roman Forum, since the site was abandoned at about the turn of the era. The agora at Morgantina, an important feature from the mid-fifth century B.C., had a road along the north side, under which stone drains carried the runoff from the hill to the north. There were springs at the northwest and northeast corners from which deep drains in a Y-pattern converged on the South Gate which led to the road down to the valley (Fig. 14.3).

In the third century the spring at the northeast was monumentalized with a fountain, and stoas were built along the north, west, and east sides. To accommodate the slope from north to south and to provide increased level area for the customary agora activities, the great steps were built about half way from north to south, roughly parallel to those sides of the public space. The steps form an irregular semihexagon, and are echoed by a second but smaller flight over to the east, laid out in a reverse semihexagon leading up to the stoa and *prytaneum* (community center). All the monumental structures and the great steps are made of the same buff-colored limestone found on the site.

Both sets of steps should be seen as the locus of informal interactions such as the exchange of political or business information, passing the

retaining wall, as a small rectangle; and a small street fountain (where the lion spout and the double pipes of Fig. 16.4 were found) below the Bouleterion, shown as a small rectangle to the right of and below the left-hand *A*. Shops are shown at *m* and *f*. A kiln was discovered at *b*, near the South Gate. Older kilns of the 6th and 5th century lay under towers *j* and *l* of the rampart. *C* is an outwork of the rampart, and *e* is the excavated inner corner of the *South Gate*, where drainage slits allowed rainwaters to exit the built-up area. On the hill to the right, *t* is the *House of the Silver Thread*, possibly fifth century; the *House of the Doric Capital* lies just below *B* and the *House of Ganymede* just below *E2*. *A, B, W1*, and *E2* are streets. The major *drains* of the Agora (not shown) formed a Y, with one arm from the northwest corner, piercing the *Great Steps* at their left corner, and joining the right arm that ran along the *East Stoa*; together they emptied out under the *South Gate*. Published by Malcolm Bell (1988): 315 and reprinted by permission.

Figure 14.3. Large drains at two levels, piercing the Great Steps in the Agora, Morgantina. The higher one to the right seems to have become necessary after the lower part of the steps had silted up. The larger opening is nearly a meter wide.

time of day with friends, negotiating a marriage, or discussing the threat of war. During the fifth, fourth, and early third centuries, these steps served for convocations of the citizens, with these functions moving to the theater when it was built in the third century. Note that the theater here occupies the southern half of the western side of the agora, convenient to all the business of the town, and directly adjacent to the western end of the great steps.

What was the source of the concept of these great steps? Some very early theaters are known to have the two- or three-sided arc configuration that is the formal pattern here (Bieber, 1961, figs. 228, 229, 231). Theaters, however, were not located intersecting the flow of space and activities in the agora. Although monumental stairways are known in Hellenistic *religious* precincts, such as the citadel at Lindos and the Asklepion at Cos, they are not known in the central agoras of either the classical or the Hellenistic eras. Whence arose this idea for the agora at Morgantina?

Control of drainage and erosion seems to have been the major impetus for the design and construction of the great steps at Morgantina. The large drain from the northwest pierces the steps at their left corner, running southward. To the north of the steps, the ground was leveled off for general use. To the south, within a very few years the process of erosion and deposit of silt had covered the bottom few steps, which therefore show little wear. Without the great steps, however, the valley between West Hill and East Hill would have deepened and widened even more than it has, as may be seen outside South Gate, where gullying is intense. Morgantina thus provides an ideal case study in the interrelationship of hydraulic engineering and urban design. This agora is rare too in having been studied by a geologist so that we know what the geological under-pinning was and how water was available here. Alternate layers of lime-stone, sandstone, sandy clay, and clay slant upwards from west to east, coming to the surface in the sloping plateau of the agora. On the west side of the space, the surface of the hill is mainly clay; on the east side it is mainly limestone. These differences explain the relatively slight foun-dation work needed for the East Stoa, and its good condition, compared with the perpetual danger of collapse in the West Stoa and the theater, which retain the clay of West Hill, but are twisted and damaged by the slippage of clay on stone. Given the geological realities, the wonder is that the great steps survive as well as they do. They certainly constitute an original and successful attempt to curtail erosion and slippage in the agora (Judson, 1959).

When the great steps were built across the middle of the agora in the third century, the builders carefully included the necessary opening for a large drain, but despite this the lower area of the agora rather quickly silted up, and a second drain had to be punched in the great steps, at a higher level. Most striking of the stone drains at Morgantina is the large one behind the East Stoa properly designed to handle rainwaters from the East Hill residential quarter (to the east) and from the roof of the East Stoa (to the west), as well as the overflow from the large fountain-house at the north end of the East Stoa. (Bell, 1982, 1983; Sjoqvist, 1964, 137–38) All these waters were channeled into the major drain along the southeast side of the agora, which joined the one running diagonally from the northwest corner of the space. The major drain was nearly three feet deep, built of unmortared slabs of stone so that the water could percolate into the soil.

CONCLUSION

Both the Sicilian tradition of architectural innovation and the geological situation at Morgantina contributed to the novel solution of the great steps. The local combination of geology, climate, topography, engineering tradition, and architectural vocabulary posed a particular challenge to the urban designer. We can understand the great steps as an elegant, inno-vative solution to the hydraulic engineering problem at the same time as they solve both urban design requirements and political-social demands for public assembly and discourse.

VII

Water System Elements Described and Quantified

15

Scale Differences: Akragas and Morgantina

The silence of pre-history ends with the arrival of the Greeks. They observed the eruptions of Mt. Etna and speculated on the nature of volcanos, leaving posterity with a body of writings in which *perceptions of Sicilian landscapes are quite explicit.* (Emphasis added)

Traces on the Rhodian Shore
—C. J. Glacken

Can we discern differences in the way water was managed at larger and smaller Greek cities? Let us take two Greek cities in Sicily as case studies, examining them in some detail as to area, population, date, geological situation, and the water system elements known at each. The aim of this exercise is to begin to understand the impact of scale differences on the clusters of water system elements in ancient cities.

Useful examples are Akragas—modern Agrigento—and Morgantina (Figs. 15.1, 15.2). Akragas is located on the south coast of Sicily, approximately in the center, and occupies a dramatic site on a hill between two rivers. The earliest settlement—and later the medieval town—were located on the highest peak of the 280–meter hill (*Storia della Sicilia*, 1979, map 1), but during classical and Hellenistic times the city spread down the hill to the wide and gentle valley to the south, which then rises again to form a ridge that separates that valley from the plain leading to the sea. In the sixth and fifth centuries B.C. a line of temples was built along the lower ridge, forming today the single largest, best preserved, and most impressive group of Greek temples anywhere. These architectural glories were possible because of the size and wealth of the city, the same factors that necessitated and made possible the extensive water system of the city.

In contrast, Morgantina was built inland, on a ridge at the juncture of the Catania plain with the plateaus of the center of Sicily. This ridge stands 578 to 656 meters above sea level, higher by 300 to 350 meters

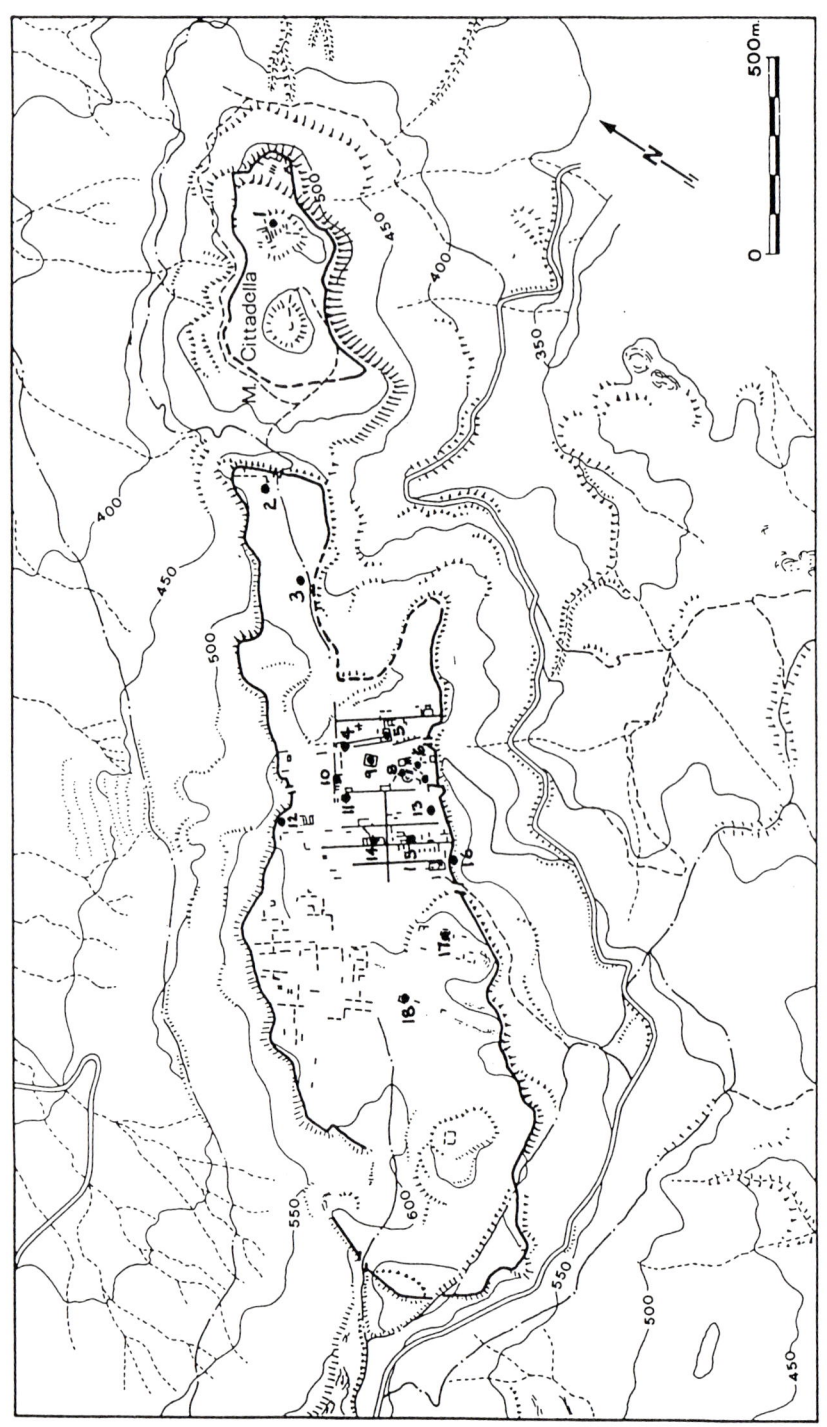

than the valleys to the north and south, but lower than the site of the nearest modern town, Aidone (885 meters), about 3 kilometers away.

Morgantina began as a prehistoric settlement of migrant tribes from Italy whose king, Morges, gave his name to the city. The earliest Sikel settlement was on Cittadella, the easternmost wedge of the ridge, during the archaic period, no later than the sixth century. By the middle of the fifth century B.C., according to Diodorus, the city was involved in Ducetius's struggle to unify the Sikels against the Greeks. He failed, and the settlement came under Syracusan control. Morgantina's location at the transition between plain and hills made the site ideal for extending Greek commerce, culture, and sovereignty into the center of Sicily. The population was removed from Cittadella hill at the eastern end of the ridge, and resettled westward along the 1800 meter ridge, where a standard fifth century type of Greek city was laid out—possibly to accommodate colonists from Syracuse—with residential quarters on top of two flat hills, and the agora area between and below them (see Fig. 5.1C). Morgantina as a colony of Syracuse may be called a "grandchild" of Corinth, the mother city of Syracuse. Shortly afterward, Morgantina was ceded by Syracuse to Camarina, in 424 according to Thucydides, but was recaptured by Syracuse in 396, remaining thereafter under Syracuse for almost 200 years (Erim, 1958, 87, citing Diodorus 11.78, and Thucydides 4.65.142), as Syracuse tried to dominate more and more of the island. Morgantina probably always had a mixed population dominated by the Greeks from Syracuse, living at first in a Greco-Sicilian mode, and later—with little effect on the water system—as Greco-Romans. The Greeks had similar situations of cultural interaction with native peoples in all their colonies, and had developed strong social defenses against the dilution of culture. Whether the settlement was a direct colony, like Syracuse, or the colony

---

Figure 15.1. Plan of Morgantina area. Water system elements, shown as heavy black circles, have been added by the author. Pipes are not shown. From right to left: *1.* Well on Cittadella, the archaic settlement. *2* and *3.* Wells in eastern part of classical and Hellenistic settlement. *4.* Northeast Fountainhouse, at north end of East Stoa. *5.* Latrine serving Prytaneion. *6.* Cistern and wells of Agora Sanctuary. *7.* Fountain. *8.* Fountain next to Theater. *9.* Tank in macellum, fed by pipes from Northeast Fountainhouse. *10.* Possible bath in Bouleterion area. *11.* Street fountain below cave spring of Fig. 17.2. *12.* Seep or spring above North Demeter Sanctuary. *13.* Spring, South Demeter Sanctuary. *14.* Arched cistern, in house of the same name. *15.* Residential area, where courtyard cisterns are common. *16.* Modern spring below the postern gate near the House of the Official. This house, lying just above the dot for 16, had its own bathroom suite which was preserved in use through later changes in ownership and in the function of the rooms of the house. *17.* So-called "Baths of Aphrodite," an area rich in cisterns and pipelines. *18.* Papa Hill where Sjöqvist found a reservoir. Plan from Princeton Morgantina files, reprinted by permission of the present excavator, Malcolm Bell.

of a colony, like Akragas and Morgantina, did not affect the self-image of the colonists as "Greek," nor their ability to carry into the new place important social and physical features of the old home, such as water management practices.

Akragas and Morgantina were quite different in size of population and in area covered by the settlement. Akragas was from 2000 to 3500 meters wide and extended 2500 meters from the lower ridge of temples up to the topmost ridge of the city. Morgantina lies on a ridge 150 to 500 meters wide and 1800 meters long plus the 400 by 600 meter wedge of Cittadella, but the built-up area as presently defined is between 325 and 1000 meters wide. Published plans of the central area indicate about 325 square meters of excavated/built-up area. However, the provision of water supply to the east and to the bath-or-sanctuary to the west (Allen, 1970,359–83) plus the structures even farther west on top of Papa Hill, called a reservoir by Sjoqvist (1964, 144–45), and recently (1988) dug by the *clandestini* (people who dig illicitly for antiquities), combine to indicate a much larger settled area in the third century B.C. at the time of greatest population.

Populations of the two cities during the Hellenistic period are harder to estimate than areas, but might approximate 50,000 to 200,000 for Akragas and 25,000 to 50,000 for Morgantina. Diodorus Siculus (13.84.2) gives a population of 200,000 at Akragas at the end of the fifth century. My estimate for Morgantina will be explained below.

As for dates of settlement and when the two cities were flourishing, we again find some contrast, although not so striking. Akragas was founded in the first quarter of the sixth century B.C. as a joint colony of Gela and Rhodes, and reached its maximum ancient population in the fourth century B.C., dwindling during the Middle Ages to the nucleus on Grigenti Hill, and only after World War II began to spread out down the hill again. Even in the mid-1980s the built-up area of the city is far less than in antiquity, although there may be increased density in some parts because of the construction of five- and six-story apartment buildings. The population today may be 52,000 or a bit more (Michelin, 1983, 273).

We have more archaeological evidence than documentary for the founding of Morgantina. From a slow start in the seventh or sixth century B.C., it grew to perhaps 50,000 people in the third century, and then was caught up in the Roman attempts to conquer Sicily. In 212 B.C. Morgantina was awarded as a prize of war to a group of Roman veterans known as the Hispanii, probably from Spain. They controlled Morgantina until the site was deserted at the turn of the era (Erim, 1958). The indigenous population declined because of the Roman-Carthaginian war, and was partially replaced by the Hispanii veterans (and possibly their families), but little change is observable in water management during the remaining 200 years or so of community life.

Since the western part of the settled area of Morgantina has not been explored in any detail, it is difficult to estimate how much of the rest of the ridge was residential, and whether residential areas took the form of town houses or villas. Thus it is difficult to give reliable estimates of the number of people living there, but somewhere between 25,000 and 50,000 in the third century B.C. seems reasonable. The smaller figure is from Professor Bell (personal communication) who is, I believe, considering only the "core" area on the East and West Hills; the larger figure is from my own studies (Crouch, 1972, 241–250) of ancient populations calculated by density, by area, by the usual proportion between rural and urban numbers, and by size of army.

Fortunately, both sites have been studied by professional geologists—rare for classical sites—and this information can be used to study the ancient settlements. As far as I know, only Pergamon among ancient Greek sites has a modern history of concurrent study of the geological, hydraulic engineering, and archaeological aspects. At Akragas, for instance, the archaeologists told me that there were no studies of the geology of the site, but at the University of Palermo, Professors Alaimo and Hauser generously shared their hydrogeological knowledge of the site and referred me to other published materials.[1] For Morgantina, Professor Sheldon Judson came from Princeton in the late 1950s to study the geology. His unpublished manuscript "Geologic and Geographic Observations at Morgantina" was made available to me by Professor William Childs who is in charge of final publications on the site, and by the former excavator of Morgantina, Dr. Hugh Allen. (Publication of his study is promised for 1992 or 1993.)

The ridge of Morgantina is formed by alternating bands of limestone, clay, and sand, with some mixtures of clay and sand, and some calcerous sandstone with or without imbedded shells. The Greeks realized that limestone, especially if combined with impervious clay, was a good source of water. The seam between stone and clay can be tapped by digging down to it or by following the seam until it surfaces. More than one such seam must have run through West Hill at Morgantina and been tapped by the wells in the House of the Arched Cistern and the House of the Official, before appearing on the southern face of the hill as a spring that still flows. Judson's manuscript includes sketches of these layers. Sometimes the water in karst areas surfaces through fissures or through shafts it has carved out from below. (see Chapter 7). Each of these behaviors of water could be utilized for human settlement, and has been at these two cities.

AKRAGAS

As the map of the geology of Akragas (Fig. 8.6) shows, the hill beneath the city is of four layers of limestone (calcarenite, with some shell sandstone, and tufa) and three of sandy-clay (sabbioso-argill) At least one

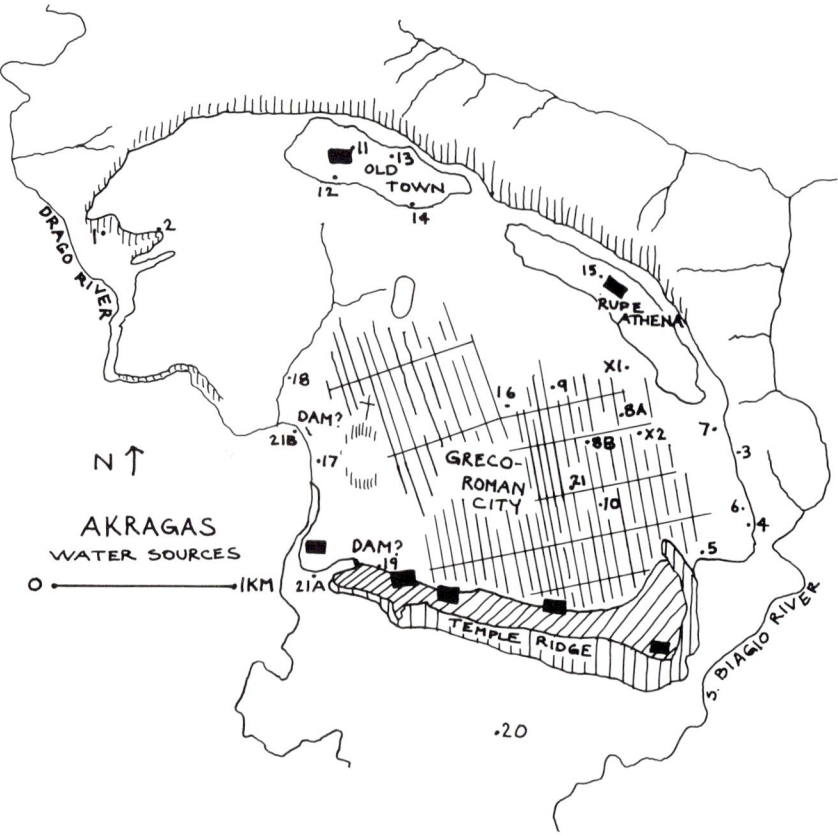

Figure 15.2. Water Sources at Akragas: *1.* Fondacazzo, near the old wall. *2.* Spring 500 m. east of Fondacazzo. *3.* Outlets at S. Biagio/Temple of Demeter. *4.* Spring 400 m. south of S. Biagio. *5.* Spring near Gate *I*. *6.* One (or two?) springs in the modern cemetery on Collo Verde. *7.* Spring to north of cemetery. *8.* Bonamorone: *8A* = Head, *8B* = outlet. *9.* Filipazzo, north of Bonamorone. *10.* Tambarello, south of Bonamorone. *11.* Spring under S. Maria dei Greci. *12.* Spring under abandoned S. Lucia. *13.* Spring or sewer line opening into Purgatorio plaza. *14.* Springs under S. Calogero. *15.* Spring on top of Rupe Athena. *16.* Possible spring. *17.* Spring below Temple of Vulcan. *18.* Spring above the sewage treatment plant. *19.* Spring in area of Castor and Pollux Temple. *20.* Spring at the Asklepion. 21. Artificial lake Kolymbetha: *21A* according to Burns; *21B* according to Crouch; probably identical with "Fischteich" on Schubring's map (frontispiece). *x1* and *x2* Caves of the side of Rupe Athena, possible water sources. To the springs published by Schubring (1870), Arnone (1942), Belloni et al. (1972), I have added those shown me by the Trasattis and the known or suspected reservoirs and two dam sites. Block rectangles are temples.

206

layer of the calcerous material is gypsum (see Fig. 8.5). The bottommost stratum at Akragas is blue clay or marl, under 10 meters of shell limestone that fissures easily so that rainwater penetrates down to the impermeable clay layer. In the walls of the valleys that flank the city, the layer of clay is visible here and there. A spring and shrine to Asklepios are located in the lower plain; such shrines frequently utilized special waters—hot or sulfurous or strongly flavored—for their cures, and here must have tapped water from the gypsum layer. The hill west of Akragas, Monserrato or C. Lo Presto, is late Pliocene limestone and today produces a sizable share of the city's water supply via the installation on top of the hill. Probably this water has always drained to the River Akragas (today Fiume Drago) that flows between the two hills (Arnone, ca. 1952; Schubring, 1870).

Akragas is thus geologically much more complicated than Morgantina, more closely following standard stream invasion and slope retreat patterns in limestone (Crawford, 1984, 295–339), with seams of water at every juncture of limestone and clay. The water naturally forms underground channels and networks, and eventually spills out on the surface (Fig. 15.2). It is my contention that here at Akragas and at many other Greco-Roman sites, the natural tendency of the water and stone to form underground networks was utilized to supply water to the neighborhoods of the city. Figure 15.3 (cf. Belloni et al, 1972, p. 100, fig. 4) is shown here as typical of the underground passages explored in the 1850's and 1860's by Schubring (frontispiece) and again in ca. 1940 by Arnone (Fig. 15.4). The hill is riddled with such passages, which exacerbate the effects of earthquake. They have been interrupted haphazardly by the foundations of new structures, and pressed into service as sewers, especially after World War II,

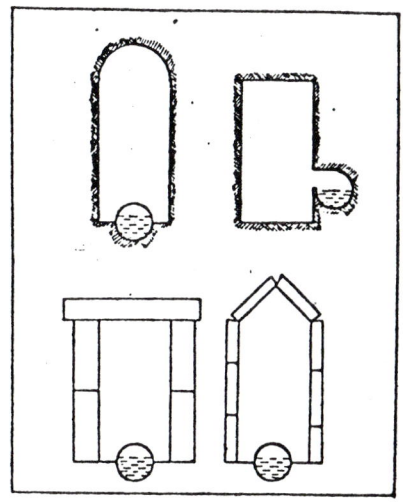

Figure 15.3. Sections of four water channels with pipes, at Akragas. Published by Pace (1935–38) and reprinted by permission of Società Editrice Dante Alighieri.

resulting in contamination of a potentially large water supply. Sr. Trassatti tells me that the official water supply of the city is 80 liters per second but that his sewage treatment plant processes between 200 and 250 liters per second; the difference is produced by the hill itself (personal communication, 1987).

As early as the sixth century B.C. the natural channels in the hill were improved for human purposes with man-made outlets and with reinforcement of weak places by inserted stone masonry. The name of the engineer Phaiax (or Phaeax) is associated with water management efforts early in the fifth century. Forbes dates the work of Phaiax to 489–472 B.C., but gives no evidence; Schubring (1870, 38–44) provides references to many ancient writers on the city. Phaiax is thought to have built aqueducts and created an artificial lake by damming the bowl-like valley at the southwestern edge of Agrigento, using the labor of captured Carthaginians. Although Arnone was able in the early 1940s to see several outcroppings of masonry attributable to Phaiax, by the 1980s I was unable to locate them or anyone who knew of them. It may be that one of the works built by Phaiax was the Purgatorio ipogeum, next to the church of the Purgatorio, as Griffo suggests (1956, 121) (Fig. 15.4). It was being restored and consolidated as of 1987–88 so that the buildings above it would not collapse into it, and so that it can possibly operate as a tourist attraction. At that time, its only liquid product was a thin trickle of sewage. The Purgatorio ipogei are one set of twenty-five described by Schubring

Figure 15.4. View of the interior of the Purgatorio ipogeum, Akragas, originally a karst passage. Drawing is the frontispiece for L. Arnone, *Gli ipogei dell'i Agrigentino* (ca. 1942); reprinted by permission.

and over thirty described by Arnone. (At Agrigento, the word "ipogei" is loosely used to refer to many kinds of underground cavities or passages.)

We can gain some idea of the size of Akragas and of the population for which water had to be supplied by listing the springs that were tapped by the ancients and are still known. Figure 8.6, a map recording the geological layers and the ten springs discovered by Dall'Aglio and Tedesco, has been redrawn to show other springs that the Trassatti's pointed out to me, and some known from nineteenth and twentith century descriptions resulting in Figure 15.2, which should be compared with the frontispiece, Schubring's nineteenth century map of the site. Note that there are undoubtedly many additional springs on the opposite west wall of the F. Drago valley also, but I made no attempt to locate them. The springs shown here are:

TO THE WEST:

1. Fondacazzo, near the old wall
2. One 500 meters east of Fondacazzo

TO THE EAST:

3. Outlets at S. Biagio/Temple of Demeter reported in *Kokalos* in 1956 as a fountainhouse.
4. One 400 meters south of S. Biagio.
5. Spring near Gate I.
6. One (or two?) in the modern cemetery on Collo Verde
7. One north of this cemetery, on a hill within the grounds of the psychiatric hospital
8. Bonamorone in 1956 was described as "excellent water" (Griffo, 1956, 48) and in 1987 was still flowing amply, but contaminated with sewage, so it is now used for washing cars and irrigating the lower orchard.
   8A = head of the spring; 8B = outlet.
9. Tambarello, south of Bonamorone among the gardens
10. Filipazzo, north of Bonamorone, just below the eastern acropolis called Rupe Athene; in Schubring's time it fed the reservoir at the church of S. Nicola (the present Museum area, indicated on the map by a cross)

AT THE TOP:

11. One under S. Maria dei Greci.
12. One under the early medieval, abandoned church of S. Lucia (not the baroque church of the same name).
13. Possibly a spring opening onto the plaza of the Church of the Purgatorio.
14. One or two very copious springs under S. Calogero just south of the plaza of the upper city. According to Sr. Trassatti, these springs

break out of confinement at frequent intervals. and cause the street to need rebuilding. The name of S. Calogero, an early missionary to the Sicilians, is also associated with a hot spring farther west along the coast, still used medicinally.

15. Probably a spring on top of Rupe Athene, to supply the first sanctuaries there and the later Norman fort. Schubring noted that a "second line opened on Rupe Athene," though he thought it supplied the area of S. Calogero. Griffo (1956,118), reports that an ipogeum was found at the summit in about 1900.

ALONG THE SLOPE:

16. A thermal spring down the western slope of the hill, at the hospital site that is being rebuilt as a university, northwest of Casa Grimaldi

It is interesting how often thermal springs and the sites of ancient and/or modern hospitals are found together. For this reason, I suspect that the modern hospital near Rupe Athene is also located to take advantage of a spring.[2]

17. Below spring No.14, and about 200 meters west of the little hill called Poggio Meta, a spring in a cave below the Temple of Vulcan.

18. A spring above the sewage treatment plant, and thus above the ancient artificial lake

Sr. Trassatti tells me that there is also an aquifer that feeds this low area and that still flows copiously; it was discovered when the sewage treatment plant was being built.

AT THE FOOT OF THE SLOPE:

19. One in the area of the Castor and Pollux Temple, towards the west end of the temple ridge

It is unclear whether the many waterlines and cisterns of the temple ridge were fed from springs on the ridge or by waterlines from higher up; however, the presence of the same kind of grotto as in the higher city suggests the same geology and hence the strong likelihood of springs, the outpourings of karst channels. (See Figs. 15.5–8.)

20. A (possibly thermal, probably sulfurous) spring at the Asklepion in the Porta Empedocles area near the beach (Fig. 8.5)

OTHER WATER SOURCES :

Near the railroad bridge, a cave with a hot water spring that has a reputation for benefiting health, but it is now closed. Since I have not seen this spring, I do not know whether it is the same as No.14.[3]

Figure 15.5. View into catacomb of San Giovani at Syracuse, similar to the ipogeum in Fig. 15.4 and the tunnel in 15.6. Natural karst channels seem to have been used in classical and Hellenistic times as aqueducts and then in early Christian times as catacombs for burials. The channel at the bottom is barely wide enough for two adult feet.

21. Giant reservoir in so-called Hellenistic quarter. Although shown on some maps and indicated here, this is actually a group of excavated houses, misinterpreted from one map to another.

22. A and B. Possible sites of the ancient artificial lake, Kolymbetha, also attributed to Phaiax, and still the goal of many of the surface streams as well as underground channels of the site.
    22A = according to Burns
    22B = according to Crouch

x1 and x2. Caves in the limestone of Rupe Athene, and since they are associated with gardens, they may be sources of water also.

Figure 15.6. View into west tunnel from Asklepion, Corinth. The regularity of this tunnel indicates its construction or enlargement by man, but given the karst features of the geology here, this tunnel in its original form is likely to have been carved by flowing water. This so-called reservoir is 2.5 meters wide.

Figure 15.7. Reservoir pool, rock-cut and stuccoed, in the area just south of the Zeus Temple, Akragas.

Figure 15.8. Farm woman doing laundry at tank that holds overflow of spring below the postern near the House of the Official, Morgantina. Tank is fed by one of up to 80 springs and seeps outside the ramparts.

With the help of the Trassatti's I have added numbers 5, 6, 9, 10, 11, 12, 13, 14, 15 17, and 18 to the list found on the map "Relievo," source of Figure 15.2. (There is no claim that my list is exhaustive.)

MORGANTINA

Let us look now at the springs of Morgantina (Fig. 15.1) Their number is much fewer, suitable for a smaller town. Perhaps four are known within the walled city limits:

1. Spring just south of the newly excavated fountainhouse in the northeast corner of the agora (Bell,1985, 1988, 313–42; Crouch 1984, 357) (Fig. 17.1).
2. Spring at the ridge-line above the North Demeter Sanctuary.
3. Spring at the northwest corner of the North Stoa, that was used to supply a small bath there (Sjöqvist, 1962, 136).
4. Cave-spring above the Doric Stoa (north end of West Stoa) along-side the street up to the residential area (Fig. 17.2).

Both 2 and 4 were discovered by the author during February 1985 and remain to be verified by excavation.

In addition, there is today one major spring at modern road level on the south slope of the ridge (mentioned earlier in connection with the seam of water under West Hill), as well as twenty to seventy outlets of water ranging in size from seep to spring around the perimeter of the ridge just below the defensive walls. (Bell gives the smaller number, Allen the larger, in personal communications.) It is interesting to note that in 1977, when I began working on the water supply of Morgantina, it was thought that there were no springs within the walled area, even though Sjöqvist had reported the one in the North Stoa. Perhaps a series of dry years had suppressed the watery evidence. My experience at the site in February-March of 1985 tends to verify the larger number.

Today there is still a spring at the very top of the nearby town of Aidone, which supports the hypothesis that spring water from that ridge could have been brought to Morgantina by long-distance pipeline over the intervening 3 kilometers. This aqueduct theory is put forth by Sr. LaSpina who manages the modern water supply and drainage of Aidone, and is supported by Allen (Allen, 1970, 360-1 and pl. 91 fig.1), who found pipes from the line along the ancient road just inside the western gate of Morgantina. A 3 kilometer supply line would have been trivial to Greek engineers (Fahlbusch, 1982).

ANALYSIS

Springs, however, are not the only elements of a water system. Each of the other elements (Table 15.1) needs to be checked briefly so that we gain a more complete picture of the arrangements at each city. It will be useful to compare the two sites as to the presence or absence of major

Table 15.1
Major Water Elements at Akragas and Morgantina

Element	Akragas	Morgantina
Water supply lines	Y*	Y
Pipes	Y	Y
Baths	Y	Y
Fittings and auxiliaries**	Y	Y
Drains	Y	Y
Springs	Y	Y
Fountains	Y	Y
Tanks and cisterns	Y	Y

*Y = Yes

**Auxiliaries can include catchment basins, lockstones, stand tanks, siphons, surge chambers, light shafts, manholes, inspection boxes, and distribution boxes. Fittings can include tubs, urinals, standpipes, well or cistern heads, laundry slabs or pithoi, footbaths, heaters for water, and washbasins/louters. Not all sites have all fittings or auxiliaries.

water elements, and then again as to fittings and other auxiliary elements (Table 15.2).

Both cities had major reservoirs that today are elusive. The huge reservoir to the west of the Hellenistic quarter at Agrigento, shown as a black rectangle on many maps, has not been described in the literature to my knowledge and is not easily accessible. The presumed reservoir on Papa Hill at Morgantina, described by Sjoqvist, was torn up by the *clandestini* in the early 1980s, and is dismissed by the present excavator.

If we look more precisely at the auxiliaries and fittings, we find in Table 15.2 a particular pattern.

Thus it seems that in their essential components, Akragas and Morgantina share all the major features of which ancient Greek water systems were composed. At Morgantina seventeen water system elements out of twenty-two have been found, compared with thirteen at Akragas. This difference is most likely a function of what has survived to be rediscovered, which is quite different at a continuously occupied site like Akragas from a site like Morgantina that has been deserted for nearly 2000

Table 15.2
Auxiliaries and Fittings at Akragas and Morgantina

Element	*Akragas*	*Morgantina*
Catchment basins	N*	Y
Surge chambers	N	N
Lockstones	N	N
Stand tanks	N	Y
Standpipes	N	Y
Siphons	N	N
Light shafts	?	N
Man holes	N	N
Inspection boxes	N	N
Distribution chambers	N	?**
Tubs	Y	Y
Urinals & toilets	N	N
Well/cistern heads	Y	Y
Laundry slabs & basins	N	Y***
Foot baths	N	Y
Washbasins (louters)	Y	Y
Heaters for water	N	N

*N = No; Y = Yes

**It is possible that the controversial bath or sanctuary of Aphrodite between West Hill and Papa Hill at Morgantina centers on a water distribution chamber like the one at Nimes (Hauck and Novak, 1988, 393–407).

***At Morgantina the laundry seems to have been done in very large semispherical pithoi set in the courtyards of houses and supplied with water from a downspout from the roof (Fig. 22.9).

years. The comparison brings out the usefulness of studying a relatively small and unimportant but undisturbed place like Morgantina for the light it can shed on the ordinary arrangements for water supply and use in the Greek world in general and in Sicily in particular.

More specifically, we can state with reasonable assurance that the water system of Akragas consisted of all the known component types of Greek systems, as did that at Morgantina. In comparison, at Priene or Rhodes, for example, some of these components have not been found at all, while others have been discovered in great profusion. Cisterns are rare at Priene, whereas Rhodes is famous for its elaborate sewer and water distribution systems. For the minor components, there is more variation, with catchment basins, stand tanks, standpipes, footbaths being found at Morgantina and not in Akragas, some question as to whether any tubs were found at Akragas, and no evidence there for laundry provisions. Light shafts seem to have been found at Akragas and not at Morgantina; these may be the air shafts of old aqueducts that have fallen into disuse so that there is no water at the bottom now, such as the shafts that illuminate the catacombs at Syracuse. The light shafts at Syracuse are published in Drögemüller (1969,107).

Only for water lines can we definitely state that the water system at Akragas was more highly developed than that at Morgantina (fontispiece). The abundance and the complexity of the separate and interlocking waterlines were impressive when Schubring studied them in 1860 and still evident 80 years later when Arnone studied them in the early 1940s with the help of the Italian army. Schubring shows the following waterlines on his map:

Sanctuario Rupestre
S. Biagio
Coddu Virdi
Filipazzo
Tamburello
Bonamorone
Giacatello
Sala-Perez
Zuccarello
Dara
Lu Coccu
Fafante
Natatello
Dovicu
Zunica
della Cava
Mirabile
della Villa Piccolo

Mirati
Fontana dei Canali
S. Lucia
Zirafa
della Acqua Amara
S. Maria dei Greci
degli Oblati

Arnone adds the following "ipogei":

Filipazzo
S. Calogero
Pipestusario
delle Forche, which includes Sotteraneo A, B, and C as well as E and F,
of the Dioscuri
Gebbca Granni
Purgatorio

and Pace (1935, 178) adds

Grotte di Fragapane, in the Christian cemetery

In his 1974 study, Alfred Burns preferred the "more realistic" descriptions of Marconi (1929, 104–08) and Pace (II, l938, 434–49) to those of Schubring and Arnone, and agreed with Pietro Griffo (1956, 28) who suggested that the pattern of water supply at Akragas was based on that of the grandmother city of Rhodes (compare Fig. 8.3 with Fig. 15.2). Not enough has been done on the particular details of the water systems of the two cities to make that comparison valid. One must be cautious of ascribing the pattern of a city that was built in the sixth and early fifth century—Akragas—to a model that we know mainly in its embodiment of the third quarter of the fifth century—Rhodes. Yet Burns' suggestion may have the merits of bringing about further study of the two patterns of water management, and of making us realize that we are dealing with a lively tradition of water management evident in all major centers of the Greek world.

CONCLUSION

It is safe to say that the geological base at Akragas was a major contributing factor in the growth and wealth of the city. The karst phenomena of multiple underground water channels, easily accessible through only ten meters of limestone or gypsum over clay, meant that there was ample water on the hill to support a large population. This population was enriched by both the agricultural wealth of the immediate area, the lumber, and other products of the interior, and the trade goods that were imported from Italy, Greece, the islands, and Carthage. Even in the present stage of incomplete excavation of the site, it is apparent that the wealth of the city was translated into comfort and beauty for the residents, and that the attractiveness of the city was increased by managing water intelligently.

Morgantina was smaller, and never grew to rival Akragas. Its site was not as easy to exploit, being farther inland, much higher above the valleys, and the underlying water much less obvious and relatively harder to discover and manage. Yet here, too, the comfort and well-being of the residents were intimately involved with the management of water. Public fountains and drainage were provided, and access to water was made as easy as possible. At least six fountains and wells were placed in and at the edges of the agora, at least two fountains in residential quarters plus numerous quasi-public wells and private cisterns. Our information about the domestic supply and use of water at Morgantina is much more complete than at Akragas, and helps us to fill out the picture for the larger city.

The size of the city and the underlying geology—and not the available technology—thus made significant differences between the patterns of water management at Akragas and at Morgantina. The available technology was the same as for the Greek world generally, but it was applied as needed, as dictated by the geology, and as could be afforded.

NOTES

1. I am grateful to former Rensselaer student, Leonardo Fodera, for arranging my meeting with these eminent hydrogeologists.

2. See the kind of reasoning called "abduction" by Pierce (1965) 5.590, as reported by Frascari (1986) 7.

3. My resourceful taxi driver reported this spring to me.

16

Clusters of Water System Elements

This study deals with the water system elements from twenty-five ancient Greek sites. The elements are grouped (as in the comparative case-studies of Chapter 15) into eight main categories, with that of "fittings and auxiliaries" subdivided into seventeen kinds of elements. Although 25 sites times 8 categories times 17 elements is 3400 possible combinations, which is more than we have room to discuss in a limited work like this, from a statistical point of view such numbers are trivial. However, scientists have recently been working with the concept of "clusters" in cases like this one where the assortments are too few for applying the methods of statistics (see H. Blalock, *Causal Inferrence in Non-Experimental Research.*) What they look for are combinations that seem to recur in meaningful patterns. One can think of a partially ordered set, where the order is apparent within categories but not over all of them. Bathtubs, for instance, can be arranged in groups of like form, but distinguishing between large bathtubs and small plunge pools may be difficult. Alternately, one may know the relative order of categories, but not their absolute magnitude. An example here is A, not knowing a language at all; B, being able to read the language; C, speaking and reading the language fluently. At what point does B grade into C? It's a judgment call. Throughout this book I have approached the material with an eye to what we can determine using irregular and "messy" data, and this concept of clusters has enabled me to appreciate the significance of the combinations of elements that have been observed at different places, times, and by different excavators, even when the number of examples is few.

Both the objects found together in clusters, and the certainty of finding them together, vary. For instance, settling or catchment basins (Figs. 16.2, 16.3) are always associated with pipes or channels to facilitate drainage. The ditch and bench supports for a latrine are frequently associated with a sewer under the street outside the building, but sometimes with a cesspool instead. Footbaths, while not unknown in private houses, are commonly associated with the multiple basins of the bathing room in

Figure 16.1. Latrine in area east of the House of the Arched Cistern, Morgantina. As in several other examples of latrines at Morgantina, this seems to be a late re-use by walling off an alley. The wall at center is about a third of a meter wide.

a gymnasium or sanctuary. Heaters for water, while not common, are as likely to be found in a public bath as in a private installation.

There are some chronological differences in the patterns of association. In the fourth century and earlier, for instance, siphons are used for public municipal aqueducts only (Fig. 13.2, 22.11–13), but by the first century A.D. in Pompeii, small siphons carried water in lead pipes up to the second floors of private houses. Thus the refinement and miniaturization of the technology made previously rare elements into common ones. It may be that the shift from terra-cotta pipes to lead pipes that we observe at many sites beginning in the second century B.C. is part of this tendency toward miniaturization.

Using the categories and data from the tables in Chapter 15, let us see what clusters occur at two sites, Morgantina and Akragas.

1. *Water supply lines.* This term covers both cut and constructed channels and pipelines. Such lines are always found with baths, fountains, and tanks/cisterns. Sometimes they are found with springs. At Akragas, the water supply lines (frontispiece) are associated with manholes (Fig. 16.11) and with well/cistern heads; wheras at Morgantina the water supply lines are associated with pipes, drains, springs, fountains, catch-

ment basins, and possibly standpipes. Probably these differences in material remains reflect the very different post-Hellenistic histories of the two sites.

2. *Pipes.* This term covers terra-cotta, lead, and stone pipes. Wooden pipes, although theoretically possible, are not known from the Greek world but from northern Roman sites in Germany. Pipes are usually found with fountains, tanks and cisterns, lockstones, stand tanks, inspection boxes, urinals and toilets, laundry basins, and heaters for hot water. They are often found with baths, springs, catchment basins, surge chambers, siphons, and distribution chambers. At Akragas, pipes are seen in the Hellenistic quarter, associated with well/cistern heads, louters, and drains. At Morgantina (Figs. 16.3, 16.4, 16.8, 17.9) they are found constituting the water supply line from Aidone, with the so-called bath on West Hill, with

Figure 16.2. Three lines of pipes in the street leading to the theater, Argos. This street has at least six sets of pipes, at different levels, plus drainage channels.

the spring/fountain house at the northeast corner of the Agora, associated with tanks and cisterns in every kind of building, and serving catchment basins, tubs, and laundry basins. Only the most preliminary dating of pipes has as yet been done (e.g., Fahlbusch,1982, 163), but both Fahlbusch and Camp are working on the problem.

3. *Baths.* This term includes both public baths in gymnasia and religious sanctuaries, and private bath suites or bathrooms in houses. At Akragas, private bathing facilities are known in the Hellenistic quarter, and several large reservoirs that may have been swimming pools are to be seen along the western part of the ridge of the temples (Fig. 15.7). At Morgantina, the House of the Official, the House of Ganymede, the House of the Doric Capital (Fig. 12.1), and the two Sanctuaries of Demeter had bathing suites, while the complex west of West Hill that Allen identified as a bath was extravagantly supplied with pipes and cisterns. (Fig. 16.3)

Figure 16.3. Pipes with V-joint, supplying the "Bath of Aphrodite" near Papa Hill in Morgantina. V-joints are known in pipelines of the Athenian Agora also. Each pipe is about .66 m long.

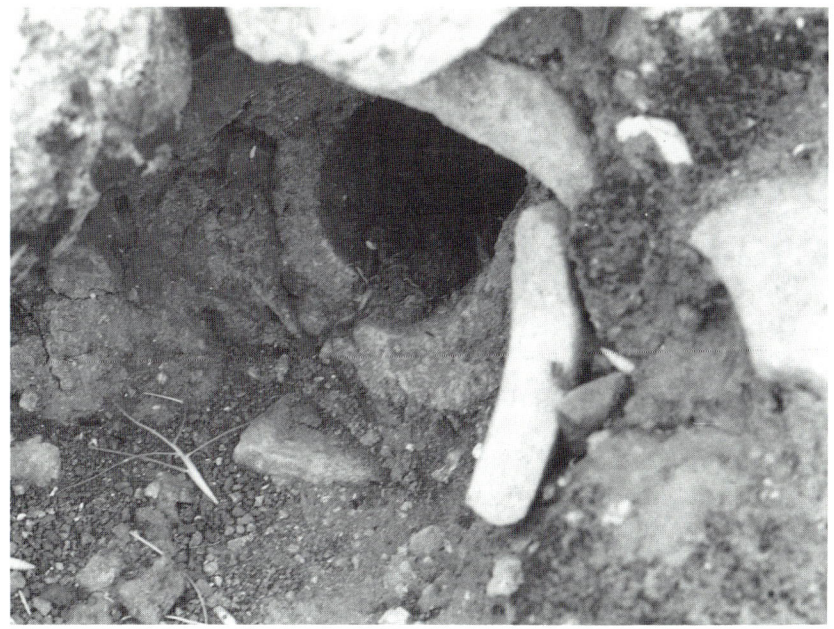

Figure 16.4. Broken pipe mended by being wrapped in additional terra-cotta pieces. This was the supply pipe for the street fountain in the northwest corner of the Agora, Morgantina. The inside pipe was approximately 10 centimeters in inner diameter.

Figure 16.5. Hellenistic pipes of stone and terra-cotta, in the storage shed near the excavation house, Pergamon. The pipes average two-thirds of a meter long.

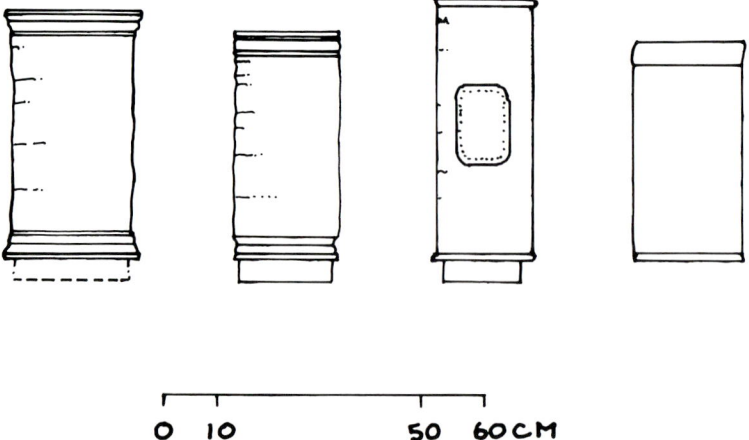

O 10 50 60 CM

Figure 16.6. Comparison of classical, Hellenistic, and Roman pipes found at Miletus. From a drawing by W. Mueller-Wiener of the German Archaeological Inst., Istanbul; reprinted by permission.

Figure 16.7. Stone elbow from pressure pipe, Miletus. The upper hole is about 18 cm. in diameter.

Figure 16.8. Terra-cotta pipe with hole for insertion of lead pipe, Morgantina. The hole is approximately 2.5 centimeters in diameter.

Figure 16.9. Lead pipe profiles, from Akragas, as published by B. Pace (1935–38) and reprinted by permission of the Società Editrice Dante Algheiri. Such pipes range from 2.5 to 12.5 centimeters, interior diameter.

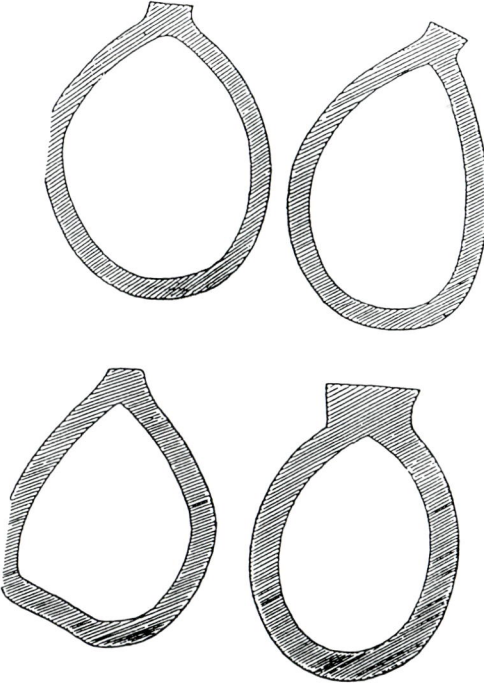

Figure 16.10. Basins in bathing room of gymnasium at Priene supplied through lion-head spouts. Source of the water was a cave spring just above the gymnasium, M in Figure 12.4 and Number 7 in Figures 12.6 and 12.7. Reprinted from Wiegand et al., *Priene* by permission from the German Archaeological Institute, Istanbul.

Figure 16.11. Manhole in courtyard of house of Hellenistic quarter, Akragas. Manholes are rare in houses, common in streets and in public precincts. This one is approximately 0.5 meter square.

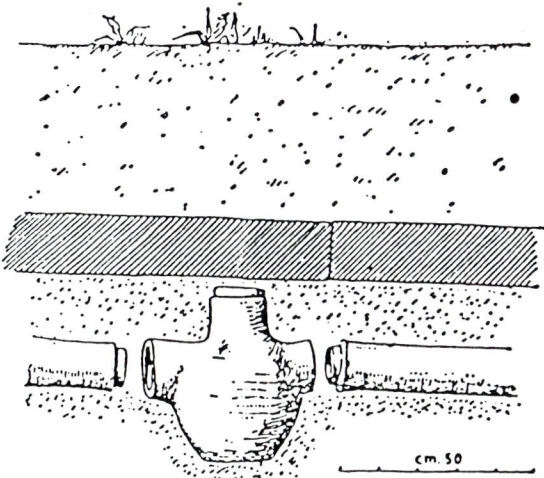

Figure 16.12. Section of settling basin, part of a waste water system, found at Syracuse. Published by Pace, 1935–38, and reprinted by permission of Società Editrice Dante Algheiri.

Figure 16.13. Large settling basin nearly one meter tall, with sides pierced to receive drain pipes, in the museum at Pergamon.

Several tubs, including a footbath tub, were found at Morgantina (Figs. 22.5, 22.6, 22.8, 22.9), but their find-spots were mostly not well recorded.

4. *Drains.* This term includes large pipe drains, ad hoc channels of reused roof tiles and pipes, and large U-shaped channels constructed of stone slabs. Owing to the downpours common in this climate, drains are essential in densely settled areas. Drains are commonly associated with catchment basins, surge chambers, manholes, urinals and toilets, cisterns, and laundry slabs and basins. At Akragas, drains from the earliest period at the hilltop site are covered by the later city, but underground they contribute to the waste water load handled by the sewage treatment plant.

Figure 16.14. Alley drain approximately .75 meter wide, along the west side of the House of the Official, Morgantina, bonded to the house foundations made of the same limestone, and hence built at the same time. Fourth or third century B.C.

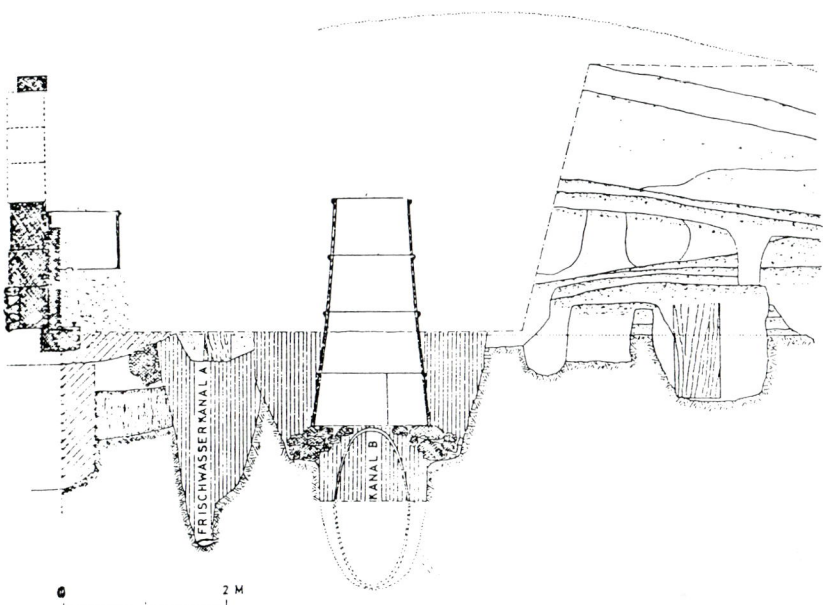

Figure 16.15. Section of two waterlines found near the Dipylon Gate in the Kerameikos area of Athens. To the left, the channel for fresh water (Frischwasserkanal A), and to the right that for waste water (Kanal B), with access shafts in the form of well mouths over the channel every six meters or so. Compare with Figure 22.15. Published by Knigge in "Keramikos Tatigkeitsbericht," and reprinted by permission of the German Archeological Institute, Athens.

They are very much in evidence in the Hellenistic quarter, running under the streets and in the alleys, in the forms of deep and large collectors as well as shallow drains of reused roof tiles. At Morgantina, drains have not been consistently distinguished from supply pipes, but true large collector drains are known to run under the Agora, and smaller stone drains lie under the North and Northwest (Doric) Stoas and in residential neighborhoods (Fig. 14.3), as well as pipe and roof tile drains on the ground surface in the South Demeter Sanctuary. Notable features of drainage at Morgantina are the large slits built into the ramparts (Fig. 12.2), and the smaller equivalents in the exterior walls of many buildings in the Agora. Drains are associated with bathrooms in the Houses of the Official and of Ganymede.

5. *Springs.* This term specifies spontaneous outflow of water at the surface of the earth. A larger number of springs is known at Akragas (Fig. 15.2) than at Morgantina (Fig. 15.1). At the former, they are associated with drains, fountains, tanks, and possibly light shafts; at the latter, with water supply lines, baths, drains, fountains, and tanks. Some of the differences in these associated groups at the two cities are due to geological

variation, and some to the fact that Akragas was at least three or four times larger than Morgantina.

6. *Fountains.* Here I distinguish between a natural outpouring of water (a spring) and the man-made architectural expression of the delivery of water to a public place (a fountain). Both sites probably had fountains, but we have much more evidence of them at Morgantina, which has been undisturbed during the past 2000 years. At Morgantina, the fountains are always associated with pipes, drains, holding basins, and some degree of architectural articulation. Although a system of cisterns and connecting channels at Akragas relates to the line of temples along the ridge, no public fountains have as yet been discovered in this area, nor do I recollect any in the Hellenistic quarter. Yet many cisterns with wellheads are evident in the houses and public buildings of the temple ridge level, especially in the residential quarter near the Temple of Hermes.

7. *Tanks and cisterns.* At neither site has there been a thorough search for municipal reservoirs, but at both there are indications that these existed. Sjöqvist (1964, 144–45) thought he found a large tank on the top of Papa Hill west of West Hill at Morgantina. A reservoir at Akragas is shown in Figure 15.7. Houses and sanctuaries from both sites show the typical Greek pattern of cisterns under the courtyard or adjacent to it, associated with pipes and drains, and accessible to louters, laundry basins, and water heaters (Figs. 12.1, 16.16, 16.17, 17.4, 17.9). [Fahlbusch (1982, 112–121) has discussed the Greek and Roman approach to reservoirs.]

8. *Fittings and Auxiliaries.* Among the seventeen elements listed in Table 15.2, the ones most often found together are washbasins and wellheads (Fig. 16.18, 16.19, 17.5), most frequently placed at the edge of the family courtyard, but also known in public buildings where they were most usually placed in the line of the colonnade. Another combination is the bathtub and the toilet facility, being frequently in the same large but subdivided space (Fig. 20.11A, C, D). Heaters for water were either the ordinary cooking apparatus in the kitchen next to the bathroom, or facilities dedicated specifically to heating water and placed in a separate room next to the bathtub. The heaters could be either free-standing, made of metal, or a built-in tank with a furnace below as we see in some sanctuaries such as Olympia. When footbaths occur, they are usually in conjunction with sets of bathtubs or basins, such as at the old bathing room of the Gymnasium at Pergamon. Other clusters of elements relate to long-distance water supply lines, such as the light shafts of the sixth to fifth century type, the manholes of all periods, and the surge chambers, lockstones, standpipes and stand tanks, inspection boxes, and distribution chambers that contributed to the successful functioning of pressure pipelines.

Only three of these fitting elements were found at Akragas: tubs, wellheads, and washbasins, while eight were found at Morgantina: catchment

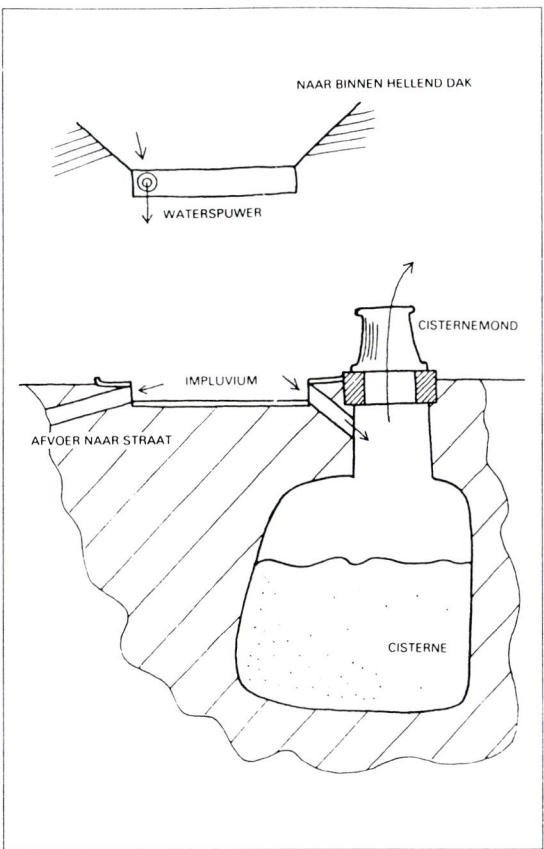

Figure 16.16. Cistern system. An example from Herculaneum. Top to bottom: "Naar binnen hellend dak" is the collecting roof, with water spout at "waterspuwer". The water lands in the "impluvium" and drains either into the "cisterne" or out to the street sewer, "afvoer naar stradt." Users draw the water up through the wellhead, "cisternemond." Reprinted from G. C. M. Jansen, "Voorzieningen van water, sanitair en afvalwaterafvoer in het Romeinse provinciestadje Herculaneum (Italie)," and reprinted by permission.

basins, stand tanks, standpipes, tubs, wellheads, laundry basins, foot-baths, and washbasins (Fig. 22.5, 22.6). Part of the reason for this variation, I think, is that a wider range of building types is known from Morgantina, owing to the accidental preservation of the site. By contrast, probably fourteen types of fittings are known at Pergamon, which was both a very large city and quite well preserved.

Figure 16.17. The rounded forms of rosemary bushes growing in cisterns along the ridge of temples at Akragas. The bushes are up to 2 m. tall. There are also some rectangular tanks, located like the cisterns on the inland side of the ridge.

Figure 16.18. Basins of two types. In the foreground, the remains of a wash-basin *(louter)* of the traditional "bird-bath" shape, about .6 m tall; behind it on the ground, a stone laundry scrubboard in a wide V shape. At Delos.

Figure 16.19. View of a house at Delos with a bathtub in the central room nearest the viewer, and a *puteal* (wellhead or cisternhead) to the left in the courtyard behind. The tub is approximately 1.5 meters long.

Figure 16.20. Boy drawing ice-cold water from a well in the courtyard of an ancient house at Delos.

SUGGESTIONS FOR FURTHER WORK

As further excavation and publication is done of Greek sites, it would be instructive to look for combinations of water system elements. From further data we will begin to get a sense of what clusters are to be associated with different eras, different geologies, and differences in ethnicity.

GENERALIZATION OF CONCEPTS

Besides considering what elements occur in what clusters, one can and must widen the focus to examine broader categories in their clusters. In Chapter 9, Urban Location Determinants, we have noted that certain clusters of favorable factors seem to occur together, contributing to the selection of a site in the first place, and to the longevity of a settlement. It might be useful to reread that chapter with this concept in mind.

VIII

Physical Constraints on Built Form

17

Urban and House Form Constrained by Water Resources—Morgantina

Everyone has to drink from his own well.
—St. Benedict, quoting Solon

Although we may think that physical form of a city is mainly the result of cultural preferences interacting with the inherent potential of local materials, there are in fact even more basic constraints that constitute the substratum of every urban form because they are the basis of life itself. These factors are food, water, and the earth that provides them and makes life possible. The urban form makes explicit how the society provides food and water for its members and how they relate to the earth. Intentionally and unintentionally, the forms of the houses, the work places, the public buildings, and the open spaces reflect the people's values and ways of behaving, as well as what they know about their environment and how they manipulate it. We are so accustomed to analyzing modern cities or "primitive" cultures in these terms that to state them is to utter a truism, but in the study of ancient cities these ideas have been applied rarely if at all.

One cannot exhaust this broad subject in one chapter, since the formal and technical details are not condensible, nor are the cultural-historic aspects susceptible to terse summary. Rather, we will take one basic constraint—water—and examine it in the light of the evidence from one particular place—Morgantina, Sicily—with just enough comparative material to make the details from Morgantina stand out clearly. This singular analysis will, I hope, suggest how fruitful it would be to study ancient urbanization in terms of the social and architectural results of resource management.

The ordinary provisions for urban form and water management as they interrelated at one ordinary site are discussed in this chapter. The desired urban form dictated placement of water system elements, and the water potential was exploited to make possible the kind of physical arrangement preferred by the urban dwellers. In this provincial town, the standard solutions for water management were applied, and the resulting urban form differed from the typical only in the feature of the great steps, which as we have seen, were specifically built to solve a drainage problem.

The street patterns of ancient Greek cities are discussed in Chapter 5, Urban Patterns. When we speak of the traditional form of an ancient city, however, we do not mean only the street pattern, no matter how distinctive. "Traditional form" also included the relationship of built to open space, the setting and the vantage point for viewing temples and other major public structures, the kinds of buildings and spaces that people provided for the activities they engaged in, and, most intimately, the shape of the house. Each of these forms is intrinsically bound with function. Again, it is not my purpose to give an exhaustive account of ancient Greek architecture. Rather, I have selected from this abundance of possibilities those elements that were given architectural expression while directly constrained by the behavior of water and the necessity for managing it intelligently and economically. The goal is a set of special insights into some practical limitations on Greek city building. We will also see how the characteristic Greek emphases on ideal form and on corporeality (Webster, 1973) are invariably manifest even in simple structures. The provincial hill town, Morgantina, with a mixed population, Greek and Sikel, is better for our purposes than one of the grand centers of Greek life, for in its modest water arrangements we can see the typical features of Greek water management during a long period of time. Morgantina has the additional advantage for our purposes of having been deserted at the turn of the era, not rebuilt in the style of Roman imperial times, but preserving Greek physical form and water arrangements.

BACKGROUND

Before turning to the details of water management as related to urban form at Morgantina, it will be useful to sketch very briefly the general environmental circumstances under which city founders and builders of the ancient Greek world (eighth to first centuries B.C.) did their work. The climate was and is Mediterranean, meaning that it is relatively mild, with a variation of perhaps 70 degrees Fahrenheit rather than the 120 degree variation that is possible, for example, in upstate New York. The "missing" 50 degrees are from the bottom of the scale, which means that winters are milder, although summer heat and the intensity of the sun require such adaptions as afternoon siestas during the hot months. Rainfall is concentrated in the winter months, which presents certain problems of timing for the growing of crops, but at least in most of the area there is enough rain to grow food and support human life.

Our clever predecessors, spurred by the essential requirement of survival, studied their environment and determined what to do to utilize its positive features and overcome its negative ones, even to the extent of being willing to move an entire city if the water supply drastically changed its location or abundance (see Part II and Chapter 9).

The technology available to city builders changed over time with an accumulating knowledge base and changing social circumstances. Only if a city were so large that it had exhausted its local water resources, or if an earthquake or other catastrophe had interfered with local water supply, would long-distance water supply lines be necessary. Only if the city were fairly rich would it have enough disposable wealth to pay for this new technology. A good example is the new type of underground aqueduct with air shafts built by sixth century B.C. tyrants who wished to gain and retain popular favor. In Samos, Megara, and Athens, these innovative rulers bolstered their power by solving ongoing problems of water supply with new long-distance waterlines. The Greeks seem to have learned of it from the Persians (Crouch, 1975, 162, n. 27; Fahlbusch, 1982), but our knowledge of the transmission process is hazy (see also Chapter 11).

Economic constraints dictated that rather than a complete shift from older methods of supplying water, there was a continuation of the old ways with new ways added on as supplements. In a small place like Morgantina, the old ways were sufficient for the most part, although in a line of pipes found along the ancient road between Morgantina and the hilltop town of Aidone to its west we catch a tantalizing glimpse of the possibility of a long-distance line that the present manager of the Aidone water system thinks tapped springs on the Aidone hill for use at Morgantina (Allen, 1970, 361 ill.2, pl.91, fig. 1).

WATER SYSTEM ELEMENTS

Parts VI and VII describe and illustrate the varied water system elements found at Morgantina—springs, fountains, wells, cisterns, reservoirs, tanks, bathrooms and their fittings (bathtubs, washbasins, footbaths), latrines, pipes, channels, drain openings, and settling basins (Crouch, 1984, 353–65, pl. 46–47). Each of these elements, in this form, manifests a sophisticated process of observing what nature has to offer, making explicit provision for use and control, and arriving at a built form that economically and efficiently signifies what it does. Let us look in turn at each of these elements as signaling a constraint, and consider the built form as combining knowledge of the natural behavior of water with civilized behavior of people.

Springs

Let us discuss only the two springs at the northeast and northwest angles of the Morgantina Agora area, since these determined the location of the Agora and allowed for the development of residential areas on the flat-topped hills flanking this lower space.

One spring, a small one, at the northeast corner, has been recognized during Bell's recent excavations of the Northeast Fountainhouse (Bell, 1985, 1988). The little cave-spring immediately south of this fountainhouse supplied the east side of the Agora and provided drinking water for the residents on East Hill for almost 200 years before the fountainhouse was built to formalize the flow (Fig. 17.1). One can still see the small cave out of which the water flowed, at the north end of the East Stoa. If there were basins or other architectural details related to the first use of the spring, they seem to have been swept away without trace when the new fountainhouse was built as part of the monumentalization of the Agora ca. 250 B.C. At that time, the three sides of the Agora were edged with stoas (west, north, and east), and this fountainhouse placed at the north end of the East Stoa, but south of the major street that ran all along the ridge and along the agora side of the North Stoa. The fountainhouse lined up with the east end of the North Stoa. In appearance, the fountain was

Figure 17.1. Small cave whence sprang the water that originally supplied the northeast fountainhouse at Morgantina. The opening is approximately .3 m tall and somewhat less than 1 m wide.

a three-sided moat, the inner wall of which supported a colonnade; this wall and colonnade separated the inner from the outer basin, a rather uncommon arrangement. Also unusual was the mixing of springwater with rain waters from the roof in the last version of the fountain, perhaps because the spring water was—as normal—cutting itself a lower outlet and no longer supplying at this level the amounts that the users of the Agora needed. Time scales for cutting actions like this are not well worked out, but a rough estimate would be 1 millimeter per year (LaFleur, 1984; Davidson, 1980, 143–158). However, abrupt dewatering caused by the water table dropping 10 to 15 meters is not uncommon (see Dreyboudt, 1990, 639–55). In its final phase, the fountain was supplied by pipes from the opposite spring (to be discussed later), running across the unpaved porch of the North Stoa.

Water from the northeast fountainhouse served the East Stoa, the macellum (market building) in the center of the Agora, and the residential area on the slope east of East Hill (Fig. 14.2). Thus this spring and its later fountainhouse

1. Induced people in the fifth century to settle here.
2. Facilitated development of the preferred urban plan for this period (residential areas on two flat hills, flanking a lower public space) (Fig. 5.1C).
3. Provided an urban design focus for the eastern side of the agora.
4. Continued the venerable tradition of placing fountainhouses at the entrances to an agora.
5. In the third century, the fountainhouse took on an open and yet monumental form appropriate for its location at the hinge between the north and east sides of the agora.
6. Later, as the supply began to diminish, reconsideration of the water supply was necessary, utilizing rainwater to supplement the spring, and (even later?) requiring further supplementing with piped water.

The northern side of Morgantina's ridge is higher than the southern and eastern sides. At many spots along the ridge where the seam between stone and sandy-clay comes to the surface, there are still today seeps and oozes and small springs along the north face of the ridge. Thus many of these springs and seeps were uphill from the Agora area. When Sjöqvist was excavating at the site in the early 1960s, he found a little spring at the northwest corner of the North Stoa that supplied the building that he thought was a bathing establishment, next to the bouleuterion (council chamber) (Sjöqvist, 1962,136). Farther up on this northern ridge, above the North Demeter Sanctuary, there was enough flowing water to supply the tank and (probable) shower bath of the sanctuary. In February 1985, I saw the remains of a catchbasin or cistern for such a spring, at the top of the ridge line, exactly on axis with the sanctuary. Both this spring and the one Sjöqvist found remain to be verified by excavation.

On the northwest corner of the Agora opposite Bell's new fountain-house and south of the main road of the town was a spring that still flows copiously today (Fig. 17.2). When I visited Morgantina in February 1985, the entire hillside below this spring was soggy wet in spite of the fact that it had not rained for a month. This spring has not been excavated, but what is visible is a large cave whose roof is encrusted with sinter, enclosed by a crude low wall of rough stones, seemingly piled up there in the Middle Ages or even later. Water from this spring spreads outward in a wide triangle from a source above or in the cave, and necessitated a network of large and small drainage channels in this corner of the Agora. Some of the channels seem to be fifth century, judging from their simple construction of large rectangular blocks of stone, just like the securely dated channel under the North Stoa, while others were probably part of that rebuilding in the third century already mentioned. Apparently the cave-spring was only one of several openings of water in this corner. Sjöqvist (1962, 136) reported "a small vein of water comes to the surface and remains available during at least part of the summer" in

Figure 17.2. View of cave-spring above the northwest corner of the Agora, Morgantina. Sinter is plainly visible on the roof of the cave, suggesting a water source above the cave. A very late wall at the bottom of the picture encloses the cave, which has not been excavated.

this corner. In 1985, the workmen told me that at any time of year when they have to dig under the paved street as it enters the Agora here, they always find wetness within a foot of ground level. The large cave-spring like its small cousin next to the East Stoa, has a street fountain associated with it. This one is in the form of a trough at the edge of the main street, supplied through a lionhead spout, with mending of the fountain's supply pipes evident from their doubled walls (Fig. 16.4). (I look forward to the excavation of this area.) Probably the spring was the focus of neighborhood life with the women of West Hill stopping there to fetch a vase of delicious fresh water for drinking, or enjoying a few minutes of conversation on their way home from the Agora, while the amphoras of others slowly filled up—the ancient equivalent of a coffee klatch. A road from behind the Doric Stoa at the northwest corner of the Agora to the houses above runs past the east edge of the cave and is clearly visible in February but completely hidden in grass and bushes in the summertime.

These two springs and their associated fountains, then, framed the north edge of the Agora and supplied both commercial and public use there as well as residential use for the people living near them. They did so with architectural expression that was competent but not aggressive, economical and elegant at the eastern springhouse, and probably so at the western one. These springs and fountainhouses explicitly united amenity and necessity into one architectural expression, transforming constraints into opportunities. Further study of other fountains and springs at Morgantina would verify that the wedding of amenity and necessity was traditional in this culture, but let us turn rather to wells and cisterns.

Wells and Cisterns

Builders of ancient Greek cities could predict where water would be found beneath the surface by careful observation of the plant coverage, since certain plants such as fig trees, brambles, and rosemary like to grow with their feet in water (Bradford, 1974, 13–24; Meinzer, 1927) (Fig. 16.17). They also examined the patterns of folded rock as revealed along the sides of hills, looking for seams between stone and clay (see Vitruvius on water and geology, in Chapter 7). Limestone, especially if combined with impervious clay, is a good source of water, and even the sandstone found at Morgantina has fissures that allow water to penetrate after storms and to collect in pockets above the impermeable clay below. In this terrain, the earliest wells were probably the natural shafts produced by this process of dissolving and weathering, but later (sixth century? seventh century? even earlier?) some daring soul would have tried digging where no such natural shaft existed, perhaps after success in enlarging an existing shaft to reach that entrapped water. On Cittadella, the hill at the end of Morgantina's ridge, where the earliest settlement was located, one well was excavated to 45 feet without reaching the bottom and in it was found pottery from the sixth century B.C. and later, the inference being that farther down in the well would have been even earlier pottery. This well was lined with masonry that had the customary hand-and-foot-holes arranged in a spiral pattern, for access. On West Hill, a well in the House of the Official was excavated even deeper, to 18.6 meters without reaching the bottom (Ostenberg excavation notebook, 1963, I, p. 89). When the workmen consider continued excavation of a well or cistern to be life-threatening, excavation is stopped and the well is refilled. Such wells, with their reliable supply of cold and delicious water were considered great treasures (Fig. 17.3, 16.20), as we can see from the fact that the plan of the house was organized around the well, and that it was necessary to pass laws to regulate use of private wells. In his life of Solon, the law-giver of 6th century Athens, Plutarch writes:

> Since the water supply of rivers, lakes and springs was inadequate, and most people dug wells, he [Solon] passed a law that wherever there was

Figure 17.3. Well section from Athens Agora, from the sixth century, judging from its masonry of small stones. Reprinted by permission of the American School of Classical Studies at Athens.

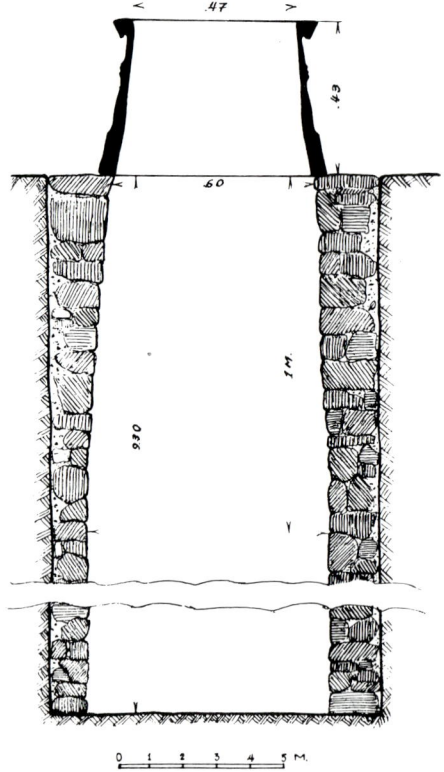

a public well within half a mile this was to be used; where it was farther away, one could dig one's own; but if, having dug to a depth of 60 feet, one did not find water one was permitted to fill a five gallon jar twice a day from one's neighbor's well; for Solon thought it right to help a man in need, but not to encourage laziness. (Plutarch, *Lives*, "Solon," XXIII, 6)

It is interesting to note the prohibition against digging a well within half a mile of a public well. The ancients seem to have understood the principle of "draw down" for wells, which means that withdrawing water from a well de-waters the ground around it. In practice, this factor limits how closely wells can be spaced. (Steel and McGhee, 1979, 61). Note too that this citation shows that a 60 foot well was normal in sixth century B.C. Athens, and thus the techniques of constructing it were commonplace.

Because of the above-mentioned danger during excavation, some water containers at Morgantina cannot be classified strictly as either wells or cisterns. One in the House of the Arched Cistern is particularly interesting. Built as part of a third century B.C. house, the Arched Cistern was finished at ground level with a rectangular draw basin topped by an arch set into the wall of the dining room of the house (Fig. 17.4). One can picture the neighbors following Solon's law and coming twice a day for cold water, not having to intrude on the private courtyard of the house, since the cistern was reached by a short quasi-public alley from the street. A similar arched water source is found on the main street at Selinus (Fig. 20.5). Both date from about the third century B.C. at the latest, and possibly from the fifth.

HOUSE FORM AND THE USE OF WATER

We have no graphic evidence from the period before Vitruvius about the reciprocal influence of house form and water management on each other. Manuscripts of Vitruvius incorporated references to traditional knowledge of Greco-Roman society about finding and controlling water, but none of the original illustrations have come down to us, and Renaissance scholars who supplied later illustrations were more interested in building form than in the technology of water management. Modern writers on Greek houses and cities (Rider, 1965, 250–55; Martin, 1956, pl. 22 and figs. 48, 49) are very little help, since they do not consider water arrangements significant and worthy of separate study. Are we, then, to continue innocent of water management questions? No, for the same curiosity that drives the study of materials for ancient buildings, or effects of urbanization on the hydrologic cycle, or analysis of ancient buildings in terms of solar heating, or the impact of karst phenomena including denudation on location and longevity of ancient cities, drives us also to ask what water and its uses had to do with the form of the Greek house.

Figure 17.4. Arched cistern 1 meter wide, from house of the same name, Morgantina. This was a semipublic opening to a cistern or well. In the last phase of use, this water-holder was filled by a lead pipe from the north.

Courtyards

The use of water in ancient Greek houses was related to each water element's function, where each was located, and what was the effect of the location, as well as the variations of placement and time period possible for these arrangements (Fig. 12.1). Sources of water supply, both within and outside the house, as well as the means and purposes of drainage, must be acknowledged. Drainage in particular affected not only the house form but also the urban form and even altered the land immediately surrounding the city. It would be only a slight exaggeration to claim that the form of the house was a series of responses to the question of water supply and use. The central courtyard was edged with porticoes covered by roofs slanting inward to facilitate collecting rainwater via downspouts. Downspouts are still in situ in Delos and Pompeii (see Fig. 17.5). Water for everything but drinking and possibly cooking was provided for each household by the rainwater cistern located under the paving of the central court of the house. This location ensured that the cistern could be easily filled, accessed, cleaned, and repaired. Sometimes a second cistern was located under the walkway around the court, making sure that even in the longest, hottest, driest summer there would be water enough for bathing, laundry, and so on. The House of the Doric Capital at Morgantina had two cisterns of the later bottle shape (Crouch,

Figure 17.5. Reconstruction of laundry and dish-washing facilities in a Morgantina courtyard. The woman is doing dishes at a *louter*, which could also be used as a table for cooking, and as a washbasin for hands and faces. Behind her the clothes dry on lines stretched between posts that held up the roof over the walkway around the courtyard. Between the two posts at left is a *puteal* (cisternhead) giving access to the cistern under the courtyard. Behind it, against the wall, a very large pithos set up on stones to be a convenient height for washing clothes, has been filled with water from the downspout recessed in the wall. Water was collected from part of the roof to fill the pithos; the rest of the roof runoff was collected into the cistern.

1984, 356, ill.3; Stillwell and Sjöqvist, 1957, pl. 50.21) (Fig. 12.1, 3.2). Judson (1959) has estimated that the amount of water falling on the roof of an average-sized house at Morgantina was enough to fill two cisterns and to last during the dry season from April to October. In case of siege, a population with cisterns had a greater chance of surviving.

In almost all the Greek houses known to us, there is an efficient grouping of kitchen, bathing facilities (whether separate room or not), and well or cistern. Sometimes there is a separate bathroom with a built-in bathtub (Fig. 17.6), a washbasin, and even—at least at Olynthos in the fourth century B.C.—a very modern-looking toilet (J.W. Graham, 1938,1191, pl. 55) (Figs. 17.7, 20.11A). Most of the houses at Delos, which flourished in the third and second centuries B.C., have separate latrines placed on the house wall nearest the street, where they could easily be flushed into the sewers. At Morgantina there are some alleyways that seem to me to have been walled up in the last two centuries B.C. for use as latrines, but this interpretation is questioned by Malcolm Bell (Fig. 16.1). Only the House of the Official and the Pryntaneion at Morgantina have spaces securely designated as latrines, suggesting that alternate, nonarchitectural arrangements such as chamber pots were also in use.

The courtyard location of the cistern meant that this was also the logical place for the washbasin that served for washing hands, faces, and dishes. Many washbasins are in situ in Greek house ruins all over the

Figure 17.6. Clay figurine of a bather in a tub, ancient Greek. Reprinted by permission of the British Museum.

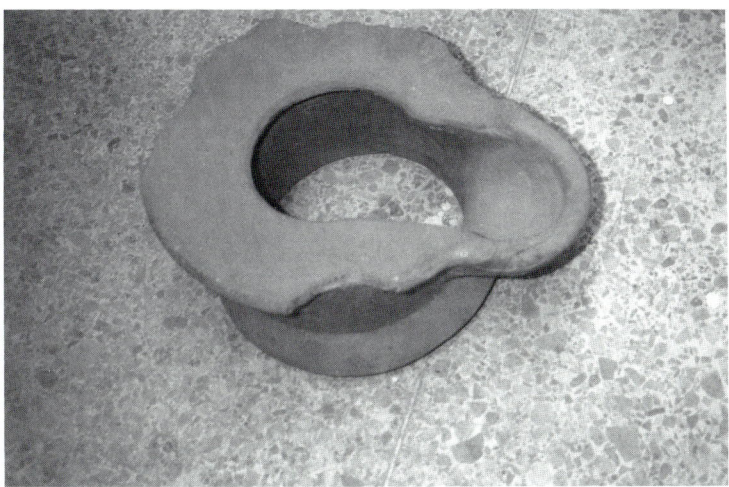

Figure 17.7. Terra-cotta toilet from Olynthos, now in the storerooms of the Archaeological Museum at Thessaloniki. Reprinted by permission of Johns Hopkins University Press.

Mediterranean. Two little figurines in the Athens museum show women washing dishes in such a stemmed washbasin (Fig. 17.8). I consider it symptomatic of the sexist approach to history that the question of where the dishes were washed in ancient Greek households has never come up before—presumably because the historians as privileged males did not have to think about this task allocated to women or slaves.[1]

Laundry arrangements in Morgantina and elsewhere were set up in the courtyard also (Fig. 17.5). The ancient courtyards had roofed walkways around them, and I imagine poles or ropes strung between their supporting posts, with the laundry spread out there and humidifying the house as it dried.

Thus the conservation and use of water directly affected the architectural form of the house, with its interior courtyard, inward slanting roofs, and placement of water-using activity spaces (bathroom, latrine, kitchen, and courtyard itself) close to one another, often with a common drain to the sewer under the street. In the Greco-Roman towns of Pompeii and Herculaneum we see the next development, small private fountains as the earliest surviving examples of enhanced aesthetic manipulation of water in the courtyards.

At a larger scale, public holding tanks for water made an architectural impact on the settlement. These could be small, like the tank in the macellum of the Morgantina Agora [Crouch, 1984, 359, based on final report (unpublished) by Nabers], medium-sized like the tank in the North Demeter Sanctuary, or large like the reservoir on the top of Papa Hill to the west of West Hill. All were rectangular and built above ground, thus dif-

Figure 17.8. Figurine of woman washing dishes at a washbasin. From the collection of the National Archaeological Museum in Athens, and reprinted by permission.

fering from the round or square cisterns recessed into the ground. Like the water in the moat section of the Northeast Fountainhouse, the water in the tank of the macellum was presumably for cleansing articles to be sold, not for bathing or drinking. Many tanks, such as the one in the North Demeter Sanctuary, held water for bathing. In the ground, particularly if deeper than about six feet down, water takes on the cool, stable temperature of the earth; above ground it more nearly approximates the temperature of the air. It was advantageous to have bathing water at a warmer temperature. Placing the tank above ground or immediately under the paving of the courtyard ensured that the water it held would warm at least to ground temperature or even to somewhere between ground and air temperature. Thus the placement of cisterns, which determines the temperature of the water, tells us whether they held drinking water or water for other purposes such as bathing.

Drains

Even so utilitarian a water system element as a drain could and did have an impact on the architectural form of the settlement. The most dramatic of the drains at Morgantina was in the angle of the great steps, an upright rectangular gap big enough for a short person to walk in (Fig. 14.3). Waters from the northwest corner of the Agora were collected and channeled through here and eventually out through the south rampart of the city. These arrangements are discussed at greater length in Chapter 14. A similar very large drain ran behind the East Stoa, joining a lower but parallel drain in the Agora and then pouring out through or rather under the South Gate. Next to that gate was one of several narrow slits in the rampart, through which storm runoff could escape; another can be seen in the stretch of wall between the postern gate near the House of the Official and the spring that lies below it (Fig. 12.2). Inside the city, some buildings of the agora have smaller drain slits proportional to the size of the building and to the amount of water that might collect either in its court—in the case of the macellum—or in the crack between the building and the hill—in the case of the granary next to the South Gate. Thus the ancient builders seem to have understood that the problems of managing storm runoff were exacerbated by the pavements (roofs, courtyards, streets) which prevented the rainwater from soaking into the ground, and they made deliberate provision for coping with the excess runoff.

We can also see the practical mind at work in the location of pipelines laid immediately beneath the cobblestone street paving in the residential area of West Hill (Fig. 17.9). By using uncemented cobblestones, the street was easy to take apart if it were necessary to have access to the water or sewer lines, and by placing the pipes immediately under this surface, they were accessible without digging. Since the ground does not freeze during the mild Mediterranean winters, the water pipes were safe enough at this level as they would not be in a more northern climate where freezing would cause bursting. In a town like Priene, where the rock of the hill comes much closer to the surface, the lines of pipes are laid in channels of semi-hexagonal shape cut into the rock and capped by slabs of stone. Here in a residential district at Morgantina, however, the pipelines were protected enough by being laid in the dirt and the street paving laid over them. Down by the northwest corner of the Agora, because of increased traffic and different soil conditions, the engineers took the precaution of cutting channels in rock and providing cover slabs wherever the levels of rock and street were too close together.

Figure 17.9. Water supply pipes running just under the cobblestone street paving on West Hill, southeast of the House of the Arched Cistern, Morgantina. Part of the street paving was removed by the excavators to inspect what was under it. The pipes are approximately 14 cm. internal diameter.

Figure 17.10. Very large drain, under the main street, Pergamon. This drain is nearly 2 meters deep.

Figure 17.11. Great drain, Athenian Agora, no later than the sixth century B.C. This drain is 1 to 1.25 meter wide and up to 2 meters deep.

PUBLIC AND PRIVATE

Architectural expression of water management at Morgantina mirrored the choices and values of the society. Security against both hostile neighbors and the vagaries of nature was enhanced by pluralism in the water supply. Neither wells nor cisterns nor springs nor pipelines alone had to carry the burden of being sole suppliers of water. Private and public activities were not assorted in the same patterns as ours but rather followed the values of that society. Small examples: most of us now do not wash our faces and our dishes in the same basin, nor do we all think of routinely combining religious ritual and bathing. Yet these actions accorded with the values of ancient Greek society.

Responsibility for different aspects of the water system was allocated to individuals, families, or the community. Building and maintaining a cistern could then as now be accomplished by a family or even by one person, but it took community effort and wealth to move the large stone slabs that formed the great drains of the Morgantina Agora, so we know that building a communal drainage system was valued enough to be an ordinary event even in small settlements.

To understand better how the water management of the society expressed the values of the society, we would have to study not only the archaeological remains but also the inscriptions, literature, sculpture and painting, and coins in order to get a fine historical sense of the culture; the geology and the geography of each site in order to know the basic resource constraints; and the technology of the time, especially hydraulic and civil engineering, in order to grasp what was technically possible. Thus we arrive again at the necessity for interdisciplinary study.

The architectural components and the urban design of even so simple a place as Morgantina show us what the Greeks accomplished within the constraints of the technology available to them, and the natural constraints of topography, climate, and resources of the site, and within their social organization and value system. What people do and make embodies their beliefs even more clearly than what they profess in words. From this modest provincial example, we see that they lived in a symbiotic relationship with the environment. Although they took what they needed in the form of raw materials and water, they returned enough to the environment that the ecological balance was preserved.

CONCLUSION

Traditional water management in ancient Greek society achieved more than a grudging minimum to make survival possible. Because it was a living tradition, able to adapt to new terrains and to incorporate innovation, it accomplished first-class solutions to the problems of necessity— solutions at once elegant and economic. What could be done privately was done that way, and what needed wider community assets and thought was done that way. The cultural tendency to make physical equivalents of intellectual understandings is just as apparent in a provincial fountain-house as in a statue by Phidias. The result was a high level of amenity that made capital use of seeming constraints.

NOTE

1. "No one seems to have studied ancient housekeeping. We don't know if the great civilizations of the past were slobs or what. I suspect the ancient Greeks were personally clean but lousy homemakers . . . I've never been able to come up with any solid historical precedent of slovenliness. . . . My best arguments against housekeeping are anthropological. The definition of dirt varies greatly from one culture to another. In societies where everyone lives in huts with dirt floors, they don't consider dirt dirt" (O'Rourke, 1987).

18

The Well-Watered Acropolis at Athens

Persons with some knowledge of the Athenian acropolis[1] are likely to be aware of the very early Mycenaean spring in the north-northwest quadrant, and of the still flowing Klepsydra Spring at the northwest corner, as well as remember stories about Poseidon's salt spring adjacent to the Erechtheum. Yet to connect the presence of water on the Acropolis with the urban history of Athens has not been explicitly done to date, even though the Acropolis has been the focus of settlement from earliest times until today. It is the purpose of this section to set out what is known about water utilization at the Athenian Acropolis, thereby suggesting firm ecological reasons why settlement should have taken place on and near the Acropolis (Fig. 18.1).

Travlos' map series of the city of Athens (1960) centered on the Acropolis show us that this hill has always been the focus of settlement, a fact well known to the ancient Athenians themselves (Thucydides, 2:15.3–6). I suggest that not only the defensive capabilities of the Acropolis but specifically its water supply made it the logical choice of location for groups who intended to live securely and to dominate the region. The number and diversity of water sources here is impressive. In each era it has been necessary to cope with the water that occurred naturally and to save for later use the rain and spring waters that drew settlers to this rocky outcropping. Let us note the locations of water on the Acropolis at several levels, with references to published accounts of some of the features and descriptions (based on surface reconnaissance and discussion with experts) of those for which I have not been able to find such accounts. Discussion of the geology of the Acropolis will be found with the paragraphs about the salt spring. After this topographical discussion, we will look briefly at the chronology of water on the Acropolis, followed by a concluding discussion of urban history.

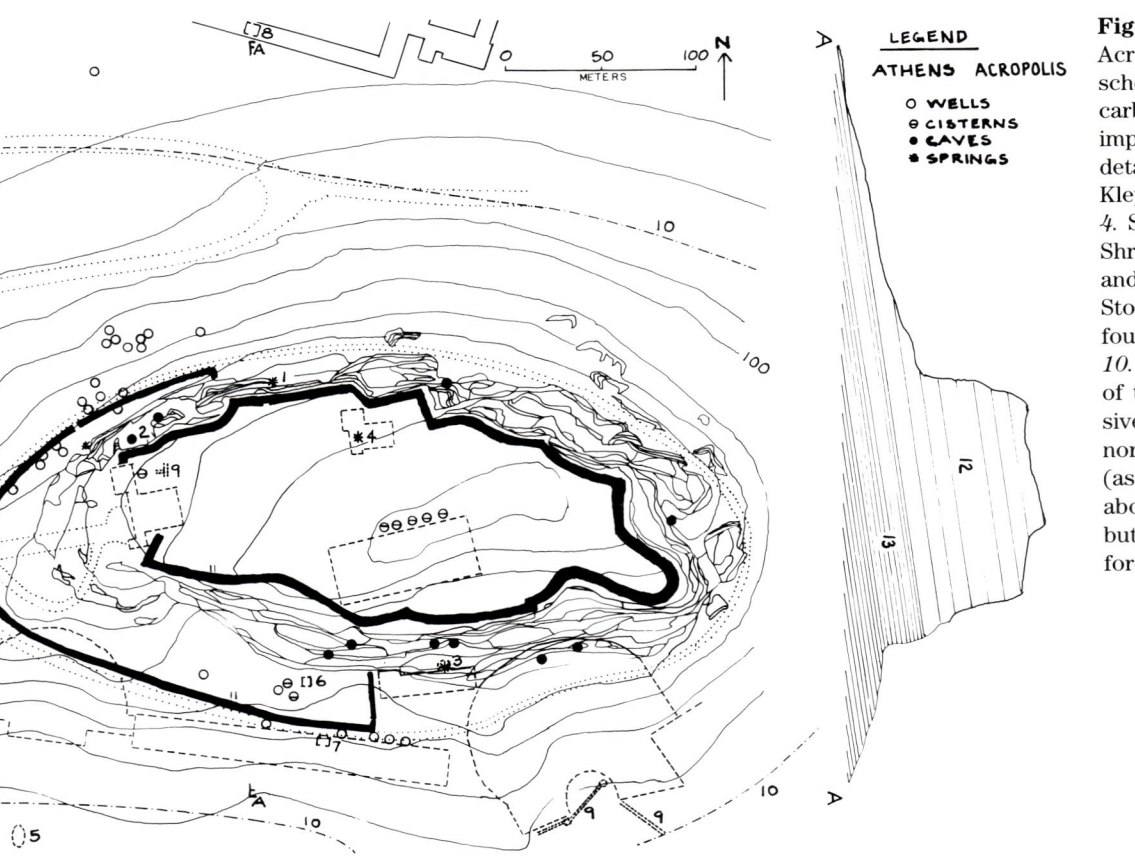

Figure 18.1. The well-watered Acropolis at Athens. At left is a schematic profile of the site, with carbonate rock (*12*) perched above impervious marl (*13*). Numbered details: *1.* Mycenaean Spring. *2.* Klepsydra Spring. *3.* Sacred Spring. *4.* Salt spring of the Erechtheum. *5.* Shrine of Nymphee. *6.* Mycenaean and archaic spring. *7.* Fountain in Stoa of Eumenes. *8.* Spring and fountain in Roman agora. *9.* Drains. *10.* Long distance water supply line of the sixth century B.C. *11.* Defensive walls. To the east of (*1*), on the north slope, other wells were found (as discussed by K. Glowacki (1991) about the wells of the North Slope) but I have not seen them and therefore do not show them on this plan.

SUMMIT

Immediately to the left of the Propylaea, inside the Acropolis wall, are rectangular cisterns dug into the rock of the surface, with rock-cut drainage channels leading to them from the central pathway. In the fall of 1988, these cisterns had been newly excavated by Tasos Tanoulas, architect of the restoration of the Propylaea, who most kindly showed them to me and explained his findings (Tanoulas, 1987, 475). What the old soundings had hinted at has been fully revealed by his excavations: very large archaic cisterns of the late sixth century B.C., covered originally with a wooden roof (long since gone) and fed with rainwater via rock-cut channels. These cisterns formed a square, divided by two cross-walls into smaller rectangular chambers, the northern two being connected by a low level drain, and excess water drained over the north wall of the Acropolis. These early cisterns lie to the east of the rectangular Roman cistern within the northeast room of the Propylaea. Such cisterns for rainwater were essential to the military role of the Acropolis. These were capable of holding several months supply of water which could be used for drinking if necessary, but usually was used for bathing and cleaning. Tanoulas's excavations revealed the patterns of supply and drainage channels in the cistern area. Further channels lie to the east of the cisterns, at several levels.

Northeast of Tanoulas' cisterns, we can look down and see the horizontal metal grating that currently blocks the way down to where the Mycenaean Fountain lay within the fold of rock. Through this barrier we can easily make out the steps that lead down within the north wall of the Acropolis to the first landing, from which one would have descended further to the fountain far below. The Mycenaean Fountain was published originally by Broneer (1939, 317–433) and well illustrated by Travlos (1980, fig. 67 no. 104, p. 72, and figs. 92–96) with a plan showing its location, a detailed section showing the stairs leading down to it, and a cross-section relating it to the Acropolis wall below, to the cave on the north slope of the Acropolis, and to the ground level to the north (Figs. 7.3, 18.2). From these illustrations we can see how the fountain related to the geology as well as to the walls and buildings of the northwest sector of the Acropolis. This water source has been dated from the thirteenth century B.C., from pottery found within it that indicates it was in use for only about thirty-five years. Travlos calls this source a spring or a well and says that the bottom of it is set into the marl that underlies the Acropolis (Travlos, 1980, 72).

It is typical of the behavior of springs to appear now here, now there, but gradually to come to the surface at lower and lower levels. Originally the water of the Mycenaean Spring was probably accessible at a higher level, but as the water receded it was necessary to build additional flights of stairs down to it. Over time, the Mycenaeans built eight flights of steps

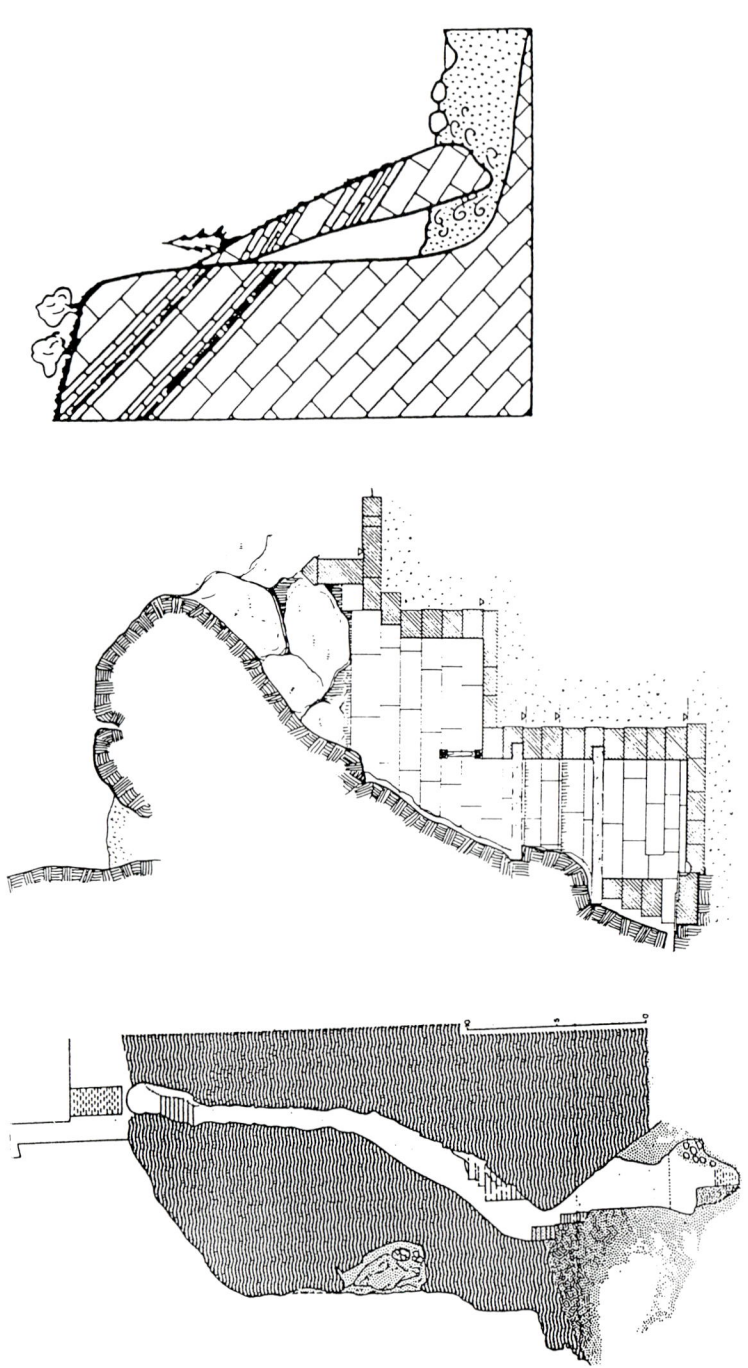

down to the surface of the water, probably cleaning out the basin each time they extended the flights of stairs. The fact that the water kept appearing at lower and lower levels could explain the apparent brevity of use. If the end of a period of danger from invasion should have coincided with the movement of water to a still lower level, this could explain what seems to be so brief a use of the fountain—the thirty-five years after the eighth flight of stairs was constructed and before they decided not to continue the process. An earth movement similar to the dislodging of great boulders that required the rebuilding of Klepsydra Spring in Roman times (see later) was probably responsible for making access to the Mycenaean fountain too difficult, or interrupting the flow of water, or both. In post-Mycenaean times the shaft probably served as a catchment for surface drainage from the Acropolis top, as is indicated by the rock-cut channels pointing toward it. Contamination from surface waters would reduce the general usefulness of the spring.

Walking eastward a little from the metal grating over the Mycenaean steps, to the Erechtheum, we are near the salt spring, most mysterious of the water sources on the Acropolis (illustrated in fig. 43 of Wycherley, 1978). The story is well-known: In the contest between Athena and Poseidon for the patronage of Athens, the goddess caused an olive tree to grow up overnight, near the site of her old temple on top of the Acropolis, and the god countered by causing a salt spring to erupt on top of the mesa. The Athenians decided they preferred her promise of oil for food and trade to his promise that he would control the sea for their benefit, and the subsequent devotion of the Athenians to this goddess was the basis of their identity as a people.

But how to explain the salt spring? How could there be such an anomaly—both so many miles from the sea and so high above sea level? Could there be any physical basis for such a story? Here modern understanding of geology, especially of the interaction of water and limestone in karst terrane is relevant, as we have discussed in Chapter 7. Already in 1893, Richard Lepsius had shown in a widely reprinted section of the acropolis in *Geologie von Attika*, pl. I, "Profile of the Hills of Athens")

Figure 18.2. Sections of caves in karst terrane. Left to right, the Mycenaean Spring and Klepsydra Spring (both of the northwest corner of the Acropolis), compared with a geological diagram of the formation of caves by collapse of sections of stone. Left, Mycenaean Spring section reprinted by permission of Greeenwood Publishing Group, Inc., Westport, CT, from *Pictorial Dictionary of Ancient Athens.* by J. Travlos, copyright in Tubingen, Germany, by Verlag E. Wasmuth, 1971; published in New York, 1971, by Praeger Publishers, reprinted 1980 by Hacker Art Books. Center, Klepsydra Spring, Parsons, 1943: 254; reprinted by permission from American School of Classical Studies at Athens. Right, Collapse cave diagram, from Jakucs (1977): 91, Fig. 27, reprinted by permission of Adam Hilger Publishing Limited.

(Fig. 18.9 here) that the Acropolis consists of an outcrop of gray limestone riding on an uptilted layer of marl, in turn above a layer of clay-schist. More recent studies of the hill's geology show that rather than one layer of marl there are a number of lenses of the impermeable stone. An exhibit, "The Acropolis at Athens: Conservation, Restoration and Research 1975–1983" held in the new Acropolis Museum in 1988 included geology maps that showed these lenses; unfortunately the geology exhibits were not included in the catalog of the exhibition (Casanaki et al., 1988), although they have been published in a 1976 study by Andronopoulos and Koukis. Springs at various levels on this hill can be accounted for by the characteristic behavior of water, limestone, and schist together in a karst terrane. The water from precipitation infiltrates the fissures in the limestone, traveling vertically or diagonally downward into the ground. When the water reaches a level of impermeable schist or marl, it turns in a direction perpendicular to the first descent. Since the bedding planes here are tilted diagonally, the water travels upward along them and appears on the surface as springs or even as artesian wells where the pressure is high enough. As Parsons writes,

> A series of small springs . . . girdle the Acropolis. They appear, typically, at the base of the cliffs, where the grey limestone cap of the Acropolis rests on layers of schist and marl. The limestone is full of crevices and cracks, and rain water which falls on the Acropolis runs off through these, and down until it reaches the relatively impermeable schist; there it collects. The limestone thus acts as a kind of gigantic reservoir, of which the schist forms the floor; it is the water seeping through wherever it can find an outlet along the "joint" which forms the series of little springs. (Parsons, 1943, 205)

Over many years, the acids dissolved in the water (CaO_3) gradually enlarge the fissures, enabling the water to penetrate more quickly, after a rainstorm for instance. This is the general circumstance of springs on the Acropolis, but what about the salt spring in question?

An article by R.C. Baker provides the necessary clue to understand the salt spring in Athens (1977, 333–39). Baker's Figure 2 (Fig. 18.3 here) and his explanation reveal that infiltrating water that passes through a bed of salt during either its vertical descent into the ground or its diagonal or horizontal passage to the surface can carry that salt out as it moves along the sloping bed, and can erupt dramatically by artesian force, when the rock above the artesian shaft becomes thin enough to collapse. The salt spring could thus appear at a particular moment, as the myth suggests, and could later disappear for one of several reasons. Either the layer of salt (deposited as was the limestone in those remote ages when present-day Greece was at the bottom of the sea) was finally washed away by the spring water, or else—more likely—the water made itself deeper paths into the earth and no longer flowed out at Poseidon's open-

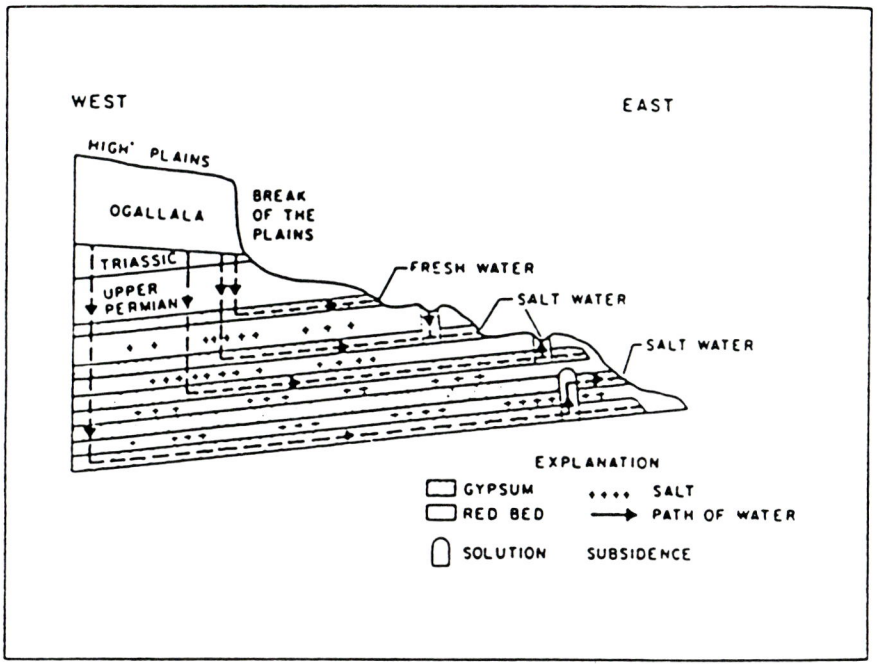

Figure 18.3. Diagram explaining a salt spring in an inland area. Water entering from the surface via vertical cracks encounters a layer of salt, dissolves some of it, and carries it either horizontally or diagonally out to a resurgence or vertically upward via a shaft that eventually pierces the overlying layers and erupts on the surface as an artesian well. Poseidon's legendary salt spring on the Athens Acropolis could be expalined by this mechanism. Reprinted by permission of Western Kentucky University Press, from R.C. Baker (1977): 336, Fig. 2.

ing, or both factors operated together. Certainly there is no longer a salt spring flowing on the top of the Acropolis. Poseidon has been vanquished.

A modern replacement of the olive tree with which Athena won the contest grows at the west side of the Erechtheum, indicating that enough water is available there to sustain its life. Two more trees grow near the steps down to the Acropolis Museum. All three require water to survive, but no source is apparent. I suggest that cistern cavities possibly dating to Mycenaean times are big enough for soil, roots, and water.

Last of the water elements on the top of the Acropolis, along the south edge of the central pathway, lie cisterns with modern lids. One is still capped with its ancient stone wellhead about 2 feet tall, sloping outward from top to bottom, and closed with a wooden lid locked in place with a modern padlock, so that one cannot look in to see whether it still holds water. Modern visitors to the Acropolis are frequently tempted to bring with them cold liquids, to offset the glare and heat of the Mediterranean sun on all that rock. Sun and rock were evident in antiquity also, and so provision had to be made for the ordinary visitor as well as for the crowds of thirsty participants during festivals. This need, I think, explains the construction and location of the five cisterns just north of the Parthenon. Without discussing or attempting to date them, Travlos (1960) shows them on his map of the "Acropolis in the fourth to second centuries B.C." (his fig. 91, p.71) These shafts date probably from the fourth century B.C., and are "the mouths of cisterns of the ordinary bottle-shaped variety," according to Homer Thompson who has suggested to me that the wellheads are likely to have been brought in from elsewhere, and probably originally supported the typical hollow cylindrical upper section of either marble or terra-cotta. In his *Politics*, (vii,1330b) written in the 320's, Aristotle asserts that "cities need cisterns for safety in war." Camp has noted that at exactly that time a severe drought extending for nearly a quarter of a century made increased efforts to save every drop of rain water essential (Camp, 1982, 9–17). This is just when cisterns began to outnumber wells in the Agora (Parsons, p.192). Cisterns on the Acropolis would have been useful also during the many later centuries when it was a fortress or a fortified village.

This completes the list of water elements on the highest level of the hill. As early as Mycenaean times, however, major water sources were known and used on the slopes of the hill, so that circuits of defensive walls were built to include them. Let's go out through the Propylaea and part way down the slope, to circumnavigate the Acropolis along the ancient Peripatos ("ring road") at a level where the hill seems to be bursting with water.

AT PERIPATOS LEVEL

First to the northwest, as one goes clockwise, comes the Klepsydra Spring, nearly invisible in the folds of rock at the northwest corner. Geologists understand this spring's setting as a cave that has gone through many phases (multiphase cave, Fig. 7.4 here) (Ford, 1981, Fig. 5). In ancient times Klepsydra was articulated by an entrance court with "impressive stone paving" which is still visible to the person walking close to the flank of the hill. The spring was beautifully published by Arthur W. Parsons (1943). This spring lies above the garden area "green today as it was in antiquity" that Parsons calls "the very heart of primitive Athens" (p. 203). As early as Neolithic times, settlers gathered here and utilized the water that never runs dry, digging no fewer than twenty shallow wells or pits to tap the water. Also early, from the Middle Bronze Age, are some deeper wells at the northwest corner of the area. Although Parsons found little evidence of settlement on the Acropolis during the Geometric period, when people seem to have preferred the level ground below, he did find wells on the terrace by the Klepsydra Spring, dating from the seventh and sixth century B.C., filled in about the middle of the fifth century just before the formalizing of this spring into a fountain-house. The rectangular underground basin of the spring has been pre-served almost intact since that first formalization, although the entrance has been moved. The "court" near the intersection of the Peripatos and the Panathenaic Way was possibly the floor of a large cistern, made of massive blocks of poros (a limestone that is not too hard and easily worked), like the Southwest Fountainhouse of the Agora. This court or cistern held the overflow from the spring and may also have stored run-off water from the slope, according to Homer Thompson, who adds, "Cut-tings in the face of the cliff above the court suggest that the court was roofed, as would be necessary for a cistern" (personal communiction; cf. Camp's discussion of the paved court as a reservoir p. 258). This spring has continued as a water source until the present, for "when Broneer began work [between the wars] on the north slope of the Acropolis, he found that women of the Anaphiotika quarter still went regularly to Klep-sydra for their water." (Parsons, 1943,193 n.4). According to Mr. Monok-roussos, engineer of the restoration of the Acropolis rock, since the spring never runs dry, the water of Klepsydra is now (1988) piped up to the top of the hill for various uses.

Continuing along the north side of the Acropolis, we pass several other caves that may once have held water that drew their associated deities into residence there: the hollows called Olympieion, Pythion, Cave of Pan, and Sanctuary of Eros and Aphrodite (Hopper, 1971, fig. 7; Travlos, 1980, fig.93). We have no evidence that these caves held water in classical times or later, but such evidence has indeed not been sought. From the same pathway one can climb a few meters and reach a cave leading to a land-ing of the Mycenaean Spring. From here one can look down where other long flights of steps once led closer to the water, but the water itself is long gone and its basin is not visible, hidden in another fold of the rock. It had been thought that in classical and Hellenistic times the nymph Aglauros was worshipped in this cave opening but now the archaeolo-gists prefer to locate Aglauros' cave and shrine farther east. The true shrine of Aglauros was detirmined to be at a very large cave on the east end of the Acropolis, just above the level of the ring road (Dontas, 1983, 48–63 and pl. 13–15; Travlos, 1980, 72–73). A stele was found in front of the cave, and Dontas called for further study of both the cave and the precinct in front of it (p. 63). Never completely excavated, the east end has in 1988–89 undergone stabilization. It is tempting to think that other visible hollows along the east side were water-bearing caves in ancient times, but they may be only recent results of the deterioration and crum-bling of this face.

It would be interesting to examine all these hollows together with a hydrogeologist.[2] In the absence of such interdisciplinary investigation, let us pass on to the south side of the Acropolis, where a series of caves mark the seam between rock layers of different hardnesses (Fig. 18.4). This seam is clearly shown on Lepsius's cross-section of the Acropolis. According to karst theory, we would expect water to appear all along the seam, as it actually does and did, so that the south side of the hill is richly endowed with water sources. One shallow cave after another has been made into a shrine—probably to safeguard the water it originally yielded, or still gives, and to give thanks for it (Rudhardt, 1971).

Already in classical times, it was the custom to set up victory columns along the Peripatos. Their present locations suggest that their original placement was concerned with the monumentalization of caves in the cliff face above the road (Wycherley, 1978, 84). First we encounter a cave below the easternmost victory column but above the Theater of Diony-

Figure 18.4. View of south side of Acropolis, Athens, from Stuart and Revett, *The Antiquities of Athens*, second edition 1825, Vol. 11 plate 37. At the top, the columns of the Parthenon lace the sky. The buttresses of the retaining wall bulk in the shadow behind the two columns of the Thrasyllos Monument, below which are the three columns of the portico of a cave sanctuary still used as a chapel. The cave, which is slightly off-axis at the top of the slope, above the Theater of Dionysius, is a karst formation; other small cave openings are visible right and left of the portico. Behind the people at the left a retaining wall casts a shadow. To its left, out of the picture, is the Asklepieion.

sos, now called the Church of the Virgin of the Cave (Panagia Speliotissa). This cave became visible in the early fourth century B.C. when the cliff was scarped back for the extension of the theater. Just as the nymphs' guardianship ensured the purity of water in ancient times, so also the Christian religion was pressed into service later on to safeguard the water (Travlos, 1980, 562).

A second cave is located at the top of the Theater of Dionysos, slightly to the west of the first. Both caves resemble the cave fountain on the Pnyx, in combining the roughness of a cave with minimum architectural intervention such as a parapet and a pair of columns at the entrance (Camp, 1979, 97).

Next we come to the temple and precinct of Asklepius, halfway along the middle level of the slope. Less accessible today than the first two caves, because of ongoing restoration work, the sanctuary comprised two stoas tucked in close to the cliff, sources of medicinal water, and a shallow terrace. Behind the eastern stoa was hidden a rounded cave-like room in the cliff, to surround and protect the original spring whose healing waters were the basis of the cures wrought here by the priest-doctors. The faithful still come to this cave to pray and take the waters, and thus it is ironic that this water was the most contaminated of the three samples I had tested (see Chapter 19, A Note on Testing Water). Since the Asklepion is currently undergoing restoration, the spring house is visible only as a tall doorway crowned by an arch (Fig. 18.5). Though its present form is late Hellenistic or Roman, the Asklepion sanctuary dates from at least as early as the end of the fifth century (Wycherley, 1978, 181–182 n.20–23).

To the west of the Asklepion stood a fountain of much greater antiquity. As early as Mycenaean times, the spring here was so important as to be enclosed in the Mycenaean fortifications of the Acropolis. The Mycenaean arrangements for this fountain were changed in the sixth century when a shaft of polygonal masonry in Kara limestone was set above the smaller round well of earlier times, filled from an underlying spring (Fig. 18.6). A fountain house that was used into the fourth century was erected to cover this well shaft (Travlos, 1980, 52, 127, 138, and fig. 188). Some evidence of a boundary dispute between the nymphs of this fountain and Asklepius, or their respective priests, may be discerned from a boundary stone set up to mark the line between them.

The copious flows of water in this area are further indicated by several cisterns of different constructions and capacities. Of the two early Byzantine (fourth or fifth century A.D.) vaulted brick cisterns, the one closer to the cliff face was fed by a spring that is chemically different from its neighbor in the Kara limestone shaft and both are different from the water in the Sacred Spring at the other end of the Asklepion. A third very large vaulted brick cistern (probably Byzantine) is located farther from the cliff, right next to the Peripatos road. Quite possibly the Byz-

Figure 18.5. View of Asklepion at Athens. At left, the cliff wall changes from carbonate rock (limestone) to clay/marl. Water typically appears along such a seam. The arched opening at right, 1 meter wide, leads to a domed cave used as a chapel for a Sacred Spring since time immemorial. See Fig. 7.3 for the geological formation of such spaces.

Figure 18.6. The shaft of the archaic water holder built on the south slope of the Athenian Acropolis, above the well/spring known since Mycenaean times, to the west of the stoas of the Asklepion. The shaft is 2 meters in diameter.

antine cisterns pertain to the church that replaced the Asklepion in the fifth century A.D. and was dedicated to the "Doctor Saints," a continuity of function (if not dogma) that was common in the ancient-to-medieval world (Travlos, 1980, 129 and Figs. 171 and 172) (cf. R. Krautheimer, 1980, chapter 2). I think that the many building periods evident here indicate there was water over a long time, but that it changed its exact outfall and rate of flow from time to time.

These structures of the Asklepion area lie at the foot of a distinctive fold in the cliff (Fig. 18.7), a narrow version of the fold that encloses Klepsydra. The Asklepion and fountain are both shown on Hopper's map, figure 14, while the fountain is shown as a spring on Travlos's map "Early Burials and Wells in the Agora and on the Acropolis" from Thompson

Figure 18.7. Drainage from the south side of the Acropolis. Top to bottom: the southwest corner of the Parthenon, Cimon's wall of the Acropolis with a cleft for drainage, buttresses of the back wall of the Stoa of Eumenes, large drain near the bottom of the hill.

and Wycherly (1972), but as a fountain on Hopper's figure 6, "The Acropolis and surrounding area in the early fifth century B.C. before the Persian sack." There will be more to say about this fold in the cliff when we discuss the fountain in the Stoa of Eumenes.

Further evidence of the management of water at the Peripatos level is to be seen in the channels, wellheads, and remains of disused cisterns that clutter the terrace (formerly the road) along the southwest side of the Acropolis, and tie in with the drainage below. These elements are especially numerous toward the west end of this terrace, clustered together where the path swerves in towards the cliff-face above the Odeion of Herodes Atticus. The channels of this area slope to the east, towards the great drain that serves the Theater of Dionysos, to be considered later. By skirting the uphill edge of the Odeion we can return to the entrance path that leads up to the Acropolis summit, thus completing the circuit of the Acropolis at the middle level.

AT THE FOOT OF THE HILL

We will turn and go downhill to the level of the foot of the theaters, set today among gardens. Turning left, we will go counterclockwise this time, back along the south slope near the bottom. The Odeion of Herodes Atticus and Stoa of Eumenes lie against the southwest edge of the Acropolis. The Odeion of Herodes Atticus was not of course a water element itself, yet near it may be found several elements for handling water. There is a very large cistern associated with the flat side of the theater, and ample provision for drainage in the form of rock-cut channels. Walking eastward from the Odeion, we pace along the wall of arches that survives from the Stoa of Eumenes. (Travlos, 1980, 540–41, fig. 677–78) The Stoa of Eumenes has not been fully published, but see Travlos (1980, p. 523) for views, plans, and some citations. This wall had the double function of terminating the space of the stoa and of supporting the Peripatos Road above, so it was important to construct behind and under it drainage channels, which still function to prevent storm and spring waters from undermining the retaining wall. Water from springs and surface drainage of that upper level is likely to have fed the fountain in the retaining wall of the stoa below, recessed within the thickness of the retaining wall, about halfway along the stoa. The fountain in the rear wall is not discussed by Travlos. Above it at the Peripatos Road level, the stone base of a wellhead is visible, and the map of the Acropolis given me by Nikos Toganidis (architect of the restoration of the Parthenon) shows the vertical shaft as having a horizontal branching into the hill, as one would expect of a karst shaft-and-channel draining impounded rain waters. (Fig. 18.8). Thus water from the top of the Acropolis finds its way from level to level in the typical karst stair-step pattern, to the springs of the Peripatos level, then down to the base of the Stoa of Eumenes, and finally to

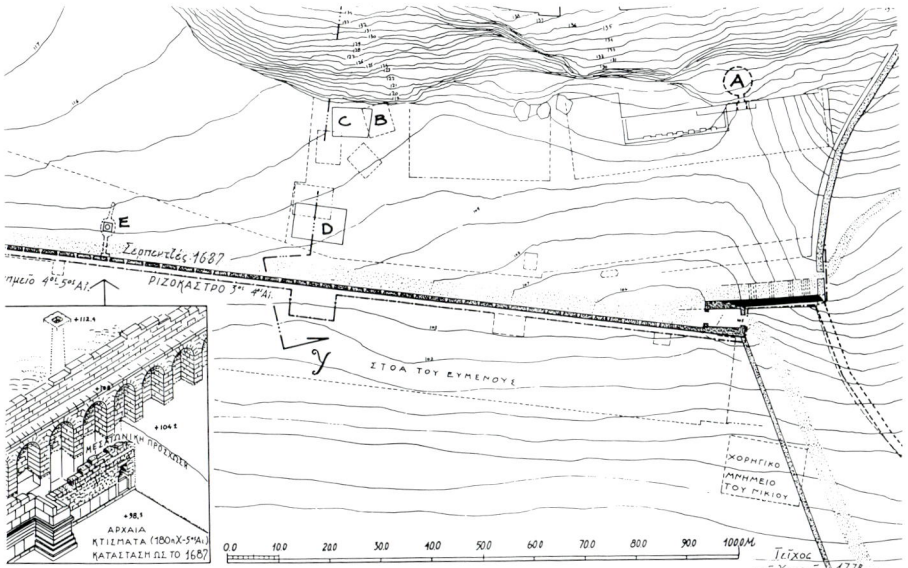

Figure 18.8. Fountain of the Stoa of Eumenes, Athens, with its channel back into the hill above the retaining wall, and access shaft to reach the water from 4 meters higher on the hill. This is a karst formation, altered by ancient builders. A. Shaft above fountain in Stoa of Eumenes. B. Medieval cistern. C. Early Christian cistern. D. Shaft of archaic well above Mycenaean Spring. E. Sacred spring of Asklepion. This is a detail of a plan prepared by the Archaeology Service in Athens preparatory to restoration work on the buildings of the Acropolis. It was brought to my attention by Nikos Toganidis, architect of the restoration of the Parthenon, and is reprinted here by permission of Peter Kaligas, Director of the Acropolis. Detail of Acropolis map by Man Korres.

the Shrine of Nymphe and the Byzantine fountainhouse near the present major street.

Note that both the upper fountain at the west of the Asklepion and lower fountain in the Stoa wall align with the constructed cleft in the southern fortification wall of the Acropolis (Fig. 18.7). This cleft may have originally been natural, but it was reinforced and regularized when the fortifications were built. It is evident that the ancient engineers took pains to control both storm runoff and surplus flowing water from the springs of the south face of the Acropolis, and to direct these waters first into the upper cleft in the southern fortification wall of the Acropolis and then on into the natural cleft below.

Downhill from the Odeion of Herodes Atticus, at the bottom of the western approach to the Acropolis but nearly 300 feet south of the path were found some ruined walls and inscriptions of a sanctuary of Nymphe, among the trees of the modern park, at about the same level as the orchestra of the Theater of Dionysos. If you know where to look, you can see it from the top of the Acropolis. Its remains abut the new boulevard of Dionysios Aeropagites and extend under the street. It was excavated by I. Miliadis in 1956–59 (Travlos, 1980, 361–64 and p. 71, where it is number 148). The Italian School in Athens discovered many signs of prehistoric habitation on the south slope of the Acropolis—habitation made possible by the permanent supply of water, and continuing during many later periods (*Annuario* IV/V, 1921–22, 490; *Bollotino d'Arte*, IV, 1924–25, 88ff). An inscribed stone found in the Agora but likely to be from the "nymphaeum sanctuary" is discussed by Parsons, who prefers a location near the cave of Pan, on the north slope, although he cites Pausanias as placing the shrine "just below the Propylaea" which could equally well be this southern location.

Farther east in the gardens we come to the drainage channels that collect water from the cliff face and lead it past the west side of the Theater of Dionysos and into the great stone drains that also receive the water from the seating and orchestra of the theater. When the Theater of Dionysos was built on and carved into the south slope of the Acropolis, careful provision was made for the drainage of the area, as reported by Broneer. Most clearly visible today, after the Roman rebuilding, are the large stone drains at the edge of the orchestra, which accepted the water from the seating area, and carried it out towards the southeast, passing under the stage building and part of the sacred precinct of the Dionysos Temple to the south. Those drains are still very impressive, and still serve to channel the storm run-off from much of the south slope over towards the valley of the Ilissos River, although the extended sequence of channels is invisible today beneath the modern traffic arteries. (von Gerkan, 1941, 163–77; Pickard-Cambridge, 1946; Dinsmoor, 1951–53, 309–30; Bieber, 1961; Travlos, 1980, Fig. 678).

If we make our way from the theater southward down to the major street, we will find just at the edge of the archaeological zone a building that seems to be Byzantine, judging from its masonry. The fact that the dividing wall between the two main rooms has an arch at floor level suggests that this too may be a fountainhouse, with provision made for the water to flow freely between the two chambers. This building, like the Shrine of Nymphe, was excavated by Miliadis in the late 1950s.

LOWEST LEVEL, NORTH SLOPE

A few remaining features of the north slope still remain to be considered, to complete the account of water and the Acropolis. To the north of the Acropolis, the lower slope is covered with the houses of the Plaka district at the level corresponding to the Theater of Dionysos on the south side. If we come down to the lowest level and enter the archaeological site that includes the Tower of the Winds and the Roman Agora, to the east of the classical Agora (Wycherley, 1978, 102) and at more or less the same elevation, we can see at the edge of the hill that water is still flowing from the rock there at sufficient volume for moss to grow in the arid Mediterranean climate. Here the gray limestone of the Acropolis tapers down to the underlying marl, and here the series of small springs at the base of the hill is most easily seen (Fig. 18.9). The edge where the floor of the agora meets the abrupt slope of the hill is so wet even today that the modern archaeologists complain that the flow seriously hampers their work, as Mrs. Touloupa told me in the spring of 1985. Individual buildings in this precinct have the usual gutters to manage rainwater from their roofs (cf. Fig. 22.1), and there is also a network of pipes and channels to handle the water running from the cliff. Those that are visible today are probably from the Roman period, but I think they replace earlier ones that had worn out. The Greeks, the Romans, and the modern excavators all have had to cope with the abundant water from the hill at this spot.

Long-distance water supply is also evident along both the north and south sides of the Acropolis, in the form of numerous pipes from the sixth century B.C. aqueduct built by the tyrants, which are stored in the Tower of the Winds, near the entrance to the Roman Agora (Fig. 18.10). They are likely to have been found not far from the tower—at least, my experience is that pipes and other water system elements have low priority as items to be cherished for their archaeological and historical significance. Therefore I infer that these are unlikely to have been brought to the tower from very far away. Homer Thompson said to me in 1988 that these pipes had only recently been placed in the Tower, but a line of the Peisistratid aqueduct was known at least by 1970 to run north of the Acropolis (Boersma, 1970, 24), and in 1988 I was shown an opening to the branch south of the Acropolis where the line runs through the gardens near the Theater of Dionysos.

Pipes similar to these supply the small fountain at the back of the South Stoa II of the Agora, as well as the Southeast and Southwest Fountainhouses at the corners of the Agora. The Peisistratid Aqueduct roughly parallels the much later Hadrianic Aqueduct. The former originates at the Kephissos Spring at the foot of Mt. Pentilicus, and is supplemented by a second line from Mt. Ymettos, which joined the first in a large reservoir. The Hadrianic Aqueduct ran from the reservoir on Lycabettus (Homer Thompson, personal communication; Judeich, 1905, 186). The air shafts of the qanat, which are 4 to 5 feet in diameter and regularly spaced at 30 to 40-meter intervals (Dorpfeld, 1898, 510) are still visible. As Dorpfeld said after his research on this aqueduct, "Only those who have taken the trouble to get right down into the tunnellings and cross tunnellings and

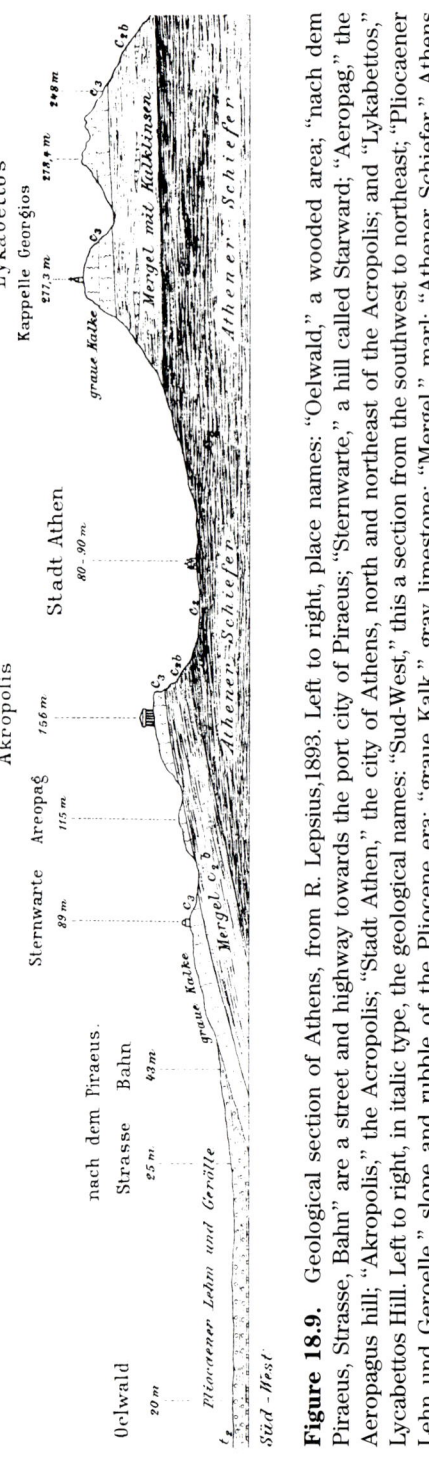

Figure 18.9. Geological section of Athens, from R. Lepsius,1893. Left to right, place names: "Oelwald," a wooded area; "nach dem Piraeus, Strasse, Bahn" are a street and highway towards the port city of Piraeus; "Sternwarte," a hill called Starward; "Aeropag," the Aeropagus hill; "Akropolis," the Acropolis; "Stadt Athen," the city of Athens, north and northeast of the Acropolis; and "Lykabettos," Lycabettos Hill. Left to right, in italic type, the geological names: "Sud-West," this a section from the southwest to northeast; "Pliocaener Lehn und Geroelle," slope and rubble of the Pliocene era; "graue Kalk," gray limestone; "Mergel," marl; "Athener Schiefer," Athens schist; "Mergel mit Kalkinsen," a mixture of marl and limestone. Note how the permeable limestone of the Acropolis—capped by the Parthenon—rides on the underlying impermeable marl, above impermeable schist. Recent geological studies have indicated a series of lenses of carbonate rocks and impermeable ones underlying the Parthenon, so that the geology of the Acropolis is more complicated than this century-old section drawing indicates.

272

Figure 18.10. Sixth century terra-cotta pipes from Peisistratid Aqueduct, Athens, stored in the Tower of the Winds. These pipes are two-thirds of a meter long, the standard length for pipes at this time.

explore them thoroughly so far as they can be explored, can form any idea of the magnitude of the work" (Dorpfeld, quoted by Harrison, 1906, 120). Some of the tunnels are the height of a man, but in others, Dorpfeld reports, one has to crawl on hands and knees. The historian Thucydides noted in the fifth century (a century or so after the Peisistratid line was built) that great water works such as those require an understanding of human nature and human needs, an understanding of the laws of nature, a great labor policy, and big expenditures (Thucydides, VI,54). The water was led by underground pipes through the city, branching into the various districts. (Leake, 1830, 385; Harrison, 1906, 120). The pipes from the aqueduct, lying on the floor of the Tower of the Winds, mutely testify to the presence of water here, to the need for more, and to its successful and sophisticated management as early as the sixth century B.C.

From the Byzantine era there is another aqueduct perpendicular to the Peisistratid Aqueduct, beginning at Klepsydra and paralleling the Panathenaic Way down the hill and into the Agora, a water line essential for the continued occupation of the Plaka area during the Middle Ages and Turkish times (Travlos' plan "Agora Excavations," as reprinted, for example, by Mattusch, 1977, pl.77; Parsons, 1943, 223). The holding tank of this branch aqueduct is dated by H. Thompson (personal communication) as fourth to fifth century A.D. Discussion of use of this water in fountains at the Agora is beyond the scope of this chapter, as are the gutters, pipes, and channels that lace the Panathenaic Way (Shear, 1973, 124). Not until Turkish times was the water from Klepsydra channeled in the direction of the area that had been the Roman Market of Caesar and Augustus (Parsons, p. 223) somewhat to the east of the classical Agora—a shift likely due to a change in residence patterns.

CHRONOLOGY

Inspection of the water system elements found on and next to the Acropolis has shown that as early as the Neolithic period (probably the third millennium B.C.), a settlement big enough to require twenty shallow wells was located on the terrace by Klepsydra Spring. From that period until the present age of scientific and touristic archeology—more than 4000 years—the great hill was not without its inhabitants. Indeed, they formed the core of every agglomeration, every version of "Athens." Instead of a topographical account, this time we will make a historical journey around the Acropolis, considering the role of available water in the development of this site.

The first stories about the Acropolis are the myths about Aegeus, Theseus, and others, which probably reflect the Mycenaean period of Athenian history. The Mycenaeans fortified the Acropolis in the last part of the second millennium B.C., to protect their palace in the same way that the palaces of Mycenae and Tiryns were fortified on their hilltops. Similar, too, were the careful provisions for obtaining water for those in the citadel, unobserved by a besieging enemy. We have noted the eight flights of stairs that led down to the Mycenaean Fountain, the most elaborate but probably not the only provision for water supply during the Bronze Age. Most likely there were also cisterns cut into the rock even at this early date. The fountain buried in the citadel wall at Athens postdates the Middle Bronze Age deep wells we noted before which had supplanted the shallow Neolithic ones of the Klepsydra terrace. These wells signify a continuing habitation of that terrace, in a pattern reminding us of the clustering of houses near the citadels of Mycenae and Tiryns. At all three settlements, the pattern was to reside comfortably on the lower slopes of the hill, but be prepared to retire into the fortress when danger from invaders threatened. The Mycenaeans buried their dead in the area that later became the classical Agora, thus that area was probably outside their settlement. We have already noted that the Mycenaean fortifications of the Acropolis enclosed the two springs now called Klepsydra and the spring to the west of the Asklepion. The builders of those walls were probably the discoverers of the spring that filled the so-called Mycenaean Fountainhouse (Travlos, 1980, 52).

It is notoriously difficult to date rock-cut channels, but quite probably some of those still visible on the top of the Acropolis were hewn out during Mycenaean times, to direct surface runoff from rain into the waiting cisterns; some may also date from the archaic period.

With the fall of the Mycenaeans, there was a period when Greece was being invaded by the Dorians, the Ionians were moving from the Greek mainland to the Ionian coast of Asia Minor, and life in Attica was so unsettled that we have no archaeological indication of urban life on the Acropolis. After the Geometric period (900–700 B.C.) however, perhaps because the trade in painted pottery had begun to restore prosperity to Athens, we again find imposing buildings on the summit, plus wells, cisterns, fountains, and channels as well as water-related shrines, which convince us of the existence of an active archaic settlement here. One theory has it that in the seventh century the Agora, formerly at the immediate western foot of the Acropolis, was moved to its present location (Wycherley, 1978, 27). Thompson, however, theorizes that there was a movable marketplace, just as in today's Athens the flea market held on Sundays occupies the streets from the ancient Agora to the Kerameikos site (personal communication).

Also during this archaic period, before the Persian Wars, some new wells were built near Klepsydra. Other new structures were the springhouse over the fountain to the west of what would later become the Asklepion, the earliest version of the precinct and Theater of Dionysos (with the concomitant need for drainage from the south slope), and the Peisistratid Aqueduct, some of whose pipes lie now stored inside the Tower of the Winds. This is a quantum jump in amount of water-management construction, focused on the Acropolis and the areas immediately adjacent to it.

From the classical period a number of water system elements still survive. They include the row of cisterns north of the Parthenon, the formal fountainhouse of the Klepsydra Spring, the first surviving buildings of the sanctuary of Asklepius, especially the round domed chamber enclosing the spring, and the sanctuary of Nymphe at the foot of the hill. At least some of the cisterns and wellheads of the southern Peripatos and their accompanying channels are likely to be from this period also.

In the Hellenistic era, the Asklepion began to take on the form we now know, and other cisterns, wellheads, and channels of this terrace were added. These constructions suggest that the water was now relatively abundant at the mid-point of the slope. The Theater of Dionysos had a complete drainage system provided during these years, and the earliest versions of the structures surrounding the Tower of the Winds were erected, including fountains and drains.

During the Roman period, the waters of the Acropolis continued to nurture life and make settlement possible here. Although an earthquake seems to have caused huge sections of the rock to collapse in on the Klepsydra Springhouse, the source was not abandoned but rather the walls of the fountainhouse were consolidated and a new access shaft built at a higher level (using characteristic Roman brick vaulting). Access from a higher level indicates that the perennial question of water for users on top of the Acropolis was to be partially answered by this new arrangement. On the south slope, the Theater of Dionysos was rebuilt with the drainage arrangements that we now see. From the second century A.D. comes the Odeion of Herodes Atticus complementing the Stoa of Eumenes of the second century B.C., with their attendant drains, cisterns, and fountains. These elements provided relief from storm waters and a supply of drinking water for those attending performances in either of the theaters. So also on the north slope, the arrangement that still survives of drains, gutters, and fountains around the Tower of the Winds is largely from the Roman period. In both locations, we may surmise that water not needed for the immediate purposes of the users of the structure at the source of the water could be and was channeled to fountains, cisterns, and animal watering troughs farther downhill for use by others.

Water seems to have continued to flow abundantly at midlevel of the slopes of the Acropolis during the Byzantine era, as we can see from the facts that the Roman chamber over Klepsydra became a Byzantine chapel, and that at least one cave of the south slope was transformed into a chapel, while the Asklepion was rebuilt as a basilica and was provided with three large vaulted cisterns (Travlos, 1980, 28–29, Fig. 172).

As Athens dwindled in importance and population during the Middle Ages, the focus of settlement remained the area immediately to the north of the Acropolis, which still benefited from the waters of Klepsydra and other springs on the north slope of the Acropolis, as well as the Peisistratid and Hadrianic aqueducts that brought water from farther to the northeast. This pattern persisted through the Turkish era, as shown in E. Burnouf's "Plan d'Athenes a l'epoque des Turcs" (1877).

CONCLUSIONS

Even a brief survey of the water elements on and next to the Athenian Acropolis is enough to make apparent that this hill has trickled water for all of its known history. People have intervened by building structures that would facilitate the use of that water and take advantage of it. The quantity and quality of the water filtered through the limestone and available in springs was the determining factor in the choice of this area as center of a settlement. Centuries of observation had made the Athenians knowledgeable about what water does, and by trial and error they had accumulated the technology they needed to harness the haphazard abundance of nature, and to ensure the survival of civilized life. Not until today, however, when humanistic history has been widened to take in all human activities including hydraulic engineering, are we in a position to understand and appreciate what the Greeks accomplished in utilizing these resources so intelligently.

NOTES

1. I am grateful to Mrs. Evi Touloupa, former director of the Acropolis excavations, who personally showed me Klepsydra and the other hidden water sources on the Acropolis and gave me access to her intelligent and helpful staff. This paper was given orally for the Geology Colloquium at Rensselaer, and for the Albany chapter of the American Institute of Archaeology; I am grateful to both groups for the insightful comments that have enabled me to correct mistakes and expand my understanding.

2. Jere Wickens has studied them more conventionally in his dissertation on "The Archaeology and History of Cave Use in Attica" (Indiana University, 1986).

Note on Testing the Water from the Asklepion Area, Athens

TEST SITE AND METHODS

These tests were performed at the Technical University of Athens, Department of Water Resources, by Assistant Professor Alexandra Katsiri during November-December 1988. The problem she was asked to investigate was in what ways these waters differed from ordinary drinking water in Athens. (I am extremely grateful to her for this gracious assistance.)

SOURCES OF SAMPLES

The waters were gathered from three separate sites in and near the Asklepieion on the south slope of the Acropolis, Athens (Fig. 18.5). Specifically, they are:

A. Sacred Spring in Asklepion
B. Archaic shaft immediately west of Asklepion
C. Byzantine cistern immediately adjacent to B, to the west

FINDINGS

Table 19.1 gives a detailed analysis of the water samples.

INTERPRETATION OF RESULTS

The fact that the figures from the three sources differ significantly indicates that the three places derive their water from different channels within the Acropolis. Thus the belief of the workmen on the site that these are different waters has been verified.

According to current American water treatment standards (supplied

Table 19.1
Analysis of Water Samples

Solids (mg/l)	A	B	C	EEC Standard
Total dissolved	1204	864	788	1500
Suspended	18	10	6	0
Turbidity (NTU)	3	6	2.4	0.4–4.0
Ammonia, N mg/l	13.7	0	1.25	0.05–0.5
Nitrate, N mg/l	50	0–4.2	15	25–50
Hardness mg/l CaCO$_3$	400	420	340	—
Chlorides mg/l	129.1	111.7	103	25
Metals mg/l				
Fe	1.03	0.55	1.63	0.05–0.2
Mn	0.29	0.12	0	0.02–0.05
Cu	0.01	0.01	0.012	0.1
Pb	0.23	0.23	0.10	0.05
Cr	0	0	0	0.05

to me by an environmental engineer), the following figures from this chart indicate the need for treatment before the water is safe for drinking:

Nitrate—over 10.1	A and C need treatment
Iron (Fe)—over 0.3	All need treatment. (These amounts of iron do not affect the safety of the water but rather its tendency to rust and stain.)
Lead (Pb)—over 0.05	All need treatment

These amounts of nitrates and ammonia classify A and C as polluted, but not B. This is interesting because, to the nonexpert observer, the water from B looked much dirtier, and indeed it is higher in turbidity.

A hardness of 400 is normal for groundwater but high for rain water. The unusual item here is that C is less hard than the other two; this suggests that it is fed more directly by rainwater.

The relatively high iron content is picked up from the strata that the water flows through. This is not surprising, since the local marble has enough iron in it that over the centuries it oxidizes to the creamy color we see now. This amount is not dangerous, but it is objectionable because of its staining qualities.

The high lead content may be from lead in the atmosphere dissolving in the water. This could be yet another effect of the serious smog problem in Athens. A more likely explanation is the actual presence of lead in the rock, as is suggested by the Athenian silver and lead mines to the south in Attica, at Laurion, where many minerals occur folded into the marble. This amount of lead is considered lethal.

The different levels of chlorides may indicate that the water found in

C flows from a clay stratum, which indeed is visible in the cliff wall at this point and to the west. Around 100 milograms per liter is a comfortable maximum for taste; beyond that, the water seems "salty." For most people, 129 milograms per liter would not be enough to taste strongly. Are 129 milograms per liter enough to establish the waters of the Sacred Spring as different from the ordinary, and capable of healing? Both the Asklepion Spring and the Erechtheum Spring were termed "of the sea" by ancient writers, suggesting to us that their salty taste was more pronounced then.

Therefore it would not be advisable to bathe in any of these waters, and they are definitely not drinkable by normal standards. Yet I saw ladles and drinking cups in the Sacred Spring, and was told that the custom still continues of praying and drinking at the spring.

It should be noted that during the fall of 1988, the Acropolis rock was being cleaned and consolidated. The process is likely to have contaminated the water in all three locations. Therefore it would be interesting to retest the water once that cleaning process is over and the hill has "settled down." I suggest that retesting in early October and late April each year for two years could assemble interesting data.[1]

NOTE

1. Initial discussion of these results was held in Athens with Mrs. Katsiri at the Technical University. I am indebted also to Jane Thapa and to Professor Emeritus Robert LaFleur of the Geology Department of Rensselaer Polytechnic Institute, an expert on groundwater hydrology, both of whom discussed these results with me and helped me to understand their significance.

IX

Amenity and Necessity

20

Architectural Expression of Public and Private Water Supply at Morgantina, Corinth, Athens, and Delos

Water in ancient Greek cities can be considered under several rubrics—aesthetic enrichment of urban spaces, ornamentation of enclosed precincts, nuisance or danger in the form of flood or excessive storm runoff, domestic amenity, public ritual and spectacle, to name a few. This chapter focuses on public fountains, which were both amenity and necessity, contrasting them with the more humble domestic arrangements of the same cities. The appearance, function, and location of fountains cannot be understood as merely visual matters, even though the form and ornamentation of fountains made significant architectural and aesthetic contributions to the cityscape. Rather, understanding the local geology and climate and the principles of hydraulic engineering makes possible a new and clearer understanding of this architectural type. The technological and geological basis of water supply is of equal weight in urban development with the formal presentation of water as an urban amenity.

PUBLIC ARRANGEMENTS

Water management in ancient Greek cities expressed in its physical forms both the simplicity and the sophistication of their hydraulic technology. The physical arrangements were expressed in the same vocabulary of the Greek orders and decorative details that were used for other buildings and fittings, and in the same range of local and imported materials. Placement of the water system elements not only facilitated their use but also indicated the high value placed on water and on its use. The dangers of too much water or not enough were not only solved by Greek technological tradition but also expressed in the physical forms given to the individual parts and to the water system as a whole.

Public Fountains

Each of the water elements I have studied is simple, fulfilling its function economically, yet each is sophisticated enough that modern day practice is just beginning to catch up with these crafty ancients. For instance, having both the flowing water of fountains and wells, and the stored rainwater of cisterns, meant that the water supply of a Greek city was diversified for greater safety in time of war or shortage, and for ecological soundness. In the late twentieth century we are just beginning to understand the utility of redundancy. The pattern of use (cisterns or fountains) was locally determined. We have seen this in the exceptional case of Pompeii, where chemical contamination of both well and aqueduct water from the volcano could make cistern water preferable for drinking.

We can read the urban value of a water system element such as a fountain from its formal development. The formal patterns manifest the values and knowledge about water management that were widely held in ancient Greek culture. Fountains added to the aesthetic appeal of a city. Both the sight and the sound of the fountain were refreshing in the arid Mediterranean context. As features in a sophisticated yet simple water system, fountains fulfilled their functions economically and expressed them in physical form. Local materials were shaped into the Greek orders for the fountains and ornamented with sculpture and painting (Figs. 20.1–20.3, 20.6, 20.7). The public outlet for the water was formalized as a fountainhouse, both to protect the purity and cleanliness of the water and to ritualize the process of obtaining the essential liquid.

A fountain is by definition a public place where fresh running water is available. Fountains were located in or near the agora or at the gateways to the city, within temple precincts, or along the main streets connecting the gates with the agora and the acropolis of a Greek city (see Figs. 15.1, 16.4, 20.1–20.6, 21.1 for individual examples, and 11.1, 11.4, 12.5–12.6, 13.1–13.2, 14.2, 15.2, 22.4 for plans of cities), because these were the places where the most people gathered every day. In all three of the cities discussed subsequently that is indeed where most fountains have been discovered. Excavators know that their chances of finding interesting materials are greater if they concentrate on the agora. Therefore one could argue that it is only accidental that they discover the fountains, pipes, drains, etc., of the water system within the agora; they might find these elements elsewhere if they dug elsewhere. Thus our knowledge of fountains in residential quarters is sparse.

The fresh-flowing water of the fountain was preferred for drinking, both for its limestone flavor and for its purity, whereas water from the domestic cistern was used for activities in which its rather flat taste was irrelevant. Some simple principles of hydraulic engineering are relevant to this study. The small pipes leading to the fountain in the macellum at Morgantina and the large pipes of the fountain next to the theater there

Figure 20.1. Sixth century fountain at Pergamon, originally marking the outfall of a karst channel at the base of the hill on which the citadel was later located. This fountain is the earliest surviving architectural monument of the site, and indicates that one reason for Alexander's selection of the site as a stronghold was its water supply. When it was recently decided to build a large modern dam and reservoir on the eastern side of the hill, this fountain had to be moved and was reerected on the main street leading up toward the gymnasium. Like the Southwest Fountainhouse at Athens, this one had columns placed within the drawbasin. The wall in the foreground is approximately .6 m. tall.

are contrasting solutions to the problem of supply, the former flowing full under some pressure, the latter flowing about half full. The presence of lead pipes at this site and of very thick stone or ceramic pipes at other sites suggests that Greek engineers understood the use of pressure systems, and had a variety of technical means available to carry out their tasks (Figs. 11.9, 15.3, 16.2, 16.7, 16.9, 22.11, 22.12).

To ground the discussion in the specific, fountains in the great cities of Athens and Corinth will be contrasted with those in the modest hill town of Morgantina. We will look at Morgantina as a provincial example, then at Corinth as a place whose fountains have been very well published but whose visible form is that of a Roman city rebuilt on a Greek site after conquest and desertion; and finally at Athens, perhaps the best studied and documented of Greek cities, with fountains going back to Mycenaean times and still operative into the twentieth century.

Figure 20.2. Fountainhouse at Megara, reconstructed. The user stands on the paved porch as she pulls her full amphora out of the draw basin. Many centuries of use have worn U-shaped depressions for the amphoras in the outer wall of the basin. A set of simple columns stands on the inner wall of the drawbasin. Behind them the octagonal piers of the reservoir stand in the dim light, some based on the floor and some on the wall that divides the reservoir into two longitudinal sections, for easier cleaning. The inlets are out of sight at the rear of the chamber. Compare with Figure 20.1. This fountainhouse has been dated as early as the seventh century, or as late as the fifth century; it is drawn as if it were built during the very late sixth century.

Morgantina

At Morgantina the geology is layers of limestone and sandy-clay, with the seam between the two strata appearing on or near the top of each flat-topped hill flanking the lower Agora. An important reason for selecting this site for settlement was that water was easily available here, since it collects along such a geological seam and appears as an oozing or as a spring. No spring has been located in the residential quarter on East Hill, although a small cave-spring at its foot in the northeast corner of the

Agora seems to have inspired and probably supplied a fountainhouse at this corner.[1] To supply the houses on West Hill, however, there was and still is a copious spring in a larger cave on the northeast corner of the hill (the northwest corner of the agora), about half way down the hill (Fig. 17.2). At least two other locations for springs are possible at the same level on this hill, one farther west on the north face of the hill and one on the southeast corner of the hill, above the South Demeter Sanctuary. Another spring is still flowing from the southwest corner of West Hill, at the road level below the postern gate near the House of the Official. Nothing is known about the ancient appearance of this spring. Only the spring at the northeast corner of the agora was given any surviving architectural decoration, to be described later.

Having thus established the water potential of the site, let us see what the Greek settlers did with it. The Agora at Morgantina is a good example of the high value placed on water in this society and of how water supply was arranged to provide for both the physical and social needs of the people. There were at least six water sources in the agora, although not all were equally public (Fig. 14.2). It was convenient for people frequenting this market to be able to quench their thirst and to have water available to wash any of their wares that needed it. Most imposing architecturally was the fountainhouse discovered in the early 1980s by Malcolm Bell of the University of Virginia (acting on my suggestion). This building had an unusual plan, with a group of columns standing up on a podium that was wrapped on three sides by a moat filled with springwater (Bell, 1983; 1985; 1988, 313–42). Inside the podium, a reservoir that (at least in its last phase) most unusually combined spring- and rainwater was the

Figure 20.3. Elevation of the fountainhouse at Olynthos just below the Agora, fed by the aqueduct from the karst springs in the mountains to the north. From Robinson, 1946, and used by permission of Johns Hopkins University Press.

Figure 20.4. Reconstruction of a fountain on the main street in a residential district of Priene. At the right of the drawing, at the foot of the wall, a large drain passed under the steps.

central feature of the fountainhouse.The fountainhouse was located at the northern end of the east side of the Agora. It formed a pivot marking the entrance/exit of the Agora, accessible from both the north and west sides.

The opposite northwest corner of the agora has at street level only a modest fountain in the form of a rectangular trough, probably filled from the cave-spring on the hillside above it. The only other surviving architectural elements from this modest fountain are the lion spout that disgorged the water, and some clumsily repaired pipes leading to it (Crouch, 1984, fig. 8 of pl. 47) (Fig. 16.4).

Another trough fountain flanked the northern retaining wall of the theater, and apparently was fed by a long large-diameter pipeline from the same northwestern cave-spring. This trough is even more crudely built than the former one, so the excavators have thought of it as late, after the city was turned over to Roman veterans in 212 B.C. The theater is from the late fourth or early third century B.C., abandoned after 211 (Allen, 1970, 363).

To the south of the theater was another small rectangular fountain,

Figure 20.5. Reconstruction of a fountain at the corner where a side street enters the main street (at left) of the Acropolis at Selinus. Still extant are the arch and some of the slabs that enclosed the basin. Probably water was delivered through a spout at the place where a small notch is cut into the stone in front of the girl's nose.

Figure 20.6. View of the fountainhouse at Megara, from the rear, showing octagonal piers and the wall that divided the reservoir so that half could be cleaned at a time. Water entered from openings in the rear wall and was drawn out from a basin at the front, half of which is visible immediately to the left of the spot of sunshine.

quite nicely finished with waterproof stucco like the one on the street to the northwest. Out in the middle of the Agora are at least two more quasi-private water outlets. Very clearly visible now is the tank within the macellum, supplied through small (3 inch) water pipes of terra-cotta from the fountainhouse in the northeast corner (Stillwell and Sjöqvist, 1957 154; Naber's unpublished report on the building). Farther south and a little to the west was the shrine of the Chthonian Divinities. Very frequently we find water in the form of a spring, well, or fountain as part of a religious sanctuary, where ritual bathing was part of the religious observance. The Asklepion at Cos is an outstanding example. We can observe vestiges of this purification process even today: The Japanese rinse out their mouths when they enter a temple, the Moslems wash their feet before praying, and Catholics cross themselves with holy water on entering and leaving a church. Not only does the Chthonian Sanctuary at Morgantina have a symbolic well called a *bothros*, but also there are other wells and a cistern that holds the water that still collects here, draining from the area of the theater (Sjöqvist, 1964, 141–44). Given the drainage patterns of the site and the way that the water-bearing limestone stratum comes to the surface along the west side of the Agora, it is not surprising that wells to tap the water and cisterns to contain it should be part of the working arrangements of this sanctuary.

It is possible that laundry arrangements at Morgantina were public and communal, as they still were at many Greek villages until about 1960. In a building at the center of many villages there are small basins to boil clothes, in which the soiled clothes are layered with ashes and a plant extract for bluing. After these are boiled together, the clothes are rinsed in cold water and then carried home to be hung up. At Morgantina today, the farm wives gather at the holding tank below the spring on the road immediately below the site. They scrub their laundry on the sloping cement coping of the tank, and take them home to hang up and dry (Crouch, 1987, 132) (Fig. 15.8). To date no such public laundry arrangements have been found at Morgantina (cf. Fig. 17.5, 22.9).

Corinth[2]

From Morgantina (which was a colony of Syracuse in turn a colony of Corinth), located in the hill country of Sicily, let us turn to one of the great cities of mainland Greece, Corinth. Corinth first came to historical notice in the late Geometric period with its fine pottery, made from the same clay that contributed importantly to the water supply of the settlement, and helped to determine both the nature of that supply and the limits of what could be done with it.

Already in the sixth century B.C., a major focal point of the Corinthian settlement was the trio of springs at the head of the receding valley leading from the port to Acrocorinth, that is, the Cyclopean Spring, Peirene, and the Sacred Spring (Hill, 1964). Since these springs have been discussed at length in Chapter 11, we will here refer to them only in summary.

These fountains stood where the agora changed levels (Figs. 11.1–2). Seams of water came to the surface in several places at the edge between the upper and lower levels of the Agora, which developed around these useful sources of water. To preserve the cleanliness of the water, by the sixth century the Corinthians had built at each outfall a small reservoir and in front of it a retaining wall of ashlar masonry, with spouts for the water. The women could place their amphorae under the spouts, as we see in scenes from vases, e.g. the cover of the booklet "Waterworks in the Athenian Agora." Glaser (1983, 181–87) states that the convention of depicting such fountains on vases is merely a convention, with no basis in reality, but I think he is overlooking examples like the Corinthian Sacred Spring. There was paving underfoot, with drains to carry away the excess water, and a roof overhead to shield the water carriers from too much sun or rain. In the third century, the Sacred Spring gradually went out of use, replaced at the upper level by a channel and basin. Construction of the South Stoa, and the consequent tapping of underground waters uphill from the Sacred Spring may have caused the latter to dry up. I think that a careful review of the geology and of the chronology of water supply elements in this Agora would provide a much clearer picture of the urban development of the site.

Because it is in the open air, the spring of Peirene is today more easily visited than the padlocked Sacred Spring (Fig. 11.2). Already in the sixth century the Greeks had begun to utilize this spring. Later they provided for it a fountainhouse with Ionic columns set between pilasters, supporting a lintel with fascias and dentils, with parapets and holding basins for the water, and with stone steps up to the level of the basins from the level of the lower agora. Vestiges of these earliest arrangements can still be seen here, as can other details from every rebuilding of the fountain. When the city was refounded by the Romans in 44 B.C., the fountain was elaborated in the current Roman mode, with new parapets, a new paved court, and large exedrae (curved alcoves) flanking the court. This fountain is perhaps the favorite spot for visitors to Corinth today.

The last of the great fountains of Corinth is Glauke, a roughly cubical mass of solid rock near the present museum, at the opposite end of the Agora from Peirene (Fig. 11.3). Possibly the rock was left over when the area was quarried for stone to build the Temple of Apollo in the sixth century B.C. or later to build some agora buildings. Many writers have thought that Glauke was originally a spring, but that in Roman times the vein of water failed and the Romans had to add a pipeline bringing water from elsewhere. The pipes are gone but the slit along the base of the rock where they were fitted in is clearly visible. However, recently the weight of opinion has swung to believing that water never did spring here naturally, but rather that the Romans—and possibly the Greeks before them—made a fountain that appeared "natural" or "geological" rather than dressed in the orders as one would expect. Thus Glauke is, I think, an extremely sophisticated metaphor for a natural, grotto-like spring and fountainhouse (Robinson, 1965,11–12; Hill, 1964, 200–24; Williams and Zervos, 1983,118–20 esp. n.3 on p. 119). This kind of architectural metaphor is known in structures of the time of Claudius, such as the Porta Maggiore at Rome, but to my knowledge no study has as yet attempted to place Glauke as late as the time of Claudius.

Our account of Corinth and its fountains would not be complete without a brief mention of the spring near the top of Acrocorinth, the great hill that looms up over the site. Settlement in ancient Corinth always clustered at or near the bottom of this hill, which was both a fortress, a source of drinking water and a place of pilgrimage. Alas! the great shrine of Aphrodite on top is now the gathering place only of goats, but the view is as splendid as ever. Just below the top, off to one side, lay a spring dignified in classical times with a stairway down to the bottom of the cave, and at the foot of the steps a Doric column set between pilasters, all three standing on a parapet and supporting a lintel. This spring bore the name Upper Peirene, perhaps because water from the hill was led to the agora in Roman times. Pausanias and Strabo write that Peirene was fed from the spring at the top of Acrocorinth, via underground channels (Hill, 1964, 3; Doxiadis, 1972, fig. 40 no.9; fig. 43 "Corinth town and acropolis—water sources," where number 17 equals Upper Peirene) (cf. Fig. 8.1 here). A large, modern lid next to this spring indicates that the output of the spring is saved today in a reservoir, proving that it still produces more water than can be exhausted on a daily basis by the goats and their shepherds. The water of Upper Peirene was in Greek times probably restricted to ritual use in the sanctuary of Aphrodite. For general use during pilgrimages, the walkway to the top has many cisterns on both sides; they would have been necessary also for the many times in history that the Acropolis has served as a fortress (Robinson, 1969, 1–35). None of these cisterns was given any architectural treatment.

Athens

The last set of public fountains we will examine are those at Athens. The most important fountains of Athens have been found at crucial points of traffic in the ancient city, quite probably because the city grew up around these nodes. As at Morgantina and Corinth, the fountains attracted much activity, making it logical to locate other community business near them. There was a fountain at the Dipylon Gate, fountains at the southwest and southeast corners of the agora (Fig. 20.7), one at the southeast edge of the Roman market, one at the northwest corner of the Acropolis and the Mycenaean Fountain just east of that, two others in the middle of and half-way down the south slope of the Acropolis, and one near the bottom of its southwest slope. In addition, there are the fountains located within the South Stoa and the Stoa of Attalos. As excavation pushes northward from the present edge of the agora archaeological site, we may expect to find other fountains at the northwest corner of the agora. (I hope that someone will soon examine each of the supposed ancient gates of the city to see if others besides the Dipylon were equipped with water fountains as well as baths and drains.)

Let us consider a few of these fountains, to distinguish their urban importance by the degree of architectural elaboration each possesses. This brief survey makes no attempt to be comprehensive. Disregarding chronology, let us place them in order of increasing architectural complication.

Mycenaean fountain. in the cleft at the northwest corner of the Acropolis, was intended to be a hidden resource, and therefore has no (surviving) architectural decoration (Fig. 18.1–2).

Klepsydra. This fountain was articulated in the fifth century B.C. with an internal stair and L-shaped platform for drawing water, and a large paved area which could have held overflow water from the spring and rainwater drained from the Acropolis (Fig. 18.2).

Enneakrounos-Kallirrhoe fountain and spring. The spring of Kallirrhoe was in the bed of the Ilissos River, southeast of the Olympieion. A system of cisterns and rock-cut tunnels collected the water into an aqueduct. The fountainhouse called Enneakrounos was built probably on the riverbank nearby, in the sixth century, by the tyrants. According to a vase painting, it had a Doric porch to protect the water carriers and the spouts of the fountain. (Travlos, 1980, 205 and fig. 154, 267–68.)

Figure 20.7. Plans (drawn to the same scale) of two fountain houses on the south side of the Athenian Agora—the Southeast Fountainhouse of the later sixth century, and the more elaborate Southwest Fountainhouse of the mid-fourth century. Both were aqueduct-fed. The Southeast Fountainhouse was 7 by 15 meters. Reprinted by permission of Greeenwood Publishing Group, Inc., Westport, CT, from *Pictorial Dictionary of Ancient Athens* by J. Travlos, published in 1971 by Praeger Publishers, reprinted 1980 by Hacker Art Books.

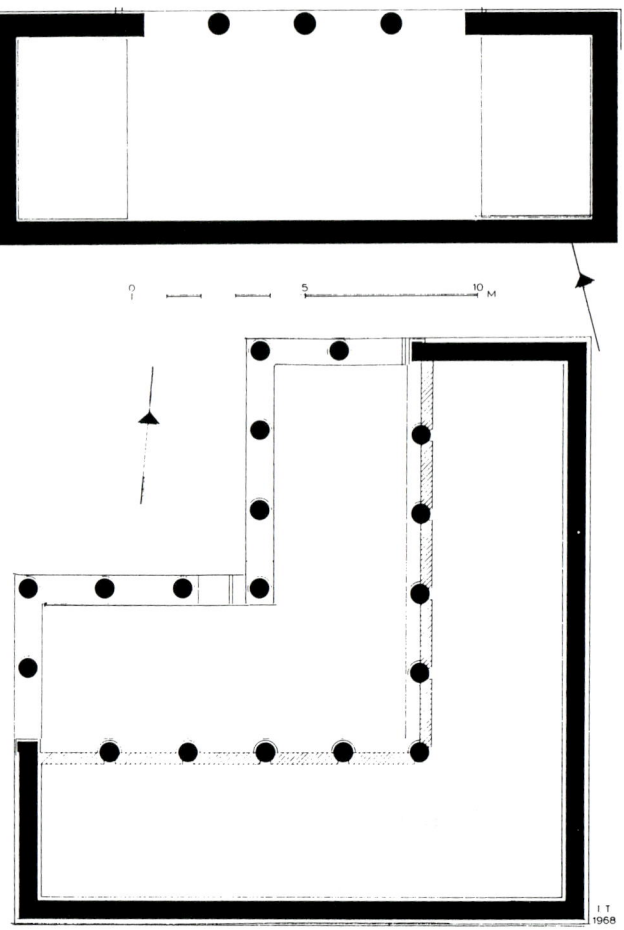

Southeast fountainhouse of the agora. Pausanias (i,14,1) describes a second fountainhouse with the name Enneakrounos, now taken to be this one (Fig. 20.7). The building stood near the corner where the diagonal Panathenaic Way left the Agora to climb to the Acropolis, a site of maximum public utility.

> The building was a long rectangle in plan with its entry from the north. At either end was a shallow basin . . . Water was delivered to a point in the middle of the back wall by a terra-cotta pipeline . . . the water was conveyed in channels in the thickness of the wall to supply a series of spouts, doubtless in the shape of animal heads . . . The overflow was carried off in an underground terra-cotta pipeline in a northeast direction to be used elsewhere. (*The Athenian Agora, A Guide,* 1962, 97)

It is significant, I think, that this fountain is the best documented example we have of a natural flow being supplemented by water from elsewhere, and a natural basin articulated by formal architecture. The *Guide* continues:

> Deep exploration around the archaic fountain house has shown, moreover, that the ground water is close to the surface in this area at all seasons, so that there may well have existed in early times a simple freeflowing spring destined to be replaced, as the needs of the community grew, by a capacious fountain house fed by a pipeline from some distant source.

Spring west of Asklepion. (Fig. 18.6). From the sixth century B.C., a small Doric springhouse stood over a square drawbasin 3.1 meters deep, fed from a smaller circular well with masonry walls some 1.25 meters deep. The well received the waters of a spring immediately to its south, judging from an opening in the south wall of the well. Travlos shows it (1980,127, fig. 188) as having a porch with three columns. At the northeast corner, part of the walls of the fountainhouse are preserved, and one can see the cutting that was made into the Acropolis cliff for the building. This fountainhouse, dating from the late sixth century, went out of use in the fourth century; it may have replaced the Mycenaean Fountain in this same area.

Springhouse east of Asklepion (Sacred Spring. *A* of table 19.1). This springhouse is set in a cave to the east and north of the later buildings of the sanctuary. Today it is accessible through an arched doorway in a beautiful wall of marble ashlars, the backwall of the two-storey Doric stoa of the last quarter of the fifth century (Fig. 18.5).

Southwest Fountainhouse. This fountain was built in the third quarter of the fourth century, at a busy entrance to the Agora (Fig. 20.7). It was supplied by a large stone aqueduct from the east, whence the earlier pipeline had also come. The L-shaped building had interior columns dividing it into an outer porch and an inner basin. As at Olynthos, there was also a separate compartment with spouts for those who did not choose to dip their water up from the basin (cf. Fig. 20.1, 20.3) (*Athenian Agora Guide*, 110)

There was also a strategically placed *fountain house just inside the Dipylon Gate* (Knigge, 1988, 73–75, her figs. 65, 66; Fig. 16.15 here).

In these fountains we have evidence of provision for water supply ranging in date from the thirteenth century B.C. to Byzantine times, and in architectural ornamentation from the lack of articulation of the Mycenaean Fountain to the complete use of the orders in the Southwest Fountainhouse. The fountains seem more likely to have been given architectural treatment if they were also a pivot or hinge of community activity, as was the Southwest Fountain, which marked the boundary of the agora. One can read not only the meaning but also the urban value of a fountain from its formal development.

DOMESTIC ARRANGEMENTS

Both the physical form of water elements and the placement of these elements in the settlement to serve public and private uses indicate the value placed on water and the principle of treating necessities as amenities. We do the same whenever we dress attractively or set the table elegantly to show off a finely cooked meal. These efforts in an ancient Greek city were not merely a matter of personal inclination but rather the actions of a society striving always to realize the ideal form for each concept (Webster, 1973, 8, 267–73) Let us consider a few examples of appropriate form in Greek domestic water arrangements, placing the private provision for drinking and cleanliness in contrast with the public display of usable water.

Any one who has sojourned for a length of time in the Mediterranean lands is aware of the dry heat that is especially enervating during the afternoon hours of summer, and making one vividly aware of water. Water to drink. Water to bathe in and cool off in. Water to sprinkle on the dust, both cleansing the air and cooling it by evaporation. These needs for water have not changed since time immemorial. The ancient Greek house, thanks to an active traditional knowledge of water management, made available to its inhabitants several arrangements, in a variety of formal patterns, that enhanced domestic life by providing water. Drinking water was carried fresh from the spring a couple of times a day or was drawn from the family well (Fig. 16.20, 20.4–5) The rest of the water that a family needed, for washing, cooking, cleaning, for domestic animals, and for craft industries, was usually supplied from cisterns (or, less often, wells; even more rarely, piped supply) in the individual houses.

Each cistern or well had its wellhead *(puteal)* of stone or terra-cotta, about 2 feet tall, set in place above the opening to the water below (Fig. 20.8–9). This well-mouth kept things and people from slipping into the

Figure 20.8. Well or cistern head on stone base (both of marble), in Agora at Athens.

opening, and made the process of drawing water easier. Often wellheads were decorated with the same strips of ornament that one could find on buildings, such as egg-and-dart or triglyph-metope friezes. Many that we find today have deep grooves inside their upper edges, worn by the friction of the rope pulling up the filled vase, repeated over many centuries. The opening to the cistern or well was usually in the open courtyard of the house, for maximum ease of access, but could be located also in the kitchen, as at Olynthos, or less commonly in the storage room—the latter location being reasonable for a well, but less convenient for a cistern that collected rainwater. When, as at Delos, we notice the wellhead embedded in a partition between rooms, we may suspect that later remodeling of a house preserved the essential access to stored water.

Arrangements for domestic water supply at Morgantina were much more modest than the agora fountains there. A few wells are known, and many cisterns, both given standard architectural elements—wellheads—

Figure 20.9.   Terra-cotta wellheads in Syracuse Museum, about .66 m tall.

to define them (Fig. 20.8–10). The arched cistern in the House of the Arched Cistern in the residential quarter of West Hill, however, was defined architecturally by a recessed arch (Fig. 17.4). The arched opening was built into the thickness of the dining room wall of the house, on the alley connecting the public street with the private courtyard of the house. Thus it would be possible for neighbors to walk in along the alley to fetch water, without disturbing the residents of the house, which makes this a quasi-public fountain. Finishing the top with a nicely curved but simple arch and providing a basin made of thin slabs of stone appropriately adjusted the arched cistern to its role and its location, without claiming for it—as columns would have—the status of a public fountain.

We are unsure whether this arched cistern was indeed a cistern or a well, because excavation stopped without reaching bottom. The issue is further complicated by finding in situ some lead pipe bringing water from the north (the location of the probable second spring on this hill) to the cistern, and on to the bathroom across the alleyway (Sjöqvist, 1962, 136). I postulate that originally the seam of water here was reached by a well that was topped by the arched opening. Later on, in the second century B.C., the water table receded and the well went dry, so a supplementary supply of water was necessary, while the old shaft continued in use as a cistern.

Unlike Morgantina, where complete bathrooms are found only in the more ample houses, the houses at Olynthos are unusual in regularly having a room for bathing, where a bathtub was built in, and where there was also a washbasin *(louter)* and sometimes an actual toilet similar to ours in size and shape (J. W. Graham, 1938, pl. 55) (Figs. 17.6, 17.7).

Figure 20.10. Wellhead of marble and wooden windlass, of the Hellenistic period, from Athenian Agora. Oblong holes in the stone base held the uprights for the bar on which the pulley was mounted to lower and raise the well bucket. Drawing by W.B. Dinsmoor, Jr., from "Waterworks in the Athenian Agora." Reprinted by permission of the American School of Classical Studies at Athens.

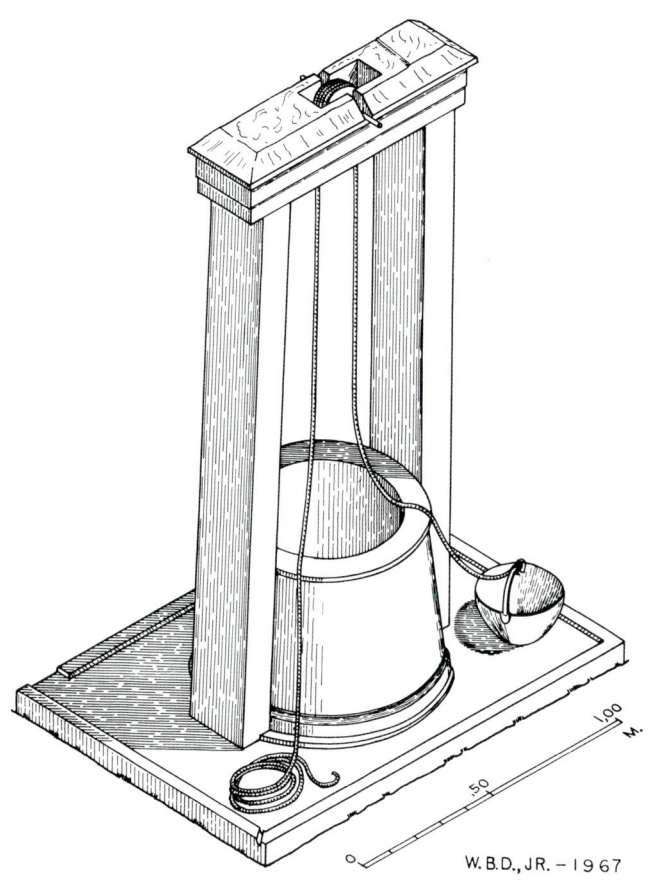

W.B.D., JR. – 1967

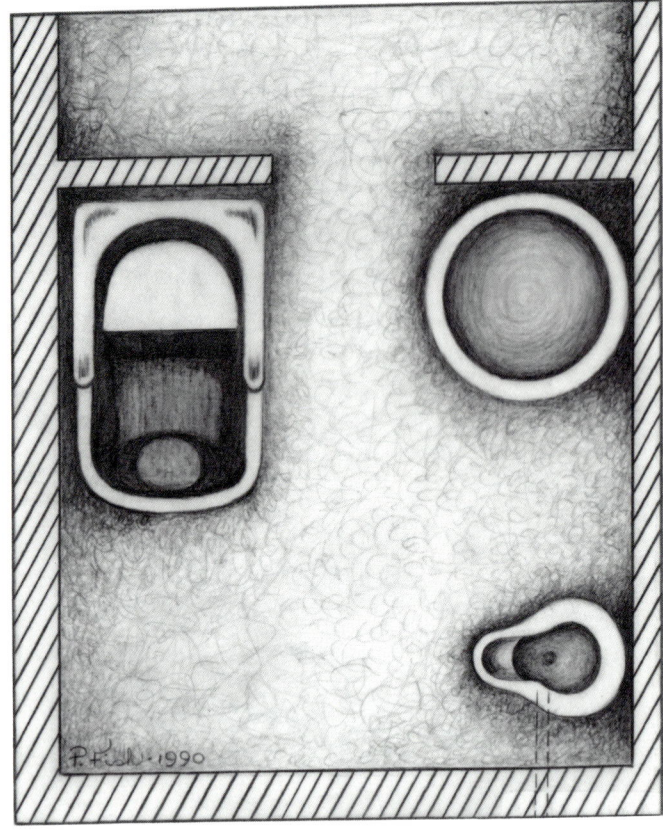

Figure 20.11A. Bath at Olynthos (clockwise from upper left) tub, *louter,* and toilet. (Based on objects found at the site, now in the storerooms of the Thessalonike Museum.) This is the most completely integrated of the domestic baths studied.

Although in other cities—Delos for example—the louters were placed in the courtyard, at Olynthos and Morgantina they are usually found also in the bathing room (Fig. 20.11A-D). When the bathing room was placed next to the kitchen, the location was ideal for sharing the warmth of the cooking fire so that bathing in cold weather was more pleasant. It was also easier to carry heated water to the bathtub. Another feature of these houses indicates the hydraulic tradition reflected in the urban plan: Each of the bathrooms was equipped with a drain to the sewer that ran along the alley or the side street between the houses. Used water from bathing and house cleaning could be utilized to flush excrement through these pipes and out to the exterior of the town (Figs. 12.7, 16.14–15, 17.10–11). There the excavators have not followed the course of the channels, but I surmise that the effluent was used as fertilizer, being too valuable to waste.

Thus the architectural form of the house reflected preferences about water as an amenity essential to the civilized life. With the cistern water saved from rainfall (or with well water) they could bathe during those hot afternoons, wash clothes and hang them to dry in the courtyard where the evaporating moisture would humidify the house, wash the floors with used bath water, and keep pots of flowers blooming to make the house more beautiful, as do the Mediterranean peoples to this day (Figs. 16.16, 17.5).

Figure 20.11B. Bathing facilities at Delos. Elements placed separately: washbasin *(1)*, cistern mouth *(2)*, and latrine *(3)*, the latter set on an exterior wall of the house, and drained into the sewer in the street. The latrine was flushed by overflow from the cistern under the courtyard at upper left. Note that the shop (crosshatching of the double row of rooms at the bottom) had its own drain to the sewer under the street. Based on plans of house 59B, published in the *Guide de Delos*, Ecole Francaise and Ed. E de Boccard, Paris, 1983; reprinted by permission.

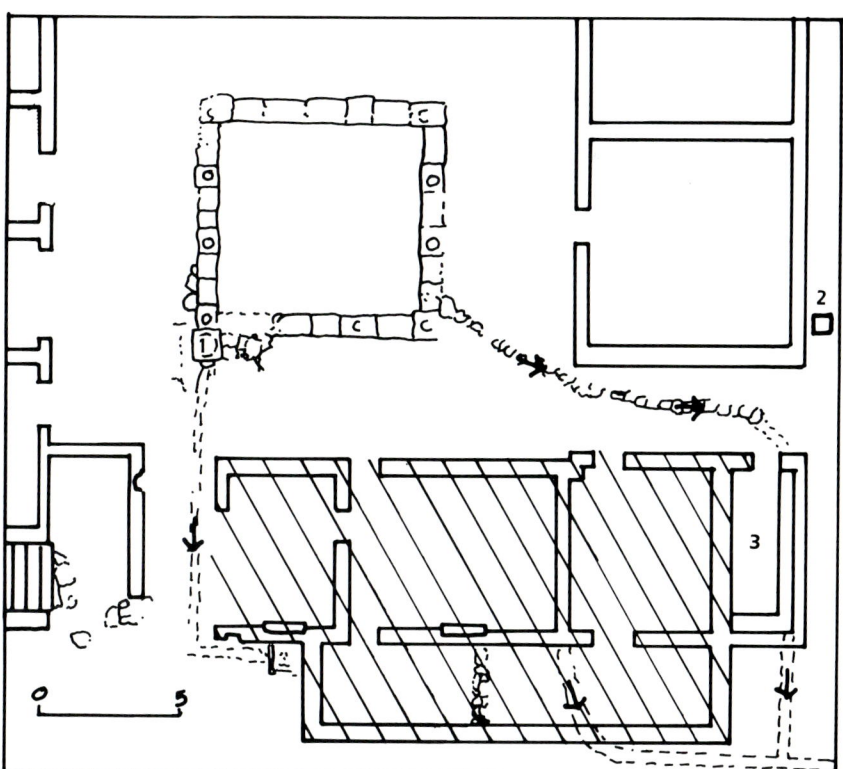

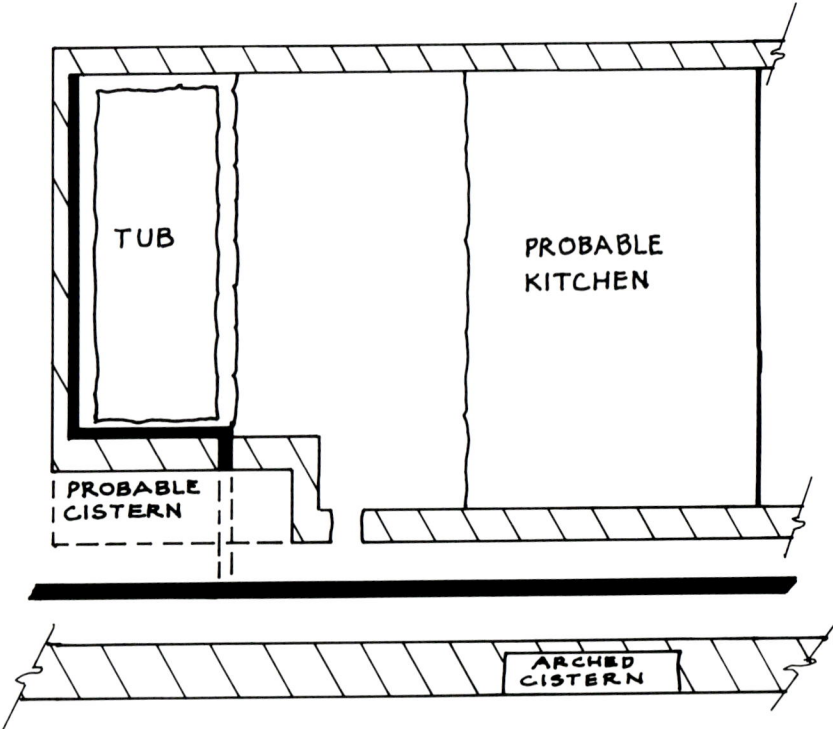

Figure 20.11C. Bathroom at Morgantina, set in an alcove off the kitchen. The tub, constructed of stone slabs, was in its last phase fed by a lead pipe shown here in black. Earlier it may have utilized water from the cistern that was set into the ground on the outer side of the end wall. This bath is in the House of the Arched Cistern. (See Figure 22.5, a photo of the tub.)

Our final set of examples of domestic arrangements is the sacred and commercial city of Delos, which played an important role in Greek religious life of all periods as the site of the birth of Apollo, and in commercial life during 314–166 B.C. as a free port (see M. Bullard et al., *L'Exploration archaeologique de Delos*, 1909–74, 30 volumes). The early city was essentially destroyed by pirates and depopulated in the first century B.C., (Stillwell, MacDonald, and McAllister, 1976, 261–64) which means that the domestic remains are mostly those of the third and second centuries. Delos is striking for its large cisterns, used to supplement the water of the Inopos River. Every house seems to have had at least one cistern. These are not of the bottle shape that we find during the same period at Morgantina, but rather are usually square, like the court that lies immediately above them. A bottle-shaped cistern has a neck big enough for a person to descend into it and carry out the mandated annual cleaning. Its long neck places it deep into the ground which keeps the water pleasantly cool. Usually at Delos, the paved court acting as lid over the square cistern insures transfer of the sun's heat to the stored water immediately below, which is fine if the chief use for the water is washing clothes or floors, but not fine if the water is for drinking. Access to the water is through a wellhead like that described earlier. From my experience of drinking ice-cold well water, I can attest that wells were a further source of water on Delos (Fig. 16.20). Finally, in the building called an inn, there is in the courtyard a very large shaft that alternately fills and empties like the poljes or estavelles of other karst areas. I think it is a karst shaft, related to the internal drainage system of the island. Perhaps its alternate filling and draining served as an ancient tourist attraction for pilgrims and traders who visited the island.

Figure 20.11D. Bathroom at Selinus. Typical built-in terra-cotta tub separated from the toilet space at bottom by a half-wall. Toilet space drained through the house wall to the drain in the street outside, and probably was flushed with used bath water. Sewer in the street is shown as a heavy black line at bottom.

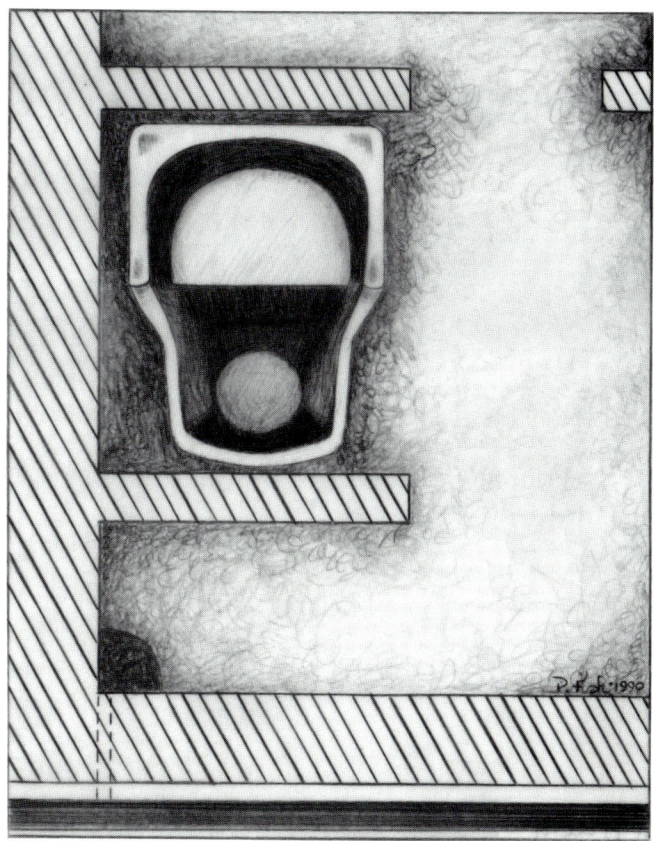

Like public buildings such as clubs and gymnasia, the houses at Delos frequently are equipped with latrines, located along the street wall, to make drainage to the sewer easier. The latrine consisted of a trench or sometimes two trenches along one or more walls, at a lower level than the floor of the room. The wooden seat or two rows of seats above the trench(s) is now gone, but not difficult to restore in imagination. Many plans of houses at Delos indicate such a latrine space (Martin, 1956, pl. 22 and figs. 48, 49; Rider, 1965, 250–55) (Figs. 12.1, 16.1, 20.11B). It is interesting to compare this routine provision of latrines with the situation in Athens, where, Travlos (1980, 342) tells us:

> Public latrines earlier than the Roman period have not been found in Athens. As early as the 5th century B.C., however, private houses had toilets located near the main entrance into the house from the street. In many instances among the excavated houses of the Agora area pits have been found, sometimes in the courtyard, mostly under the surface of the road near to the main entrance of a house; these rectangular pits, lined with masonry, were used as cesspools. From the fourth century onwards the system of cesspools was abolished and waste products and rainwater were drained off by means of branch drains leading into the main system of drain channels under the streets.

Finally, a word about the distribution of bathroom elements at Delos. We have just noted that latrines are in separate rooms. I saw very few rooms with bathtubs, but many courtyards with louters, usually adjacent to the wellhead of the cistern. Placement of washing facilities in the courtyard facilitated access to the water, at the same time reducing privacy. Complete bathing could be done at a gymnasium or sanctuary, or in a portable tub set up in the kitchen or bedroom. Since dining often took place in the courtyard, having the louter in the court was convenient for doing the dishes (Figs. 17.5, 20.11B). Court placement of the louter in the late years of the Hellenistic era seems to presage the proliferation of louter-fountains in courtyards at Pompeii and Herculaneum in the first century A.D.

Louters, wellheads, even laundry tubs are often made of white marble at Delos, where that material was in plentiful supply, or of a dark blue-grey stone (Fig. 16.18–20). Usually these practical elements have re-strained ornamentation or none at all. At other sites the same elements may be made of stone or terra-cotta ornamented with traditional architectural mouldings such as dentils or bead-and-reel.

CONCLUSION

These few examples are enough, I hope, to suggest the careful thought that the ancient Greeks gave to water as both amenity and necessity. Whether for private or public use, for propaganda or utility, water was considered significant in the urban fabric. The relative splendor of public fountains makes explicit the cultural value of water, while the provision of domestic water—in a system at once thorough, economical, and modest—suggests that it was not only in literature and politics that the Greeks have left us models we strive in vain to equal.

Indeed, during the many centuries of Western history when our cultures deemphasized cleanliness, it was the military prowess or oratorical subtlety or aesthetic idealism of the Greeks that appealed to us. Only in late Victorian times, when the pleasures of indoor plumbing had been rediscovered, could we begin again—in the person of Arthur Evans, excavator of Knossos—to learn about their pioneer work in the provision of water for urban populations, as both amenity and necessity.

NOTES

1. The cave was identified as the probable location of a spring by U. Özis who teaches hydraulic engineering at the Technical University at Izmir, Turkey, and who has, with his students, made detailed studies of the ancient water supply systems of Ionia, and by R. LaFleur, hydrogeologist at Rensselaer Polytechnic Institute, both working from photographs.

2. I should like to thank Charles Williams, excavator at Corinth for the American School of Classical Studies, and the staff of the museum and site for many courtesies extended to me, such as entry to the Sacred Spring, and also discussions of my research and their knowledge. They were very helpful.

X

Conclusions: Learning from Greek Experience

21

Profile of Individual Water User

One way to show our understanding of ancient Greek management of water is to follow an ordinary person in her daily patterns, observing when and how she uses water. This schedule ignores differences that derive from local geology, climate, or customs, but rather tries to set out the common patterns.

1. *At daylight.* Wake up. Go to room or alcove set aside for excreting and do that. Rinse with previously used water. Then go to courtyard, pull up bucket of water from cistern, pour into louter, and wash face and hands. Save water for re-use (Fig. 13.3).
2. *First meal.* Fix breakfast, using water from cistern for any cooking. Water donkey, dog, house plants, with water from cistern or re-usable water from cooking or bathing.
3. *Work.* Morning and mid-afternoon to late day:
   A. Do family laundry—use giant pithos or scrub-board at edge of courtyard, filled from downspout from roof or with buckets of water from the cistern; hang clothes to dry on poles or rope strung between posts (columns) supporting roofs around courtyard. Alternate: laundry might be done communally at a large tank that received the overflow from a fountain near the agora, and the wet clothes carried home and spread out to dry, as above (Fig. 17.5).
   B. Or do craft activity such as making pottery, using courtyard and water from cistern.
   C. Or go out to farm. Excrement and garbage were probably carried daily to the farm for fertilizer. An important farming task was to monitor the irrigation of timber lots, fields, orchards, and vineyards with waste water from the town or with spring or river water or dispersed rainwater.
   D. Or do shopping and/or selling. Periodically carry craft items to Agora to sell them. If need be, rinse items such as vases in public fountains to show off their best colors. In Athens, women

participated in the markets, selling lettuce and other farm or craft products, but in some Greek cities shopping and selling were solely masculine activities.

4. *Recreation.*
   A. Talk with cousin from the country who waters his donkey at the public trough in the Agora.
   B. On the way home stop at neighborhood fountain to chat with other people fetching water to drink (Fig. 21.1).
   C. On special occasions (marriage, birth) go to a sanctuary for a ritual bath. (Fig. 6.1).
5. *Main meal.*
   A. Fetch jug of fresh water from nearest fountain, for drinking, or send daughter to fetch it (Fig. 20.4–5).
   B. Cook meal using cistern water.
   C. Wash dishes using cistern water and louter (Fig. 17.8).
6. *Heat of the day, in early afternoon.* Bathe, using cistern water (some of which may have been heated on the lunchtime cooking fire). Alternate: bathing may take place at a temple on ritual occasions (for both sexes) or at the gymnasium (usually for men only)

Figure 21.1. Women at a fountain with lion-headed spout. From a late sixth century B.C. vase in the British Museum. Reprinted by permission.

or from the fifth century B.C. on, at a public bath (for both sexes) (Figs. 17.6, 22.2, 22.7).

7. *Late afternoon and early evening.*

    A. Clean house, washing floors etc. with previously used bath water.

    B. Wash children (hands and faces) and send them to bed.

    C. Refreshed with clean hands, face, and clothing, enjoy the cool of the evening in the courtyard or on the roof, with family members.

In ancient Greek society, service activities that used water, such as carrying drinking water, cooking, laundry, and dishes, were done by women and girls or sometimes by male slaves. Yet even the free adult males who were citizens were involved with water use and management in their roles as farmers, athletes, and civic officials, as well as in their professions as architect-engineers, potters, fullers, etc. Depending on family composition, some young boys would have the experience of carrying water, as we see in Greek settlements today (Fig. 16.20). Since a larger proportion of male life was public and communal, it is not surprising that more of their bathing activities, for instance, took place in gymnasia than was true for their female counterparts (Fig. 16.10). Social pressure about bathing was one way the society brought about a minimum of cleanliness necessary for health, and thus ensured the well-being of athletes who competed in the inter-city games, and the well-being of soldiers who defended the city.

It is likely that individual householders built or at least maintained their own domestic cisterns (Fig. 3.2, 16.16). At least once a year it was necessary to climb down into the cistern and clean out any objects that had fallen in and any silt that had collected at the bottom. At this time the waterproof stucco that lined the cistern would be inspected and repaired if necessary. This annual cleaning would usually be done in the fall before the rainy season began, when the level of stored water was at its lowest. Probably annual attention to the various drains of the houses was useful also, not to mention clearing out the cesspool. A time for this clearing out would be chosen at the point in the annual agricultural cycle when the contents of the cesspool could lie on the fields biodegrading into useful fertilizer, before the major planting in October. In a neighborhood, people might cooperate to clean out one cistern at a time, so that the shortage of water was minimized.

22

Discoveries About Greek
Water Management

Looking back through twenty years of work on this topic, I can sum up what I have learned under two major categories: general truths and site-specific insights. Within each of these categories, I differentiate between items that were not known by me when I started and items that as far as I can tell were not known at all.

GENERAL FINDINGS

First let us consider the findings that have general application. Primary are findings connected with the geological basis of Greek settlement. The ones in italics have not been known before at all, as far as I can tell. For each discovery, there is a brief discussion.

1. *Relation of karst patterns to settlement in the ancient Greek world.* In Part IV of this volume we have discussed this topic in a preliminary fashion. As is the case with so many details of the human situation, the relevant knowledge is in the hands of two disciplines that rarely perceive that they have any questions in common. Karst has been studied by hydrogeologists and ancient Greek settlements by classicists, with an impenetrable membrane separating the two fields of knowledge. Nevertheless, my study has conclusively demonstrated that one cannot understand either the choice of an ancient Greek site or the subsequent history of the settlement without factoring in the geological base and the water resources this base provided (Fig. 7.1). It is a pity that the lead of the noted classicist Judeich (1905 and 1931) was not followed sooner, since he illustrated his section on water supply with a geological map and section.

2. *Utilization of karst in urban water systems.* The work of modern engineers and geologists in such countries as Yugoslavia makes us aware that karst waters can be tapped or, to put it more strongly, harnessed for settlements. Many of their modern solutions are not dependent on advanced technology but rather on careful observation and clever manipu-

lation. The ancient Greeks were fully capable of both. The famous pine-cone experiment on the Tripoli plain of the sixth century B.C. is strong indication that the ancient engineers were examining data with an eye to manipulating karst for human purposes, and in fact we have a story, from the same area, of water being diverted down a sinkhole to drown out an unsuspecting enemy settlement.

3. *Origin of qanats.*

4. *Origin of wells.* In Chapter 10 I have sketched a hypothesis about the origin of wells and qanats possibly even before Greek times, based on careful observation of the behavior of water in karst terrane. Both qanats and wells retain their "natural" form, though both can be amplified, remodeled, and redirected by humans, as they definitely were during the Greek period studied here. The tribes in Iran whose hereditary work is the building and maintenance of qanats bring such traditional knowledge into the twentieth century.

5. Karst terrane tends to self-destruct, by stripping soil from rock, carrying it down through shaft and cave system, and depositing it at a considerable distance downstream. This is a fact. What a society will do about this fact varies considerably from place to place and time to time. A community can decide, "There's no use being careful, since the terrane self-destructs." Or they can decide, "We need to be gentle and keenly aware of the results of all our actions, since this terrane is so delicate and tends to self-destruct. We certainly don't want to make matters worse." Modern study of the island of Melos shows that the known destruction of the soil of that island is independent of human actions. The Greeks may have been unduly blamed for the deforestation of the Mediterranean countryside, since my studies indicate rather a careful attention to ecological balance. Many communities understood "reinvestment" into the natural environment to keep it in long-term balance. Certainly the long droughts of the eighth and fourth centuries B.C. would have forcefully reminded the Greeks of how precarious was their standing in the natural world.

6. This study has begun to suggest what the ancient engineers and city founders had to know about water to make viable plans for new human settlements. In so doing, the study indicates additional reason for respecting the accomplishments of our Greek forebears. Just because we are naive and ignorant about water management does not mean they were! It is even possible that the ancient city founders and their engineers were able to plan for the long-range effects of urbanization on weather cycles, water runoff, and infiltration.

7. Economic depression is harder on marginal lands than is total economic collapse. The argument here is that with total economic collapse, there is no use at all of marginal lands, so they are relatively safe. During economic depression, however, the lands are misused and no maintenance is given to such features as terraces, so the end result is much

worse in terms of erosion. I'd like to see Hellenistic history reexamined in terms of drought, inflation, and economic depression. We know, for instance, that the enormous amounts of gold from the Americas in the sixteenth and seventeenth centuries gave Spain a brief Golden Age followed by centuries of depression. Could it be that Alexander's conquest of the rich Persian Empire had the same boom-and-bust effect on the Greek lands? This economic pressure would have coincided with volcano-induced cold and a serious drought just after Alexander's death.

8. *Cities were centered on water system elements especially springs and fountains, because they were developed around such nodes.* The point here is that the locations of water delivery nodes were not accidental nor unconscious. Athens and Corinth are notable examples of great cities whose physical extent and historical impact owed much to their abundant water resources (Figs. 8.1, 18.1).

9. *Greek use of three qualities of water.* This is, to me, one of the most surprising findings of this study. It is not generally realized that the redundancy in water supply at these settlements was deliberate. Nor that this is a most intelligent method of developing water resources.

A. *Water storage was a family responsibility, while drainage was a joint responsibility of families and the whole community.* Drainage from individual houses was the responsibility of the family (Figs. 16.11–15) but major collector drains, being frequently constructed of large heavy stones, could not have been built by an individual or a family (Figs. 12.7, 16.15, 17.10–11, 22.15). *Flowing water* for fountains, supplied by long-distance water supply lines, *was a muncipal responsibility* (Fig. 22.10). *These findings about the management of water resources tell us things we had not previously known about the ancient Greeks, and provide models for solution of modern water problems.*

B. Use of wells, cisterns, and fountains, in both public and private buildings. Fountain water was preferred for drinking, but cistern water was possible for drinking in case of real necessity and for a wide range of other activities. The water of wells was allocated depending on its palatability—at Delos for drinking, at Pompeii for subpotable uses.

C. Use and reuse of water. I approached this study with the unthinking modern American notion that all water users in all times and places use water use as I do. A severe water shortage in California first alerted me to the possibility of other patterns of use. Finally, hearing and reading about modern water management problems made explicit the range of solutions that are possible.

D. "Only 6 percent of water used for drinking" is a truism in modern hydraulic engineering, but was news to me as an urban historian, and still is not common knowledge among humanists and classicists.

10. *Relation of irrigation to waste water drainage.* Once I began to see every drop of water as an important resource, the previous distinction between "good" unused water and "bad" used water broke down.

Figure 22.1. Eaves gutter and settling basin, gymnasium, Pergamon. The gutter is approximately 25 centimeters interior width.

All water in the ancient Greek world was potentially valuable, since there were *defined uses for every quality of water.* Even salty or sulfurous or hot waters could be used at health spas (Fig. 8.5), and domestic used water (free from not-yet-in-use soaps and detergents) could be re-used several times. Once water had reached maximum use-and-reuse, it was fed into the drainage channels where it was joined by runoff from storms. These combined waters flushed public latrines and sometimes cesspools, and were carried out of town through the communal sewers, to be reused in irrigation when the local terrain permitted agriculture.

11. *Drainage being as important as supply.* When I began this study, I concentrated on aqueducts and other supply elements, not realizing that if water were brought to a site and used there, it must also be evacuated, for both health and aesthetic reasons (Figs. 12.7, 13.2). The proliferation of drain pipes, gutters, and channels at the Greek sites I have visited soon made me realize that drainage received every bit as much thought and

effort as supply, because drained water was as valuable a resource as fresh water.

12. Maintenance of an ecological loop. During the twenty years of this study, "sustainable architecture" has gradually come to be a major concern in schools of architecture such as the one at Rensselaer where I spent nearly fifteen years. Naturally I turned the light of this concept on the Greek sites I was studying and asked how did a little place like Morgantina survive for 450 years, or a great place like Syracuse for 2700 years? Very carefully, with lots of attention to reinvestment in the natural resource base, so that the great-grandchildren and their great-grandchildren could also survive and thrive in the same settlement. Basic reinvestment was to put waste water back into the ground so that it could be purified naturally and drawn up again for later human use. Growing trees also was an investment in the environment that paid off for fuel and building materials and for filtering water into the underground water table, making purified water available in perennial springs and wells.

13. *Beauty of site as location determinant since Minoan and Mycenaean times* (Fig. 22.13). This was another surprising finding of the study. Although everyone knows of the beauty of Greek towns, there is a vague feeling that this beauty is an accident. On the contrary, I think now that the beauty of site was a deliberate choice and was deliberately fostered, partly through placement of water system elements where they would enhance the experience of the place.

14. How culture-bound we are in reading evidence! For example, *use of water for wiping in latrines in Greco-Roman times.* Visits to Nepal, where toilet facilities are similar to ancient Greek ones, opened my eyes to how naive I was on this topic. This explanation makes clear why Roman latrines, such as the one in Hadrian's bath at Leptis Magna, which were flushed out with dirty water from the swimming pools, also had a small stream of water running at the feet of the users, who may have dipped small sponges into the water for wiping, as we would use paper. Nothing in my own modern toilet usage pattern explained this little stream of water, but the cross-cultural insight made it clear.

15. Water management challenges were different north and south of the Mediterranean Sea, with relatively more emphasis on drainage to the north and on saving water to the south.

16. Fahlbusch's study of the evolution of technology for long-distance water supply came out in 1982 and has made possible the comprehension of how many previously unrelated elements comprise the water system of an ancient city. Specifically, municipal reservoirs (Fig. 15.7), underground aqueducts (Fig. 22.14), and pressure lines (Figs. 11.7, 22.10), are now seen to be in widespread use during the period studied. Previously pressure systems had been thought rare; Fig. 16.7, an elbow from such a line at Miletus, is one of many that could be cited. It is particularly sig-

nificant that thick-walled pressurepipes are known from a sixth century context at Olynthos, where in any case they cannot be later than the end of the fourth century B.C. This evidence may push the date for pressure systems back to the sixth century, which is a hundred years earlier than had been supposed.

In addition to these general findings, which I postulate as true for Greek sites as a group, there are other findings that are specific to one or more places. I will discuss them under the heading of the particular site related to their discovery. Again, those in italics are the ones that I think were not known at all when I began this study.

SITE SPECIFIC FINDINGS

Akragas

Gypsum layer correlates with spring in Asklepion (Fig. 8.5). Another example of geologists and classicists being interested in different aspects of a site, and not talking to each other about that site. At a couple of Sicilian sites I was assured by archaeologists that there had never been any geological study of that site, only to find that the geologists had in fact been hard at work, but it had apparently not occurred to anyone to correlate the geological with the historical and archaeological aspects of the site. Since Asklepions frequently occur where there are special waters, it is gratifying rather than surprising to learn that such is the case at Akragas.

Correlation of springs and urban form (Fig. 15.2). The map of the springs of Akragas suggests a strong correlation between those water sources and the urban development of the site, a history of water use related to urban form that has continued through the medieval, baroque, and modern times here.

Immense drainage problems. The truth about how complicated drainage is in karst areas has been out of fashion at Akragas for many centuries. Consequently, post-World War II construction has taken place without regard to the constraints of this kind of drainage, and with the expectable results—too much of the wrong kinds of water, shortage of pure water for drinking.

Additional springs at Akragas. Fourteen? more?—certainly not the ten shown on geology maps of the site. Desperately needed for Agrigento is an accurate block-by-block map of ancient water sources and drains, related to the present coverage of the site by buildings. The map published here (Fig. 15.2) shows the fourteen springs I have been able to determine.

Argos

City as focus of resources: fishing, farming, grazing, water. Argos has made me aware of the importance for urban location of water and any two of the other three factors. With these resources, the community can survive. With all three plus water, the town can flourish, as Argos has done during many centuries. Careful inspection of Argos—incompletely excavated and scantily published as it is—shows water system elements at every turn, indicating a profound understanding, on the part of its ancient builders, of water as a natural resource to be manipulated for human purposes.

Abundance of water at the site. None of the accounts I have read of Argos make a point of how much good water is available here, yet inspection of the site makes it clear that karst water was a major factor in determining location and development of the settlement.

Relation of springs at Argos to sinkholes on Tripoli plateau. Here again the geologists and the classical historians have separate but dovetailing information about the hinterland of Argos.

Assos

Usual combination of cisterns and springs, especially on the Acropolis. Although Assos is situated on an extinct volcano, there are also limestone strata through which some karst channels flow. Thus the site does not depend only on cisterns but also on at least one important spring just above sea level, a spring that probably drew the Ionians here in the third millennium B.C.

Relation of site to very large thermal spring, west of Assos. This spring depends on the volcanic nature of the terrain. Thermal springs were foci for major settlements, as we have seen also in the case of the thermal spring at the top of Akragas.

Athens

Athenian Acropoolis as well-watered center of urban history (Fig.18.1). When I began this study, I knew and believed the stories about how the Athenians had so little water that it was a serious problem. Now I think the history was much more complicated, with droughts in the eighth and fourth centuries plus city growth (especially in the fifth century) beyond what the existing water supply could handle. Yet throughout all its history, the Acropolis of Athens produced valuable water for its immediate vicinity.

Aqueducts as supplementary water supply are first heard of in the sixth century, when several of the Greek tyrants competed to build long-distance water supply lines according to the newly imported technology from the East (Figs. 4.1, 8.4, 13.1, 18.1, 22.3, 22.10). The Peisistratid Aqueduct built at Athens in the sixth century was a major contribution to the political dominance of this family (Fig. 18.10).

The fourth century drought in Attica caused changes in local water management. For instance, wells were filled in and cisterns built, suggesting that the water table had dropped. Water has a range of behaviors in any given climate and terrain. The Athenians might have remembered the eighth century drought, and been prepared, but perhaps that is too much to ask of human nature!

Corinth

Water system as karstic. The springs and fountains of Corinth have been given exemplary publication in the series of excavation reports from the site, and yet neither a hydraulic engineer nor a geologist seems to have been consulted. It was a happy discovery that many of the water system elements here fit readily into the pattern of karst features, and to conclude that the ancient Greeks had deliberately utilized these karst features in constructing this water system (Fig.11.1).

The number of cisterns on Acrocorinth showed me that the history of that citadel extends far beyond the Greco-Roman period, as does that of the citadel of Larissa at Argos. Cisterns were basic to the ability of any garrison to hold out on this mountaintop, since the one spring that is recorded (Upper Peirene) did not give enough water for a large garrison.

An unanswered question here is whether the construction of the South Stoa not only coincided with but was the cause of the drying up of the Sacred Spring, since the stoa tapped the water channels farther upstream.

Delos

There is a river on Delos, not just cisterns and wells. Reading the excavation reports, I had the mistaken notion that all houses relied on cisterns because there was no flowing water here. To the contrary, there were wells, cisterns, a river flowing from a spring—all of the possible sources of water.

Variation in shape and placement of cisterns from the flask-shaped kind I knew so well at Morgantina; the cisterns at Delos are usually square or rectangular underground boxes, their lids the pavement of the courtyard above them. Since most of the surviving houses are third or second century, this difference cannot be accounted for by claiming that they are early and primitive. Rather, I think that there was enough very cold water from wells so that the rainwater retained in cisterns could be used for washing and cleaning, purposes for which warmer water is better. There was no incentive to place the cisterns deep in the earth to keep the water cool.

Water holder in the so-called "inn" as a probable karst shaft. The story that I was told about this large shaft (8–10 feet in diameter, at least 30 feet deep) is that it inexplicably fills up with water and empties out "as if it had a leak." This is just the way a karst doline behaves, depending on the time of year and amount of rainfall upstream.

Delphi

Dominance of karst in visible springs, seeps, etc. has been studied by Burdon and other karst experts. This is one ancient site where the karst features are well known in geological circles (Fig. 8.2). Location of major buildings depends on water sources. A fine example is the gymnasium along the terrace of the upper end of a valley, where it receives the abundant outpouring of springs in the cliff-face above the modern road. The upper stadium and the Roman-period bath near the top of the sanctuary also are located to receive the output of springs high on the mountain, the flow of the perched water tables so commonly found in karst terranes.

Gela

Bath near modern hospital (Fig. 22.2). To my knowledge, no excavations have been done below the hospital to trace earlier health establishments, yet such would not be unlikely. At Akragas a spring within the grounds of the modern psychiatric hospital cries out for similar investigation of previous health care facilities on the site.

The bath at Gela seems to be of the fourth century or early third century at the very latest. If it is from the fourth, it is early for a bath with several rooms each with banks of tubs, and with a below-floor heating room. It reminds us of the fifth century bath found just outside the

Figure 22.2.   View of the fourth century B.C. baths at Gela, next to the modern hospital.

Dipylon Gate at Athens. Gradually we are becoming aware that public baths of several rooms, with provision for heated water and oriented to the south for solar heating of the spaces, are a standard feature of Greek water management from the fifth century on, rather than being a development of the Romans.

Gortys

Spring-fed river is perpetual not seasonal. So unusual is this kind of perennial river in the Mediterrranean lands that its occurrence called for establishment of health facilities related to the worship of a god. The abundant flow was possible because of karst springs and channels in the mountains to the east. Bath had solar heating.

Istanbul (Byzantium, Constantinople)

Repeated urban renewal with water renewal. Long-distance water supply lines here seem to be Roman and later, but cisterns are known from Greek times, in the oldest part of the city where the Topkapi Museum now stands. Almost nothing has been done at Istanbul to trace water system elements from Greek times. It is significant that the modern effort to renew the physical fabric of Istanbul includes both an impressive renovation of the Cistern of 1000 Columns next to the site of Hagia Sophia, and a much more ambitious and expensive effort to rehabilitate the arm of water called the Golden Horn, which has served as an open sewer for generations, and transformation of a moat into a park.

Lindos

Besides cisterns on the sanctuary-citadel and elsewhere, the town was watered by aqueducts from the mountainous karstic interior of the island, from whence waterlines were also led to supply the city of Rhodes.

Megara

Ample water but not enough land. The only ancient Greek remains visible here to date are the famous fountainhouse of the fifth century B.C. (Fig. 20.6).

Miletus

How big Miletus is and how much there is to see there is not at all evident from maps, since in most books Miletus and Priene each take up one page, although the two cities are quite disparate in size. Miletus takes hours to walk around and across (Fig. 22.3). It was the leading Greek city of the eighth century, before its destruction in the Persian Wars and its rebuilding in classical and Hellenistic times. Consequently there are many water system elements visible here and many more still to be discovered.

Miletus as a perfect example of a city in karst terrane. The hills to the southeast and east of Miletus are karstic and a number of mountain

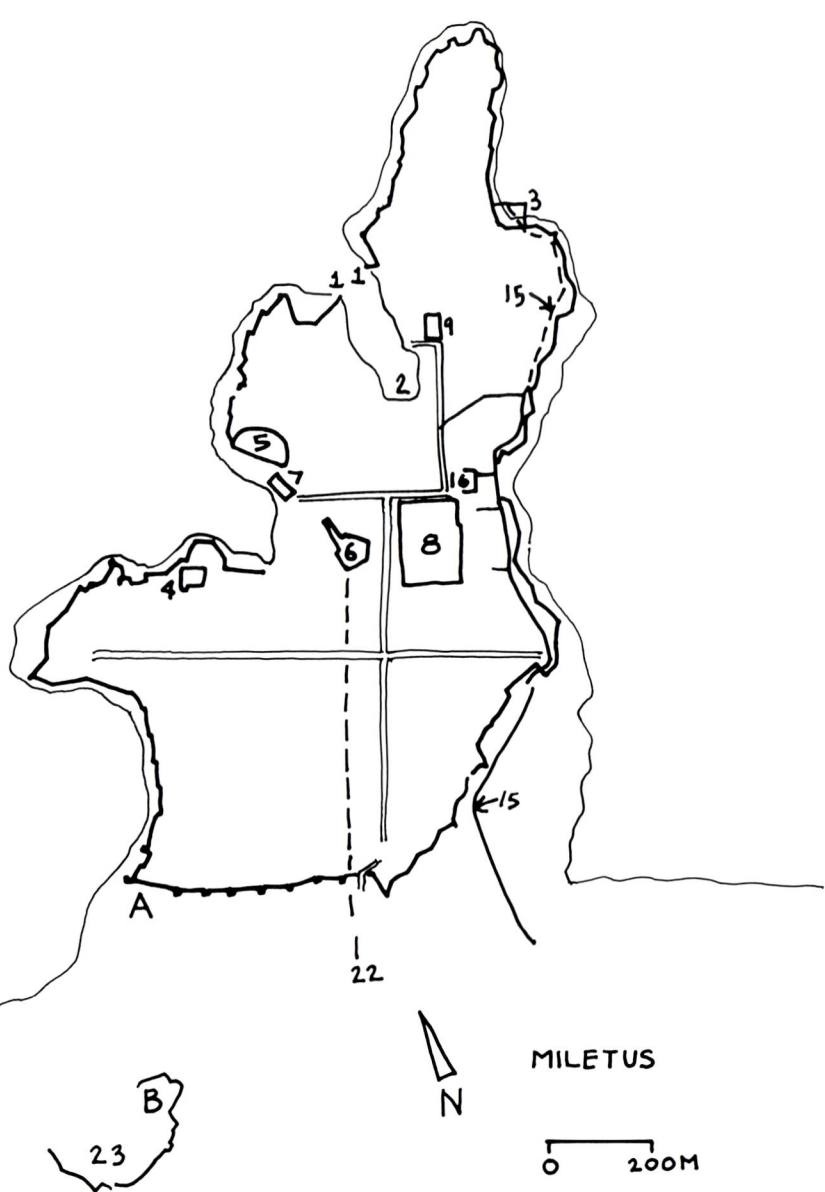

Figure 22.3. Map of Miletus, showing water supply elements: *1, 1.* Gate of the Harbor of the Lions. *1–2.* Southwest shore of Harbor of Lions is rich in water from the hill behind the shore. Numerous cisterns are related to the theater on the other side of the same hill. *3.* Recently discovered but unexcavated bath, probably fed from the high waterline on arches (15), coming from the mountains, which also supplied the Nymphaeum and other baths to the south, along the east side of the city. *4.* Bath (so-called Hamei Tepe Bath). The peninsula southwest of this bath was the site of a Mycenaean settlement. *6.* Faustina Bath (Roman), typically Greek in its association with a palestra. *7.* Seljuk caravanserai, recently rebuilt as a tourist facility, indicating the persistence of water at this outlet. *8.*

springs were tapped for the water system of the city, still supplying the villages of this edge of the Meander River valley (Fig.7.1). A detailed study of the Roman and earlier water lines here would be very useful (Fig. 16.6–7, 22.4).

The settlement pattern of Miletus was quite unlike what I had thought, in its historical development. The separate nodes of the archaic town on its mesa and the archaic and earlier port (beyond the modern tourist facilities) have yet to be connected satisfactorily in a coherent urban history of the site. Yet in spatial distribution of the extant ruins, the Hippodamean pattern of the fifth century and later city is clear, and matches what I had expected from reading the literature.

Morgantina

Several bathtub types are known from Morgantina and a few are beautifully displayed in the Morgantina Museum in the town of Aidone. Not known from any other site are the *stone bathtubs at Morgantina, lined with cubes of glazed brick* (Fig. 22.6)

Five springs (not one) *at Morgantina and their relationship to urban form* (Fig. 14.2, 15.1). Knowing Morgantina in as much detail as I do made the conclusion inescapable that the urban form—while embodying a general pattern also found in many Western Greek cities of the fifth century—was in its details dependant on the specific location of water sources around which the city developed.

Ample evidence of use of several classes of water such as fresh running water from springs, cold still water from wells, rainwater captured in cisterns, and drainage water carefully led out of town to the hillsides below, made me ponder the why and how of this redundant water use. The data from Morgantina made me critical of water usage patterns at other sites.

The specifics of water use in one industry at Morgantina was illuminating about the careful thought given to management of this resource.

Water in (mostly unexcavated) South Market is indicated by abundance of brambles. *9.* Hellenistic bath. *15.* Aqueduct (solid line) and its supposed extension (dashed line) to the bath at 3. *16.* Nymphaem. *22.* Probable aqueduct supplying the Serapeion fountain and the Faustina Baths. *23.* Excavations of the archaic period settlement on this hill reveal not only houses but a probable fountain at the base of the eastern side of the hill. The flat-topped hill was formed by karst erosion processes, being made of a soft chalky carbonate rock topped by a very hard caprock of limestone. Redrawn and water system elements added, from a map of the German Archaeological Inst., Istanbul, by permission. *A*, Greco-Roman city. *B*, Archaic settlement. The public water elements of Figures 22.3 and 22.4 total 23; no attempt has been made to map the cisterns, wells, fountains of private houses.

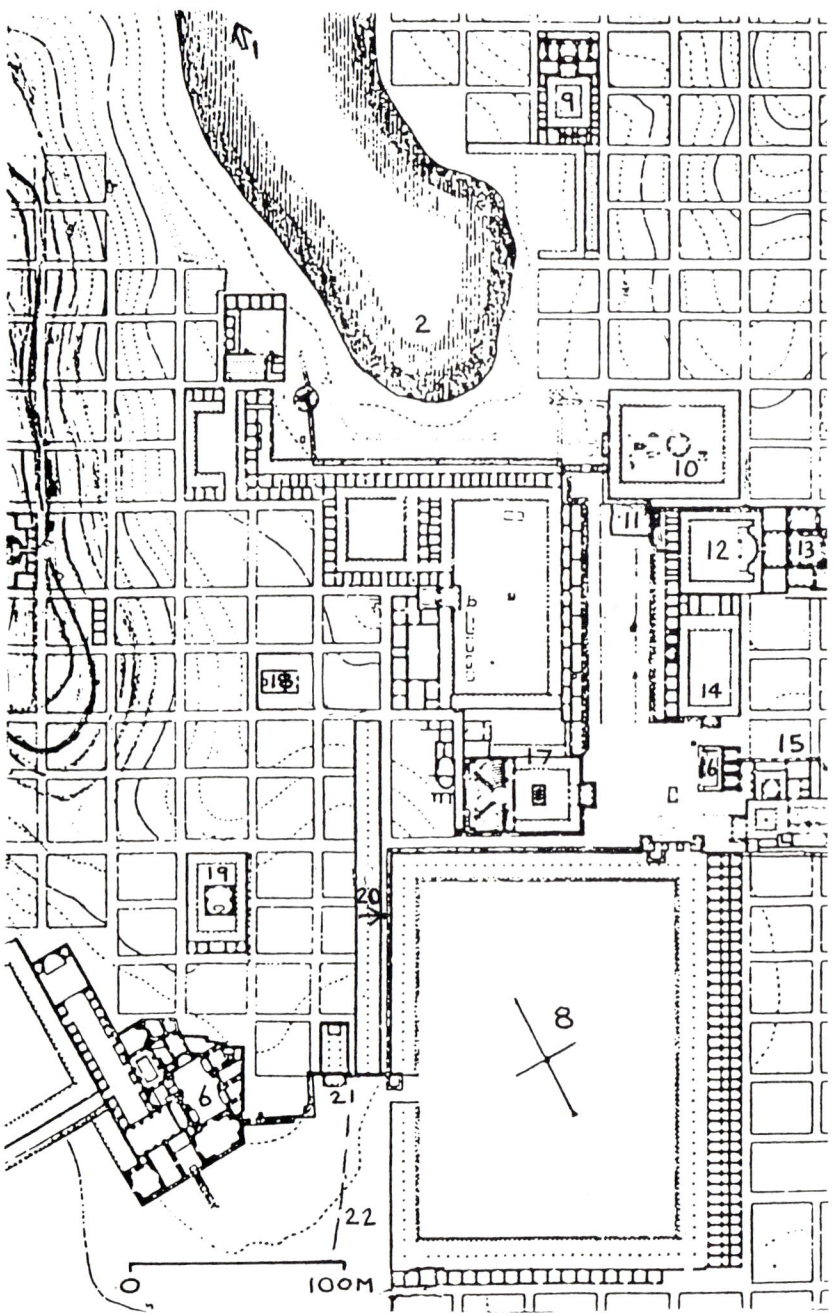

Figure 22.4. Miletus, detail of central district, with same numbering as Fig. 22.3, but also showing the famous grid system associated with Hippodamus of Miletus, of the fifth century B.C. *1–2.* Southwest shore of Harbor of Lions is rich in water from the hill behind the shore. Numerous cisterns are related to the theater on the other side of the same hill. *6.* Faustina Bath of the Roman period, with its Greek-style palestra to the left. *8.* Water in the mostly unexcavated South

Figure 22.5. Tub of stone slabs, in House of the Arched Cistern, Morgantina, approximately 0.66 by 1.25 meters. Just across the wall in the foreground was a floor cistern, and the tub seems to have also been supplied from a lead pipe that ran in a groove where the line of shadow is at left. See plan, Figure 20.11C.

Market is indicated by the abundance of brambles. *9.* Hellenistic bath. *10.* Pipes and channels are visible in and along the edges of the Delphinion. *11.* Seljuk bath. *12.* Capito bath. *13.* Large structure behind Capito Bath. The baths (12 and 13) may have originated in the Hellenistic period or even earlier, and seem to have persisted in use through the Byzantine period, possibly being transformed into a large church. *14.* Gymnasium. *15.* Aqueduct, shown as a dotted line. *16.* Nymphaeum. *17.* The Bouleterion courtyard and especially the porticoes between it and the small temple to its north are rich in waterlines and cisterns. *18.* Pipes and cisterns are visible in the precinct of the Early Christian church and bishop's house. *19.* Water supply pipes are visible in the courtyard alongside the Heroon, having been excavated since 1983. *20.* Street has several water lines that utilize the siphon principle. The long narrow building to the left of the street is an early Greek warehouse, so the waterlines may well be fourth or fifth century B.C. *21.* Serapeion and fountain. *22.* Probable aqueduct, shown as a dashed line, supplying the Serapeion fountain and the Faustina Baths. Redrawn from a map of the German Archaeological Institute, Istanbul, and used by permission.

Figure 22.6.　Stone tub about 1.25 meter long, lined with 2.5 centimeter square terra-cotta cubes glazed in red. At Morgantina.

Figure 22.7.　Vase painting of bather with sponge and towel, about to step into a bi- or tri-level tub having a metal stand. As published in J. Delorme, *Gymnasion* (Paris: E. de Boccard, 1960). Reprinted by permission.

Figure 22.8. Classical tub shape with three interior levels, designed to have a metal stand or be built in. This shape was typical of the fifth and fourth centuries B.C., and has continued to be used in Greece until present times.

Figure 22.9. Giant pithos about 1 m. in diameter, in north room of House of Arched Cistern, Morgantina, possibly for washing clothes and bathing.

- *Potters' kilns at Morgantina where water and clay were conveniently near one another:*

    In North Stoa—clay from uphill used with water from the springs of the northwest corner of the agora.

    In the Chthonian Sanctuary in the Agora, using water from theater hill and clay from the Agora side of West Hill.

    In the granary, using water draining from East Hill, or a still-unidentified spring in East Hill behind the granary, *which may have fed the large drain through the granary.* The clay for this kiln seems to have come from just outside South Gate.

    Even a seep would be enough water for a pottery.

Mycenae

Possible use of "French drain" as the aqueduct supplying the famous under-the-wall water-postern. A "French drain" is a ditch dug between a water source and outfall, then filled with stones through which the water would flow more quickly and easily than through undisturbed land, and finally covered with soil so that it is invisible. Although earlier than the period studied, such a construction is thought-provoking for what it suggests about the possible sophistication of pre-Greek water management and the oral tradition that may have passed this information on down to the archaic Greeks.

Olynthos

Strong role of geology in viability of site. The broad wheat fields of today indicate what the Athenian colonists saw as valuable at the site. But this obviously valuable feature of the area had to be supplemented by the abundant water potential of the karstic hills to the north in order for the settlement to become rich and successful. The aqueduct discovered by the excavators, first built in the sixth century, speaks to the primacy of water supply in the development of the town. If the aqueduct is sixth century, it preserves the *earliest known use of a pressure pipeline.* Even if a fully developed pressure system came later, this line had to include siphons to carry the water from the hills down into the vally to the north of the settlement and then up onto the fortified hill.

Pella

Well-developed drainage system and still-visible water system. At a site noted for its magnificent pebble mosaic floors and sumptuous houses, it is gratifying to see that equal attention was paid to water management.

Pergamon

Details of urban design at Pergamon as related to water need a lot of work. Some questions:

1. What was the function of the building with a great arch in the wall (near the tourist stand at the entrance to the upper city)? It seems to me to be a cistern and fountain placed as was traditional next to the main gateway. I have not been able to discover a published explanation of it.
2. Was there an original spring within the citadel, possibly in the caves of barracks area? Another in what are today damp and overgrown rooms of the palace area?
3. Drainage patterns of the upper city need to be traced in detail. Particularly mysterious is a cleft behind the buildings and retaining wall to the left in the theater area, which reminds me of the clefts of the Athenian Acropolis. I think it is, like them, a natural cleft that was pressed into service as a drain. It would be logical for the substructures of the theater terrace to serve as storage reservoirs for rainwater to be used in the lower city.

Even at Pergamon, with over a century of modern study of the water supply, *no one has studied the distribution pattern of the municipal water supply.* (Fig. 22.10 is a map of the supply lines outside the city.) Such a study has been done only at Pompeii, and for only the Roman period there. I·have discussed this issue with Professor Garbrecht, who has led the modern effort to understand the water supply of Pergamon, and it may be that a student of his will undertake such a detailed study of water distribution at this site.

For a great city such as Pergamon, water supply and drainage were as complicated and sophisticated then as now. This principle is based on the fact that for a site to be densely settled, attention must be paid to sanitation and water supply, as matters of survival but even more of maximizing the potential of both site and occupants.

Petra

Water was essential to survival here in the rocky desert, and carefully managed. Even here where one would think water was available for only the most essential uses, there were street fountains to enliven the central business and ceremonial area, and public baths just off the main street.

Pompeii

This is the only water distribution system completely studied, *yet even here there is no understanding of the way cistern and fountain water differed and how differently they were used, no study of the sources and long-distance water lines outside the city, and no attempt to write a profiile of water use by individuals.*

Posidonia (Paestum)

Ample evidence of karst here. This colonial settlement was deliberately located on a site where traditional knowledge of managing karst could be utilized.

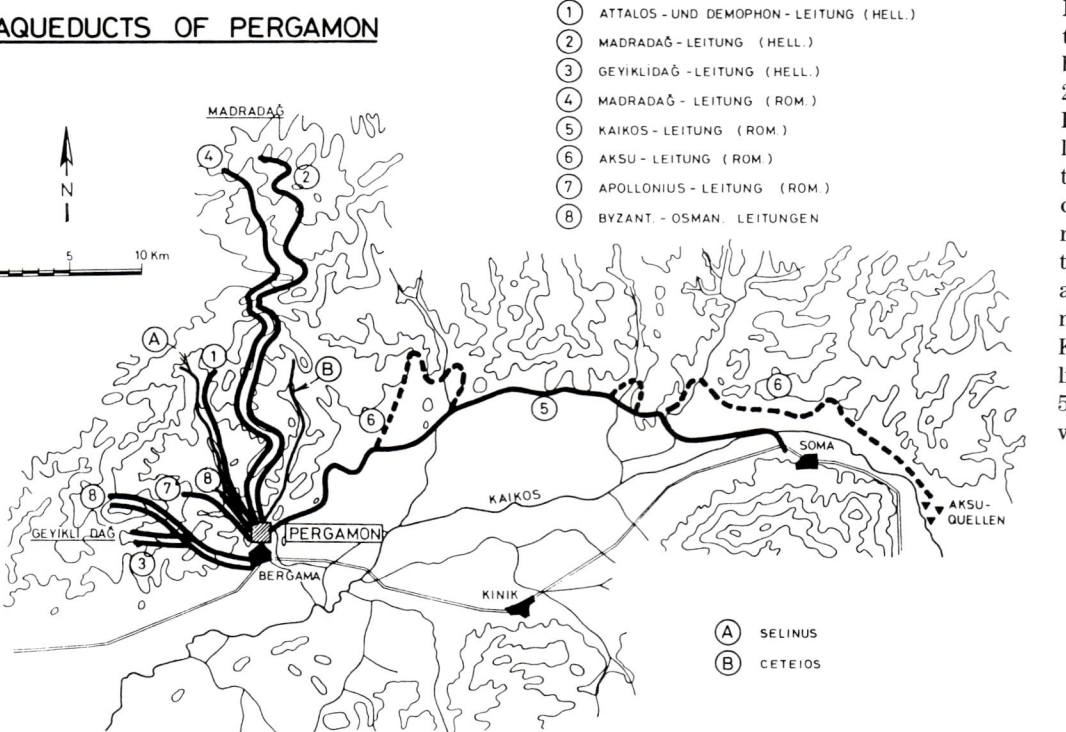

AQUEDUCTS OF PERGAMON

1. ATTALOS - UND DEMOPHON - LEITUNG (HELL.)
2. MADRADAĞ - LEITUNG (HELL.)
3. GEYIKLIDAĞ - LEITUNG (HELL.)
4. MADRADAĞ - LEITUNG (ROM.)
5. KAIKOS - LEITUNG (ROM.)
6. AKSU - LEITUNG (ROM.)
7. APOLLONIUS - LEITUNG (ROM.)
8. BYZANT. - OSMAN. LEITUNGEN

Ⓐ SELINUS
Ⓑ CETEIOS

Figure 22.10. Plan of the long-distance water supply lines of Pergamon, both Hellenistic and Roman. A and 1, 2, 3. Hellenistic lines; B and 4, 5, 6, 7. Roman lines; 8. Byzantine and Turkish lines. The ancient city of Pergamon and the modern town of Bergama are adjacent. Geyikli Dag and Madradag are nearby mountains whose springs fed all the lines except 5 and 6. Aksu-quellen are the springs that fed the Aksu line, number 6, some 65 kilometers long. Kaikos is the river whose waters fed line 5. From a plan of G. Garbrecht (fig. 57 in *Wasser*, Deutsches Museum, Rowohlt, 1985); reprinted by permission.

Figure 22.11. View of the Hellenistic pressure pipeline north of Pergamon, shown by its lockstones still in situ; the lead pipes have been robbed out but left traces of lead in the soil under the line. This photo was published by H. Graber, in "Die Wasserleitungen von Pergamon," 1888; he was one of the hydraulic engineers brought in by the early excavators to investigate the water supply of the site. Graber reported finding slivers of lead between the lockstones.

Priene

Few cisterns in Priene because of abundance of flowing water. Priene was a useful corrective for my conceptual understanding of Greek water management, because it forced me to deal with how local variations in geological base and in climate made immense differences in the patterns of water management. Every "general law" about ancient Greek water management is qualified by many exceptions and qualifications.

Rhodes

Subtlety of the proportional street system at Rhodes forces us to re-examine the meaning of the Hippodamean street plan, and the promulgation of this plan in the fifth century Greek world (Fig. 8.3).

A study of Rhodes's street plan from water and sewer pipes indicates

Figure 22.12. Largest lockstone of the pressure pipeline at Pergamon, perhaps 2 meters in width, and placed at the top of the hill shown in Fig. 22.13, where the pressure put the greatest strain on the siphon system.

Figure 22.13. Line of arches of the Roman aqueduct at Pergamon appears here as a dark line at the center, running toward the top of the photo. Parallel to it were the earlier underground Hellenistic lines that appear here as "light shadows" in the grass to the right of the line of arches. This photographic effect is due to different grasses growing in the more shallow soil over the buried remains of the early water channel. Looking north from the citadel.

the valuable knowledge to be derived from close examination of pipelines and other water system elements at other sites, particularly the patterns and clusters in which these elements are found.

The ability of Greek water engineers of the fifth century to harness karst water from the interior and deliver it to Rhodes was undoubtedly significant in the viability of the new city.

Rome

Water system as karstic. We have quite a bit of knowledge of the manmade aspects of this water delivery system, but now that data needs to be correlated with geological information. The initial study by Bauer of the Cloacca Maxima needs to be expanded to a general study of drainage (ancient and modern) of the city of Rome.

Samos

The famous sixth century tunnel was succeeded by later lines for same purposes, supplying the city (now called Pythagorion) and the Hellenistic-and-later baths on the south coast (Fig. 22.14). A history of the development of water supply here would go a long way to account for history of settlement in this area. For instance, on old maps reproduced in Kienast's dissertation about the ramparts of Samos (1978), there is evidence of aqueducts coming to Pythagorion from the northwest.

Some geological studies of Samos already exist, which will make possible a closer reading of the relationship between resources base, settlement history, and water management.

Selinus

Relation of spring Gaggara and Temple M on the edge of the hill west of the Acropolis, to the street pattern on the tableland of Manuzza inland from the Acropolis (Fig. 12.3). Another case of geological studies bringing out the significance of archaeological work.

Both the modern managers of tourism at the site and the ancient founders and builders of Selinus have seen and acted upon the necessity of drains and manholes to handle abundant winter rains.

Not every human activity has an architectural solution—a fact evident from the absence of toilets from the excavated domestic bathrooms here (Fig. 20.11D). One must infer, e.g., *chamber pots*.

Syracuse

So strong is the *correlation of the history of Syracuse with karst phenomena* that it is really not possible to understand the form of the city without this information. By including hydraulic engineering information in our study of the urbanization of Syracuse, we achieve not only a more accurate perception of how the city worked and why the residential areas were placed as they were on the landscape, but also greater respect for

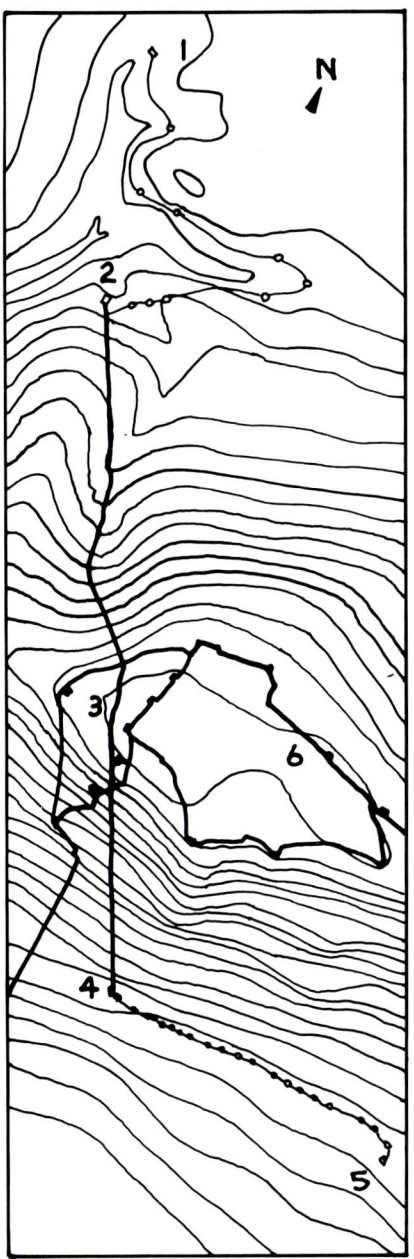

Figure 22.14. Plan of the tunnel of Eupalinos at Samos (present-day Pythagorion). Direct distance from the spring to the city is 1700 m. but the water line is longer because it partially follows contours. The parts of the waterline are spring (1), contour channel from the spring to the tunnel (1–2), north entrance (2), place where the two halves of the tunnel met (3), south entrance (4), and contour channel from the tunnel to the city (4–5) . Published by H. Kienast in "Der Tunnel des Eupalinos auf Samos," *Mannheimer Forum,* 86/87 Abb. 25b, and reprinted by permission.

Figure 22.15. Water channel at Selinus, covered with stone slabs. A wellhead gives access to the flowing water below. Compare with Fig. 16.15, a very similar arrangement at Athens. The channel held runoff water which could be re-used to water animals, for crafts manufacturing in domestic courtyards or shops, and to water down the streets for evaporative cooling.

Greek accomplishments, since they succeeded in efforts of water management that are of high value to us. The contributions of the geological and engineering disciplines to a more complete and satisfying account of each particular city's history are evident (Figs. 8.4, 11.4).

Springs in Ortygia and in the harbors as karstic. Until now, no viable explanation for the harbor springs has been put forth, in spite of centuries of discussion (Fig. 7.9–10).

The lower level of the fountain between amphitheater and the arch near it is not indicated in the published materials about this arch. Such a detail reminds us of how essential it is to check published data with the circumstances at the site itself, and to be skeptical of published plans.

Other disciplines may not take the architectural historian's or urban historian's view of the importance of three-dimensional relations between buildings and spaces in the urban landscape. Few in any discipline are trained to ask what the information and working methods from another discipline can do to help them understand the urban data they are working with. Yet a city is so complex an artifact that no single discipline nor even two or three disciplines can hope to account for all its features.

Reuse of abandoned water channels as catacombs suggests new insight into *origins of catacocmbs*, for instance at Rome where we know there was karst activity (Fig. 15.4–6).

Thasos

Abundant karst water has never, as far as I know, been factored in as significant in the development of this site, even though that same abundance makes possible the rich green vegetation that is one's chief impression of the island, and lures both Greek and Yugoslav tourists here as it lured settlers before and during the archaic period. The water is strongly correlated with the excellent quality of building stone being quarried at the island today as in the past.

Troy

Although of the pre-Greek period that lies outside this study, Troy has visible water system elements that—like those at Mycenae—make us wonder about the content and continuation of an oral water management tradition in the Greek world. Specifically, there is a drain under the sixteenth century B.C. gate, so similar in form and function to drains under the Dipylon Gates at classical Athens and under the Roman gates at Palmyra, as to reinforce the principle that since water still behaves as it always has, many solutions to managing it remain constant from age to age and culture to culture.

In outline, these are the major findings of this study.

23

Thoughts on the History of Greek Urbanization

What raised man above the level of barbarism . . . and enabled him to develop the higher faculties . . . to live well instead of merely living, was his membership in an actual, physical city."
—Collingwood and Myres,
Roman Britain and the English Settlement

Today we are facing constraints on the use of water. Some cities have astronomically high densities or unusually low access to fresh water while still others may have only enough water that is not contaminated with heavy metals or pesticides to cover the 6 percent allocated for drinking but not enough of that highest quality for the rest of domestic use. In all of these cases, modern hydraulic engineers are experimenting—though often without realizing it—with a set of solutions that are at least 2500 years old. These solutions were appropriate quality of water for each use, plus reuse to the extent feasible. Both solutions were determined then and are implemented now on a cost-benefit basis. Those who understand the lessons of history of water management can repeat them more quickly and efficiently than those who, for instance, have to re-invent a three-tiered water system from scratch.

This is where the urban historian can play the role of interpreter, to help us understand in a way that the recital of disconnected facts never can. The historian recovers the plan of the past—both the physical form and the social intention. From the point of view of the development of architectural and urban history and theory, this approach to the data involves humble acknowledgment of ignorance, careful amassing of facts, meditation on the facts to see what principles they suggest, and utilization of both data and methodology from many different disciplines. Then the principles derived from one site can be tried to facilitate the understanding of another site, and a body of theory develops strongly bolstered by facts as well as principles and insights.

From the site-specific facts about water management in the ancient

Greek world, I have provisionally arrived at the following elements for a theoretical position about the role of water in the formation of traditional settlements:

1. Founders of these settlements used traditional knowledge to find and develop water resources.
2. Their methods were positive for long-term water resource management.
3. Water of several qualities was allocated to its best use.
4. House design and city form reveal the society's means of collecting and using water, as well as constraining that use.
5. Even in the absence of written records, careful study of the geological base, of archaeological remains, and of visual representations of water system elements can tell us much about how the ancient Greeks managed water to make settlement possible, sustainable, and amenable.

Greek cities were carefully sited according to a traditional process, so they would have at least two of the food possibilities (fishing, grazing, farming) plus readily available water. Residents were drawn to these sites precisely because of their resources. Traditional water knowledge relied on geological and meteorological observation plus social consensus and administrative organization, and developed chronologically as listed in Table 23.1:

Table 23.1
Chronology of Water Knowledge

Prehistorical period	Springs
3–2nd millennium B.C.	Cisterns
*3 millennium B.C.	Dams
3 millennium B.C.	Wells
? Probably very early	Reuse of excrement as fertilizer
*2 millennium B.C.	Gravity flow supply pipes or channels and drains, pressure pipes (subsequently forgotten)
8th–6th c B.C.	Long-distance water supply lines with tunnels and bridges, as well as intervention in and harnessing of karst water systems
6th c. B.C. at latest	Public as well as private bathing facilities, consisting of: bathtubs or showers, footbaths, washbasins, latrines or toilets, laundry and dishwashing facilities
6th c. B.C. at latest	Utilization of definitely two and probably three qualities of water, potable, sub-potable, and non-potable including irrigation using storm runoff, probably combined with waste waters
6th–3rd c. B.C.	Pressure pipes and siphon systems

*indicates an element discovered, probably forgotten, rediscovered later.

? indicates an educated guess.

The pressure of population and increased complexity of the organization of work/production went together with increased complexity of water supply and drainage. Because they had cisterns and wells and had harnessed the flow of springs, the ancient Greeks were less dependent on any one source of water. Reuse and multiple supply meant that a given amount of rainfall could support more activities and more people. A city the size of Alexandria is unthinkable if based solely on cistern water, because of the paucity of rain in Eqypt, but the wells of the city tapped an aquifer more than 60 feet below the surface, and we suspect that long-distance supply lines brought water from outside the city to supply the published bath and other public facilities.

If a modern city were emulating the Greeks in using the three-tiered system of water supply, and showed as much care to return used waters to the environment, they would win much praise for their ecological soundness. It seems unlikely that the Greeks carried out a similar process unconsciously.

The close symbiosis between settlement and setting was an unexpected finding of this study. These findings force further reexamination of the history of cities on a geographical, especially a geological, basis. As a historian, I have deliberately opted to try "to see the land with the eyes of its former occupants, from the standpoint of their needs and capacities" (Sauer, 1956, 287–99).

Water management in Greek times was nicely balanced between elements that people could build, maintain and use privately, and those that required communal effort and provided communal rewards. Understanding this requires us to reevaluate what we know about the ancient Greeks from purely literary remains which are, of course, skewed towards upper class male views of the Greek urban experience. It takes more thought than money to live well—comfortably, graciously, nonexploitatively. In spite of marked differences between the roles, functions, and powers of men and women, free and slave, daily life among the ancient Greeks was pegged at a level of equity and comfort rarely equaled in human history. Both the daily routine and the built containers for that routine (houses and public buildings and spaces) were pleasant for most people. Water arrangements played an important role in making this so.

CONCLUSIONS

Part I. *Purposes and Methods. Difficulties of Cross Disciplinary Research.* As one pursues a major, long-term project like this, purposes and methods change as the topic expands, clarifies, and ramifies. Of the twenty years I have spent on this work, it took fourteen to realize what the questions really were, and where to look for the answers, as well as how to read those answers for which I had previously not had questions. Much of this delay was due to my own ignorance, and to the necessity of gaining skills in other disciplines than art history. An additional factor was prematurity, so that even as I began to understand and be able to explain the problem, I had to develop an audience that could hear me. (See "Prematurity and Uniqueness in Scientific Discovery," by Gunther S. Stent, *Scientific American.* (Dec. 1972) 84–93.)

Particularly important was the realization that I had to bend object-related research data to new uses in a system-oriented study. Although I worried about the resultant distortion of the data, I was encouraged by the remarks of other scholars such as J. W. Bennett (1976). The question of causation is complex, he wrote, emphasizing the concept of SYSTEM, in which both behavioral (or cultural) and environmental (either/or physical and social) factors are seen to be in a reciprocal process of interaction (p. 1). Systems theory is a method for studying complex situations to include the largest number of interdependent factors (p. 21). "The question that should underlie the study of human systems is when and under what circumstances these teleological and causative elements characterize human systems and how important it may be to include them in the analysis." For example, in " the increasingly complex cases of resources exploitation and economic handling . . . *research on sociona-tural systems . . . must unravel the very many feedbacks*, before restraint (if that is required) can be exercised" (p. 22) (emphasis added). In a nutshell, that is my work: *research on socionatural urban systems.*

Part II. *Modern Questions about Ancient Water Control.* We are accustomed to reading plays, poetry, temples and sculpture as evidence of Greek civilization. Revisions in the methodology and slant of history during the past decade or two have, however, taught us to look for other aspects of the recent and distant past, as being equally worthy of our interest, and as fruitful for new understandings of our predecessors—and ourselves. Just so, we can now see Greek cities in quite a new way when we see them as containers for water systems and made up of people who designed, built, maintained, and used water systems. How they did all that may be old data, but it is news.

So too, when we turn back to Greek times with new questions, we find ourselves looking for new kinds of information, and reexamining old data. For instance, G.V. Blackstone, (1957) "properly" begins his book with basis in classical precedent, referring on p. 4 to a Roman pump found at Bolsena and another found at Silchester (Fig. 23.1). Both were based in turn upon inventions of Ctesibius of Alexandria, as described by Hero in the third century B.C.: "a machine which expels water to a great height." (Reference from Howard Blyth.) Who knows how many fragments are lying about in museum storerooms or at sites, unrecognized? So, too, other elements from Greek water systems may come into our consciousness, forcing us to revise our data and our evaluation of the Greek experience.

Part III. *Greek Urbanism—Data and Theories.* When I began this study I believed that there were two basic patterns of Greek cities, the grid of Hippodamos and the fan blades of "scenographic urbanism". Reality turned

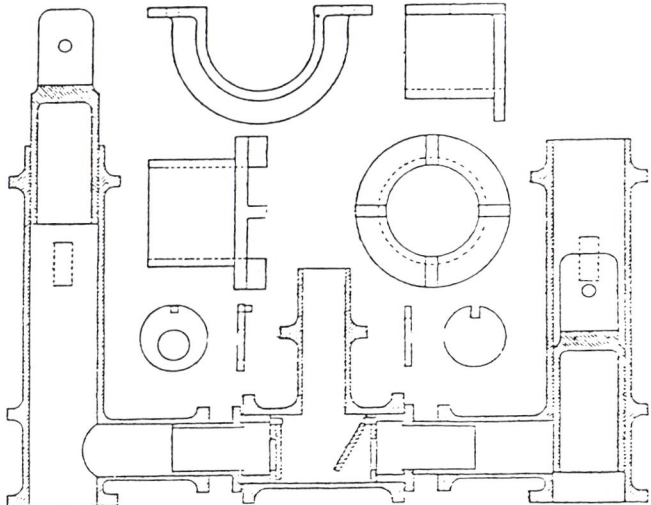

Figure 23.1. Diagram of a Roman pump found at Bolsena, in the British Museum, based on the work of Ctesibius of Alexandria, third century B.C, as published in G.V. Blackstone, *A History of the British Fire Service* (London: Routledge and Kegan Paul, 1957). Reprinted by permission from Routledge.

out to be more complicated, with five basic patterns (Fig. 5.1A-E). So I should not have been surprised that neither the central place theory nor the network economic theory of urban location was sufficient to account for locations of Greek cities (Fig. 9.1). Rather, a combination of both, and factoring in a strong element of geological determinism, and we begin to see the why of the where. In Volume II I expect to delve further into the way that urban location factors at the macro-scale, local geology, and groups of water system elements occur together in some of these ancient Greek settlements. The purpose of both volumes of this study is to understand the past in a new way and to extrapolate those lessons to our own situation today, in a world of increasing resource restraint.

Part IV. *Geography and Geology.* This part makes explicit one facet of the interplay between history and its geographical setting. As Captain John Smith said in 1624:

> Geography without History seemeth a carcasse without motion; so History without Geography wandereth as a Vagrant without a certaine habitation. (*National Geographic*, Sept. 1988)

That interplay [termed geosophy, or geographical knowledge by C. J. Glacken (1967)] is studied here as it is revealed in one aspect, karst geology. I have very much enjoyed the flash of insight based on karst knowledge that enabled me to perceive natural models for wells, cisterns, and other water system elements. It is a truism that science progresses when people reexamine the obvious.

Part V. *Planning.* Long association with modern urban planning, both personal and professional, has meant that I could not study Greek cities without trying to understand their planning. Planning has both physical and social aspects, but to make the subject manageable here I have concentrated only on the planning of water quality management. Selecting two cities, I asked, "What did they have as water resources? What did they do with them?" Without exhausting the topic, the answers are instructive—good examples of circumstances alter cases.

Part VI. *Supply, Distribution, Drainage.* Chapter 11 was the last written, except the Conclusion. It was necessary to pause and consider all that I had learned before I was ready to tackle one city frozen in its tracks before the end of the fourth century B.C. and another known mainly in its first century A.D. manifestation. It was fascinating to see how much of sixth century Olynthos was still evident in the fourth century new town, and how much of the preceding five centuries of life at Pompeii was still discernable in the ruins of that Roman city. Landscapes are not just contemporary; they carry residual effects of earlier eras which both obscure contemporary processes and constrain them, according to Thornes and Brunsden (1977). A good example is the earliest cistern-well arrangement at the Stabian Baths in Pompeii, which was basic to every remodeling of that structure for over 500 years. Even at Morgantina, which initially I knew in much greater detail than any other city, the realization of the role of the drains in the design of the Agora came on me gradually as I worked on the material and meditated on the ancient patterns.

Part VII. *Water System Elements Described and Quantified.* Morgantina again proved a useful standard for comparing the system of a small town with the larger, more complicated water system of the large city of Akragas. It was fascinating to see how much could be gleaned from a numerical comparison of the two sites, especially considering how partial our data are. Again and again I had to find research tools outside of the art history and classical archaeology methodologies that I had learned in graduate school. The concept of clusters is being used in biology, for instance, in situations where clear-cut statistical comparisons are not possible; it has proved useful in this study also.

Part VIII. *Physical Constraints on Built Form.* It is said that a problem is an opportunity cleverly disguised as an impossibility. Thus the constraints on ancient Greek urban and residential form, especially the water constraints, could have forced them to give up completely. What is significant is that they took these constraints and made beautiful and comfortable built forms, which still stand as "best examples" for us. How could the barren rock of the Athenian Acropolis be such a permanent magnet for settlement (Fig. 18.1)? One answer was "a solid base of flowing water." Another was the intelligence and resourcefulness of the ancient Athenians.

Part IX. *Amenity and Necessity.* The nuances of private and public display of water were quite interesting to examine. "Of course" public fountains had columns, and "of course" private wells did not—until we stop and try to understand what the message is in each level of articulation. Then the economy of means in architectural articulation is seen to perfectly complement the economy of means in water supply and usage (Fig. 20.3, 20.10). Most of us are more ready to admit conscious thought in architectural articulation than in management of water resources. Perhaps this inclination is due to repeated exposure to discussions of articulation as compared with consistent ignoring of questions of resources management, whether past or present.

Part X. *Learning from Greek Experience.* For me it is impossible to write history without contemplating what history is and what I am doing. History can be said to be

- everything that ever happened, or
- what is recorded about what happened, or
- what historians do

I have come to believe that a delicate reliance on incomplete data must of necessity describe the historian's work. Now I see my task as using incomplete but fascinating data to make a story about what happened at some earlier time, told in a way to bring out the meaning for today's people and relevance to their problems.

At the end, I sat down to examine what I had learned. It was a great deal more than I had, until then, realized. Besides the text, another part of that learning is shared with you in the photographs, maps and drawings of reconstructions, part of it in the selected bibliography of most important works cited and consulted. If this work can motivate others to study ancient and modern cities as users of water and builders of water management systems, view modern or ancient resource constraints critically, and nudge them to incorporate new and pragmatic questions into their study of the past or the present, I shall feel that the effort has been worthwhile.

Water is basic for life. Water is amenity and necessity. Water management is essential to urban life, and defines how people will live in their settlements. In the end the poet Pindar from Thebes, the best-watered of all classical cities, has said it correctly:

Water is the best thing.

Glossary

Aqueduct.   A long-distance water line, whether underground, on the surface, or raised in the air on bridges. Contrary to American usage, in German the term is used only for bridge sections supported on arches.

Artesian well.   Water under pressure flows upward to the surface; a vertical spring.

Baths.   Public buildings for bathing, usually having arrangements for groups of people to bathe together at the same time, and often providing waters of different temperatures. Distinguished here from *bathrooms* in private houses.

Cistern.   A water-holder carved or constructed below the ground surface, and waterproofed.

Fountain.   A natural outpouring of water (a spring) is different from the man-made architectural expression of the delivery of water to a public place (a fountain).

French drain.   A ditch dug between a water source and outfall, then filled with stones through which the water would flow more quickly and easily than through undisturbed land, and finally covered with soil so that it was invisible

History   is a term with three levels of meaning: everything that ever happened, or what is recorded about what happened, or what historians do—a delicate reliance on incomplete data.

Hydrogeology   deals with the occurance and distribution of underground water.

Impluvium.   The flat basin at the center of an atrium, made to receive rainwater, and fitted with openings to the cistern below.

Karst.   An area of calcium carbonte rocks (limestone, dolomite) having surface openings, pinnacles, blind valleys, and underground drainage channels. Also used of the interactive process between rocks and water in such terrane. Named after the area in Yugoslavia where karst was first identified.

Nymphaeum.   A large public fountain, often elaborated with architectural detail and with statues.

A *polje*   differs from a lake in its drainage pattern, since not only can all the water drain out abruptly, like pulling a plug, but also water can under some circumstances flood up into the polje from its shaft. Another name for this kind of feature is an *estavelle*.

Qanat. An underground aqueduct developed in Armenia in the eighth century B.C. and characterized by regularly spaced air shafts to the surface. Water-bearing strata, usually limestone, were "milked" with a number of access channels and the water collected into a single passage in which it flowed as much as 100 kilometers to its urban destination. Adopted by the Greeks in the seventh and sixth centuries, when its use spread also to Egypt and as far east as Afganistan. The term is Arabic (also spelled *kanat*); known as *karez* in Persian and *foggara* in Berber Arabic.

Reservoir. A large (usually municipal) water holder.

Source. Thing or place from which something comes; place of origin of a stream or river. In archaic English and modern French, a natural spring.

Spring. The resurgence of an underground water channel, at the surface of the ground or in a cave.

Tank. Used here to denote a water holder built above the ground surface.

Terrane. A special geological spelling of the word terrain, used here to signal that a geological point of view is operative.

Urbanism is the life of people in cities, wheras *urbanization* is the process of making cities.

Washbasin (louter). A large flat dish with a rim, supported on a stem, and set up in a courtyard, where it was used for washing hands, faces, and dishes, and for preparation of food. The washbasin was made of terra-cotta or stone. It had the same form as a modern birdbath.

Water management has two levels of meaning: the formulation of strategic water goals and policies, and the tactical administration of the chosen means of implementation (Lindh and Berthelot, 1979, 6). The term is used here precisely because of this double level of meaning.

Water table is an underground surface beneath which soil and rocks are saturated with water. In karst terrane, there may be localized water tables at different heights; these are called *perched nappes*.

Well. A shaft dug into the ground to reach the water table, into which water seeps and can be drawn up. An *artesian well* is a vertical spring from which the water erupts at the surface, under pressure.

Wellhead or cisternhead *(puteal).* A cylinder or truncated cone of terra-cotta or stone, used to guard the opening to an underground water-holder and to permit access to the water. It could be set directly on the floor of a courtyard or on the stylobate between columns of a building, but frequently had as a base a large square stone pierced with a hole of the same diameter as the wellhead. Sometimes fitted with a pulley and rope; often it became marked with grooves along the inner lip, where ropes had been pulled against the stone for many centuries.

Bibliography

Adamesteanu, D. "Osserviazioni sulla battaglia di Gela del 405 a.C." *Kokalos* 2(1956):142–58.

Adams, R. McC. *Heartland of Cities: Surveys of Ancient Settlement and Land Use on the Central Floodplain of the Euphrates.* Chicago: University of Chicago Press, 1981.

Adams, R. McC. and Kraeling, C. *The City Invincible*, University of Chicago Press, 1960

Allen, H. "Excavations at Morgantina (Serra Orlando), 1967–69: Preliminary Report X." *American Journal of Archaeology* 74 (1970): 359–83 and pl.91–98.

Altertumer von Pergamon I, 3. German Archaeological Institute, Berlin: W. Spemann, 1885–.

Ancient Corinth (guide), American School of Classical Studies at Athens, 1954.

Andronopoulos, B., and Koukis, G., *Geologiki-geotechniki meleti tis periodis Akropoleos Athinon.* Athens: Institute for Geology and Subsurface Research, 1976.

Annuario della Scuola Archaeologia de Atene IV/V (1921–22): 490, about Italian excavations on the south slope of the Acropolis, Athens.

Aristotle *Meteorologia* Book I, chapter XIII, 349b.

Aristotle *Nicomachean Ethics* ix.10.3

Aristotle *Politics* vii,1330a-b; xii, 678, 1269a, 1328a; viii,4.

Arnone, L. "Gli Ipogei dell'Agrigento." Agrigento: Edizioni Ente Provinciale per il Turismo, n.d., ca. 1952.

Aschmann, H. "Man's Impact on the Several Regions with Mediterranean Climates," which incorporates "Human Activity Affecting Mediterranean Ecosystems." In di Castri and Mooney, 1973, 362–71.

The Athenian Agora, A Guide, American School of Classical Studies, 4th edition, 1990.

Baker, M. N. and Horton, R. E. "Historical Development of Ideas Regarding the Origin of Springs and Ground Water." *EOS*, Transactions of the American Geophysical Union 37(1936): 395–400.

Baker, R. C. "Hydrology of Karst Features in Evaporite Deposits of the Upper Permian in Texas." In Dilamarter and Csallany, 1977, 333–39.

Baszin, H., translator into French. *Xenophon's Lacedemonian Republic* 15, 6, Paris: Leroux, 1885.

Bell, M. Oral report on the new fountainhouse at Morgantina, at the AIA meeting in Philadelphia, 1982; abstract published in *American Journal of Archaeology* 87(1983) 226.

Bell, M. "La fontana ellenistica di Morgantina." *Quaderni dell'Instituto di Archeologia* (Messina) 2 (1985).

Bell, M. "Excavations at Morgantina, 1980–85: Preliminary Report XII." *American Journal of Archaeology* 92(1988): 313–42.

Belloni, S., Martinis, B., and Orombelli, G. "Karst of Italy", in Herak and Stringfield, 1972, 85–128.

Belson, R. P. "The Hydrology of Karst Urban Areas." In Dilamarter and Csallany, 1977, 162–75.

Bennett, J. W. *The Ecological Transition: Cultural Anthropology and Human Adaptation.* New York: Pergamon Press, 1976.

Berard, J. *"La Colonisation grecque de l'Italie Meridoniale et de la Sicilie dans l'antiquite: L'histoire et la legende*, Paris: E. de Boccard, 1941.

Berard, J. *Bibliographie topographique des principales cites grecques de l'Italie meridoniale et de la Sicile dans l'Antiquite.* Paris, 1941.

Berthelot, R. M. and Lindh, G. *Socio-economic aspects of urban hydrology.* Paris: UNESCO Studies & Reports in Hydrology, #27, 1979.

Bieber, M. *History of the Greek and Roman Theater.* Princeton, N.J.: Princeton University Press, 1961.

Biers, J. C. *The Great Bath on the Lechaion Road, Corinth XVII.* Princeton, N. J.: American School of Classical Studies at Athens, 1985.

Binford, L. R. *In Pursuit of the Past.* London: Thames and Hudson, 1983.

Binford, L. R. *Debating Archaeology.* New York: Academic Press, 1989.

Bintliff, J. "Mediterranean alluviation," *Proceedings of the Prehisitoric Society,* 41(1975): 78–84.

Bintliff, J. "The Plain of Macedon and the Neolithic Site of Nea Nikomedeia." *Proceedings of the Prehistoric Society.* 42(1976): 241–262.

Bintliff, J. "Sediments & Settlement in So. Greece." In Davidson and Shackley, 1976.

Bintliff, J.L. *Natural Environment & Human Settlement in Prehistoric Greece.* Oxford: BAR Supp. Series 28 (i & ii) 1977.

Bintliff, J. L., Davidson, J. A., and Grant, E. G. (eds.) *Conceptual Issues in Environmental Archaeology.* Edinburgh: Edinburgh University Press, 1988.

Blackstone, G.V. *A History of the British Fire Service.* London: Routledge and Kegan Paul Ltd., 1957.

Blinkenberg, C., Kinch, K.F. and Dyggve, E., *Lindos, Fouilles et recherches,*1(1931); 2(1941); 3(1960). Paris: French School of Archaeology.

Board, C., et al., eds. *Progress in Geography* . London: E. Arnold, 1971.

Boardman, J. *The Greeks Overseas.* New York: Harmondsworth, 1964, reprinted 1973, 1980.

Boersma, J. S. *Athenian Building Policy.* Groningen: Walters-Noordhoff Pub., 1970.

Boehringer, E. (ed.) *Pergamon Gesammelte Aufsätze.* Vol. 1, "Pergamenische Forschungen" includes G. Garbrecht, "Fragen der Wasserwirtschaft Pergamons", 43–48. Berlin: W. de Gruyter for the German Archaeological Institute, 1972.

Bogli, A. "Corrosion by Mixing of Karst Waters." *Transactions* of the Cave Research Group of Great Britain. 13/2(1971): 109–14.

Bogli, A. "Shafts." *Actes 3eme Congress Suisse Spelolog. 1967.* 17–18.

Bogli, A. *Karst Hydrology and Physical Speleology.* Berlin: Springer-Verlag, 1980.

Bollotino d'Arte, IV, 1924–25, 88ff, about the excavations of the Italian School at Athens, on the south slope of the Acropolis.

Bradford, J. *Ancient Landscapes*. G. Bell & Sons, 1957; reprinted Bath: C. Chivers Ltd., 1974.

Brinker,W. Dissertation on cisterns at Pergamon, under the direction of G. Garbrecht. Technical University, Braunschweig, Germany,1990.

Brinkmann, R. *Geology of Turkey*. Amsterdam: Elsevier, 1976.

Broneer, O. "A Mycenaean Fountain House." *Hesperia* 8 (1939): 317–433.

Broneer, O. *The South Stoa and Its Roman Successors, Corinth,I pt. IV*, American School of Classical Studies, 1954.

Bulard, M., general editor, *L'Exploration archaeologique de Delos*, 1909–74, 30 volumes, French School of Archaeology, Athens.

[Burdon, D.], *Karst Groundwater Investigations: Greece*. Rome: FAO, 1964.

Burdon, D. "Hydrogeology of Some Karstic Areas of Greece." *Hydrology of Fractured Rocks. Proceedings of the Dubrovnik Symposium, Oct. 1965*. Centbrugee: AIHS, 1967, 308–16.

Burnouf, E. *La ville et l'acropole d'Athenes aux diverses epoques*. Paris: Maisonneuve & Cie., 1877.

Burns, A. "Ancient Greek Water Supply and City Planning: A Study of Syracuse and Agrigento." *Technology and Culture* 15 (1974): 389– 412.

Butzer, K. W. "Holocene Alluvial Sequences: Problems of Dating and Correlation." In Dilamarter and Csallany, 1977, 66–68.

Butzer, K. W. "Accelerated Soil Erosion." In Manners and Mikesell, 1974., 66– 68.

Cahill, N. Dissertation on spatial and social city planning at Olynthos, in progress at University of California at Berkeley, Program in Ancient History, 1991–.

Camp, J. M. *Water Supply of Ancient Athens*. Ph. D. dissertation, Princeton University, 1979.

Camp, J. M. *The Athenian Agora: Excavations in the Heart of Classical Athens*. London: Thames and Hudson, 1972.

Camp, J. M. "Drought and Famine in the 4th Century B.C." In "Studies in Athenian Architecture, Sculpture, and Topography presented to Homer A. Thompson," *Hesperia*, Supp. XX (1982):. 9–17.

Camp, J. M. "A Drought in Late 8th Century B.C." *Hesperia* 48 (1979): 397– 411.

Camp, J. M. *The Athenian Agora*. New York: Thames and Hudson, 1986.

Campbell, A.S., ed. *Geology and History of Turkey*. Petroleum Exploration Society of Libya, 13th Annual Field Conference, 1971.

Carter, J. M. "Athens, Euobea and Olynthus," *Historia* 20 (1971) 418–29.

Casanaki, M. et al., *The Acropolis at Athens: Conservation, Restoration and Research 1975–1983*. Athens: Committee for the Preservation of the Acropolis Monuments,1988.

Castri, see di Castri.

Cavallari, F. S. *Die Stadt Syrakus in alterthum*. Strasburg: J.H.E. Heitz, 1887. German edition of Cavallari, F. S. and Holm, A. *Topografia archeologica di Siracusa*. Palermo, 1883.

Changes of Climate. Proceedings of the Rome Symposium organized by UNESCO and the World Meteorological Organization. Paris: UNESCO, 1963.

Changnon, S. A. Jr., "Inadvertent Weather and Precipitation Modification by Urbanization." *Journal of Irrigation and Drainage Development*, (March 1973) 27–41.

Clarke, J. T. *Report of the Investigations at Assos, 1881*. Papers of the Archaeological Institute of America I. Boston: A. Willimans and Co., and London: N. Trubner, 1882.

Collingwood, R. G. and Myres, J. N. L. *Roman Britain and the English Settlements.* Oxford: Clarendon Press, 1936.

Commoner, B. *The Poverty of Power* . New York: Knopf, 1976.

Cook, J. M. *The Greeks in Ionia and the East.* New York: Praeger, 1965.

Constantinopoulos, see Konstantinoupoulos.

Crawford, N. C. "Karst Landform Development along the Cumberland Plateau Escarpment of Tennessee." in LaFleur, 1984, 294–339.

Crouch, D. P. "Palmyra." Ph. D. dissertation, University of California at Los Angeles, 1969.

Crouch, D. P. "A Note on the Population and Area of Palmyra." *Melanges* of the University of St. Joseph, Beirut, 47(1972): 241–50.

Crouch, D. P. "The Water System of Palmyra." *Studia Palmyrenskie* 7 (1975): 151–87.

Crouch, D. P. "The Hellenistic Water System of Morgantina, Sicily: Contributions to the History of Urbanization." *American Journal of Archaeology,* 88(1984): 353–65, pl. 46–7.

Crouch, D. P. "Water System Evidence of Greek Civilization," in Wunderlich and Prins, 1987, 125–138.

Crouch, D. P. "Water management at Agrigento and Morgantina", *Mitteilungen* of the Technical University of Braunschweig, Germany, Vol. 103(1989): 155–74.

Crouch, D. P. "Roman Models for Spanish Colonization," *Columbian Consequences Vol. 3, The Spanish Borderlands in Pan-American Perspective.* edited by D.H. Thomas. Washington, D.C.: Smithsonian Institution Press, 1991, 21–35.

Crouch, D. P. "Spanish Water Technology in the American Southwest—Transfer and Alteration," Proceedings of the Frontinus Society meeting in Spain, October 1991, forthcoming in the *Mitteilungen* of the Leichtweiss Institute for Water Research, Technical University, Braunschweig, Germany.

Crouch, D. P., Garr, D. J., and Mundigo, A. I. *Spanish City Planning in North America.* Cambridge, Mass.: M.I.T. Press, 1982.

Cullingford, R. A., Davidson, D. A., and Lewis, J. (eds.) *Timescales in Geomorphology.* Chichester: J. Wiley & Sons, 1980.

Curtius, E. and Kaupert, J. A., *Atlas von Athen.* Berlin: Verlag von Dietrich Reimer for the German Archaeological Institute, 1878.

Cvijic, J. "The Dolines." In Sweeting, 1981: 23–41.

Dall' Aglio, M. and Tedesco, C. "Studio geochemico ed idrogeologico di sorgenti della Sicilia." *Rivista Mineraria Siciliana* Vol. 19 parts 109–11 (Jan.-June 1968)

Dall' Aglio, M. and Tedesco, C., "Studio geochimico ed idrogeologico di sorgenti della Sicilia." *Rivista Mineraria Siciliana,* Vol. 19 parts 112–14 (July-Dec. 1968):171–210, with map of Agrigento, 208.

Davidson, D. A. "Erosion in Greece during the First and Second Millennia B.C." In Cullingford et al., 1980:143–58.

Davidson, D. A. and Shackley, M.L. (eds.), *Geoarchaeology,* Boulder, Colo.: Westview Press, 1976.

Davis, W.M. "Origin of Limestone Caverns." In Sweeting, 1981:136–59.

Deb, A.K. "Dual water supply for future urban water management." In Wunderlich and Prins, 1987: 221–230.

de la Geniere, J. "La Colonisation grecque en Italie Meridionale et en Sicilie et l'acculturation des non-grecs." *Revue archeologique* 2 (1978): 257– 76.

Delbruck, R. and Vollmöller, K. G. "Das Brunnenhaus des Theagenes." *Mittheilungen des Deutschen Archaeologischen Inst. Athen*, 25(1900): 23–33 and pl. vii-viii.

Delorme, J. "Recherches au Gymnase d'Epidaure." *Bulletin de Corespondence Hellenique*, 70(1946):108–19.

Delorme, J. *Gymnasion: etude sur les monuments consacres a l'education en Grece*. Paris: A. & J. Picard, 1956; Ed. de Boccard, 1960.

Demand, N. H. *Urban Location in Archaic and Classical Greece: Flight and Consolidation*. Norman, Oklahoma: University of Oklahoma Press, 1990.

De Miro, E. "La Fondazione di Agrigento e l'ellenizzazione del territorio fra il salso e il platani." *Kokalos* 8(1962): 122–52.

De Miro, E. "Il quartere ellenistico-romano di Agrigento." *Academie Nazionale dei Lincei, Rome*. Classe di Scienze Fisiche Mathematiche e Naturali. Rendiconti. Series 8 vol. 12(1957): 135–40 and 4 pp. of plates.

De Miro, E. "I recenti scavi sul poggetto di S. Nicola in Agrigento." *Cronache de Archeologia e di Storia dell'Arte* #2(1963) (U. of Catania): 57–63.

Demosthenes *De Falsa Legatione* 426, cited in *Olynthos* II, 97.

de Waele, J. A. *Acragas Graeca*. Arch. Studien van het Nederlands Historisch Inst. te Rome, 3(1971) (kindly translated for me from the Dutch by Saskia de Melker).

di Castri, F. and Mooney, H. A., (eds.) *Mediterranean Type Ecosystems*. New York:Springer Verlag, 1973.

Diels, H. *Antike Technikk*. Leipzig: 1920.

Dietz, S. and Papachristodoulou, I., (eds.) *Archaeology in the Dodecanese*. Copenhagen: National Museum of Denmark, Dept. of Near Eastern and Classical Antiquities, 1988.

Dilamarter, R. R. and Csallany, S. C., (eds.), *Hydrologic Problems in Karst Regions, Proceedings of the International Symposium, April 1976*. Bowling Green, Ky.: W. Kentucky University Press, 1977.

Diller, A. *The Textual Tradition of Strabo's Geography*. Amsterdam: Hakkert, 1975.

Diller, J. S. "Notes on the Geology of the Troad. " *Memoires* du Museum National. Sci. de la Terre Vol. 3 #1(1881): 634.

Diller, J. S. "The Geology of Assos." in Clarke, 1882; 166–77.

Dinsmoor, W. B. "The Athenian Theater of the Fifth Century." in Mylonas, G. 1951–53, 309–30.

Diodorus Siculus, 11.78; 14,18.

DiVita, A. "La penetrazione siracusana nella Sicilia sud-orientale alla luce delle piu recenti scroperte archeologiche." *Kokalos* 2(1956): 177–205.

Dontas, G. "The True Aglaurion." *Hesperia* 52(1983): 48–63 and pl. 13–15.

Dorpfeld, W. "Die Ausgrabungen und der Enneakrunos." KDAI Athens, *Archaeologischer Anzeiger* 19(1894): 143–51.

Dorpfeld, W. ["Report on old waterline between Pnyx and Areopagus"], *J. für Gasbeleuchtung & Wasserversorgung* 41(XII Jahrgang, 1898): 510.

Doxiadis, C.A. *Architectural Space in Ancient Greece*. Published in German in 1937, and in English in 1972 by MIT Press.

Doxiadis, C. A. *The Method for the Study of the Ancient Greek Cities* (5 vol.). Athens: Ekistics Center, 1972, especially maps "Colonies of Corinth established between 880–733 B.C." (including Syracuse); maps of c. 700 and c. 550 B.C., with a total of 14 colonies; fig. 43 "Corinth town and acropolis—water sources."

Drachmann, A. G. *The Mechanical Technology of Greek and Roman Antiquity; A Study of the Literary Sources.* Copenhagen: Munksgaard, and Madison: University of Wisconsin Press, 1963.

Dreybrodt, W. "Karstification: A Model." *Journal of Geology* Sept. 1990: 639–55.

Drögemüller, H.-P. *Syrakus.* Heidelberg: C. Winter, University Press, 1969.

Dufaure, J. "Neotectonique and morphogenese dans une peninsule mediterraneene," *Revue de Geographie Physique et de Geologie Dynamique* 19 (1977): 27–58.

Dyggve, E. *Lindos Fouilles et recherches. III pt. 1,2 Le Sanctuaire de Athana Lindia et L'architecture Lydienne avec un catalog des sculptures trouvees sur l'Acropole.* Berlin: Walter de Gruyter, 1960.

Dyggve, E. *Lindos, Fouilles de l'acropole 1902–1914 et 1952.* II. Berlin: Walter de Gruyter & Cie, 1931 and 1960.

Erim, K. "Morgantina", *American Journal of Archaeoelogy.* 62(1958): 79–90, citing Diodorus 11.78 and elsewhere, and Thucydides 4.65.142.

Ervin, M. "The Sanctuary of Aglauros on the South Slope of the Acropolis and its Destruction in the First Mithridatic War." *Arxeiov Povtou.* 22 (1958): 129–166.

Eschebach, H. "Die Gebrauchwasserer sorgung des Pompeii." *Antike Welt* 10 (1977): 3–24.

Eschebach, H. *Die Stabianer Thermen in Pompeii.* Berlin: W. de Gruyter, 1979.

Eschebach, H. "Katalog der Pompeiianischen Laufbrunnen." *Antike Welt* 13(1982): 21–26.

Eschebach, L. "Pompeii." In "Bildanhand: Beispiele antiker Wasserversorgungsanlagen." In Frontinus-Geschellschaft, *Die Wasserversorgung antiker Stadt,* Band 2, Mainz am Rhein: Verlag Philipp von Zabern, 1987: 202–5.

Evanari, M. and Koller, D. "Ancient Masters of the Desert." *Scientific American* 194 (Apr. 1956): 39–45.

Evans, A. *The Palace of Minos. I.* New York: Biblo and Tannen, 1964 reprint of 1921–35 edition. Vol. I esp. 142–3, 226–30.

Fabbriocotti, E. "I bagni nelle prime ville romane." *Cronache pompeiana* 2(1976): 2–111.

Fabricius "Polycrates at Samos." *Mitteilungen* des Deutschen Archaeologischen Inst. Athen, 9(1884), 165 ff.

Fahlbusch, H. *Vergleich antiker griechischer und romisher Wasserversorgungsanlagen.* Mitteilungen of the Leichtweiss Inst. für Wasserbau, Technical University of Braunschweig, Germany, Heft 73/1982.

FAO (Food and Agriculture Organtization of the United Nations), "Economic Survey of the Western Peloponnesus, Greece." Vol. 4 & 5 "Land and Water" part 1. Rome: FAO 1966.

FAO, "Groundwater Resources in the Greek World." Computer generated map in color, made available to me at FAO headquarters in Rome.

FAO, "Soil Map of the World." Vol. V: Europe (2 maps, east and west). Paris: UNESCO, 1981.

Fekete, K. "The Development and Management of Karst Water Resources in the City of Pecs and its Vicinity, Hungary." In Dilamarter and Csallany (1977): 279–85.

Feldhaus, F. M. *Die Technik der antike und des mittelalters.* Wildpark-Potsdam: Akadenische verlagsgesellschaft Athenaion, 1931.

Finkel, H. J. "Water Resources in Arid Zone Development," 440–76, which includes "Recycling Urban Sewage," 466–70. In G. Golany (1976, 1979).

Flemal, R. C. and Melhorn, W. N. (eds.) *Theories of Landform Development.* London: George Allen and Unwin, 1975.

Forbes, R. J. "Water Supply." *Studies in Ancient Technology 1.* Leiden: Brill, 9 vol. 1955–1964: 145–89.

Forbes, R. J. "Hydraulic Engineering and Sanitation." In Singer et al. (1956): 663–94.

Forbes, R. J. and Dijksterhuis, E. J. *History of Science and Technology,* 2 vol. Baltimore: Penguin, 1963.

Ford, D. C. "Geologic Structure and A New Explanation of Limestone Cavern Genesis." In Sweeting (1981): 187–200.

Frascari, M. "Semiotica Ab Edendo, Taste in Architecture." *Journal of Architectural Education* 40 (Fall 1986).

Frazer, J. G. (ed.) *Pausanias's Description of Greece I-IV.* London: Macmillan, 1898, 1913, etc.

Frontinus, S. J. *The Two Books on the Water Supply of Ancient Rome.* Clemens Herschel, translator and editor. New York: 1913; see more recently G. Kuhne's translation of and commentary on Frontinus in *Die Wasserversorgung der antiker Rom,* published by Frontinus- Gesellschaft, Munich & Vienna: R. Oldenbourg Verlag, 1983, 81–128.

Frontinus-Gesellschaft, *Wasserversorgung Antiker Stadt.* Munich and Vienna: R. Oldenbourg Verlag, 1983, Vol. I, "Sextus Iulius Frontinus + Curator Aquarum." Vol. II, "Pergamon + Recht/Verwaltung + Brunnen/ Nymphaen + Bauelemente," III "Mensch und Wasser + Mittel- europa + Thermen + Bau/Materialien + Hygiene" and IV "Die Wasserversorgung im Mittelalter,"of this series are published at Mainz am Rhein: Verlag Philipp von Zabern, 1987, 1988, 1990.

Furon, R. "Introduction a la Geologie et Hydrogeologie de la Turquie." *Memoires du museum national d'histoire naturelle.* Serie C. Sciences de la terre. Tome III, Paris:1952-3, 1–99

Gage, M. "The Tempo of Geomorphological Change." *Journal of Geology,* Vol. 78 (1978): 619–25.

Garbrecht, G. "Fragen der Wasserwirtschaft Pergamons." In Boehringer, (1972): 43–48.

G. Garbreccht et al., reports on longdistance water lines at Pergamon in the *Mitteilungen* of the Leichtweiss Inst. für Wasserbau of the Technical Univeristy of Braunschweig, Germany, constituting volumes 37(1973), 44(1975), 60(1978), 61(1978), 78(1983) text and plates.

Gerkan, Armin von. See von Gerkan, Armin.

Gentile, G.V. "Siracusa—Scoperte nelle due nuove arterie stradali . . ." *Academia nazionale dei Lincei,* Roma. 23(1951):261–334.

Giebeler, C., and Graber, B. "Die Antike Hochdruck-Wasserleitung der Berg Pergamon." *Journal für Gasbeleuchtung und Wasserversorgung,* 40 (20 March 1897):185–6.

Ginouves, R. "Une salle de bains hellenistique à Delphes." *Bulletin de Correspondence Hellenique* 76(1952): 541–61.

Ginouves, R. *L'etablissement thermal de Gortys de Arcadie.* Paris: J. Vrin, 1959.

Ginouves, R. *Balineutike: recherches sur le bain des antiquite grecque.* Paris: Ed. de Boccard, l962.

Glacken, C. J. *Traces on the Rhodian Shore.* Berkeley: University of California Press, 1967.

Glaser, F. *Antike brunnenbauten (KPHNAI) in Griechenland.* Vienna:Verlag der Österreichischen Akademie der Wissenschaften, 1983.

Glover, T. R. *The Challenge of the Greeks.* Cambridge University Press, l942.

Glover, T. R. *Springs of Hellas.* Cambridge University Press, l945.

Glowacki, K., *Topics Concerning the North Slope of the Akropolis at Athens (Greece).* Ph. D. dissertation, Bryn Mawr College, 1991.

Golany, G. (ed.) *Arid Zone Settlement Planning* (title of 1979 reprint of *Water Resources in Arid Zone Development*) Rehovet, Israel: International Irrigation Information Center, 1976; reprinted New York, l979.

Goodfield, J. "The Tunnel of Eupalinus." *Scientific American,* (June l964): 104–12.

Graber, B. "Die Enneakrunos." Deutsches archaeologisches Institut *Athens Mitteilungen.* 30(1905), 5–64.

Graber, H. "Die Wasserleitungen von Pergamon." *Abhundlingen der Deutschen Akademie der Wissenschaften zu Berlin.* l888, 1–19, 26–31 and 2 pl.

Graham, A.J. *Colony and Mother-city in Ancient Greece.* Manchester University Press, l964; Chicago: Ares Publications, 1983.

Graham, J.W. *The Hellenic House. Excavations at Olynthus,* VIII. Baltimore: Johns Hopkins University Press, l938.

Griffo, P. *Agrigento, Guide to the Monuments and Excavations.* Agrigento, Superintendant of Antiquities, 1956.

Griffo, P. and von Matt, I. *Gela.* Wurzburg: Echter-Verlag, l964 and New York: N.Y. Graphic Society, l968.

Gruben, G. "Das Quellhaus von Megara." *Deltion,* 19(1964): A 37–41.

Grund, M. A. "The Geographical Cycle in the Karst." In Sweeting (1981): 54– 59 .

Hammond, P. "Desert Waterworks of the Ancient Nabataeans," *Natural History* 76(June-July 1967): 38–47.

Harrison, J. E. *Primitive Athens as Described by Thucydides.* Cambridge University Press, 1906.

Hauck, G. F. W., and Novak, R. A., "Water Flow in the Castellum at Nimes," *American Journal of Archaeology* 92 (July l988): 393–407.

Herzog, R. *Kos. I Asklepieion.* Berlin: H. Keller, l932.

Herak, M., and Stringfield, V. T. (eds.) *Karst: Important Karst Regions of the Northern Hemisphere.* Amsterdam: Elsevier, l972; see especially chapter 2, by the editors, "Historical Review of Hydrogeological Concepts,"19–24.

Herodotus *History* 6.76. London: Penguin, 1972.

Higgins, C. G. "Caves of the Acropolis of Athens." *Geomorphological Abstracts. Papers of the Michigan Academy of Science, Arts, and Letters.* 47(1962):13–18.

Hill, B. H. *The Springs . Corinth I, pt. VI,* Princeton, N. J.: American School of Classical Studies at Athens, l964.

Hippocrates, *Airs Waters Places.* Translated by W. H. S. Jones. Loeb Library, l923.

Hodge, A. T. "A Roman Factory." *Scientific American* 292(Nov. 1990) 106–11.

Hoepfner, W. and Schwandner, E.-L. *Haus und Stadt im klassischen Griechenland.* Munich: Deutscher Kunstverlag, l985.

Hohenberg, P. M. and Lees, L. H. *The Making of Urban Europe, l000–l950.* Cambridge, Mass.: Harvard U.niversity Press, 1985.

Hopper, R. J. *The Acropolis,* New York: Weidenfield and Nicolson, 1971.

Huelsen, J. *Das Nymphaeum.* Berlin: Walter de Gruyter, 1919. Vol.1 part 5 of *Milet, Ergebnisse der Ausgrabungen und Untersuchungen seit dem Jahre 1899*

Hulot, J., and Fougeres, G., *Selinonte—La Ville, L'Acropole et les Temples.* Paris: Schmid, 1910.

Huntington, E. "The Karst Country of So. Asia Minor," *Bulletin of the American Geographical Society of New York* (1911): 91–106.

Hydrology of Fractured Rocks. Proceedings of the Dubrovnik Symposium, Oct. l965. Paris: UNESCO,1967 (published in French and English). Also published jointly by IAHS and UNESCO at Louvain, Belgium, 1967.

Implications de l'Hydrologie dans les autres Sciences de la Terre. I.H.R.S. Symposium, Montpellier, France, Sept. 1978. Memoire hors serie CERGH-USTL Montpellier.

Infrastructure and Urban Growth in the Nineteenth Century. Chicago: Public Works Historical Society, 14, 1985, especially J.A. Tarr, "Building the Urban Infrastructure in the Nineteenth Century: An Introduction." 61–85.

Institute of Geology and Mineral Exploration, "Geological Map of Greece" (1:500,000). Athens, 1983 (second edition).

Institute of Geology and Mineral Exploration, "Geology of Greece" series (1:50,000). Athens, 1984 etc.

Izmirligil, U., "Side Su Yollari" *VIII Turk Tarih Kingresi'nden ayribasim.* Ankara: Turk Tarih Kurumu Basimevi, 1979.

Izmirligil, U., "Die Wasserversorgungsanlagen von Side," Garbrecht, G. (ed.) *Symposium uber Historische Wasserversorgungsanlagen.* I.T. U. Istanbul, June, 1979. Mitteilungen of the Leichtweiss-Institut für Wasserbau of the Technical University of Braunschweig, Heft. 64 (1979).

Jacobs, J. *The Economy of Cities.* New York: Random House, 1969.

Jakucs, L. *Morphogenetics of Karst Regions.* Bristol: Adam Hilger, 1977.

Jansen, G. C. M. "Water systems and Sanitation in the houses of Herculaneum." *Papers* of the Netherlands Inst. in Rome: Antiquity, 50, (1991): 145–66.

Jashemski, W. E. *The Gardens of Pompeii.* New Rochelle, N.Y.: Caratzas Bros., 1979.

Jennings, J. N. *Karst.* Cambridge, Mass.: MIT Press, 1971.

Jones, J. L. "The Laurion Silver Mines: A Review of Ancient Research and Results." *Greece and Rome* 29 (1982): 169–83.

Jones, W. H. S., translator. *Hippocrates, Airs Waters Places.* Loeb Library, 1923.

Judeich, W., *Topographie von Athen* in I. von Muller, *Handbuch der klassischen Altertumwissenschaft* Band 3 Abt. 2 Halfte 2. Munich: 1905; second edition, 1931.

Judson, S. "Geologic and Geographic Observations at Morgantina" Unpublished manuscript in the Princeton University Morgantina files, 1959. Forthcoming in a book with M. Bell.

Kahn, F. A. *The Indus Valley and Early Iran.* Karachi, Pakistan: Dept. of Archaeology and Museums, 1964.

Kallergis, G. (ed.), *Proceedings of the VIth Colloquium on the Geology of the Aegean Region Athens l977.* Athens: Inst. of Geological and Mining Research.

Kardos, L. T., and Soper, W. E., "Renovation of Municipal Waste Water through Land Disposal by Spray Irrigation." In Soper and Kardos (1973): 148–63.

Karst Groundwater Investigations: Greece. Rome: FAO, 1964. By D. Burdon, although not so stated on the title page.

Kashot, A. A. I., "On the Management of Karst Aquifers in Saudi Arabia." In Dilamarter and Csallany (1977) 311.

Kastning, E. H., "Faults as Positive and Negative Influences in Groundwater Flow and Conduit Enlargement." In Dilamarter and Csallany (1977): 193–201.

Kelley, R., "The Interplay of American Political Culture and Public Policy: The Sacramento River as a Case Study." *Journal of Policy History* 1(1989): 1–23.

Kienast, H. J., *Die Stadtmauer von Samos.* Bonn: Habelt Verlag, 1978.

Kienast, H. J. "Der Tunnel des Eupalinos auf Samos." *Architectura* 77 (1970): 97–116.

Kienast, H. J. "Der Tunnel des Eupalinos auf Samos" (different content) *Mannheimer Forum* [19]86/87: 179–241

Klemes, V. "Dilettantism in Hydrology: Transition or Destiny?" *Water Resources Research* 22(Aug. 1986):177S-88S.

Knauss, J., *Die Melioration des Kopaisbeckens durch die Minyer im 2 Jt.v. Chr.* Kopais 2. Bericht Nr. 57 of the Inst. fur Wasserbau, Technical University of Munich, 1987.

Knauss, J., *Wasserbau und Geschichte Minysche Epoche - Bayerische Zeit* . Kopais 3. Bericht nr. 63 of the Inst. für Wasserbau, Technical University of Munich, 1990.

Knauss, J., Heinrich, B., and Kalcyk, H., *Die Wasserbauten der Minyer in der Kopais—die älteste Flussregulierung Europas* . Kopais I. Bericht Nr. 50 of the Inst. fur Wasserbau, Technical University of Munich, 1980.

Knigge, U., *The Athenian Kerameikos: History - Monuments - Excavations*, Athens: German Archaeological Institute and Krene Editions (1988, in German) 1991, in English.

Komatina, M. "Artificial Works and Efficient Interception of Groundwater in Karst." In Dilamarter and Csallany (1977): 286–96.

Konstantinopoulos, G., "Rhodes, New Finds and Old Problems." *Archaeology*, 21(1968):115–23 and pl. 21.

Kraeling, C., and Adams, R., *The City Invincible.* Chicago: University of Chicago Press, 1960.

Kraft, J. C., *"A Reconaissance of the Geology of the Sandy Coastal Areas of E. Greece and the Peloponnese.* College of Marine Studies, University of Delaware, Technical Report 9, July 1972.

Kraft, J. C., and Rapp, G. R., Jr., "Geological Reconstruction of Ancient Coastal Landforms in Greece with Predictions of Future Coastal Changes." In Marinos and Koukis (1988):1545–56.

Kraft, J. C., and Rapp, G. R., Jr., "Late Holocene Paleogeography of the Coastal Plain of the Gulf of Messenia, Greece. . . ." *Geological Society of America Bulletin* 86(1975):1191–208.

Krautheimer, R., *Rome, Profile of a City.* Princeton, N.J.: Princeton University Press, 1980.

Kuhne, G. "Die Wasserversorgung der antiken Stadt Rom (Ubersetzung der Schrift von Sextius Iulius Frontinus)." In *Wasserversorgung der antiker Rom*. Munich: R. Oldenbourg Verlag, 1983, 81–128.

Kunz, H., *The Grid and Urban Space: A Study of Patterns and their Geocultural Determinants*. Master of Architecture thesis, Rensselaer Polytechnic Institute, 1985.

Kunze, E., and Schleif, H., "Die Bader." *Bericht uber die Ausgrabungen in Olympia*, Vol. IV, 1944.

Kwitny, J., "The Great Transportation Conspiracy: How GM and its Allies Dismantled America's Mass Transit," *Harper's* (Feb. 1981): 14–21.

LaFleur, R. G. (ed.) *Groundwater as Geomorphic Agent*. Boston: Allen and Lenwin, 1984.

Lang, M., *Waterworks in the Athenian Agora*. Princeton, N.J.: American School of Classical Studies at Athens 1968.

Larsen, J. D., "The Water Towers in Pompeii." *Annalecta Romana Inst. Danici*, 11 (1983): 411–67.

Last, J. S., "Kourion: The Ancient Water Supply." *American Philosophical Society* 119, nc.1(1975): 39–72.

Lavendan, P., *L'histoire de l'urbanisme*. Paris: H. Laurens, 1926.

Lazaridis, D., "Thasos and its Peraia." Vol 5 of Doxiadis, 1972.

Leake, W. M., *Travels in the Morea*. London: J. Murray, 1830.

Leake, W. M., *Topographie Athens*. Zurich: 1844; *Topography of Athens*, second edition, London:1841.

LeGrand, H. E., "Hydrological and Ecological Problems of Karst Regions," *Science* 179 (1973): 859–64.

LeGrand, H. E., "Karst Hydrology Related to Environmental Sensitivity." In Dilamarter and Csallany (1977): 10–18.

LeGrand, H. E., "The Geographical Cycle in the Karst." In Sweeting (1981): 54–59.

Lepsius, R., *Geologie von Attika*, Berlin: D. Reimer, 1893.

Levensohn, M., and Levensohn, E., "Inscriptions on the South Slope of the Acropolis." *Hesperia*. 16(1947):63–74, followed by "Notes on South Slope Inscriptions" by Merkel, W.R., 75–77.

Lindh, G., "Water Resources Management Problems in Urban Agglomerations." In Wunderlich and Prins (1987): 191–200.

Lindh, G., and Berthelot, R.M., *Socio-economic Aspects of Urban Hydrology*. Paris: UNESCO Studies & Reports in Hydrology, No. 27, 1979.

Loicq-Berger, M.-P., "Syracuse: Histoire culturelle d'une cite grecque." *Latomos (Revue d'etudes latines)*. Bruxelles: 1967.

Loy, W.S., *The Land of Nestor: A Physical Geography of the Southwest Peloponnese*. National Academy of Science, Foreign Field Research Program, No. 34 (n.d.: field work 1965–66).

Lucretius, *De Rerum Natura*.

MacDonald, W. L., *The Architecture of Imperial Rome*, Vol. II. New Haven: Yale University Press, 1986.

Mackay, P. A., "The Fountain at Hadji Mustapha." *Hesperia* 36 (1967):193– 95.

Maiuri, A. "Pompeii Pozzi e condotture d'acqua . . ." and "Scoperta di grandi conditture in piombo dell'acquedoto urbano." *Notizie degli Scavi di Antichita* 7(1931): 546–76.

Manners, I. R., and Mikesell, M. W., *Perspectives on Environment.* Assn. of American Geographers, Pub. No. 13 (1974): 66–68.

Marconi, P., *Agrigento: Topografia ed Arte.* Firenze: Vallecchi Editore, 1929. Not to be confused with his small guide *Agrigento,* published at Rome in 1933.

Marinelli, O., "Materiali per lo studio dei fenomeni carsici, 3. Fenomini carsici nelle regioni gessose d'Italia." *Mem. Riv. Geograf. Ital.* 34: 263– 416 (1917), quoted in Belloni et al., "Karst in Italy."

Marinos, P. G., and Koukis, G. C. (eds.) *The Engineering Geology of Ancient Works, Monuments and Historical Sites, 4 Vols.* Rotterdam, A.A. Balkema, 1988.

Marinos, P. G., "Les conditions hydrogeologiques et la disposition des dechets municipaux dans un haut plateau karstique (Grece-Poloponnese centrale)." In *Implications de l'Hydrologie dans las autres Sciences de la Terre* (1978): 537–51.

Martin, R., "Aesclepieion d' Athenes." *Bulletin de correspondance hellenique* 68–69(1944–45): 434–38.

Martin, R., *L'urbanisme dans la Grece antique.* Paris: A. & J. Picard, 1956.

Martin, R., "Rapport sur l'urbanisme de Selinunte." *Kokalos* 21 (1975): 54–67.

Martini, W., *Das Gymnasium von Samos.* Bonn: German Archaeological Institute and P. Von Zabern. 1984. Vol. 19 of the excavations of Samos.

Matusch, C. C., "Bronze- and Ironworking in the Area of the Athenian Agora." *Hesperia* 46 (1977): pl. 771.

Mau, A., *Pompeii, its Life and Art.* New York, 1899, 1907 new edition translated by F.W. Kelrey; New York: Macmillan, 1902; reprinted New Rochelle, N.Y.: Caratzas Bros., 1982.

Maurin, Z.W., and Zoetl, J., "Salt-water Encroachment in Low Altitude Karst Water Horizons, in "*Hydrology of Fractured Rocks* (1967): 423–38.

McPherson, M. B., *Hydrological Effects of Urbanization.* Paris: UNESCO, 1974.

Meiggs, R. *Roman Ostia,* Oxford: Clarendon Press, 1960; second edition, 1974.

Meinzer, O. E., *Plants as Indicators of Ground Water.* U. S. Geological Survey Water Supply Paper 577, 1927.

Melhorn, W. N., and Flemal, R. C., (eds.) *Theories of Landform Development.* London: George Allen and Unwin, 1975.

Mendelssohn, K., *The Riddle of the Pyramids,* New York: Thames and Hudson, ca. 1974.

Merkel, W. R., "Notes on South Slope Inscriptions." *Hesperia* 16(1947): 75–77, following Levensohn, M. and Levensohn, E. "Inscriptions on the South Slope of the Acropolis." 63–74.

Metraux, G., *Western Greek Land Use and City Planning in the Archaic Period.* New York: Garland, 1978.

Meulenkamp, J. E., de Mulder, E. F. J., and van de Weerd, A., "Sedimentary History and Paleogeography of the Late Cenozoic of the Island of Rhodes." *Z. Deutsch. Geol. Ges.,* Band 123, 541–53 and 4 maps. Hanover: 1972.

Michelet, *L'histoire de France.* London: Whittaker, 1844 and many 19th century French editions.

Michelin tourist guide, *Italy.* Clermont-Ferrand, France,1983.

Mijatovic, B. "Current Problems in the Rational Exploitation of Karst Water." In Dilamarter and Csallany (1977): 262–79.

Milanovic, P. T., *Karst Hydrogeology.* Littleton, Colo.: Water Resources Publications, 1981.

Miliadis, I., Reports on the excavations of the south slope of the Acropolis at Athens, *Praktika.* 1955: 50–52; 1956: 262–65; 1957: 23–26.

Mistardis, G. G., "Recherches (Hydrogeologiques) dans la region des lacs karstiques beotiens." In *Hydrology of Fractured Rocks, 1965.* Louvain, Belguim: IAHS and UNESCO, 1967: 162–70.

Moehring, E. P., "Public Works and Urban History: Recent Trends and New Directions." *Essays in Public Works History* 13. Chicago:Public Works Historical Society, Aug. 1982.

Mooney, H. A., and di Castri, F. (eds.), *Mediterranean Type Ecosystems.* New York: Springer Verlag, 1973.

Morgan, C.H. "Excavations at Corinth 1938." *American Journal of Archaeology* 43(1939): 255–67.

Mueller-Wiener, W., "The south dig on the Kalabaktepe hill, Milet 1986," *Ist. Mitt.* 37(1987): 666–733 and pl. 2–19.

Mumford, L. *The City in History.* New York: Harcourt, Brace and World, 1961.

Murano, D., *Pompeji, donde venivano le acque potabili ai castelli acquarii.* Naples: A. Morano, 1894.

Mygind, H., "Pompeijis Vandforsyning." in Mygind, H., *Pompeiistudier.* Copenhagen 1977: 77–157, also published at Copenhagen in *Janus* 1916–7: 294–35.

Mylonas, G., *Mycenae and the Mycenaean Age* . Princeton, N.J.: Princeton University Press, 1966.

Mylonas, G. (ed.), *Studies Presented to David M. Robinson,* I & II. St. Louis: Washington University Press, 1951–53.

Nabers, N. "Macellum Report." Princeton University Morgantina files

Naveh, Z., and Dan, J., "Human Degradation of Mediterranean Landscapes in Israel." In di Castri and Mooney (1973): 373–90.

Neuburger, A., "The Story of Water Supply." *The Technical Arts and Sciences of the Ancients.* Leipzig, 1919; New York: Methuen & Co., 1930.

Norton, P., (ed.) *Guide to the Geology and Culture of Greece.* Petroleum Exploration Society of Lybia, 1965.

O'Rourke, P. J., *Bachelor Home Companion.* New York: Pocket Books, 1987.

Orlandi, P., "Storia e topografia de Gela dal 405 al 282 a.C. alla luce delle nuove scoperte archeologiche." *Kokalos,* 2 (1956): 150–76, with plan.

Orlandi, P., "L'espansione de Gela nella Sicilia centro-meridonale." *Kokalos* 8(1962): 68–121.

Orsi, P., "Avanzi di fabbricato nel podere de Matteis sul l'Acradina." *Notizie degli Scavi di Antichita* 1900: 207–8.

Ostenberg, C. E., excavation notebook I, 1963, Princeton University Morgantina files.

Ostenberg, C. E., "City Walls." Unpublished final report in Princeton University Morgantina files.

Ovid *Metamorphoses* Book 15, 570–643.

Özis, U., "Assessment of Karst Water Resources." IWRA 5th World Congress on Water Resources, Brussels, 1985, paper 31a, 95–102.

Özis, U., "Environment and Underground: Karst Waters of Anatolia." Proceedings of V. Turk-Alman Cevre Muhendisligi Symposium, held 1984 in Izmir, Turkey.

Pace, B., *Arte e civilita della Sicilia antica, II and IV.* 4 vol. Milano: Ed. Dante Alighieri, 1935–38.

Palmer, J., *Ground Water Flow Patterns in Limestone Solution Conduits.* Ph. D. dissertation. State University of New York (Oneonta), 1976.

Palmer, A. N., "Geomorphic Interpretation of Karst Features." in La Fleur, (1984): 173–209.

Palmquist, R. C., "Distribution and Density of Dolines in Areas of Mantled Karst." In Dilamarter and Csallany (1977): 117–29.

Parsons, A. W., "Klepsydra and the Paved Court of the Pythion." *Hesperia*, 12(1943):191–267.

Pausanias *Description of Greece.* edited by C. Habicht. Berkeley : University of California Press, 1985. i,40,1; ii.24; iv,35,8–12; v.7.3) . See also the J. G. Frazer, *Pausanias* edition especially for the citation of Pseudo-Dicaerchus or Herakleides, introduction XLii ff.

Pedersen, P. "Town-planning in Halicarnassus and Rhodes." In Dietz and Papachristodoulou (1988): 98–103.

Pergamon waterlines: *Mitteilungen of the Leichtweiss Institut für Wasserbau,* Brandschweig Tecchncical University, Germany, Vol. 37 (1972), 44 (1975), 60–61 (1978), 73(1982), 78(1983).

Petroleum Exploration Society of Libya, *Excursion in Sicily May 27–30, 1960* Rome: Topografia del Senato, 1960.

Petroleum Exploration Society of Libya, *Guide to the Geology and Culture of Greece.* P. Norton (ed.) 1965.

Pfister, F., *Die Reisenbilder des Herakleides.* Vienna, 1956.

Picard, L., "Development of Underground Water Resources in Greece." 5 reports prepared for the Government of Greece through the U.N. Technical Assistance Program, 1956–1958.

Picard, L., "Karst Groundwater Investigations—Greece." Final Report of the UNSF/ FAO Project. Rome: FAO, 1964.

Pickard-Cambridge, A. W., *The Theater of Dionysos in Athens,* Oxford: Clarendon Press, 1946.

Pierce, C. S., *Collected Papers.* Cambridge, Mass.: Harvard University Press, 1965, 5.590, quoted in Frascari, M. (1986):7.

Pinchon, J. F., "Une transversale dans la zone Pelagonienne . . . ." In Kallergis, 1977: 168ff.

Pindar, *The Odes,* translated with an introduction by C.M. Bowra. London: Penguin Books, 1969.

Pirenne, H., *Medieval Cities.* Princeton, N.J.: Princeton University Press, 1934.

Plato, *Critias* iii D-El and 1176; *Laws* 761C and 8.884; *Phaedo.*

Pliny, *Natural History* XXXI 21, 1.2, on water.

Plutarch, *Lives,* "Solon" XXIII,6, 23.

Pohl, E. R., "Vertical Shafts in Limestone Caves." *Occasional Papers of the Speleological Society* (April 1955): 5–21.

Polybius, *History* IX, 27; X, 28 (re qanats of Achaemenian kings). Loeb edition, translated by W.R. Paton, 1925.

Pope, K. O., and Van Andel, T.H., "Late Quaternary Alluviation & Soil Formation in the So. Argolid: its History, Causes & Archaeological Implications." *Journal of Archaeological Science* 11(1984): 281–306.

Prince, H. "Real, Imagined and Abstract Worlds of the Past." In Board et al., 1971.

Princeton Encyclopedia, see Stillwell.

Pritchett, W. K., "The Waters of Ancient Hellas." Lecture given March 19, 1963, and preserved in the library of the American School of Classical Studies, Athens.

Pritchett, W. K., *Studies in Ancient Greek Topography*. Berkeley: University of California Press, 1965.

"Qanats of Armenia." *L. A. Times*, Sept. 29, 1971. See also Polybius, *History* X, 28.

Quinlan, F., *Types of Karst with Emphasis on Cover Beds in their Classification and Development*. Ph.D. dissertation, University of Texas (Austin) 1978.

Rapp, G.,Jr. and Gifford, J. A. (eds.), *Archaeological Geology*. Yale University Press, 1985.

Renz, C., "Geologische untersuchungen auf den Inseln Cypern und Rhodos", *Memoires* du museum national d'histoire naturelle. Nouvelle serie. Serie C. Sciences de la terre. Tome III, fasc. 1929, pp. 308–14.

Richardson, L. Jr., *Pompeii: An Architectural History*. Baltimore: Johns Hopkins University Press, 1988.

Rider, B. C., *The Greek House*. Cambridge University Press, 1965.

Robertson, D. S., *A Handbook of Greek and Roman Architecture*. Cambridge University Press, second edition, 1964.

Robinson, D. M., "The Third Campaign at Olynthos." which includes "The Fountain House," 219–20. *American Journal of Archaeology* ' 39(1935): 210–47.

Robinson, D. M., (general ed.) *Excavations at Olynthus*. Baltimore: Johns Hopkins University Press,1929 on, especially:

Robinson, D. M., *Architecture and Sculpture: Houses and Other Buildings*. Part II, 1930.

Robinson, D. M., *The Terra-cottas of Olynthus Found in 1931*. Part VII, 1933.

Robinson, D. M., and Graham, J. W., *The Hellenic House*. Part VIII, 1938, which includes "Water Supply and Drainage," 307–11.

Robinson, D. M., and Clement, P.A., *The Chalcidic Mint and the Excavation Coins Found in 1928–1934*. Part IX, 1938, which includes material on the aqueduct and fountainhouse.

Robinson, D.M., and Mylonas, G. E., *Domestic and Public Architecture*. Part XII, 1946.

Robinson, H. S., *The Urban Development of Ancient Corinth*. American School of Classical Studies, Athens, 1965.

Robinson, H. S., "A Sanctuary and Cemetery in Western Corinth." *Hesperia* 38 (1969): 1–35.

Robinson, H. S., "Excavations at Corinth: Temple Hill 1968–1972." *Hesperia* 45 (1976).

Roebuck, C., *The Asklepieion and Lerna. Corinth, XIV*. Princeton, N.J.: American School of Classical Studies at Athens, 1951.

Rostovtzeff, M. *Social and Economic History of the Hellenistic World*. 3 vol. Oxford: Clarendon Press, 1941, and several reprints.

Rudhardt, J., "Le theme de l'eau primordiale dans la mythologie grecque." *Travaux* Publies sous les auspices de la Societe Suisse des Sciences Humaines, 12. Berne, Switz.: Editions A. Franke, 1971.

Runnels, C. N., and Van Andel, T.H. "The Evolution of Settlement in the South Argolid, Greece: An Economic Explanation." *Hesperia*. 56(1987): 303–34.

St Clair, D. J., "The Motorization and Decline of Urban Public Transit, 1935– 1950." *Journal of Economic History.* 41(Sept. 1981): 579–600.

Sakellariou, M. and Faraklas, N., "Corinthia-Cleonea." In C. Doxiadis, 1972.

Sauer, C. O., *The Morphology of Landscape.* University of California Publications in Geography 2:11(1925): 19–54; 1956: 287–99.

Schubring, J., "Die Bewasserung von Syrakus." *Philologus* 22(1865): 577– 638, with map. In E. Von Leutsch, "Zeitschrift fur das Klassische Alterthum."

Schubring, J., "Historische Topographie von Akragas in Sicilien." *Philologus.* Leipzig, 1870, 38–44 plus map. Also available in Italian as "Topografia Storica di Agrigento" 1887 and reprinted as No. 86 of *Bibl.Istorica della Antice e Nuova Italia,* by Arnoldo Forni Ed. (n.d.).

Schwandner, E-L. and Hoepfner, W., *Haus und Stadt in klassischen Griechenland.* Munich: Deutscher Kunstverlag, 1985.

Scranton, R. L., *Greek Walls.* Cambridge: Harvard University Press for American School of Classical Studies, 1941.

Scully, V., *The Earth, the Temple, and the Gods: Greek Sacred Architecture.* New Haven: 1962; New York:1969.

Seneca, *Natural Questions* book 3 "On forms of Water."

Shalhevet, J., Mentel, A., Bieloral, H., and Shimski, D., "Irrigation of Fields and Orchard Crops under Semi-arid Conditions" in Golany, 1976.

Shaw, B. D., "Water and Society in the Ancient Maghrib. Technology, Property, and Development." *Antiquites Africaines* 20(1984): 121–73.

Shear, T.L., Jr., "The Athenian Agora: Excavations of 1971." *Hesperia* 42(1973): 124.

Singer, C., Holmyard, E. J., Hall, A. R., and Williams, T. I., *A History of Technology.* 8 vol. Oxford: Clarendon Press, 1954–1984.

Sjöqvist, E., "Excavations at Serra Orlando, Preliminary Report II." *American Journal of Archaeology* 62(1958): 155–64.

Sjöqvist, E., "Excavations at Morgantina (Serra 0rlando) 1961: Preliminary Report VI." *American Journal of Archaeology* 66 (1962):,135–144 and pl. 29–36.

Sjöqvist, E., "Excavations at Morgantina (Serra Orlando) 1963: Preliminary Report VII." *American Journal of Archaeology* 68 (1964):137–47, pl. 41–46.

Smith, Capt. John, quoted in the *National Geographic* vol. 174 (Sept. 1988): 430.

Smith, N., *Man and Water: A History of Hydrotechnology.* New York: Charles Scribner's Sons, 1975.

"Solon" XXIII,6 in Plutarch' s *Lives.*

Soper, W. E., and Kardos, L. T., (eds.), *Recycling Treated Municipal Waste Water and Sludge through Forest and Cropland.* University Park, Pa.: Pennsylvania State University Press, 1973.

Squyres, C.H. (ed.), *Geology of Italy.* Earth Sciences Society of the Libyan Arab Republic, 1975.

Steel, E. W., and McGhee, T. J. *Water Supply and Sewerage.* New York: McGraw Hill, 1979, fifth edition esp. Chapter 4, "Ground Water."

Stent, G. S., "Prematurity and Uniqueness in Scientific Discovery." *Scientific American.* 227(Dec. 1972): 84–93.

Stevens, G. P., "The Periclean Entrance Court of the Acropolis." *Hesperia* 5(1936): 444–520.

Stevens, G. P. "The Setting of the Periclean Parthenon." *Hesperia* Supplement 3 (1940).

Stillwell, R., "Excavations at Serra Orlando, 1958: Preliminary Report III." *American Journal of Archaeology* 63(1959): 167–73 and pl. 39–44.

Stillwell, R., "Excavations at Morgantina (Serra Orlando) 1962." *American Journal of Archaeology* 67(1963): 63–72.

Stillwell, R., MacDonald, W. L., and McAllister, M., *Princeton Encyclopedia of Classical Sites.* Princeton, N.J.: Princeton University Press, 1976.

Stillwell, R., and Sjöqvist, E. "Excavations at Serra Orlando: Preliminary Report." *American Journal of Archaeology* 61(1957):151–59 and pl.53–60.

J. Stiny, *Die Quellen.* Viena: Springer Verlag, 1933.

Storia della Sicilia I, Soc. editrice Storia di Napoli, del Mezzogiorno continale e della Sicilia, 1979.

Strabo, *Geography* translated by H. L. Jones, Loeb edition, London: W. Heinemann; New York: G. P. Putnam's Sons, 1917–32. On Upper Peirene spring, subterranean water connections, and wells, Book 8.6.21. on tracer experiments, 6.8.371, and 9 on deforestation.

Stringfield, V. T., and Herak, M. (eds.), *Karst: Important Karst Regions of the Northern Hemisphere.* Amsterdam: Elsevier, 1972.

Stringfield, V. T., and Le Grand, H. E., " Relation of sea water to fresh water in carbonate rocks." *Journal of Hydrology.* 9(1969): 307–404.

Stringfield, V. T., and Rapp, G., Jr., "Progress of Knowledge of Hydrology of Carbonate Rock Terranes—A Review." In Dilamarter and Csallany (1977): 12.

Sweeting, M. M., "Some Factors in the Absolute Denudation of Limestone Terranes." *Erdkunde,* 18 (1964): 92–95.

Sweeting, M. M., *Karst Landforms.* New York.: Columbia University Press, 1973.

Sweeting, M. M., *Karst Processes.* Berlin: Gebr. Borntraeger, 1976.

Sweeting, M. M. (ed.), *Karst Geomorphology.* Stroudsburg, Pa.: Hutchinson Press, 1981.

Symeonoglou, S., *The Topography of Thebes.* Princeton, N.J.: Princeton University Press,1985.

Tanoulas, T., "The Propylaea of the Acropolis at Athens since the 17th Century, Their Decay and Restoration." *Jahrbuch des deutschen archaeologischen Institut.* 102(1987): 475.

Tarr, J. A., "Introduction" to a special issue on "The City and Technology." *Journal of Urban History* 5 (1979): 276ff.

Tarr, J. A., "Building the Urban Infrastructure in the Nineteenth Century: An Introduction." In *Infrastructure and Urban Growth in the Nineteenth Century.* Chicago: Public Works Historical Society 14, 1985, 61–85.

Tennyson, L. C., and Settergren, C. D., "Subsurface Water Behavior and Sewage Effluent in the Missouri Ozarks." In Dilamarter and Csallany, (1977): 411–18.

Thatcher, E. D., "Solar and Radiant Heating—Roman Style: The Open Rooms of the Terme del Foro at Ostia." *Journal of the American Institute of Architecture* (March 1958): 116–29, condensed from 1956 article in the *Memoires* of the American Academy at Rome. See also a newer article by Jordan and Perlin in *Solar Heating Journal,* 1979.

Theodorescu, D, "Remarques preliminaires sur la topographie urbaine de Selinonte." *Kokalos,* 21(1975): 108–20.

Thompson, H. A. and Wycherley, R. E., *The Athenian Agora XIV.* Princeton, N.J.: American School of Classical Studies at Athens, 1972.

Thornes, J. B., and Brunsden, D., *Geomorphology and Time.* New York: J. Wiley and Sons,1977.

Thrower, N. J. W., and Bradbury, D. E., "The Mediterranean Type Region." In di Castri and Mooney (1973): 40ff.

Thucydides *Peloponnesian War* I, 58; II:15.3–6; IV.65.142; VI,54.

Tölle-Kastenbein, R., *Antike Wasserkultur.* Munich: Verlag D.H. Beck, 1990.

Tolman, C. F., *Groundwater.* New York: McGraw-Hill, 1937.

Toutain, J., "Le culte des eaux (sources, fleuves, lacs) dans la Grece antique." *Nouvelles etudes de mythologie et d'histoire des religions antiques.* Parie: Jouve & Cie, Eds. 1935.

Travlos, J., *Poleodomike Exelixis ton Athenon.* (A history of Athens in maps, in Greek.) Athens, 1960.

Travlos, J., *Pictorial Dictionary of Ancient Athens* . New York: Praeger, 1971; reprinted by Hacker Art Books, 1980.

Travlos, J., *Bildlexikon zur Topographie des antiken Attika.* Tubingen: E. Wasmuth, 1988.

Tuan, Y.-F., *Topophilia.* Englewood Cliffs, N.J.: Prentice-Hall Inc., 1974.

Van Andel, T. H., Jacobsen, T. W., Jolly, J. B., Lianos, N., "Late Quaternary History of the Coastal Zone near Franchthi Cave, So. Argolid, Greece." *Journal of Field Archaeology.* 7 (1980): 389–402;

Van Andel, T. H., and Pope, K. O., "Late Quaternary Alluviation & Soil Formation in the So. Argolid: its History, Causes & Archaeological Implications." *Journal of Archaeological Science* 11(1984): 281–306.

Van Andel, T. H., and Runnels, C. N., "The Evolution of Settlement in the South Argolid, Greece: An Economic Explanation." *Hesperia* 56(1987): 303– 34.

Van Andel, T. H., Runnels, C. N., Pope, K. O., "5000 Years of Land Use and Abuse in the So. Argolid, Greece." *Hesperia* 55(1986): 103–28.

Van Andel, T. H., and Sutton, S. *Landscape and People of the Franchthi Region.* Bloomington, Ind.: Indiana University Press, 1987.

Vergil, *Aeneid* 3.692–97.

Vita-Finzi, C., *The Mediterranean Valleys.* Cambridge University Press, 1969.

Vitruvius, *Ten Books on Architecture,* especially book VIII. Translated by M.H. Morgan. New York: Dover Publications, 1960.

Vollgraff, W., "Le Sanctraire d'Apollon Pytheen à Argos." *Etudes Peloponnesiannes,* Ecole Francaise d'Athenes. Paris: J. Vrin, 1956, 38– 52.

von Gerkan, A., *Griechische Staedteanlagen,* Berlin: Walter de Gruyter, 1924.

von Gerkan, A., *Kalabaktepe Athenatempel und Umgebung,* Vol. 1 pt. 8, 1925. of T.Wiegand (general ed.), *Milet.* Berlin: Reimer Verlag, 1906–36.

von Gerkan, A., "Die neronische Scaenae Frons des Dionysos-Theaters in Athen." *Jahrbuch des deutschen archaeologischen Inst.* 56 (1941), 163–77.

von Gerkan, A., *Thermen und Palaestren.* Vol. 1 pt. 9, 1928, of Wiegand, *Milet.*

Von Leutsch, E., "Zeitschrift für das Klassische Alterthum." *Philologus* 22(1865): 577–638.

Wagstaff, J. M., "A Note on Settlement Numbers in Ancient Greece", *Journal of Hellenic Studies,* 95 (1975):163–68.

Wallace, P. W., "Strabo on Acrocorinth." *Hesperia.* 38(1969): 499.

Walter, H., *Die vegetation der Erde III.* Jena: G. Fischer Verlag, 1986.

Wasserversorgung der antiken Rom. Published by the Fontinus- Gesellschaft, at Munich & Vienna: R. Oldenbourg Verlag, 1983.

Waterworks in the Athenian Agora, American School of Classical Studies, Princeton, N.J., Picture Book No. 11, 1968 (n.p.). By Mabel Lang, although not so listed on the title page.

Webster, T. B. L., *Athenian Culture and Society*. Berkeley: University of California Press, 1973.

Weinberg, S. A. "Cross-section of Corinthian Antiquities." *Hesperia*, 17(1948): 198–241.

Weinberg, S. A. "Investigations at Corinth, 1947–48." *Hesperia*, 18(1949): 148–58.

White, D., excavation notebook 1961, II, Princeton Univeresity Morgantina files.

White, W. B.,"Conceptual Models for Carbonate Aquifers: Revisited." In Dilamarter and Casallany (1977): 176–87.

White, W. B., "Rate processes: chemical kinetics and karst landform development." In R. LaFleur, 1984: 227–48.

White, W. B. and White, E. L., *Karst Hydrology*. New York: Van Norstrand Reinhold, 1989.

Wickens, J., *The Archaeology and History of Cave Use in Attica, Greece*. Ph.D. dissertation, Indiana University, 1986.

Wiegand, T., "Die griechische Hochdruck-Wasserleitung in Pergamon." *Das Gasund Wasserfach* 76: 26–52(1933) 513–16. .

Wiegand, T., *Milet*. Berlin: Reimer Verlag, 1906–36, which includes Huelsen, J., *Das Nymphaeum*, Vol. 1 pt. 5, 1919; von Gerkan, A. *Kalabaktepe Athenatempel und Umgebung*, Vol. 1 pt. 8, 1925; von Gerkan, A., *Thermen und Palaestren*. Vol. 1 pt. 9, 1928.

Wiegand, T., and Schrader, H., *Die Wasseranlagen*. Vol.IV of *Priene*. Berlin: Reimer Verlag, 1904

Williams, C.K., II and Fisher, J. E., "Corinth 1970." *Hesperia* 40(1971) ;12.

Williams, C.K., II, " Corinth." *Hesperia* 45 (1976): 109–15.

Williams, C.K., II, " Corinth." *Hesperia* 46 (1977): 40–53.

Williams, C.K., II and Russell, P., "Corinth Excavations of 1980." *Hesperia* 50(1981); 1–44, esp. p. 5 b & c.

Williams, C.K., II and Zervos, O. H., "Corinth, 1981: East of the Theater." *Hesperia* 51(1982): 115–63 and pl. 37–46.

Williams, C.K., II and Zervos, O. H., "Corinth 1982: East of the Theater." *Hesperia* 52(1983): 118–20 with map and plan.

Williams, C.K., II and Zervos, O. H., "Around the Fountain House of Glauke" in "Corinth 1983." *Hesperia* 53(1984): 97–101, fig. 2 and pl. 24b.

Winter, F. E., *Greek Fortifications*. Toronto: Toronto University Press, 1971.

Wiseman, J., "The Fountain of the Lamps." *Archaeology* 23(1970):130–37.

Wiseman, J., "The Gymnasium Area at Corinth 1969–1970." *Hesperia* 41(1972): 1–42 and pl. 1–11.

Wiseman, J., "The Land of the Ancient Corinthians." *Studies in Mediterranean Archaeology* 50(1978): 82–119. Goteborg: P. Astrom.

Woodhead, A. G., *The Greeks in the West*. New York: Praeger, 1962.

World Meteorological Organization, *Changes of Climate*. Proceedings of the Rome Symposium 1961, organized by UNESCO and WMO, especially pp. 127–129 on climate change induced by volcanos during Greek times. Paris: UNESCO, 1963.

Wunderlich, W., and Prins, J. E. (eds.,) *Water for the Future*. Rotterdam: A.A. Balkema, 1987.

Wycherley, R. E. "Notes on Olynthus and Selinus." *American Journal of Archaeology*. 55(July, 1951): 231–36.

Wycherley, R. E., *How the Greeks Built Cities*. London: Macmillan & Co. Ltd., 1962.

Wycherley, R. E. *The Stones of Athens*, Princeton, N.J. :Princeton University Press, 1978.

Wycherley, R. E., and Thompson, H. A. *The Athenian Agora*. Princton, N.J.: American School of Classical Studies at Athens, 1972.

Xenophon, *Lacedemonian Republic* 15,6. translated into French by H. Baszin, Paris: Leroux, 1885.

Ziller, E., "Wasserleitung von Athen,." *Mitteilungen* of the DAI Athens, 2(1877), 107–31.

Zotl, J. G., "Results of Tracing Experimnets for Construction of Reservoirs in Karstic Regions." In Dilamarter and Csallany (1977) 450–58.

Index